Woolf Studies Annual

Volume 16, 2010

Pace University Press • New York

Pace University Press
41 Park Row, Rm. 1510
New York, NY 10038

Printed in the United States of America

ISSN 1080-9317
ISBN 0-944473-99-7 (pbk: alk.ppr.)

Member

Council of Editors of Learned Journals

Paper used in this publication meets the minimum requirements of American National Standard for Information Sciences–Permanence of Paper for Printed Library Materials, ANSI Z39.48–1984

Editor

Editorial Board

Many thanks to readers for volume 16: Elizabeth Abel (U of California Berkeley); Kristin Czarnecki (Georgetown C); Kathy Hill-Miller (Long Island U); Emily Hinnov (BGSU Firelands C); Karen Levenback (Independent Scholar); Brenda Lyons (Everest C); Gabrielle McIntire (Queen's U); Eleanor McNees (U of Denver); Jeanette McVicker (SUNY Fredonia); Ruth Saxton (Mills C); Helen Southworth (U of Oregon); Diana Swanson (Northern Illinois U); Miriam Wallace (New C of Florida); Janet Winston (Humboldt SU).

Woolf Studies Annual is indexed in *Humanities International Complete, ABELL* and the *MLA Bibliography.*

Contents

*W*oolf *S*tudies *A*nnual

Volume 16, 2010

REVIEWS

Abbreviations

AHH	*A Haunted House*
AROO	*A Room of One's Own*
BP	*Books and Portraits*
BTA	*Between the Acts*
CDB	*The Captain's Death Bed and Other Essays*
CE	*Collected Essays (4 vols.)*
CR1	*The Common Reader*
CR2	*The Common Reader, Second Series*
CSF	*The Complete Shorter Fiction*
D	*The Diary of Virginia Woolf (5 vols.)*
DM	*The Death of the Moth and Other Essays*
E	*The Essays of Virginia Woolf (6 Vols.)*
F	*Flush*
FR	*Freshwater*
GR	*Granite & Rainbow: Essays*
JR	*Jacob's Room*
L	*The Letters of Virginia Woolf (6 Vols.)*
M	*The Moment and Other Essays*
MEL	*Melymbrosia*
MOB	*Moments of Being*
MT	*Monday or Tuesday*
MD	*Mrs. Dalloway*
ND	*Night and Day*
O	*Orlando*
PA	*A Passionate Apprentice*
RF	*Roger Fry: A Biography*
TG	*Three Guineas*
TTL	*To the Lighthouse*
TW	*The Waves*
TY	*The Years*
VO	*The Voyage Out*

"Tilting at Universities": Woolf At King's College London

Christine Kenyon Jones and Anna Snaith

Women's education was a constant concern for Virginia Woolf. She read widely about the historic exclusion of women from higher education, the social reformers who fought for women's higher education, and the prejudices that persisted even after colleges opened their doors to women. Her novels are full of female characters—Clarissa Dalloway, Mrs. Ramsay, Eleanor Pargiter—lamenting the insecurity and constraint bred by their lack of education. It was not enough that women's colleges such as Newnham at Cambridge, Somerville at Oxford, or Bedford in London simply existed; Woolf's writing continually questions the nature, aims and methods of education itself. Particularly during the 1930s as she was writing *The Years* and *Three Guineas* she considered the psychological effects of the inequities between male and female education. Her 1937 novel is full of evidence of the untold emotional divisions between siblings caused by the amount of money and time spent on educating boys as opposed to girls.[1] As research for *The Years* she read and collected quotations from scores of memoirs and biographies about Victorian education and attempts to reform the provision for girls and women. In this period, too, she was forever "tilting at Universities," arguing in particular that the roots of imperial and patriarchal violence lay in the training boys received at public school and Oxbridge (*D*4 79). In the notes to *Three Guineas* she argues that

> psychologically eminence upon a platform encourages vanity and the desire to impose authority. Further, the reduction of English literature to an examination subject must be viewed with suspicion by all who [...] wish to keep one art at least out of the hands of middlemen and free, as long as may be, from all association with competition and money making. (*TG* 379)

Given the prevalence of questions of gender and pedagogy in Woolf's own writing it is curious that her own formal education has received relatively little attention. Recently examined archival records at King's College London reveal that Woolf had much more first hand experience of women's higher education than either she or her biographers have acknowledged. Her extended studies at King's College Ladies' Department brought her into direct contact with some of

[1] The Schools' Inquiry Commission in 1867-68 reported that, although middle-class girls might be sent to boarding school between the ages of 12 or 13 and 17, and might attend "finishing" school, the aims of this kind of education were social, not academic (Dyhouse 1981: 41).

the early reformers of women's higher education such as Clara Pater, George Warr and Lilian Faithfull.[2] This article will not only reproduce, for the first time, the enrolment lists, syllabi (course reading lists) and examination pass lists relating to Virginia and her sister Vanessa's studies at King's College between 1897 and 1901, but will also place those studies in their institutional context. We will link aspects of the ethos and environment of King's Ladies' Department to Woolf's later writings. The absence of references to her early education in her subsequent writing career has meant that this important archival material has gone unnoticed, and also that the impact of her studies on her later theories of education has not been explored. Biographical material from Woolf's teenage years is sparse—only intermittent letters and journals remain—therefore this discovery provides valuable information about a relatively undocumented portion of her life.

The impression given by Woolf's biographers, and indeed by Woolf herself, is that she was almost entirely self-educated. The appended chronology in Quentin Bell's biography of Woolf does list attendance at King's College in November 1897 (Greek and History), January 1898 (Greek with Dr. Warre [sic]), October 1898 (Latin with Miss Pater and Greek with Dr. Warre [sic] and October 1900 (Bell 191-2). In the biography itself, however, her attendance at King's is not mentioned, just her private tuition with Clara Pater. When Bell outlines a typical day in the Stephen household he depicts Vanessa cycling off to her art classes at Mr. Cope's School, and Virginia left alone in the nursery at the top of the house reading Greek (Bell 68 and 73). In 1972, Bell thus sets the narrative in place which will be perpetuated by future biographers. Jean O. Love mentions only Woolf's private tuition with Clara Pater and Janet Case (156). Phyllis Rose's biography, published a year later in 1978, mentions Woolf's Greek studies, but sets them firmly within the home, her father and his library her only teachers (21). Following the publication of the early journals and letters, biographers mention Woolf's attendance at King's College London but only in the briefest terms. No one consults the archival records. John Mepham and James King note that she attended lectures on Greek and history at King's College, London (Mepham 10; King 69). Panthea Reid mentions King's briefly but states that Woolf did not sit for exams (Reid 51, 54, 56). The *Oxford Dictionary of National Biography* entry by Lyndall Gordon states that "Virginia Stephen was educated at home," and that she was

> largely self-educated, and continued with a programme of reading throughout her life. Her only sustained formal study was in Greek. At fifteen she attended a few Greek classes at King's College in London.

[2] We would like to thank Professor Rick Trainor, Principal of King's College London, and Professor Michael Trapp and Dr Trudi Darby both of King's College London, for their suggestions and comments.

Hermione Lee's biography describes how, after a two-year gap following the death of her mother, Julia, "in which she wrote nothing and had no lessons," Virginia was writing and "gobbling up" the books belonging to her father Leslie Stephen almost faster than he approved (Lee 143). Lee then notes briefly that during the "years of lonely self-education" in the autumn of 1897 Virginia "started classes in Greek and Latin with Dr George Warr [...] one of the founders of the Ladies Department of King's College, in Kensington. She didn't take the exams"(143). She then moves on to discuss Woolf's private tuition with Clara Pater and Janet Case. These accounts suggest attendance at classes outside the home that was at best sporadic.

Virginia herself presents a similar impression of her own lack of formal education, writing, for example, to her brother Thoby in 1903:

> I dont get anybody to argue with me now, and feel the want. I have to delve from books, painfully and all alone, what you get every evening sitting over your fire and smoking your pipe with Strachey etc. No wonder my knowledge is but scant. Theres nothing like talk as an educator I'm sure. (*L*1 77)

In the draft of a talk Woolf gave to sixty girls at Hayes Court School in 1926, she begins: "In the first place I am going to confess a crime—not my own doing however—I have never been to school" (Daugherty, "Virginia Woolf's" 161).[3] In 1932, in response to a request for biographical information from Harmon Goldstone who wanted to write a book on her, Woolf wrote: "Partly from reasons of health I was never at any school or college. My father allowed me to read any book in his library when I was a girl; and it was a large library" (*L*5 91). In that same year when she was invited to deliver the Clark Lectures at Cambridge University (given by her father in 1883) she felt that the invitation was an affirmation of her years of studying by herself:

> This, I suppose, is the first time a woman has been asked; & so it is a great honour—think of me, the uneducated child reading books in my room at 22 H. P. G.—now advanced to this glory. (*D*4 79)

So important to her, however, was her outsider position, and so abhorrent to her the lecture form, that she refused the invitation.

The archival material we have examined substantially alters the narrative of Woolf's early formal education as intermittent, brief, or even non-existent. Detailed enrolment records and syllabi (course catalogues) show that Adeline

[3] For the transcription of this talk, which eventually became "How Should One Read a Book?" in the *Second Common Reader*, see Daugherty, ed. "Virginia Woolf's."

Virginia Stephen, as she then was, studied at King's College Ladies' Department for five years between 1897 and 1901, between the ages of 15 and 19.[4] She was not only registered for courses in a range of subjects, but reached degree-level standard in some of her studies, and also took examinations. The archives show that Vanessa Stephen was also registered for classes at the Ladies' Department of King's College London between 1898 and 1900 and that the sisters studied Latin together there under Clara Pater.[5]

The Ladies' Department at 13 Kensington Square (now London W8), was part of King's College London, itself founded in 1829 and one of England's oldest university institutions. Oxford and Cambridge universities were medieval foundations, but the early nineteenth century saw the development of several new institutions in England offering boys and young men a variety of new opportunities for post-secondary education, including degree-level studies. These included University College London (founded in 1826), King's College London (1829), and the University of Durham (1832).

When the University of London was founded by the government in 1836, University College and King's College became its two constituent colleges, making them both eligible to educate and enter students for its degrees. Entry to the London bachelor's degree was dependent on passing the matriculation examination (broadly equivalent to modern English Advanced or "A" level, or the International Baccalaureate) and achieving this degree required three years of full-time study, progressing through intermediate, pass and honors examinations, to a level broadly equivalent to a modern English or US first degree. From the 1860s the University of London offered a Special Examination for Women, and in 1878 it became the first university in England to offer women the opportunity to take its degrees.

Distinctions between institutions of "secondary" and "higher" education were less clear in the nineteenth century than they are now, and until the 1890s King's College London incorporated both a Junior and a Senior Department in its premises at the Strand (now London WC2), with the Junior Department offering secondary-level education and the Senior one offering a variety of courses to boys from age 16 upwards. These included not only studies leading to University of London degrees, but also professional courses and preparation for the entrance exams of Oxford and Cambridge. Between 1848 and 1850, from the age of 16 to

[4] King's College London Archives, KWA/RAD 3-7, KW/SYL 6-9 and KWA/R1.

[5] King's College London Archives, KWA/RAD4, KWA/RAD5 and KWA/RAD6. The registrations in this year are for Vanessa as "Miss Stephen" at 22 Hyde Park Gate, and for Virginia as "Miss AV" Stephen or "Miss V" Stephen at the same address. In the years when Vanessa did not attend the Ladies' Department, Virginia is sometimes referred to as "Miss Stephen."

18, after leaving Eton, Virginia's father Leslie Stephen studied at King's for his entrance to Cambridge University.

Residential and non-residential colleges catering to women's higher education began to be established from the middle of the century. King's College London launched its "Lectures for Ladies" in 1871 in Richmond, and this enterprise then moved to Kensington and grew into the Ladies' Department of King's College, formally so constituted in 1885. By the time Virginia was there, the King's Ladies' Department had over 500 students and was offering a wide variety of courses at a range of educational levels, requiring varying amounts of commitment, and including preparation for London and Oxford university degree exams. In 1902, just after Virginia had left, the Ladies' Department became the King's College Women's Department, and then, in 1910, King's College for Women. The arts and sciences departments of King's College for Women were merged with the "main" King's College in 1915, when the women students joined their male colleagues at the Strand.[6] King's College London is now a research-led, co-educational, multi-faculty university institution with some 22,000 students, part of the University of London but awarding its own degrees, and ranked among the world's top twenty-five university institutions.[7]

A vivid picture of the Department at the time of Woolf's attendance is provided in the memoirs of Lilian Faithfull (1865-1952) who was the Vice-Principal of King's in charge of the Ladies' Department from 1894 to 1907 (Faithfull 101-20). Faithfull identifies three main types of student: first, a large number of middle- and upper-class women who had "developed the lecture habit" as essentially a leisure pursuit, and followed for interest and pleasure courses of lectures given by (male) professors from the "main" King's College, without on the whole taking any examinations (Faithfull 111). Second, there was a small but growing minority of self-funding, regular, "matriculated" students (i.e. those who had passed the entrance exam for University of London degrees), much encouraged by Faithfull, who were studying for degrees of the University of London or for the Oxford Women's Examinations.[8] Third, there were students who were intending to

[6] See Oakeley, Appendix A, 489-509.

[7] *Times Higher Education* League Tables, 2007 and 2008.

[8] The Oxford Women's Examinations were set and marked by the University of Oxford Delegacy of Local Examinations and were available to women over 18 not attending the University's women's colleges. The Oxford First Women's Examination was similar in standard to London University's Matriculation exam, while the Second or Higher Examination had different levels at pass and honors, equivalent in standard to final bachelor's degree exams. See "Local Examinations Delegacy LE.pdf", available through the Oxford University Archives website [http://www.oua.ox.ac.uk/index.html, accessed 25 February 2009], 31, and Oxford University Archives, ref LE 110/2, cited in an email message from Meirian Jump, Archives Assistant, Oxford University Archives, to Christine Kenyon Jones, 1 April 2009.

become teachers who held scholarships from the Technical Education Board and were also reading for London degrees.

The classes Virginia attended were open to students of all three types, and Faithfull describes how

> [w]omen and girls of all ages from seventeen to seventy came to the lectures, some only to do one course, once a week, and some to several. Old ladies followed a favourite Professor and came year after year. [...] Married women arrived gasping for a 10 o'clock lecture, having snatched an hour with difficulty from their household duties at that time in the morning. And there were innumerable girls who had just left school and were anxious to continue their education, and others who were in the hands of governesses unable to teach them this or that subject, and glad to supplement their lessons by lectures. (Faithfull 105)

Virginia and Vanessa do not quite seem to fit any of the types of student Faithfull describes: they were perhaps more assiduous than those who only wanted to attend lectures as a leisure pursuit, but they were not matriculated students, regularly following a course of study leading to a London or Oxford University degree. Faithfull might have categorized them as some of the "innumerable girls," although the Stephen sisters had neither attended school nor outstripped a governess. The courses at the Ladies' College at this time were in a state of transition between fulfilling a leisure role and providing a basis for university qualifications, and the pattern and type of Virginia's studies reflect this.

Comparing King's Ladies' Department with the residential women's colleges at Oxford and Cambridge, Faithfull believed it had "some advantages":

> Our students were older. They had read more and thought more than the undergraduate fresh from school, and lived in the midst of London, with its cosmopolitan life and interests. They were familiar with cultivated people in their own homes and they brought some independent critical judgement to bear on the books they studied. Many of them had never been at school, and were either self-taught or at all events home-taught, with a keen appetite not blunted by text-books, but rather sharpened by browsing in a library. (Faithfull 113)

The number of students registered at the Ladies' Department in the Michaelmas term of 1897 was 593, of whom seven were described as "private" students. In the Michaelmas term of 1901 there were 524 students, of whom 70 were said to be "private."[9]

The King's records show Virginia's sustained enrollment in a range of subjects at the Ladies' Department, including History (Continental and English), Greek

[9] King's Archives KWA/R2.

(Intermediate and Advanced), Latin and German (see "Virginia's Registrations," below).[10] Besides the classes in Latin which Vanessa took alongside Virginia in 1898-99 and 1899-1900, the King's records show that Vanessa also studied elementary Italian at the King's Ladies' Department in the Michaelmas term of 1898; Architecture in the first two terms of 1899-1900; and Art in the Michaelmas term of 1900.[11] The cost of registration in 1897-98 was one guinea (in modern terms, one pound and five pence) for each of these subjects per term, although divinity classes were apparently half-price.[12] The College year comprised thirty weeks of classes, and in 1897-98 the Michaelmas (autumn) term ran from Monday 11 October to Friday 17 December; the Lent (spring) term from Monday 17 January to Friday 25 March, and the Easter (summer) term from Monday 2 May to Friday 8 July.[13]

[10] King's Archives, KWA/RAD3-KWA/RAD7. "King's College London Ladies' Department Syllabus of Lectures, 1897-8" 1. King's College London Archives, KW/SYL 6-9.

[11] From 1896 Vanessa was also attending art classes at Cope's School in South Kensington, and in 1901 she began to study at the Painting School of the Royal Academy (see Lee 142 and Dunn 49). According to the King's Ladies' Department "Syllabus of Lectures 1899-1900" (King's Archives KW/SYL8: 50-51), Vanessa's architecture course at King's comprised a series of lectures on "English Architecture" given by W. Church Howgate ARIBA, which covered the topic from the 15th to the 18th century. Her "Art" registration would have been in the Ladies' Department's Art School, which included life classes, "antique" drawing (i.e. drawing plaster casts of ancient sculpture), still-life drawing and painting. The syllabus for 1899-1900 (52) lists the staff of the Art School as Professor Albert W. Holden, Professor of Fine Arts at King's College London and "Exhibitor, Royal Academy," and the Assistant Art Master, Thomas Speight, with the historical and portrait painter John Seymour Lucas RA (1849-1923) as the Art School's "Hon Visitor." Neville Marsh, in *The History of Queen Elizabeth College*, says that the painter Rex Vicat Cole (1870-1940) was "an additional Lecturer in Landscape Drawing" at the Ladies' Department from 1894 to 1910 and describes how he encouraged his pupils to join him in the country during August (21-2). In 1898 he took his classes to the picturesque village of Headcorn in Kent and 1899 to Bolton Abbey in Yorkshire. In *The Pargiters*, Milly makes do with "a sketching club which went for expeditions in the summer–and painted flowers in her bedroom" because "painting at the Slade meant painting from the nude" (*P* 30 and 29). As Woolf writes in "Two Women": "If women wanted to paint, there was, up to the year 1858, only one life class in London where they could learn" (*M* 160). Vanessa is, however, likely to have found interesting companions in her classes: Faithfull describes the students in the Art School as "inflammable material [...] a set of wild but very attractive students, many of them daughters of artists in and around Kensington" (119).

[12] "Syllabus of Lectures, 1897-8," 51-2. Edith Morley reports that students could register for half a term or a whole one, and a half-term's divinity course cost five shillings and three pence (qtd. in Dyhouse 1995: 204).

[13] *The Calendar of King's College London 1897*-8, 293, "Department for Ladies."

Figs. 1a-f. *Registrations for "Miss V Stephen" and "Miss Stephen" between 1897 and 1901 from the King's Ladies' Department registers, (KWA/RAD 3-7). Courtesy of King's College London Archives.*[14]

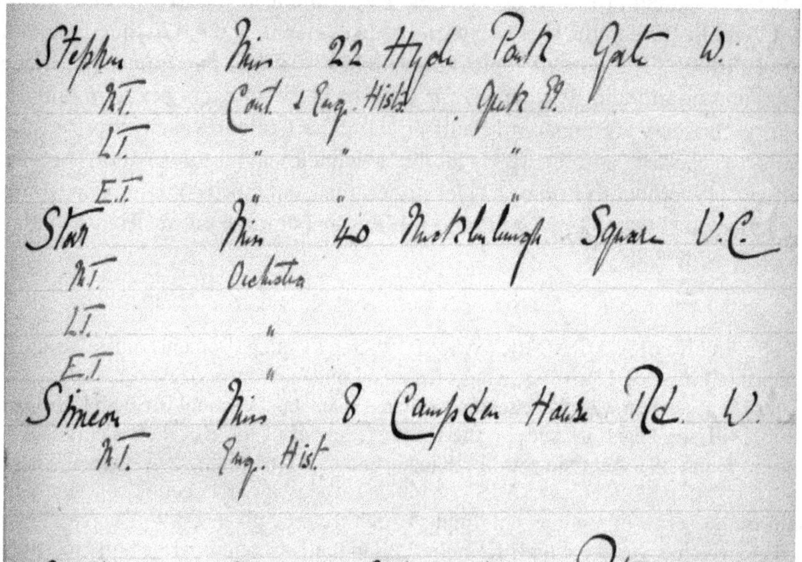

Stephen Miss 22 Hyde Park Gate W.
M.T. Cont. & Eng. Hist.
L.T. " "
E.T. " "
Starr Miss 40 Mecklenburgh Square W.C.
M.T. Orchestra
L.T. "
E.T. "
Simeon Miss 8 Campden House Rd. W.
M.T. Eng. Hist.
Sparks Miss Suffolk House Putney Hill
M.T. Geology
L.T. "
E.T. Botany (2)
Stronge Miss 21 Upper Addison Rd W.
M.T. Vict. Era Eng. Lit. (Shuttleworth)
L.T. "
E.T.
Slade Miss 38 Holland Park W.
M.T. ~~Roman Hist~~

Fig. 1a.

[14] Our thanks to Katherine Godfrey and Frances Pattman of King's College London Archives for their assistance and archival expertise.

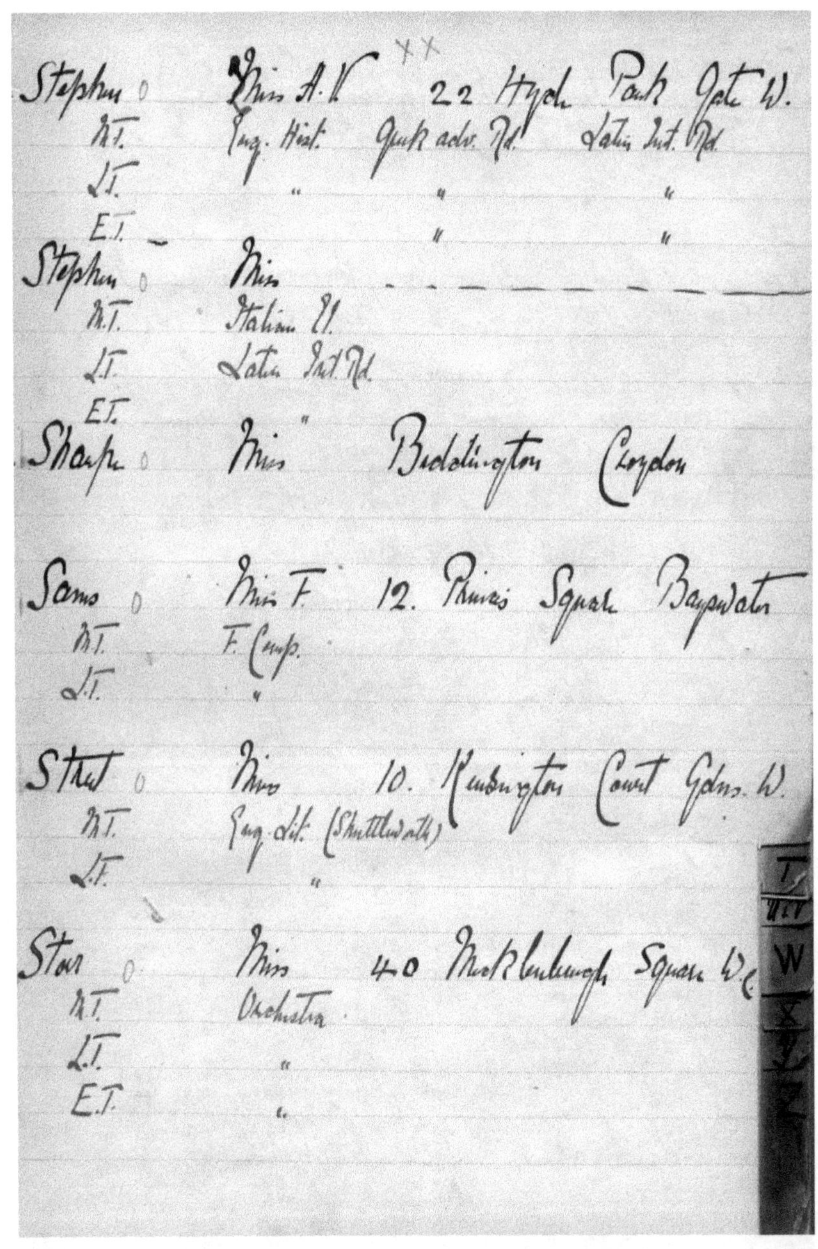

Stephen 0 Miss A.V. 22 Hyde Park Gate W.
M.T. Eng. Hist. Greek adv. Rd. Latin Int. Rd.
L.T. " " "
E.T. " "
Stephen 0 Miss
M.T. Italian El.
L.T. Latin Int. Rd.
E.T.
Sharpe 0 Miss " Beddington Croydon

Sams 0 Miss F. 12. Princes Square Bayswater
M.T. F. Comp.
L.T. "

Street 0 Miss 10. Kensington Court Gdns. W.
M.T. Eng. Lit. (Shuttleworth)
L.T. "

Storr 0 Miss 40 Mecklenburgh Square W.C.
M.T. Orchestra
L.T. "
E.T. "

Fig. 1b.

Smith ✓ Miss Ridley 12 Eaton Place S.W.
M.T. Italian adv. Pl. Sci.
L.T. Dante "

Stephen Miss 22. Hyde Park Gate S.W.
M.T. Architecture Latin int.
L.T. Arch. Latin int
E.T.

Steele ✓ Miss 43. Kensington Square W. xx
M.T. Art (2 V.C.) Perspective, Visits.
L.T. " (3 ") "
E.T. " 1 P. Out door Sketching

Shand ✓ Miss Park Holme Elm Park Gdns S.W. xx
M.T. Divinity
L.T. Divinity
E.T.

Stebbing Miss S. Keith Pk Walton on the Hill Epsom
M.T. Philosophy Art (H.1)

Solomons Miss 46 Westbourne Terrace W. xx
M.T. Philosophy Ethics
L.T. Fr. Lit. Philosophy.

Fig. 1c.

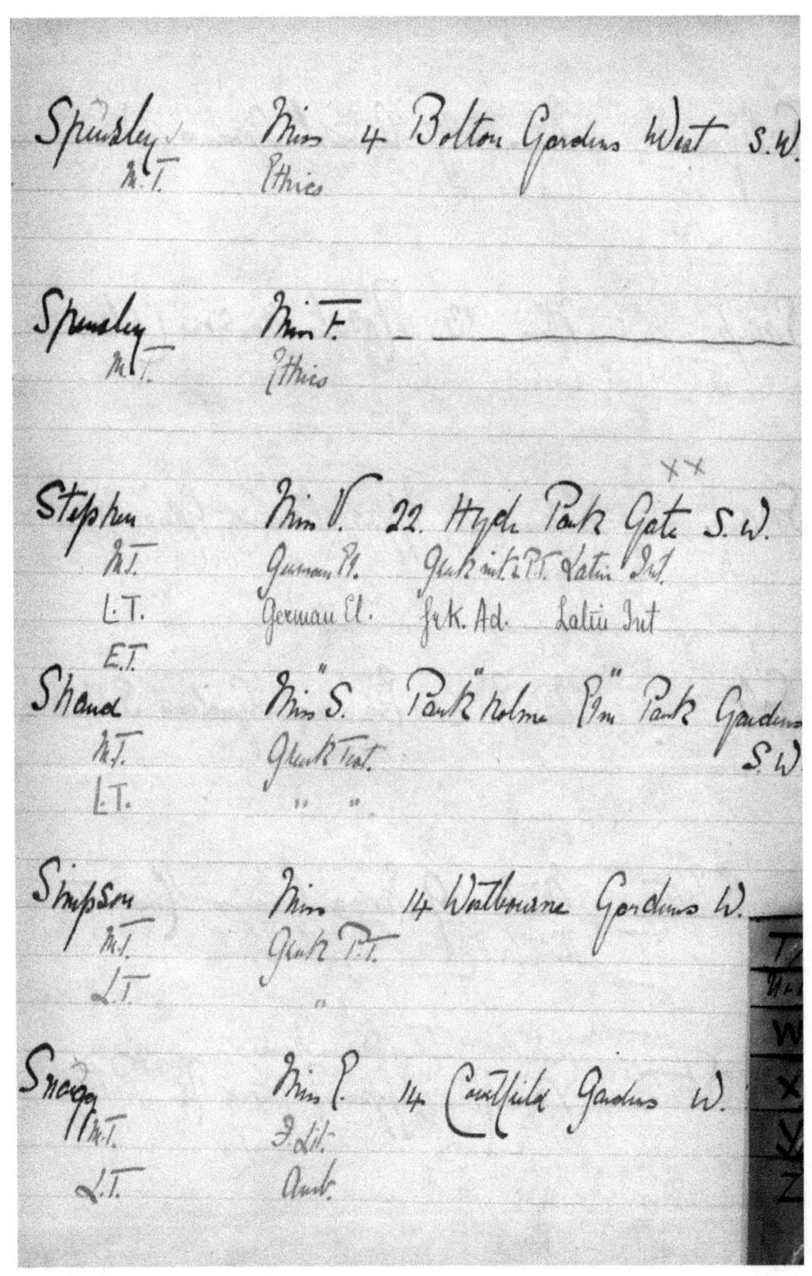

Spurdley — Miss — 4 Bolton Gardens West S.W.
M.T. — Ethics

Spurdley — Miss F. — ———
M.T. — Ethics

Stephen — Miss V. — 22. Hyde Park Gate S.W. ××
M.T. — German Pt. — Greek int. & P.T. — Latin Int.
L.T. — German El. — Grk. Ad. — Latin Int.
E.T.

Shand — Miss S. — Park Holme Elm Park Gardens S.W.
M.T. — Greek Text.
L.T. — " "

Simpson — Miss — 14 Westbourne Gardens W.
M.T. — Greek P.T.
L.T. — "

Snagge — Miss E. — 14 Courtfield Gardens W.
M.T. — Eng. Lit.
L.T. — Anat.

Fig. 1d.

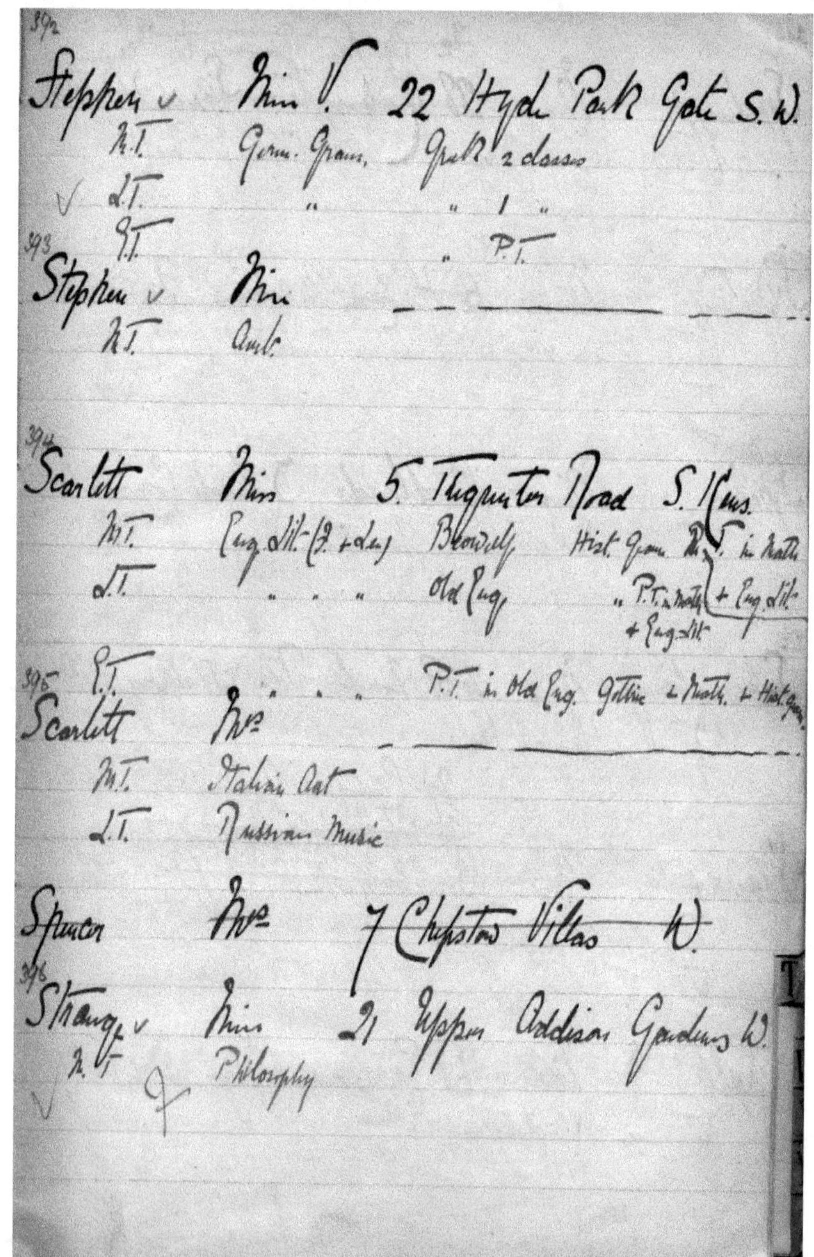

392 Stephen ✓ Miss V. 22 Hyde Park Gate S.W.
M.T. Germ. Gram. Greek 2 classes
✓ L.T. " " 1 "
S.T. " P.T.
393 Stephen ✓ Miss ——————
M.T. Arith.

394 Scarlett Miss 5. [illegible] Road S. Kens.
M.T. Eng. Lit. (3. + Lec.) Browning Hist. Gram. [illegible] in Math
L.T. " " " Old Eng. " P.T. in Math + Eng. Lit. + Eng. Lit.
S.T. " " " P.T. in Old Eng. Gothic + Math. + Hist. Gram.
395 Scarlett Mrs ——————
M.T. Italian Art
L.T. Russian Music

Spencer Mrs 7 ~~Chepstow Villas W.~~
396 Strange ✓ Miss 21 Upper Addison Gardens W.
M.T. Philosophy

Fig. 1e.

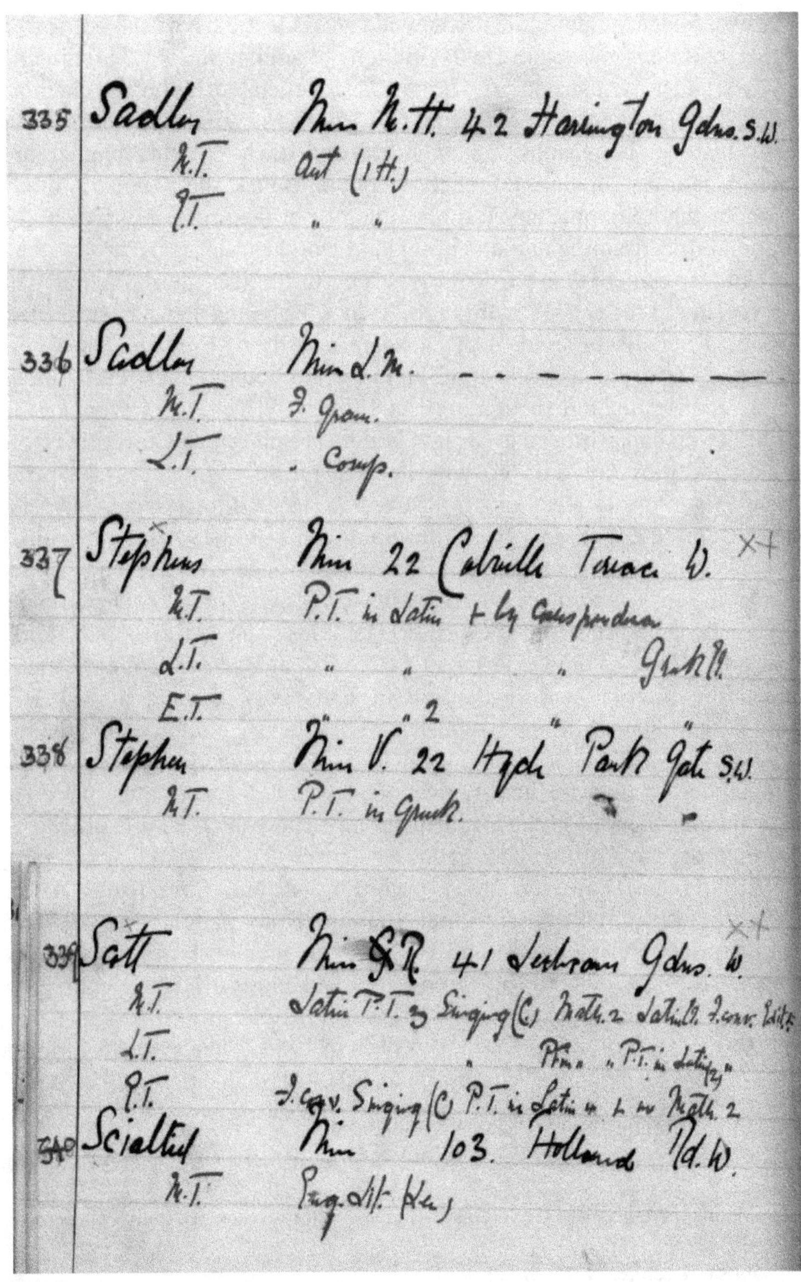

335 Sadler — Miss N. H. 42 Harington Gdns. S.W.
M.T. — Out (1 H.)
[illegible] — " "

336 Sadler — Miss L. M. — — — — —
M.T. — [illegible] Gram.
L.T. — " Comp.

337 Stephens — Miss 22 Colville Terrace W.
M.T. — P.T. in Latin + by Correspondence
L.T. — " " " Greek [illegible]
E.T.

338 Stephen — Miss V. 22 Hyde Park Gate S.W.
M.T. — P.T. in Greek.

339 Scott — Miss [illegible] 41 [illegible] Gdns. W.
M.T. — Latin P.T. [illegible] Singing (C) Math. 2 [illegible]
L.T. — " [illegible] " P.T. in Latin (2) "
[illegible] — [illegible] Singing (C) P.T. in Latin " + in Math. 2

340 Scialtiel — Miss 103. Holland Rd. W.
M.T. — [illegible]

Fig. 1f.

The College syllabi indicate the wide and eclectic list of subjects offered at the Department in the late 1890s, including "animal biology," architecture, art and art history, astronomy, "botany and vegetable biology," chemistry, divinity, English literature (including Old English or Anglo-Saxon), geology, Greek, history, household management and thrift, Latin, mathematics, modern languages (including French, German, Italian, and Spanish), nursing, philosophy, photography, physics, physiology, political economy, psychology, recitation, voice training and elocution, and wood carving.

The Department was particularly strong in English literature, but Woolf never registered for classes in this subject at King's, and as we have seen, she later stated her disapproval of the academic study of English. The English staff at the Department in her time included the young Ernest de Selincourt (then a lecturer in English literature at University College, Oxford); Lilian Faithfull (who had achieved first-class honors at Somerville College, Oxford), and Edith Morley (1875-1964) who became the first woman professor at a British university, at Reading, in 1908.[15] In 1899, Morley and her fellow Ladies' Department student, Caroline Spurgeon (1869-1942), both gained a "First Class at Oxford in the English School," becoming the only London students to do so, through their studies at King's Ladies' Department.[16] Spurgeon became Professor of English Literature in the University of London in 1913 and Head of the Department of English at Bedford College, and she founded the International Federation of University Women in 1919. Her lecture notes taken while she was at King's frequently quote Leslie Stephen's *Dictionary of National Biography* and *Hours in a Library* as sources she was recommended to read for her studies.[17] The Stephen sisters must have been somewhat conspicuous at the Department as the daughters of a man who was well-known to most of their teachers.

Virginia did, however, study both English and Continental History, which were taught by Professor (later Sir) John Knox Laughton (1830-1915), naval historian, Nelson expert and Professor of Modern History at King's.[18] Over the year 1897-8 both the Continental and English History courses (on Tuesdays and Fridays respectively at 10am) covered the historical periods from 1660 to 1702, 1702 to 1748, and 1748 to 1789.[19] The syllabus describes these as "subjects prescribed for the London B.A. Examination, 1898," and the

[15] "Syllabus of Lectures, 1897-8," 15; Oakeley 495-9.

[16] *Historical Sketch, King's College Ladies' Department, 13 Kensington Square*, King's Archives KW/EPH1, 21.

[17] Royal Holloway Archives, Collection PP7 (Papers of Professor Caroline Spurgeon) PP7/2/2-PP7/2/5.

[18] "Syllabus of Lectures, 1897-8," 11.

[19] "Syllabus of Lectures, 1897-8," 10-13.

King's College Calendar for this year states that "For those who are able to pursue a systematic course of study, Lectures have been so arranged as to offer a complete preparation for the Final Pass BA and Intermediate BSc Examinations of the London University."[20] It is therefore clear that these were lectures pitched for students studying at degree level, although a considerable amount of further reading and written study would have been necessary to acquire the standard needed to achieve passes in these exams. Virginia seems to have gone at least some way down this route and, writing to Thoby about the beginning of her studies in October 1897, she reports: "I have to write essays upon historical subjects for my history class, and on Tuesday I am going to have my first essay given back to me with the masters corrections" (*L*1 11). The English History lectures in 1898-99, again given by Laughton (on Fridays at 10am), covered the period from the accession of Queen Elizabeth I to the restoration of the monarchy in 1660.[21]

From autumn 1897 to summer 1900 Virginia studied Greek at the Ladies' Department with George Charles Winter Warr, Professor of Classical Literature at King's. In 1897-98 she took Warr's "Elementary Class" in Greek on Mondays from 2pm to 3.30pm, and in 1898-99 (on Mondays at 3.30pm) she took his "Advanced Grammar and Reading Class" in Greek, studying Sophocles' *Oedipus Coloneus* and "Greek Prose," which were "prescribed for final pass B.A., London 1899."[22] In the Lent and Easter terms of 1900 Virginia was again registered for Advanced Greek with Warr on Mondays at 3.30pm, studying "Thucydides, Book II" which was also prescribed for the final pass BA exams of the University of London.[23]

Warr (1845-1901) was one of the foremost Greek scholars of his day. He had been the prime mover, with King's College's Principal the Reverend Dr. Alfred Barry and Mrs. William Grey, a leader in women's education, in the establishment of the College's "Lectures for Ladies" in the 1870s (Oakeley 491). One of the early fundraising ventures for the Ladies' lectures was the staging of Warr's *Tale of Troy, or Scenes and Tableaux from Homer*, performed in 1883 and 1886. The play, which raised £650 for the Ladies' Department, involved the collaboration of a list of Victorian notables: Lord Leighton designed the opening tableaux; John Ruskin and the Prime Minister William Ewart Gladstone were in the audience, and the performers included Herbert Beerbohm Tree and his wife Helen, Jane Harrison as Penelope, and Woolf's cousin J. K. Stephen as Hector in the Greek performance (Oakeley 492).

[20] *The Calendar of King's College London 1897-8,* Department for Ladies, 294, "Examinations and Certificates and Diplomas"; and "Syllabus of Lectures, 1897-8," 11.
[21] "Syllabus of Lectures, 1898-9," 15.
[22] "Syllabus of Lectures, 1898-9," 20 and 22.
[23] "Syllabus of Lectures, 1899-1900," 22.

Figs. 2a-l. *Syllabi or course catalogues for classes taken by Miss V Stephen and Miss Stephen between 1897 and 1900 (King's College Archives, KW/SYL6-9) in History, Greek, Latin, German, Art and Architecture. Courtesy of King's College London Archives.*

10 DEPARTMENT FOR LADIES.

4. The Invasion of Rome by the Gauls.
5. The War with Pyrrhus.
6 and 7. The Punic Wars.
8. The Conquests of Rome in the East.
9. The Life and Character of the Romans.
10. Recapitulatory Lecture.

Continental History.

PROFESSOR J. K. LAUGHTON, M.A.

Tuesday, 10 a.m.

Michaelmas Term.

* 1660–1702.

France, under the personal rule of Louis XIV., becomes the dominant power in Europe—Colbert, Louvois, Condé, Turenne, Vauban, Duquesne, Tourville—Death of Philip IV. of Spain—Portugal regains its Independence—War between France and Spain—The Triple Alliance—John De Witt—War of France against Holland, Spain, and the Empire—Devastation of the Palatinate—Peace of Nimeguen—Invasion of the Empire by the Turks—Sobieski—Bombardment of Algiers—Revocation of the Edict of Nantes—League of Augsburg—General European War—Peace of Ryswick—The Partition Treaties—Death of Charles II. of Spain.

Lent Term.

§ 1702–1748.

War of the Spanish Succession—General Coalition against France—Overthrow of the French Supremacy—Treaty of Utrecht—Death of Louis XIV.—Relations between France and Spain—Dubois, Alberoni—Elizabeth the "Termagant"—The Quadruple Alliance—War of the Polish Succession—The "Pacte de Famille"—The Pragmatic Sanction—Death of the Emperor Charles VI.—Frederick II., King of Prussia—Maria Theresa—War of the Austrian Succession—General European War—Treaty of Aix-la Chapelle.

* Subjects prescribed for the London B.A. Examination, 1898.
† Subjects prescribed for the Oxford Higher Local Examination, 1898.
‡ Subjects prescribed for the London Intermediate B.Sc. Examination, 1898.
§ Subjects prescribed for the Cambridge Higher Local Examination, 1898.

Fig. 2a.

Easter Term.

§ 1748-1789.

The Seven Years' War—Peace of Paris—Joseph II., Emperor—Partition of Poland—Death of Louis XV. of France—Gustavus III., King of Sweden—War of American Independence—The State of France—Financial Confusion—The Revolt of Opinion—Its spread through Germany—Social and Economical Ferment—France on the verge of Bankruptcy—Meeting of the States General—Outbreak of the Revolution.

English History.

PROFESSOR J. K. LAUGHTON, M.A.

Friday, 10 a.m.

Michaelmas Term.

* 1660-1702.

Charles II.—The Restoration—The Clarendon Code—The Second Dutch War—The Cabal—The Triple Alliance—The Secret Treaty of Dover—The Third Dutch War—The Test Act—Shaftesbury in Opposition—The "Popish Plot"—Impeachment of Danby—The Habeas Corpus Act—The Exclusion Bill—The Rye House Plot—Death of the King.

James II.—Illegal Levy of Taxes—Monmouth's Insurrection—The Bloody Assize—Case of Sir Edward Hales—Attacks on the Rights of the Universities—The Declaration of Indulgence—Arrest and Trial of the Seven Bishops—Birth of the King's Son—Invitation to the Prince of Orange; his Declaration; his Landing—Flight of the King—Meeting of the Convention—Declaration of Right.

William III.—The Convention made into a Parliament—The Non-Jurors—War against France—War in Ireland—Bill of Rights—Massacre of Glencoe—The National Debt—The Bank of England—The Triennial Act—Death of the Queen—Sir John Fenwick's Plot—Peace of Ryswick—Act of

* Subjects prescribed for the London B.A. Examination, 1898.
† Subjects prescribed for the Oxford Higher Local Examination, 1898.
‡ Subjects prescribed for the London Intermediate B.Sc. Examination, 1898.
§ Subjects prescribed for the Cambridge Higher Local Examination, 1898.

Fig. 2b.

Resumption—The Partition Treaties—Act of Settlement—The Kentish Petition—Death of James II.—Death of the King.

Lent Term.

§ 1702–1748.

Anne.—War with France—Marlborough and the Duchess; Rooke; Peterborough—The Union with Scotland—Harley leaves the Ministry—Dr. Sacheverell—Mrs. Masham—Dismissal of Marlborough and Godolphin—Creation of Twelve Peers—Treaty of Utrecht—Intrigues of Bolingbroke—Death of the Queen.

George I.—Inquiry into the conduct of the late Ministry—The Rebellion in Scotland—The Septennial Act—The Triple Alliance—War with Spain—The South Sea "Bubble"—Walpole—War with Spain—Death of the King.

George II.—Treaty of Seville—The Excise Bill—Porteous Riots—Death of the Queen—The Wesleys—Jenkins' Ear—War with Spain—Walpole's Resignation—War with France—The '45—Peace of Aix-la-Chapelle.

Easter Term.

§ 1748–1789.

George II. continued.—Lord Hardwicke's Marriage Act—The Seven Years' War—The "Glorious Year"—Death of the King.

George III.—Bute, Prime Minister—The Peace of Paris—Wilkes; George Grenville—The American Colonies—Their Discontents—The Stamp Act—The Rockingham Ministry—The Grafton Ministry—The Middlesex Election—The North Ministry—The Liberty of the Press—The Royal Marriage Act—Troubles in America—The Boston Port Bill—Revolt of the Colonies—Declaration of Independence—War with France; with Spain; with Holland; in India—Rockingham's Ministry—Shelburne's Ministry—Peace of Versailles—The Coalition—Pitt, Prime Minister—His Peace Legislation.

* Subjects prescribed for the London B.A. Examination, 1898.

† Subjects prescribed for the Oxford Higher Local Examination, 1898.

‡ Subjects prescribed for the London Intermediate B.Sc. Examination, 1898.

§ Subjects prescribed for the Cambridge Higher Local Examination, 1898.

Fig. 2c.

junction. Their relationship and history. The place of Interjections. Prefixes and Suffixes.

Easter Term.

Common Errors in written and spoken English. Hints on Composition. History of some common forms of English versification.

Latin.

PROF. G. C. W. WARR, M.A.

ELEMENTARY CLASS.

Thursday, 2.30 p.m.

The Text-books used are "Via Latina," by Dr. Abbott (Seeley), and "Exercises in Unseen Translation," by Welch and Duffield (Macmillan).

† HIGHER CLASS.

Thursday, 4 p.m.

Livy xxi., Horace, Sat. I., Epp. I.
Latin Syntax and Translation at Sight.

Greek.

PROF. G. C. W. WARR, M.A.

ELEMENTARY CLASS.

Monday, 2—3.30 p.m.

Text-books: Mayor, "Greek for Beginners" (Macmillan); Morice, "Stories in Attic Greek."

A portion of the time is reserved for those who are prepared for less elementary work.

* HIGHER CLASS.

Monday, 3.30 p.m.

Michaelmas and Lent Terms.

Aeschylus, "Septem contra Thebas"; Plato, "Phaedo."
Greek Composition and Translation at sight.

* Subjects prescribed for the London B.A. Examination, 1898.
† Subjects prescribed for the Oxford Higher Local Examination, 1898.
‡ Subjects prescribed for the London Intermediate B.Sc. Examination, 1898
§ Subjects prescribed for the Cambridge Higher Local Examination, 1898

Fig. 2d.

DEPARTMENT FOR LADIES. 15

English History.

PROFESSOR J. K. LAUGHTON, M.A.

Friday, 10 a.m.

Michaelmas Term.

England at the accession of Elizabeth—Its relations with Scotland—with France—with Spain—The State of Ireland—Civil and religious discord—War with Spain—The Queen's last years—Burghley—Howard—Drake—Essex.

Lent Term.

The accession of James I.—Condition of the Catholics—The question of 'Impositions'—Proposals for a Union—The French Treaty—The French War—Petition of Right—Ship Money—The Bishops' War—Raleigh—Buckingham—Wentworth—Laud.

Easter Term.

The impeachment of Strafford—The Grand Remonstrance—The State of Ireland—The Civil War—The King beheaded—The war in Ireland and in Scotland—The First Dutch War—Cromwell Protector—War with Spain—The Restoration.

English Literature.

MISS L. M. FAITHFULL,

Vice-Principal of King's College, Ladies' Department.

Tuesday, 12 noon, *beginning the second week in each Term.*

Michaelmas Term.

‖ PROSE LITERATURE OF THE AGE OF DRYDEN AND POPE.

The beginning of a great epoch in Prose Literature—Late development of Prose—Comparison of the general features of the Prose before and after 1688. Influence of France upon style. Pioneers in the development of Prose. Dryden as a Prose Writer. Sir William Temple. Writers on

* Subjects prescribed for Matriculation, London, 1899.
† Subjects prescribed for Intermediate B.A., London, 189
‡ Subjects prescribed for Intermediate B.A. Honours, Lon on, 1899.
§ Subjects prescribed for Intermediate B.Sc., London, 1899.
‖ Subjects prescribed for Final Pass B.A., London, 1899.
¶ Subjects prescribed for Final Pass B.Sc., London, 1899.
** Subjects prescribed for B.A. Honours, London, 1899.

D

Fig. 2e.

20 DEPARTMENT FOR LADIES.

**§|| Old English.

E. DE SELINCOURT, M.A.,

Monday, 2 p.m.

A class will be held for the study of Old English Grammar, Gothic, and Philology. Special attention will be paid to the following texts. Anglo-Saxon Reader, I. XXI., Beowulf.

Latin.

PROFESSOR G. C. W. WARR, M.A.

ELEMENTARY CLASS.

Thursday, 2.30 p.m.

The Text-books used are "Via Latina," by Dr. Abbott (Seeley), and "Exercises in Unseen Translation," by Welch and Duffield (Macmillan).

* READING CLASS.

Thursday, 3.30 p.m.

Cicero in Catilinam.
" pro M. Marcello.

MISS PATER.

† INTERMEDIATE READING CLASS.

Tuesday, 2 p.m.

Michaelmas Term.

Virgil, Aeneid, IX. X.

Lent Term.

Livy, IX.

Easter Term.

Revision of the above mentioned books.

* Subjects prescribed for Matriculation, London, 1899.
† Subjects prescribed for Intermediate B.A., London, 1899.
‡ Subjects prescribed for Intermediate B.A. Honours, London, 1899.
§ Subjects prescribed for Intermediate B.Sc., London, 1899.
|| Subjects prescribed for Final Pass B.A., London, 1899.
¶ Subjects prescribed for Final Pass B.Sc., London, 1899.
** Subjects prescribed for B.A. Honours, London, 1899

Fig. 2f.

22 DEPARTMENT FOR LADIES.

PROFESSOR G. C. W. WARR, M.A.

‖ ADVANCED READING AND COMPOSITION CLASS.

Monday, 3.30. p.m.

Michaelmas Term.

Sophocles, Oedipus Coloneus. Greek Prose.

Lent Term.

Demosthenes, Meidias and Androtion. Greek Prose.

French.

A. ESCLANGON.

* ADVANCED GRAMMAR.

Wednesday, 10 a.m.

Explication détaillée des difficultés de la *syntaxe* et des *verbes réguliers et irréguliers.*

Étude des *homonymes*, des *idiotismes*, des *synonymes*, des *préfixes*, des *suffixes* et de la *formation de la langue.*

Comparaison entre la *langue française* et la *langue anglaise.*

Premiers principes pour *bien traduire.*

Règles élémentaires d'une *bonne prononciation.*

† COMPOSITION CLASS.

Wednesday, 11 a.m.

Principes de *composition* et de *style.*

Divers genres de style.

Étude des règles nécessaires pour *se former à la composition.*

Étude des *divers genres* de composition—Descriptions—Narrations—Lettres.

Exercices variés de *style* et d'*analyse littéraire.*

Étude complète des *règles de la traduction.*

De l'art *de bien dire.*

* Subjects prescribed for Matriculation, London, 1899.
† Subjects prescribed for Intermediate B.A., London, 1899.
‡ Subjects prescribed for Intermediate B.A. Honours, London, 1899.
§ Subjects prescribed for Intermediate, B.Sc. London, 1899.
‖ Subjects prescribed for Final Pass B.A., London, 1899.
¶ Subjects prescribed for Final Pass B.Sc., London, 1899.
** Subjects prescribed for B.A. Honours, London, 1899.

Fig. 2g.

DEPARTMENT FOR LADIES. 21

Latin.

PROFESSOR G. C. W. WARR, M.A.

ELEMENTARY CLASS.

Thursday, 2.30 p.m.

The Text-books used are "Via Latina," by Dr. Abbott (Seeley), and "Exercises in Unseen Translation," by Welch and Duffield (Macmillan).

* READING CLASS.

Thursday, 3.30 p.m.

Cæsar de Bello Gallico, IV. 20—V. 23.

MISS PATER.

† INTERMEDIATE READING CLASS.

Tuesday, 2 p.m.

Michaelmas Term.

Horace, Odes, I.-III.

Lent Term.

Horace, Odes, IV. and Epodes.

Easter Term.

Cicero de Officiis, III.

† INTERMEDIATE GRAMMAR CLASS.

Friday, 2 p.m.

Prose Composition, Unseen Translation.

PROFESSOR G. C. W. WARR, M.A.

‖ ADVANCED GRAMMAR AND READING CLASS.

Wednesday, 3 p.m.

Advanced Latin Prose Composition and Syntax.
Lucretius de Rerum Nat. V., Cicero pro Sulla.

* Subjects prescribed for Matriculation, London, 1900.
† Subjects prescribed for Intermediate B.A., London, 1900.
‡ Subjects prescribed for Intermediate B.A. Honours, London, 1900.
§ Subjects prescribed for Intermediate B.Sc., London, 1900.
‖ Subjects prescribed for Final Pass B.A., London, 1900.
¶ Subjects prescribed for Final Pass B.Sc., London, 1900.
** Subjects prescribed for B.A. Honours. London, 1900.

E

Fig. 2h.

Greek.

PROFESSOR G. C. W. WARR, M.A.

ELEMENTARY CLASS.

Monday, 2—3.30 p.m.

Text-books: Mayor, "Greek for Beginners" (Macmillan); Morice, "Stories in Attic Greek."

A portion of the time is reserved for those who are prepared for less elementary work.

MISS PATER.

† INTERMEDIATE READING CLASS.

Tuesday, 11 a.m.

Michaelmas Term.

Plato, Ion.

Lent Term.

Sophocles, Antigone.

Easter Term.

Revision and Unseen Translation.

† INTERMEDIATE GRAMMAR CLASS.

Thursday, 11 a.m.

Michaelmas, Lent, and Easter Terms.

Syntax, Prose, and Unseen Translation.

PROFESSOR G. C. W. WARR, M.A.

‖ ADVANCED READING AND COMPOSITION CLASS.

Monday, 3.30. p.m.

Michaelmas Term.

Aristophanes, Vespae. Greek Prose.

Lent Term.

Thucydides, Book II. Greek Prose.

* Subjects prescribed for Matriculation, London, 1900.
† Subjects prescribed for Intermediate B.A., London, 1900.
‡ Subjects prescribed for Intermediate B.A. Honours, London, 1900.
§ Subjects prescribed for Intermediate B.Sc., London, 1900.
‖ Subjects prescribed for Final Pass B.A., London, 1900.
¶ Subjects prescribed for Final Pass B.Sc., London, 1900.
** Subjects prescribed for B.A. Honours, London, 1900.

Fig. 2i.

26 DEPARTMENT FOR LADIES.

German.

MISS E. S. BUCHHEIM

ELEMENTARY CLASS.

Monday, 12 noon.

Reading of Easy German Books suitable for beginners.

Accidence: Theory and Practice.

Learning of Poetry by heart.

Books recommended:—

Aue's "Elementary German Grammar." (Chambers.)

Buchheim's "German Reader," Part I. (Clarendon Press.)

The Clarendon Press "German Poetry for Beginners."

* GRAMMAR AND READING CLASSES.

Monday, 11 a.m.

Advanced German Readings.—Easy composition.

Accidence and Elementary Syntax.

Books recommended:—

(*a*) Aue's "Advanced German Grammar." (Chambers).

(*b*) The Clarendon Press Elementary Prose Composition.

(*c*) Buchheim's "Modern German Reader," Part II. Clarendon Press.

[Under Professor Buchheim's Superintendence.]

HERR H. MENKEN.

Assistant Lecturer.

† INTERMEDIATE GRAMMAR AND COMPOSITION CLASS (1).

Wednesday, 11 a.m.

Advanced German Readings — Grammar — Translation from, and into, German.

* Subjects prescribed for Matriculation, London, 1900.
† Subjects prescribed for Intermediate B.A., London, 1900.
‡ Subjects prescribed for Intermediate B.A. Honours, London, 1900.
§ Subjects prescribed for Intermediate B.Sc., London, 1900.
‖ Subjects prescribed for Final Pass B.A., London, 1900.
¶ Subjects prescribed for Final Pass B.Sc., London, 1900.
** Subjects prescribed for B.A. Honours, London, 1900.

Fig. 2j.

GREEK.

Elementary Class. *Monday*, 2—3.30 *p.m.*

G. C. W. WARR, M.A., PROFESSOR.

Text-books: Mayor, "Greek for Beginners" (Macmillan); Morice, "Stories in Attic Greek."

A portion of the time is reserved for those who are prepared for less elementary work.

† Intermediate Reading Class. *Monday*, 3 *p.m.*

MISS PATER.

Michaelmas Term. Lysias. Eratosthenes and Agoratus.

Lent Term. Aeschylus. Septem contra Thebas.

Easter Term. Revision and Unseen Translation.

† Intermediate Grammar Class. *Thursday*, 11 *a.m.*

MISS PATER.

Syntax, Prose, and Unseen Translation.

‖ Advanced Reading and Composition. *Monday*, 3.30 *p.m.*

G. C. W. WARR, M.A., PROFESSOR.

Michaelmas Term. Homer, Iliad XXII.-XXIV. Greek Prose.

Lent Term. Herodotus, Book II. Greek Prose.

* Subjects prescribed for Matriculation, London, 1901.
† Subjects prescribed for Intermediate B.A., London, 1901.
‡ Subjects prescribed for Oxford Higher Local, 1901.
§ Subjects prescribed for Intermediate, B.Sc. London, 1901.
‖ Subjects prescribed for Final Pass B A., London, 1901.
¶ Subjects prescribed for Final Pass B.Sc., London, 1901.
** Subjects prescribed for Oxford Honours, English Lang. and Lit.

Fig. 2k.

Conversation. *Friday*, 3 *p.m.*

VICTOR SPIERS.

Composition—French Plays—Debates.

N.B.—The Classes are limited to five.

GERMAN.

Elementary Class. *Monday*, 12 *noon.*

MISS E. S. BUCHHEIM.

Reading of Easy German Books suitable for beginners—Accidence: Theory and Practice—Learning of Poetry by heart.

*** Grammar and Reading Class.** *Monday*, 11 *a.m.*

MISS E. S. BUCHHEIM.

Advanced German Readings. — Easy Composition—Accidence and Elementary Syntax.

Books:—The Clarendon Press Edition of Minna von Barnhelm. (Lessing.)

‡† Intermediate Grammar and Composition Class.

H. MENKEN. *Wednesday*, 2 *p.m.*

Advanced German Readings—Grammar —Translation from, and into, German.

Books recommended:—

(*a*) Schiller's "Wallenstein's Tod" (Buchheim's edition).

(*b*) Freitag, "Ingraban."

(*c*) Buchheim's "Prose Composition." (Bell.)

(*d*) For Students preparing for the Intermediate Pass Examination:—Buchheim's "Modern German Reader." Part II. (Clarendon Press.)

* Subjects prescribed for Matriculation, London, 1901.
† Subjects prescribed for Intermediate B.A., London, 1901.
‡ Subjects prescribed for Oxford Higher Local, 1901.
§ Subjects prescribed for Intermediate B.Sc., London, 1901.
‖ Subjects prescribed for Final Pass B.A., London, 1901.
¶ Subjects prescribed for Final Pass B.Sc., London, 1901.
** Subjects prescribed for Oxford Honours, English Lang. and Lit.

Fig. 2l.

Between the autumn of 1899 and the spring of 1901 Virginia studied German at the Ladies' Department, and in the Department's "Class List" for the Michaelmas term 1899 "Miss V Stephen" appears among those who had passed an examination in "German (Elementary)," achieving "class II," while in the Lent term 1901 "Miss Stephen" is again recorded as having achieved "class II" in "German Grammar and Reading."[24] It appears that these were College exams, set and marked by the tutors at the Ladies' Department. The syllabus of lectures for 1897-98 states that "College Examinations are held at the conclusion of each Course of Lectures, but attendance at such Examinations is voluntary. Certificates will be given to those Students who have attended regularly and passed Examinations satisfactorily for three Terms."[25] The Elementary German class Virginia took in Michaelmas 1899 (taught by Miss Emma S. Buchheim on Mondays at 12 noon) is not designated as one aligned to London University exams, but the German Grammar and Reading class in 1900-01 (also on Mondays at 12 noon) did include "subjects prescribed for Matriculation, London, 1901."[26] The question papers and scripts are no longer extant, but Virginia's two "class II" passes (there were three grades of achievement) represent good but not outstanding performances at a level broadly equivalent to university entrance.

Woolf's decision to sit these exams is interesting in light of her ideas in *Three Guineas*, quoted above, on the error of distilling learning down to a single exam paper, but also comments made in her 1927 review "Two Women." Ostensibly a review of a biography of Emily Davies, founder of Girton College, Cambridge, and the *Letters of Lady Augusta Stanley*, this piece is, in fact, a key treatise on women's education. In the review she contrasts these two women, the middle-class reformer and the "court lady," imagining that from their union may spring "some astonishing phoenix of the future who shall combine the new efficiency with the old amenity" (*M* 164). She discusses the obstacles Davies faced in improving education for Victorian women. Their positive education stopped at "a little Latin, a little history, a little housework" but it was the "negative education" that taught women not what they could but what they couldn't do that "cramped and stifled" (*M* 159). Even when women got through the doors of a college, the taboos and obstacles surrounding their learning remained strong. Important for our context here, Woolf's review quotes from an article in the *Saturday Review* about examinations.

[24] "Class List" inserted in *King's College Magazine, Ladies' Department*, number X, Lent term 1900, 1 of the "Class List" (King's College London Archives, K/SER1/170), and *King's College Magazine, Ladies' Department*, number XII, Lent term 1901, 32.

[25] "Syllabus of Lectures, 1897-8," 2-3.

[26] "Syllabus of Lectures, 1899-1900," 26, and "Syllabus of Lectures, 1900-01," 19.

HECTOR

(THE LATE J. K. STEPHEN)

From a photograph by Mendelssohn

Fig. 3. *J. K. Stephen as Hector in the Greek version of the 1883 "Tale of Troy," written by Professor George Warr to raise funds for the King's Ladies' Department. Virginia's cousin performed the role on 30 May 1883, the English version having been given the day before with Herbert Beerbohm Tree as Hector. The photograph appears with Warr's account of the production in the* King's College Magazine, Ladies' Department, *number VII, Lent term 1899, 16-25 and 27-9. King's College London Archives, references K/SER1/170. Courtesy of King's College London Archives.*

THE PLEDGE OF APHRODITE REDEEMED

Her presence softly brooding, for an hour,
Seemed to the town a trance
As of the waves at rest,
A jewel smiling fair on Ilium's breast,
A gently darted glance
Of love, that burgeoned into poignant flower.

ainted by Matthew W. Webb, from the original designs
the late Lord Leighton and Sir E. J. Poynter, P.R.A.

Photographed by Holly

Fig. 4. *"The pledge of Aphrodite redeemed": painted by Matthew W. Webb, from the original designs by Lord Leighton and Sir E. J. Poynter, for the opening tableau of Professor George Warr's* Tale of Troy. *Reproduced from* King's College Magazine, Ladies' Department, *number VII, Lent term 1899, 20. Courtesy of King's College London.*

> The idea of submitting young ladies to local university examinations "almost takes one's breath away" [...] it would be "next to impossible to persuade the world that a pretty first-class woman came by her honours fairly [...] there is a strong and ineradicable male instinct that a learned or even an accomplished young woman is the most intolerable monster in creation." (*M* 161-2)

With hindsight, Woolf's decision to sit her German exams seems a rebellious act.

Woolf's attendance at King's College also required her to face male disquiet closer to home. In November 1897 Leslie Stephen wrote to his friend George Warr:

> My daughter is attending your Greek class. I hope you will allow me to give you one hint. She has been in a very nervous state, wh[ich], though [...] explicable, has given me some anxiety. I have allowed her to go to the class, for wh[ich] she was very anxious; because I think that it does her some good to have the occupation. [...] I should be grateful if you would just remember this & let her off with light work.[27]

Stephen's special pleading for his daughter, and his fear that the classes will be too much for her, certainly underestimates the vigor with which she pursued her studies and the pleasure she derived from the intellectual stimulation. Stephen, though, had reason to be concerned about his daughter's health. In 1895, following the death of her mother, she had suffered a serious breakdown, and her illness was exacerbated by the death of her half-sister, Stella, in July 1897. Despite her father's dismissive focus on the "therapeutic" nature of his daughter's study at King's, Virginia's letters and intermittent diary entries from this period show sustained references to her studies.

In September 1898 Virginia tried to recruit her cousin Emma Vaughan to study with her at King's:

> I have thoughts of learning *Latin* next term at King's College. Would you come too? You know some and I know a little, and it would be great fun going together. Besides you would make the acquaintance of dear old Warr. (*L*1 20)

Six days later she wrote again:

> I find that my beloved Warr gives his Latin classes on a day which is impossible for me, so that I mean to go to Miss Paters Intermediate Latin

[27] Quoted in Dalgarno (41). The original letter is now in the Archives of American Art at the Smithsonian Institution, Washington DC, catalogue identifier AAA 3480.

Fig. 5a-b. *Class List–Exam Results from Michaelmas term 1899 and Michaelmas term 1900 (King's College Archives, KWA/R1). Courtesy of King's College London Archives.*

KING'S COLLEGE, LONDON

LADIES' DEPARTMENT

13, KENSINGTON SQUARE, W.

MICHAELMAS TERM, 1899

CLASS LIST

The mark * implies special distinction

Certificates will be granted in accordance with the regulations in the last issue of the Syllabus and Prospectus. Applications for such Certificates to be made to Miss FAITHFULL, 13, Kensington Square, W.

THE FOLLOWING STUDENTS HAVE PASSED THE OXFORD FIRST WOMEN'S EXAMINATION:

Miss Bray
„ Fraser
„ MacSwinney
„ E. MacSwinney
„ Rutherford

ARCHITECTURE

Class I.	Class II.	Class III.
	Miss E. Greenwood	

BOTANY

Class I.	Class II.	Class III.
Miss Renshaw	Miss Kaye	Miss Manners

ENGLISH LITERATURE (Miss FAITHFULL)

Class I.	Class II.	Class III.	Class IV.
Miss Locock	Miss Rücker	Miss White Miss Lloyd	Miss Cockerell

GERMAN (*Elementary*)

Class I.	Class II.	Class III.
Miss M. Cadman Miss E. Murphy Grimshaw	Miss G. Baggally Miss M. Murphy Grimshaw Miss V. Stephen	

GERMAN (*Grammar and Reading*)

Miss H. Gurney
Miss Hawkins

Fig. 5a.

Michaelmas Term 1900

KING'S COLLEGE MAGAZINE

CLASS LIST.

*The mark * implies special distinction.*

English Language and Literature.

(*Old English.*)

Class I.	*Class II.*	*Class III.*
	Miss Sanderson Miss Selby Lowndes Miss Robinson	Miss Verran

(*Literature*, Miss Faithfull.)

Class I.	*Class II.*	*Class III.*
Miss De Rougemont Miss Scarlett Miss Henty	Miss Shea Miss O. Bray	

(*Literature*, Miss Lee.)

Class I.	*Class II.*	*Class III.*
Miss K. Locock	Miss Scarlett	Miss Henty

(*Outlines*, Miss Morley.)

Class I.	*Class II.*	*Class III.*
	Miss Sanderson Miss C. Hancock	Miss Solomon

German.

(*Elementary.*)

Class I.	*Class II.*	*Class III.*
Miss B. Hales Miss Lightbody	Miss Evans Miss Wedgewood	

(*Grammar and Reading.*)

Class I.	*Class II.*	*Class III.*
Miss Hawkins Miss Owen	Miss Cadman Miss Stephen Miss Tweedie	

32

Fig. 5b.

> class, on Tuesdays at 2. You only do reading Virgil–with her–wont you come to that? I should think it was quite amusing. (*L*1 20)

Emma's older sister Margaret (Marny) was already studying with Warr (*L*1 13). The "Latin Intermediate Reading" classes that Virginia and Vanessa took on Tuesdays with Clara Pater in 1898-99 studied Virgil's *Aeneid* books IX and X, and "Livy, X," and these are described as "subjects prescribed for Intermediate BA, London 1899."[28]

Clara Pater (1841-1910) had tutored students in Classics at Oxford from 1879, and she later became Vice-President of Somerville College, Oxford, and was active in the promotion of higher education for women. It was when she moved to Kensington after her brother's death in 1894 that she became tutor of Greek and Latin at the King's Ladies' Department. In autumn 1899 Virginia began studying Greek as well as Latin with Pater, and the Greek Intermediate class she took with Pater that term (on Tuesdays at 11am) read Plato's *Ion*, a subject prescribed for Intermediate London BA exams.[29] By the summer of 1900 Virginia felt that her studies were paying off, and knew she would sign up again for the following year, asking Emma Vaughan to "diverge into King's College one day [...] and buy me a Syllabus, the biggest kind they have–Price 3d."(*L*1 25). Referring to Pater as "perfectly delightful," she wrote:

> I am, however, feeling a little triumph over the Latin language as though I had stolen a march on it–great rough beast that it is! As for Greek, it is my daily bread, and a keen delight to me (*L*1 26 and 35).

Lyndall Gordon records that in October 1900 Virginia

> began private lessons with old Clara Pater, [...] in an atmosphere of Persian cats and Morris wallpaper, but these lessons proved too undisciplined, and in 1902 Miss Pater was replaced by Janet Case, one of the first women to pass through Girton College, Cambridge, who gave Virginia the only systematic tuition she ever had and introduced her to the feminist cause.[30]

The edition of the Department's magazine published in summer 1901 speaks of Pater's "enforced resignation" (presumably on health grounds) from class teaching at the Department, although it appears that Virginia's continued private

[28] "Syllabus of Lectures, 1898-1899," 20.

[29] "Syllabus of Lectures, 1899-1900," 22.

[30] *ODNB* online, entry for "Virginia Woolf". The Ladies' College's syllabus for 1899-90 states that "Private tuition can be provided in any subject, by special arrangement with the Vice-Principal" (5).

studies with Pater were registered through King's until the end of 1901.[31] Pater's departure was described as "a great loss to our present and future students," and the magazine records that

> Miss Pater's long and close connection with Somerville College was from the first a matter for our pride and congratulation; but these became greater as we watched individual students developing under her influence; as we saw as well as heard them bear testimony to the ambition for good work, the hatred of slovenliness and above all the passion for the best literature she always induced. Many of her students speak warmly of the debt they owe to her for the introduction to some of the highest and noblest pages in literature.[32]

Her place at King's was taken by a "Miss Lucas, fresh from Oxford" but there is no evidence of Virginia having studied with her.

Pater's teaching fostered Virginia's lifelong engagement with Greek literature. The history tutor, Miss Craddock, with whom Kitty studies in Oxford in the 1880 section of *The Years*, is modeled in part on Pater, as is the figure of Julia Craye in the short story "Moments of Being: 'Slater's Pins Have No Points.'" Biographical details link Craye to Pater: she is a music teacher in Kensington whose "well-known" brother has died (*CSF* 215). But the erotic desire and adoration Fanny Wilmot feels for her teacher, Miss Craye, perhaps speak more to Pater's early influence on Woolf and the attraction she felt for the independent, educated women who mentored her early in her life. Only a few years later, in 1905, Woolf would become a teacher herself, teaching history and literature classes at Morley College for Working Men and Women in Lambeth, South London (see Daugherty, "Virginia Woolf Teaching," and "Teaching Woolf").[33]

Apart from their teachers, other details of the environment in which Virginia and Vanessa studied resonate with Woolf's later writings. The key source for this information is the Department's magazine, published two or three times a

[31] *King's College Magazine, Ladies' Department,* number XIII, Easter term 1901, 6.

[32] *King's College Magazine, Ladies' Department,* number XIII, Easter term 1901, 6-7.

[33] Beth Rigel Daugherty's extensive work on Woolf, education, class and reading is an invaluable contribution to a relatively unexplored aspect of Woolf's writing life. Daugherty is currently working on *The Education of a Woman Writer: Virginia Woolf's Apprenticeship*, a book-length project about the impact of Virginia Stephen's education–homeschooling, Morley College teaching, and reviewing–on Virginia Woolf's work as an essayist. This new archival research, however, slightly alters not only Daugherty's claim that "Virginia Woolf basically educates herself," but also that she has "next to no experience as a student" ("Virginia Woolf Teaching" 61 & 62). Although the class composition of students at Morley College was, of course, very different to that at King's Ladies' Department, by the time she started teaching, Woolf would have had a fair amount of exposure to different teaching styles and methods.

year between 1896 and 1914. Assuming that Woolf read the magazine, she must have seen familiar names as well as subjects close to her heart. The Department's library, for instance, grew from a base of 800 volumes during Virginia's time, thanks to donors listed in the magazine, including Jane Harrison, who donated some of her own works.[34] In 1901 the Librarian recorded a characteristic gift from Leslie Stephen, of "Chalmers' *Biographical Dictionary* in thirty-two volumes."[35] Throughout her career, Woolf championed the support of libraries, particularly public libraries and libraries for women, largely because of the opportunity they offered for serendipitous, unconstrained and untutored learning. In the 1930s she gave sustained support, in the form of money and books, to the Women's Service Library, of the London Society for Women's Service (a direct descendant of the first women's suffrage committee; see Pawlowski). One would imagine that she found the Ladies' Department's library not only a useful supplement to her father's library, but also a peaceful escape from the emotionally tangled rooms of 22 Hyde Park Gate.

Other facilities at the Ladies' Department by the time of Virginia's attendance there included classrooms, laboratories, studios, music rooms and a common room for the use of students "in which silence is observed from 10 to 2."[36] In 1897 the Department opened King's Hall, a "house of residence" for students at 28 Kensington Square, run by Lilian Faithfull's sister Eveline, "late student of Somerville College Oxford."[37] "The House is arranged on the usual College principles. Each student has one bed-sitting room fitted up as a study, besides having the use of general sitting-rooms," the Department's Syllabus for 1899-1900 explained.[38]

The Department's magazine indicates a busy extra-curricular life, including hockey, tennis, boating and bicycling clubs and a gymnasium class, a Ladies' Orchestra, a Browning Society under the guidance of Edith Morley, and a dramatic club which aimed to give performances once a term (W. S. Gilbert's *Pygmalion and Galatea* was performed on 13 December 1898 and Sheridan's *The Rivals* was given "by the amalgamated clubs of the Ladies' Branch and King's College, Strand" on 9 February 1899).[39] A King's College Guild was founded in March 1898 to support the Women's Settlement in Stratford (a poor area of London's East End).[40] There was a literary and debating society in which "party spirit" ran high, and in 1901 a society for scientific discussion was formed (Oakeley 499).

[34] *King's College Magazine, Ladies' Department,* number VII, Lent term 1899, 28.
[35] *King's College Magazine, Ladies' Department,* number XII, Lent term 1901, 30.
[36] "Syllabus of Lectures, 1897-8," 2.
[37] "Syllabus of Lectures 1899-1900," 4.
[38] King's College London Archives KW/SYL8.
[39] *King's College Magazine, Ladies' Department,* number VII, Lent term 1899, 30-1.
[40] *King's College Magazine, Ladies' Department,* number VI, Michaelmas term 1898, 1.

Some features in the magazine hint at discussions held at the Ladies' Department that may have contributed to Virginia's later thinking and writing on women's lives and work. In autumn 1897 the "opening address" of the Department's year was given (for the first time by a woman) by "Mrs. Creighton," probably Louise Hume von Glehn Creighton (1850–1936, wife of Mandell Creighton, Bishop of London), who became well-known as a moderate voice in the women's suffrage movement and had been one of the first to pass the University of London's Special Examination for Women in the 1860s. Taking as her subject "Fanny Burney," Mrs. Creighton opined that "with all her advantages the modern woman is not necessarily more cultured than her grandmothers"; this perhaps sowed the seeds for Woolf's call, in *A Room of One's Own*, for women to "think back through their mothers" (*AROO* 99).[41]

Closer Woolfian foreshadowings can perhaps be found in an article on "College Education for Women" by Lilian Faithfull, which was printed in the Lent and Michaelmas 1900 editions of the Department's magazine, and quoted at length in Faithfull's memoirs, published in 1924.[42] Faithfull was well-placed to describe the variety of higher education opportunities available to women, since she had been an undergraduate at Somerville College, Oxford, and had taught at the women's residential Royal Holloway College in Egham for five years before she came to King's. After leaving King's, in 1907, she went on to follow Dorothea Beale (whose biography Woolf read while researching *The Years*) as Principal of Cheltenham Ladies' College (which at this stage offered studies at degree level as well as secondary schooling). She became a leading member of the Association of Head Mistresses, and one of the first women to be appointed as a magistrate in England.

Many of Faithfull's discussions of the benefits of women's education prefigure the portrait of Fernham in *A Room of One's Own* but, in contrast to Woolf, assume the return of women to the home following their studies. In her 1900 article for the Ladies' Department's magazine, for example, Faithfull describes the movement for the higher education of women as having made a "wonderful advance" in the last 20 years:

> I do not want merely to contend that College life does not do the harm that was prophesied, but that it does infinitely more good than was anticipated; that it developes [sic] girls morally and socially as well as mentally. That it tends to implant in them certain qualities in which women are too often lamentably deficient, and that it adds greatly, not only to the happiness of a

[41] *King's College Magazine, Ladies' Department*, number IV, Michaelmas term 1897, 4.
[42] *King's College Magazine, Ladies' Department,* number X, Lent term 1900, "College Education for Women" by L M Faithfull, 6-10; *King's College Magazine, Ladies' Department,* number XI, Michaelmas Term 1900, "College Education for Women *(continued)*" by L M Faithfull, 5-9, and *In the House of my Pilgrimage*, 61-8.

> few years when a woman is most impressionable, most full of the capacity for enjoyment, when her vitality is most abundant, but also provides her with a deep and permanent source of happiness for after life.[43]

In the "London and non-resident colleges," she says,

> there is for a true student the difficulty of satisfying the demands of home and college, of her domestic and intellectual life. [...] For many girls the home life is, I know well, a necessity–they cannot be spared; and then a compromise is all that can be achieved, but it is effected at considerable cost to the worker and to the work. There is no question that the dual life is difficult and wearing, and for any girl who has the instinct of a scholar, I would plead that she should be given, if possible, freedom from home ties for a time, with the certainty that she will chafe less, and return to them more willingly, when her ambitions have been somewhat satisfied.[44]

In the "resident colleges," Faithfull describes how

> [t]he greater part of each day is spent by the student in her own room. Sometimes girls prefer to work together, but as a rule they seem to find that solitude conduces to concentration, and that a self-imposed isolation is advisable. This solitude in a corporate life is surely most valuable, and the necessity for it is too often forgotten in home life. [...] The possession of a castle of one's own is, perhaps, the first keen joy of College life.[45]

Faithfull goes on to warn that residential college friendships "too often degenerate into a sentimental devotion, good neither for the worshipper nor the one worshipped." Her observation that these "absurd relationships" lead invariably to "loss of dignity and self-respect" seems to foreshadow Woolf's later reading about Dorothea Beale's horror at "the unhealthy attachments" fostered at women's schools and colleges, and the depiction of homoerotic relations between Kitty and her tutor Miss Craddock in *The Pargiters* (*P* 80), or as described above in "Moments of Being: 'Slater's Pins Have No Points.'"

Faithfull's phrase "a castle of one's own" resonates, of course, with Woolf's 1929 essay, *A Room of One's Own*. As a non-residential student, Woolf would have to wait until her move to Bloomsbury for her room of her own, but she may well have enjoyed the freedom and female company found in the Department's communal spaces. Unfortunately, Woolf does not comment on her fellow students, and does not seem to have forged any lasting friendships during her time there. The Department's records indicate that, while many of the "Ladies" had addresses

[43] *King's College Magazine, Ladies' Department*, number X, Lent term 1900, 6.
[44] *King's College Magazine, Ladies' Department*, number X, Lent term 1900, 8.
[45] *King's College Magazine, Ladies' Department*, number XI, Michaelmas term 1900, 5-6.

of equal social prestige to Virginia's, such as those who lived in Hyde Park, Bayswater, Knightsbridge, and Regent's Park, and that some had aristocratic titles, many others (probably particularly those training to be teachers) came from areas of London that were then poorer, such as Streatham, Brixton, Lewisham, Stepney, Lambeth, New Cross Gate, and Fulham.[46] Although Faithfull was keen to develop "a band of more ambitious spirits, able and willing to give up their days to study and take a University Degree" she also welcomed the diversity of students at King's Ladies' Department, commenting on how "the amateur, with her wider knowledge, her familiarity with standards of taste unknown to the professional, and her love of learning for its own sake, corrected the too utilitarian attitude of the over-worked student in training" (Faithfull 109 and 112).

A Room of One's Own, The Years, and *Three Guineas* make much of the economic disparity between funding for men's and women's colleges, and the discrepant amounts spent by fathers on educating their sons and daughters. Faithfull too describes the funding of the Ladies' Department as a constant concern, remarking that "we were desperately poor [...] We had no endowment, no scholarships, and a debt on our buildings" (Faithfull 110). After the gravy soup and yellowed sprouts served up at Fernham, the narrator in *A Room of One's Own* considers the meager results of the women's college's fund-raising efforts: "to raise bare walls out of bare earth was the utmost they could do" (*AROO* 29). In *Three Guineas*, in response to a letter from the treasurer of a women's college asking for a contribution to their rebuilding fund, Woolf dissects more closely the correlation between the relative poverty of women's colleges and resistance to women's education. Even in 1937, "colleges for the sisters of educated men are, compared with their brothers' colleges, unbelievably and shamefully poor" (*TG* 194). The self-perpetuating cycles of women's exclusion from education, or education solely as preparation for marriage, mean that colleges like Newnham continue to struggle to exist. One excerpt from the "Notes and Suggestions" page of the *King's College Magazine Ladies' Department* (1898) reads as though it comes straight out of *Three Guineas*:

> An anonymous friend has given £15,000 towards the liquidation of the College debt [...] We in Kensington, are, however, just a little envious. A quarter of that sum would enable the Committee to make all sorts of improvements in the Ladies' Department,–perhaps even to found

[46] King's College London Archives, KWA/R3a (records of classes paid for). An analysis of the College enrolment records (which includes addresses) for students for 1897-98 (KW/RAD3) records Virginia's fellow students in the Continental and English History classes as coming almost entirely from similar upper-middle-class areas to the Stephens at Hyde Park Gate.

> Scholarships, and to supply the Library with some of the many books of reference of which we stand so sorely in need.[47]

For Woolf, though, such poverty was something of a blessing; she found the effects of wealth, ceremonies, traditions and treasures stultifying, incompatible with adventurous and transgressive education:

> The aim of the new college, the cheap college, should be not to segregate and specialize, but to combine. It should explore the ways in which mind and body can be made to cooperate; discover what new combinations made good wholes in human life [...] People who love learning for itself would gladly come there (*TG* 200).

In her essay "Why?" she asks

> Why, since life holds only so many hours, waste one of them on being lectured? [...] why continue an obsolete custom which not merely wastes time and temper, but incites the most debased of human passions–vanity, ostentation, self-assertion, and the desire to convert? [...] Why not invent human intercourse?"(*DM* 146-7)

Recent scholarship has explored Woolf's alternative sites of pedagogy, in particular the democratizing concept of the active, dialogic common reader (see Daugherty, "Virginia Woolf Teaching"; "Readin'"; "Teaching Woolf"; and Cuddy-Keane). King's Ladies' Department may not have been Woolf's utopian space of learning, but it was certainly diverse in its constituency and adventurous in its aims. It is curious that Woolf did not draw more directly on her experience at King's in her writing, given that she had such sustained exposure to a women's college from the inside.[48] Perhaps she preferred to think of herself as an autodidact and felt that her real learning had taken place outside institutional walls.

[47] *King's College Magazine, Ladies' Department*, number V, Lent term 1898, 1.
[48] "A Woman's College from the Outside" (*CSF*). This was originally published as Woolf's contribution to *Atalanta's Garland, being the book of the Edinburgh University Women's Union* (Edinburgh UP, 1926).

Virginia's registrations at King's Ladies' Department

1897	Michaelmas (autumn) term	Continental History English History Greek Elementary
1898	Lent (spring) term	Continental History English History Greek Elementary
1898	Easter (summer) term	Continental History English History Greek Elementary
1898	Michaelmas term	English History Greek Advanced Reading Latin Intermediate Reading
1899	Lent term	English History Greek Advanced Reading Latin Intermediate Reading *(and Vanessa)*
1899	Easter term	Greek Advanced Reading Latin Intermediate Reading *(and Vanessa)*
1899	Michaelmas term	Greek Intermediate and private tuition Latin Intermediate (*and Vanessa*) German Elementary Passes German Elementary exam
1900	Lent term	Greek Advanced Latin Intermediate (*and Vanessa*) German Elementary
1900	Easter term	Greek Advanced Latin Intermediate (*and Vanessa*) German Elementary
1900	Michaelmas term	Greek (two classes) German Grammar Passes German Grammar and Reading exam
1901	Lent term	Greek (one class) German Grammar
1901	Easter term	Greek (private tuition)
1901	Michaelmas term	Greek (private tuition)

Vanessa's registrations at King's Ladies Department

1898	Michaelmas term	Italian Elementary
	Lent term	Latin Intermediate Reading
	Easter term	Latin Intermediate Reading
1899	Michaelmas term	Architecture
		Latin Intermediate
1900	Lent term	Architecture
		Latin Intermediate
1900	Easter term	Latin Intermediate
1900	Michaelmas term	Art

Works Cited

Bell, Quentin. *Virginia Woolf: A Biography*. London: Grafton Books, 1987.

Cuddy-Keane, Melba. *Virginia Woolf, the Intellectual and the Public Sphere.* Cambridge: Cambridge UP, 2003.

Dalgarno, Emily. *Virginia Woolf and the Visible World.* Cambridge: Cambridge UP, 2001.

Daugherty, Beth Rigel. "Readin', Writin' and Revisin': Virginia Woolf's 'How Should One Read A Book?'" *Virginia Woolf and the Essay*. Ed. Beth Carole Rosenberg and Jeanne Dubino. New York: St. Martin's, 1997: 159-75.

——. "Teaching Woolf/Woolf Teaching." *Woolf Studies Annual* 10 (2004): 275-307.

——. (ed). "Virginia Woolf's 'How Should One Read a Book?'" *Woolf Studies Annual* 4 (1998): 123-85.

——. "Virginia Woolf Teaching/Virginia Woolf Learning: Morley College and the Common Reader." *New Essays on Virginia Woolf.* Ed. Helen Wussow. Dallas: Contemporary Research Press, 1995: 61-77.

Dunn, Jane. *A Very Close Conspiracy: Vanessa Bell and Virginia Woolf.* London: Jonathan Cape, 1990.

Dyhouse, Carol. *Girls Growing up in Late Victorian and Edwardian England.* London: Routledge and Kegan Paul, 1981.

——. *No Distinction of Sex? Women in British Universities 1870-1939*. London: UCL Press, 1995.

Faithfull, Lilian M. *In the House of my Pilgrimage*. London: Chatto & Windus, 1924.

Gordon, Lyndall. "Woolf, (Adeline) Virginia (1882-1941)," *Oxford Dictionary of National Biography*, Oxford University Press, 2004; online edn, May 2005 [http://www.oxforddnb.com/view/article/37018, accessed 2 Feb 2010].

King, James. *Virginia Woolf.* London: Hamish Hamilton, 1994.

King's College Archives. Registration records for King's College Ladies' Department 1897-1901 (KWA/RAD 3-7); Syllabi for King's College Ladies' Department 1897-1901 (KW/SYL 6-9); King's College Magazine, Ladies' Department 1897-1901 (K/SER1/170); Class List–Exam Results 1899 and 1900 (KWA/R1); Historical Sketch, King's College Ladies' Department (KW/EPH1); King's College Ladies' Department records of classes paid for (KWA/R3a).

Lee, Hermione. *Virginia Woolf.* London: Chatto and Windus, 1996.

Love, Jean O. *Virginia Woolf: Sources of Madness and Art.* Berkeley: U of California P, 1977.

Marsh, Neville. *The History of Queen Elizabeth College*. London: King's College London, 1986.

Mepham, John. *Virginia Woolf: A Literary Life*. London: Macmillan, 1991.

Oakeley, Hilda D. "King's College for Women." *The Centenary History of King's College London* by F. J. C. Hearnshaw. London: Harrap, 1929: 489-509.

Pawlowski, Merry M. "The Virginia Woolf and Vera Douie Letters: Woolf's Connections to the Women's Service Library." *Woolf Studies Annual* 8 (2002): 3-62.

Reid, Panthea. *Art and Affection: A Life of Virginia Woolf.* Oxford: Oxford UP, 1996.

Rose, Phyllis. *Woman of Letters: A Life of Virginia Woolf.* London: Routledge, 1978.

Spurgeon, Caroline. Unpublished papers. Archives of Royal Holloway, University of London. Collection PP7.

Woolf, Virginia. *The Complete Shorter Fiction.* Ed. Susan Dick. London: Grafton, 1991.

——. *The Death of the Moth and Other Essays.* London: The Hogarth Press, 1942.

——. *The Diary of Virginia Woolf.* Vol. 4. Ed. Anne Olivier Bell and Andrew McNeillie. London: Hogarth Press, 1982.

——. *The Flight of the Mind: The Letters of Virginia Woolf.* Vol. 1. Ed Nigel Nicolson and Joanne Trautmann. London: Hogarth Press, 1975.

——. *The Moment and Other Essays*. London: The Hogarth Press, 1947.

——. *The Pargiters: The Novel-Essay Portion of* The Years. Ed. Mitchell A. Leaska. London: The Hogarth Press, 1978.

——. *A Room of One's Own* and *Three Guineas*. Ed. Morag Shiach. Oxford: Oxford UP, 1992.

——. *The Sickle Side of the Moon: The Letters of Virginia Woolf.* Vol. 5. Ed. Nigel Nicolson and Joanne Trautmann. London: Hogarth Press, 1979.

Posthumous Was a Woman: World War I Memorials and Woolf's Dead Poet's Society

Bette London

Now my belief is that this poet who never wrote a word and was buried at the crossroads still lives. . . . for great poets do not die; they are continuing presences; they need only the opportunity to walk among us in the flesh.
—Virginia Woolf, *A Room of One's Own*

When Virginia Woolf wrote these words, she was not, of course, referring to the dead soldier-poets of World War I: the men who also "died young," their gifts still unrealized, and who were buried where they fell in the battlefields of Belgium and France.[1] Yet Woolf's invocation of Shakespeare's sister, coming as it did ten years after the Peace was declared, followed a period of national obsession with the fate, in spirit if not name, of Shakespeare's brothers—the men, as David Cannadine puts it, "of brilliance, promise and innocence, who were snuffed out in the carnage of the First World War" (199). And these war dead—these dead poets, as they were most commonly figured—were still very much alive in the public consciousness when, in *A Room of One's Own*, Woolf took up the woman writer's cause. The years immediately succeeding the war, in fact, saw an unprecedented display of public and private acts of commemoration, most notably the erection of the Cenotaph, or "the empty tomb," in Whitehall in July 1919 and the burial of the Unknown Warrior in Westminster Abbey on Armistice Day 1920, timed to coincide with the unveiling of a new Cenotaph, now made permanent by popular demand. The response was not one that could be easily forgotten: "by the end of the week, it was estimated that one million people had visited the Cenotaph and the graveside, and that no less than 100,000 wreaths had been laid either in the Abbey or in Whitehall" (Cannadine 224).

[1] Edna Longley notes that "during the war 'soldier poet' was a tautology—('almost as familiar as a ration-card,' says Edmund Blunden)—rather than a problematic category" (58). Samuel Hynes notes, "In 1916 it was decided that no bodies should be returned to England, but that they should be buried where they fell (more or less: there were more than twelve hundred patches of soldiers' graves in France alone at the end of the war, and these were eventually consolidated)" (271). In 1920, after considerable discussion culminating in a debate in Parliament, the decision was reaffirmed: it was decided that there would be no repatriation of dead soldiers or private memorials: "All British and Empire soldiers would be buried—or would remain buried—where they fell . . . the name of every soldier who died would be recorded, either in a cemetery or—where no body was found—on one of a number of memorials" (Dyer 12). This decision contributed to the immense popularity of war memorials on home ground, where they served for many as substitute graves.

And the process did not stop there; what, as Karen L. Levenback reminds us, Woolf called the "lurid scene" of the "night of the Cenotaph"—a scene "like one in Hell"—was followed by "approximately forty thousand memorials throughout England," reaching their height in the early 1920s, when memorial tributes and "unveilings" could be observed on a daily basis (Levenback 31; 39).[2] In East London alone, Mark Connelly has identified "the unveiling and dedication of some twenty-six memorials in East and West Ham between January 1919 and Armistice Day 1921, forty-one in the City, twenty-two in Tower Hamlets, ten in Ilford and three in Romford" (143). Elsewhere in London, notable memorials, impossible to miss, included the London and North Western Railway memorial obelisk in Euston Station (1921) and the Royal Artillery Memorial at Hyde Park Corner (1925). And throughout the 1920s, Sir Edwin Lutyens, the designer of the Cenotaph and one of the key architects for the Imperial War Graves Commission, continued to leave his mark on other London structures, including the Royal Naval Division memorial at Horse Guards Parade (1925) and the Mercantile Marine memorial at Tower Hill (1928). The London Woolf so avidly longed for with the return of peace could be seen, then, as an urban landscape that was being transformed into a testimonial tract.[3] Indeed, as Geoff Dyer has argued, in the postwar years, Britain entered a "phase of protracted mourning" only "formally completed with the inauguration of the Memorial to the Missing of the Somme at Thiepval in 1932" (30-31).[4] This essay proposes to read *A Room of One's*

[2] In her diary entry for 12 December 1920, Virginia Woolf writes: "I forget my first view of Molly [Hamilton], going down the Strand the night of the Cenotaph; such a lurid scene, like one in Hell. A soundless street; no traffic; but people marching. Clear, cold, & windless. A bright light in the Strand; women crying Remember the Glorious Dead, & holding out chrysanthemums. Always the sound of feet on the pavement. Faces bright & lurid . . . .A ghastly procession of people in their sleep" (*D2* 79-80). As Levenback notes, "The actual number [of war memorials] is in doubt. The National Inventory of War Memorials by the Imperial War Museum, begun in 1989, estimates that there are 54,000 war memorials in the British Isles, most of which were erected after the First World War" (31n19). The figure of 40,000 represents K. S. Inglis's speculation, arrived at before the work of the National Inventory was completed. Levenback cites Eric Homberger, "The Story of the Cenotaph," *Times Literary Supplement*, 12 Nov. 1976, 1429-30, for the daily occurrence of unveilings in the early 1920s.

[3] Recent scholarship has increasingly investigated Woolf's engagement with the culture of monuments and memorialization. See, for example, Jeanette McVicker's probing analysis of Woolf's critique of monumentalization and her interrogation of the remapping of the urban landscape and its implications for gender in "Six Essays on London Life." Vara Neverow illuminates the place of war memorials in *Jacob's Room* in her annotated edition of the text. David Bradshaw explicates the culture of commemoration in *Mrs. Dalloway*, including an extended discussion of the Cenotaph.

[4] The Memorial to the Missing of the Somme at Thiepval, Britain's largest war memorial,

Own through and against this postwar context. The culture of remembrance, it suggests, provides an important frame of reference for understanding Woolf's own meditation in *Room* on the absent and the missing. But in invoking—and inhabiting—the tropes of remembrance, *Room* also displaces them, allowing the text to both engage and critique the official structures of memorialization.

Formal monuments were not the only way memorialization was being performed at this time, nor were they unique in the way they entwined and impressed on the public mind the cult of the dead soldier-poet and the idea of a lost or missing generation. The "immense investment in war poetry as 'marketable sentiment' in newspapers and anthologies," already evident by the middle of the war, continued unabated in the immediate postwar years (Haughton 422), and Woolf's densely allusive text is also attentive to these alternative structures of remembrance. If the first phase of this enthusiasm found its apotheosis in the canonization of Rupert Brooke, himself, Robert Wohl suggests, transformed into "a patriotic monument of marble" almost immediately upon his death (Wohl 91),[5] the counter story of war that increasingly took hold with the posthumous collections of Wilfred Owen (1920) and Isaac Rosenberg (1922) did not so much displace the central icon of the lost/doomed youth of unfulfilled promise as deromanticize it, resituating the locus of tragedy in the horror of war and in the fate of a generation callously delivered to meaningless slaughter.[6] The decade's end, moreover, as historians of

---

was also designed by Sir Edward Lutyens; along with the Cenotaph at Whitehall, it is Lutyens' most influential memorial. Lutyens was a central architect of the war cemeteries in Belgium and France. He designed more than fifty memorials in cities, towns, and villages in Britain and abroad, and his designs were frequently copied and adapted by other war memorial designers; he also reused his own motifs in multiple memorials. The Cenotaph, for example, was especially popular, and memorial cenotaphs were common throughout the UK and abroad. See Skelton and Gliddon for illustrations of Lutyens' war work. See also King for Lutyens' influence on other memorial artists.

[5] Hynes makes a similar point: "Rupert Brooke had become a monument" (300). Churchill's eulogizing of Brooke, when news of his death reached London, turned Brooke into an instant "icon in which an entire class could recognize itself and by means of which it could justify the sacrifice of its sons, whose slaughter was assuming alarming proportions" (Wohl 91). This reputation was cemented with the posthumous publication, in 1915, of *1914, and other poems*, with its infamous portrait of Brooke, and *Collected Poems*, with a biographical note by Margaret Lavington; Brooke's iconic status was revived and consolidated with the publication in 1918 of *Collected Poems, with a memoir* by Edward Marsh.

[6] These were, of course, supplemented by notable publications of "living poets"—most influentially, perhaps, Siegfried Sassoon, reviewed twice by Virginia Woolf in the *TLS*, but also Robert Graves, six of whose books were published by the Hogarth Press between 1923 and 1926, and Ivor Gurney. These survivors of the war frequently represented themselves as, in effect, already dead, thus casting their work as, in some sense, posthumous.

the war have frequently noted, saw "a rash of books about the generation of 1914 and their war experiences, many of which became runaway best-sellers," with 1929, the year *A Room of One's Own* was published, the "big year for war books in England" and 1928, the year Woolf delivered the lectures upon which she based her text, a close second (Wohl 105, 106).[7]

S. P. Rosenbaum's publication of the manuscript versions of *A Room of One's Own* makes clear that "the fiction of Shakespeare's sister was not part of Woolf's original Cambridge talk" (Woolf, *Women & Fiction* xxvi). Nor was the trope of "the blank spaces on the shelves," of "looking about the shelves for books that were not there" (*AROO* 54, 47). The evolution of these motifs in the year between the talk and the publication of *Room* locates these developments at precisely the moment a new orthodoxy of disillusionment with the war was being consolidated in belated war memoirs and the moment, Wohl suggests, the idea of a "lost" generation, initially associated with disorientation and discontinuity, "was increasingly being equated with [a] 'missing' generation," and "the suggestion of physical absence" (Wohl 112). When, in *A Room of One's Own*, then, Woolf writes, "When the guns fired in August 1914, did the faces of men and women show so plain in each other's eyes that romance was killed?" (15), she echoes what surely must have seemed, at that moment, a familiar anti-war refrain: the death of romance. Indeed, in focusing on the ugly truths the war brought to light, Woolf aligns her work with the gritty realism and new truth-telling that defined those works. The romance, however, so systematically dismantled in the war books of the late 1920s was romance of a different kind from the one Woolf spotlights—the romance of war. For these works had as an implicit target the idealistic rhetoric—of adventure, heroism, patriotism, glory, and self-sacrifice—that the experience of trench warfare quickly shattered. And when Woolf prefaces this passage, her most extended and explicit reference to the war in this text, with the question "Shall we lay the blame on the war?" (15)—indeed, when she inserts the question in this seemingly unlikely place (a discussion of dead vs. living poets)—she does so at a moment when "blaming it on the war" had become something of a fashionable pastime, a point her holograph insertions to the Fitzwilliam manuscript of *Women & Fiction* underline.[8]

[7] For other discussions of this boom in war books, see Fussell, and Hynes (423-469). Hynes locates *A Room of One's Own* as part of this moment, aligning it with works like those of Graves, Sassoon, and Blunden (468). As Hynes points out, the Hogarth Press was one of the first to take up works expressing these anti-war sentiments, with its publication in 1925 of Herbert Read's *In Retreat*—a text he had been unable to publish in 1919 when the world was not yet ready for "the simple facts" of the war (298-299).

[8] See, for example, this allusion to the scapegoating of the war: "<the war is made the scapegoat for / simply>," and this noting of the ubiquity of such sentiments; "<One has only to> /<read novels, newspaper; to hear people [say?]" (*Women & Fiction* 20). Wohl

This passage, culminating in the only half-rhetorical question, "But why say 'blame'? Why, if it was an illusion, not praise the catastrophe, whatever it was, that destroyed illusion and put truth in its place?" (*AROO* 15), is cited frequently in Woolf scholarship. What is less frequently noted is the way the passage specifically invokes the postwar literature of disillusionment from which it takes off—both literally and figuratively: "For truth . . . those dots mark the spot where, in search of truth, I missed the turning up to Fernham" (15).[9] Woolf's recognition of the importance of the war in opening careers for women, a point she makes in distinguishing "the chief occupations that were open to women before 1918" (37) from those now before her audience, has also been noted as a crucial context for *A Room of One's Own*, making possible Woolf's appeal to her audience to do the work that would give "the dead poet who was Shakespeare's sister" the "opportunity to walk among us in the flesh" ([118], 117). Yet despite the acknowledged importance of these moments, and despite a growing consensus that Woolf, throughout her career, was deeply engaged with issues of war, *A Room of One's Own* has not generally been read as one of Woolf's "war books."[10] Nor does the text, for the most part, call attention to what Teresa Winterhalter has called its "lexicon of war," and what I would like to call its "lexicon of war

---

suggests that by 1929, an effort was already underway to counter the monolithic view of the war perpetrated by the new surge of "anti-war" publications. Charles Carrington's *A Subaltern's War* was published in 1929 and reissued in 1930; Douglas Jerrold's *The Lie About the War* was published in 1930 (108-09). Wohl also cites T. E. Lawrence's resistance to the war book craze: "In 1929, when the war-book boom was getting underway and self-pity among the survivors had become a respectable and financially profitable attitude, Lawrence warned his friends against blaming all their current problems on the war. . . . When the translation of *All Quiet on the Western Front* appeared in England, Lawrence dismissed it as 'postwar nostalgia shoved into the war period' and 'the screaming of a feeble man'" (120). Hynes also catalogs the resistance to the new orthodoxy of disillusionment in what he calls the "The War Books Controversy" (see especially, 449-459).

[9] As this line suggests, "truth" for Woolf is always at least half in quotation marks. As in her refocusing of the question of romance earlier in the passage, Woolf's mimicry allows her to both participate in and distance herself from the postwar truth-telling project.

[10] *Virginia Woolf and War* (1991), edited by Mark Hussey, has played a crucial role in extending to wide audiences a new understanding of Woolf as a "theorist of war" and promoting the recognition of "the centrality of war in her life's work" (Hussey 3). Karen L. Levenback's *Virginia Woolf and the Great War* (1999) remains a landmark work in this area of Woolf studies. Christine Froula, *Virginia Woolf and the Bloomsbury Avant-Garde: War, Civilization, Modernity* (2005) is an important recent contribution. For exceptions to the view that *A Room of One's Own* is *not* a war book, see Levenback, "Teaching" and Marts; both these essays document, from a teacher and student's perspective respectively, the experience of studying *A Room of One's Own* in the context of the Great War. See also Barrett and Winterhalter.

memorialization," as often as not representing it through a rhetoric of indirection and displacement.[11]

What would it mean, then, this essay asks, to read Woolf's influential contribution to a history and theory of women's authorship against this largely unspoken backdrop, to uncover the memorial culture that underwrites the work in which Woolf both does and does not take part? For a start, Woolf's homage to the Unknown Poet she calls Judith Shakespeare, the commemorative gesture that forms the centerpiece of her work, could be seen as precisely that: a commemorative act.[12] And Woolf's spectacular fiction of this unknown poet's life might be heard to echo —indeed, to answer and improve— "the fanciful essays in which the life of the Unknown Warrior was re-created" in the newspapers of the time of the 1920 Armistice Day rites (Cannadine 224). Indeed, Woolf's extended meditation on "Women and Fiction," even as it shifts the discourse away from Men and War, draws on precisely the tropes Jay Winter has identified as comprising the distinctive logic of the memorialization project that followed the Great War: the return or rising of the dead; the obligation of the living to make good their sacrifice; the dialogue with the dead through the conferral of a posthumous voice.[13] When Woolf enjoins her audience to "let flowers fall upon the tomb of Aphra Behn" (69)—in Westminster Abbey, no less—and dedicate themselves to bringing Shakespeare's sister (back) to life, she is evoking, I want to suggest, the well-established rituals of collective mourning which she then displaces with her own idiosyncratic rites. And when she confers on Shakespeare's sister the promise of belated authorship and a posthumous life, she is carving out a space

[11] Scholars who have studied the manuscript versions of the text generally note the erasure or toning down of war references in the published version of the text. For a discussion of some of the ways *A Room of One's Own* calls attention to its war references, see Barrett.

[12] Referring to Vanessa Bell's jacket design for the Hogarth Press publication of *A Room of One's Own*, Jane Marcus writes: "She has managed to articulate absence, to suggest infinite possibility, to design a monument for Judith Shakespeare, to picture the tomb of the 'Unknown' woman artist. It is both a memorial and a stage set for a resurrection" (48). Marcus suggests that *A Room of One's Own* might be read as an "unmarked grave" (Marcus 4), and she acknowledges that she has always read it as "an elegy for the lost women artists of the past" (17). Marcus's essay, however, in its concern with the lack of proper upkeep of Woolf's name in her native country, and with "the rescue and resurrection of Virginia Woolf's reputation" (4), follows very different lines from mine.

[13] See *Sites of Memory, Sites of Mourning*. In this, I am suggesting, *A Room of One's Own* bears certain resemblances to *Mrs. Dalloway*, where, as David Bradshaw has noted, "In fact, at one point or another, just about every aspect of the formal culture of remembrance is evoked" (107). In Bradshaw's reading, *Mrs. Dalloway* "not only opposes the official memorialization of the dead" but also "contributes to the culture of remembrance" (118). Like Bradshaw, I am interested in illuminating the doubleness of Woolf's engagement with the rituals of commemoration.

for the emergence of a novel form of women's authorship in a territory newly excavated by the war.

For World War I posed in particular and pressing ways the problem of posthumous authorship, if for no other reason than that it "produced a phenomenal number of poets who wrote a vast quantity of verse," and it produced an extremely large number of deaths among this poetry-writing class.[14] If, in *A Room of One's Own*, Woolf is prompted to speculate about a female Shakespeare by the absence of women writers in an age "when every other man, it seemed, was capable of song or sonnet" (43), the Great War seemed another such time of creative outpouring, leading at least one contemporary critic to dub its fallen heroes, "The New Elizabethans": "They were all scholars and sportsmen and poets—even if they did not write poetry, they had a conviction that life ought to be lived poetically. They had the Elizabethan exuberance" (Osborn 3).[15] As a publisher, a reviewer, and an avid reader of newspapers where such works were regularly noted, Woolf would have been well aware of this flood of war poetry appearing in monographs, books, anthologies, newspapers, as well as postcards, pamphlets, broadsides, and other ephemera. In her published essays, and even more in her letters and diaries, Woolf expressed a certain ambivalence about the poetry of the living war poets—Sassoon, Graves, Blunden, Thompson—many of whose volumes the Hogarth Press published over the course of the 1920s. But as her *TLS* essays suggest, she was even more keenly aware of the peculiar delicacy of judging posthumous works, of which there were so many, given, as she put it in one review, the "large number of . . . young men who left behind them enough verse to fill a little book before they were killed" ("These Are the Plans" *E*3 73).

These little books, of radically uneven quality and often published as tributes by family and friends, appeared literally as well as figuratively as voices from the dead. This was no less true of what we have come to see as the major and defining war poetry of the period as it was of its more minor and private manifestations. Wilfred Owen, for example, who published only five poems before his death in battle one week before the end of the war, could be said to be defined by his posthumousness, his public literary career emerging, Geoff Dyer suggests, not so much as protest to the nation's official rites of remembrance but rather as one of the coordinates: "the Unknown Soldier and the poet everyone knows" (Dyer 29).[16] When Edith Sitwell brought out the first edition of Owen's poems in 1920,

[14] Reilly xiii. Reilly identifies 2,225 English poets in her bibliography.

[15] E. B. Osborn's *The New Elizabethans: A First Selection of the Lives of Young Men Who Have Fallen in the Great War*, was published in 1919. Osborn was also the editor of an anthology of war poems, *The Muse in Arms*, first published in November 1917.

[16] There is some discrepancy in accounts of the number of poems Owen published in his lifetime. Dyer lists five poems, while many other sources note only four. Seven poems appeared in Edith Sitwell's 1919 edition of the anthology *Wheels*. Mark Rawlinson also

Siegfried Sassoon, in his now famous introduction, insisted that Owen's poems (poems Owen himself had called "elegies") could "speak for him" and turned the poems, in effect, into Owen's elegies for himself: "All that was strongest in Wilfred Owen survives in his poems," Sassoon wrote; "these poems survive him as his true and splendid testament" (Owen 1).[17]

Yet if Owen's words bear witness from the other side of death, they require, as in any form of posthumous authorship, the efforts of the living to reach an audience. More common than the case of Owen, however, were the volumes of posthumous poems by authors of admittedly lesser genius—volumes published in small runs as acts of private, or semi-private commemoration. Virginia and Leonard Woolf, for example, along with Leonard's brother Philip, published in 1918, as the second publication of the Hogarth Press, a posthumous edition of Cecil Woolf's poems, for private distribution among family and friends. As Philip's dedication intimates, these were poems that were perhaps not yet ready for publication, poems that were, like their author, prematurely released: "Had he lived longer, some of these poems, revised and re-polished, might have appeared one day in a volume under both our names. Now that he is gone, I dedicate them as they were left, to the memory of the dearest and bravest brother that a man was ever loved by."[18]

But by far the most striking instances of what I am calling posthumous authorship were ones that didn't explicitly announce themselves as such: the spate of private memorials to the countless young men who died before making their name, to the "dead poets" who, like Woolf's Judith Shakespeare, "never wrote a word," and whose "lives," reconstructed by family and friends, stood in the place of their posthumous poems. Alongside the public display of the war memorials, these "lives of the obscure" testified to the way, as Winter argues "[c]ommemoration also happened on a much more intimate level, through the preservation in households of possessions, photographs, personal signatures of the dead" (*Sites* 51); these private memorials, I would add, also happened through

---

notes the significance of Owen's posthumousness: "A further issue in evaluating Owen is the posthumousness of his public literary career. From this point of view, he is identical with his reception and publication histories, not differentiated from them and the uses to which he has been put (as in the case of Keats or Bob Dylan). Notably, the poet was revealed to his growing public in a process which reversed his poetic development, a factor which has perhaps given renewed life to the legend of the poet made by the war, which his early death helped to cement" (118).

[17] According to Longley, "Elegy is arguably both a genre and the over-arching genre of war poetry. Indeed, the Great War may have made all lyric poetry more consciously elegiac and self-elegiac" (78).

[18] The dedication is quoted in Spater and Parsons (102). Cecil Woolf was killed in the Battle of Cambrai on 3 December 1917. The same shell injured his brother Philip.

the collection of these and other items into commemorative volumes that bore the dead man's name. So common had these books become that in 1924 Woolf could introduce a book review thus:

> The war has made us familiar with the type of book of which Mr Graham's is a good example. A young man impresses his friends with his powers, writes one novel of great promise, and is killed at the age of thirty. The friends then attempt to record what he was to them, and to adumbrate what he might have been to the world. Those who did not know him follow with sympathy, but necessarily with some bewilderment. (*E*3 409)[19]

The war, it could be added, made post-war audiences familiar with another type of book even more likely to leave its readers in a state of confusion and puzzlement: the memorial volume with a spiritualist cast. The most famous of these was undoubtedly *Raymond; or Life and Death*, published in 1916, by Sir Oliver J. Lodge, a distinguished physicist. Part memorial to his youngest son who died at Ypres at the age of twenty-six, part collation of evidence for the "survival" of his son, including transcripts of séances in which "Raymond" communicated from the other side, part theoretical explication of the spiritualist hypothesis, *Raymond* "went through a dozen printings between 1916 and 1919 and was republished in abridged form as *Raymond Revisited* in 1922" (Winter, *Sites* 62).[20]

Successors to *Raymond*—in published volumes and in private records of sessions with mediums—were part of the daily fare of the postwar reading public, though few commanded the public attention Lodge's original volume generated. In their sheer persistence, however, these acts of remembrance remind us that the revival of spiritualism, especially among the educated classes, was one of the striking effects of the war, and an occasion for new forms of posthumous

[19] Review of *The Life and Last Words of Wilfrid Ewart* (G. P. Putnam Sons, 1924) by Stephen Graham. Ironically, although Ewart had in fact served in the war, as a Captain in the Scotts Guards, he did not die in the war; he was killed in 1922 by a stray bullet while in Mexico. See *E*3 409.

[20] Lodge was a Professor of Physics and Mathematics at University College, Liverpool, and Principal of Birmingham University. By the time he published *Raymond*, his scientific scholarly work had earned him election to the Royal Society, a knighthood and international recognition. From 1901-1903 he served as President of the Society for Psychical Research. The full title of the book reads, *Raymond; or Life and Death: With Examples of the Evidence for Survival of Memory and Affection After Death.* Like other memorial volumes, *Raymond* contains as a frontispiece a photograph of the soldier in uniform. Divided into three parts, its first part, or "Normal Portion," follows the pattern of other memorial texts, including an "In Memoriam" section, copies of Raymond's letters from the Front, and condolence letters from officers.

authorship and posthumous publication. As testimonials like Lodge's suggest, moreover, in their hybrid commemorative/spiritualist structure, the argument for "life" after death is the ultimate extension of the memorial impulse: they materialize the assertion that the dead survive, as Woolf would say, as "continuing presences" (*AROO* 117).[21] As such, these works make explicit what is already inherent in memorial tracts produced without what Lodge calls "supernormal" assistance. For in these volumes, the dead survive, quite literally, in pieces and fragments: family reminiscences, autobiographical fragments, obituary notices, representative letters (from childhood, from school, from the battlefield), lists of favorite books, scraps of papers, inventories of possessions, photographs, transcriptions of poems, commemorative odes, letters from officers, fellow soldiers, and friends, remembrances in letters of condolence. Of little independent interest or merit, these fragments speak through their representativeness, and they testify to the problem of memorializing a life cut off too soon to provide the proper materials of a biographical effort: they lack, as Lodge acknowledges, "marriages, births of children, productive years," and hard evidence of special achievement (Lodge, *Raymond* 4).

As Woolf wrote in her review of the *Collected Poems of Rupert Brooke, With a Memoir* (1918), "the biographers of those who have died with undeveloped powers, tragically, and in the glory of public gratitude" are beset with "enormous difficulties": "They [the dead] leave so little behind them that can serve to recall them with any exactitude. A few letters, written from school and college, a fragment of a diary—that is all" (*E*2 278). Such memoirs, she concluded, must be "inevitably incomplete" (277), and in the case of Brooke, her own personal knowledge of the subject—knowledge that did not and could not find its way into such an official record—left her "sceptical of the possibility of any biography of a man dying, as he died, at the age of twenty-eight" (278).[22] In like manner, Raymond's brother explains in his personal reminiscence, "fame has but a narrow circle in a life of twenty-six years"—hence the need to memorialize Raymond,

[21] For a discussion of the revival of spiritualism and its relationship to the culture of memorialization, see Winter, *Sites of Memory*, 54-77. As Winter reminds us, "the cause of spiritualism was promoted by well-known public figures" (58), including Sir Arthur Conan Doyle. After the loss of his son, his brother, and his brother-in-law in the war, Conan Doyle became a kind of evangelist for the spiritualist cause, publishing *The New Revelation* in 1918, a book that grew out of a series of lectures to the London Spiritualist Alliance, undertaking lecture tours of the United States and Australia, and helping to found a spiritualist church in London in 1923 (58-59).

[22] As many critics have noted, Woolf's published remarks radically understate the outrage she felt at the posthumous distortion of Rupert Brooke's reputation. In her diary, for example, she wrote, "The book is a disgraceful sloppy sentimental rhapsody, leaving Rupert rather tarnished" (*D*1 171).

not in monuments of brass and stone, but in emulation of his life and sacrifice. Himself a poet, the younger Oliver Lodge ["O.W.F.L."] had sent a volume of his poems to his brother, who carried them with him as he moved across the battlefields of France, but in his own poetic tribute to his brother, he laments the failure of words to convey the knowledge of such an unknown and ultimately unknowable life: "They cannot know the man we knew, / Our words go down the wind like rain" (Lodge, *Raymond* 6).

For Christopher Coombe Tennant, the subject of another memorial volume compiled by Lodge, *Christopher: A Study in Human Personality* (1919), the problem is exacerbated. The son of close family friends, Christopher died at age nineteen, three days after his arrival at the Front. "This is not an attempt at autobiography," Christopher wrote in the locked manuscript book found among his effects and transcribed in the memorial volume, "it is merely an attempt to set down a few incidents of my past life, an attempt which, writing as I do at the age of 19 years 9 months, must necessarily be incomplete and lacking in detail" (Lodge, *Christopher* 104). Writing as he did for no eyes but his own, the fragment, not seen by anyone until after his death, allows Christopher to speak once more from the afterlife, but the picture remains incomplete. As Lodge explains, "The autobiographical fragment breaks off—perhaps fortunately—at the end of his experience of the Preparatory School. What he felt afterwards in his main school days can only be gathered between the lines of his letters home, for apparently he had not the heart to confess it even to his locked book" (Lodge, *Christopher* 50). In the place of detail and completeness, what we get is, on the one hand, a collection of fragmentary documents that, even as they pile up, can only display how little there is to tell (how much, that is, we must make up by reading between the lines), and on the other hand, Lodge's tribute to "latent capacity" and "nascent genius," the "altar" he feels compelled to raise to the memory of doomed youth: "It is mainly of these unfledged songsters, these undeveloped athletes, these youths of blighted promise, that I write" (*Christopher* 12).

Asking in "Youth and the War," the introduction to *Christopher*, the fundamental question, "Why pick out for special remembrance one rather than another of the glorious company of those who have sacrificed themselves in this high cause?" Lodge rationalizes his choices for their typicality: "Each has done his duty, each is one of a type." Offering *Christopher* as, in effect, a sequel to *Raymond*, Lodge explains that, having already dealt with "the engineering practical type" in that earlier volume, he is now attempting to limn "the more artistic type, the undeveloped man of letters . . . the youth of intelligent and cultivated emotion" (Lodge, *Christopher*15-16). As with the Cenotaph, with its blank marble surface and empty center, and as with the blank slate of Shakespeare's sister, Lodge's "incomplete" memorialized "lives" remain to be completed by what his readers project onto them: "Each may stand for a multitude, and I trust that many parents will realise, in one or the other of those commemorated, a sufficient picture of what their own son was like, and will feel that in endeavouring to commemorate a few we are really commemorating a large and increasing number" (Lodge, *Christopher* 16).

Part personal memoir, part exposition, *Christopher* is, like *A Room of One's Own*, a meditation on genius, as Lodge's opening words suggest: "In this great massacre of youth, in which we are all, to the best of our ability, heavily engaged . . . what slaughter of heaven-sent genius must there inevitably be!" (Lodge, *Christopher* 11). Like Woolf, moreover, Lodge recognizes that genius rarely flourishes where the necessary conditions have not prevailed (birth, education, wealth, a congenial family environment): "One undoubtedly who possessed such advantages is the subject of this memoir" (*Christopher* 17).[23] Like so many others, however, Christopher's genius is not allowed the opportunity to bear fruit: he is nearly stifled first by the uncongenial atmosphere of the Public School, then by the demands of the war that shut him out from "his cherished ambition to go to Cambridge" and force him to abandon "the anticipated enjoyment of rooms in the Great Court of Trinity, wherein, when he tried for his scholarship, he had passed a glorious week" (*Christopher* 28); in the place of such rooms of his own, Christopher experiences the oppressive discipline of Sandhurst and the grim realities of the trenches, where he is quickly struck down. More interesting, perhaps, than this familiar recital of promise, however, is the digression Lodge allows himself in order to lament the daily slaughter of genius among those of the lower social ranks, simply by virtue of their class: "Of the wastage we hear less, but it must be appalling. Slaughter in war is but another and more obvious form of slaughter; it attracts more attention, but, save in quantity, it need hardly be more repined than the less obtrusive moral and intellectual slaughter always going on in time of peace" (Lodge, *Christopher* 18).[24]

[23] This, of course, is the gist of Woolf's parable of Shakespeare's sister: "That, more or less, is how the story would run, I think, if a woman in Shakespeare's day had had Shakespeare's genius. But for my part, I agree with the deceased bishop, if such he was—it is unthinkable that any woman in Shakespeare's day should have had Shakespeare's genius. For genius like Shakespeare's is not born among labouring, uneducated, servile people. It was not born in England among the Saxons and the Britons. It is not born today among the working classes" (*AROO* 50).

[24] Sir Arthur Quiller-Couch may be Lodge's source here for the class-based analysis of genius; he was the authority Woolf invoked to legitimate her claim that "Intellectual freedom depends upon material things": "Nobody could put the point more plainly. 'The poor poet has not in these days, nor has had for two hundred years, a dog's chance . . . a poor child in England has little more hope than had the son of an Athenian slave to be emancipated into that intellectual freedom of which great writings are born.'" From this, Woolf concludes,

The stories of latent genius snuffed out by the War—of those "mute and inglorious Miltons" who never got to express themselves in song—would have been only too familiar to Woolf when she imagined "some mute and inglorious Jane Austen" (51) as *A Room of One's Own* took shape in her mind. And the would-be poets trapped in soldiers' bodies and forced to bring their mangled work out before its time—poets of whom Woolf wrote on more than one occasion—may well have cast their shadow as she pondered "the heat and violence of the poet's heart when caught and tangled in a woman's body" (50),[25] leading her to speculate, "Indeed, I would venture to guess that Anon, who wrote so many poems without signing them, was often a woman" (51). As it did for Lodge, the much celebrated slaughter of war provided Woolf with the occasion to repine—and thus to make "obtrusive"—"moral and intellectual slaughter" of another kind, although for Woolf that other kind had more to do with gender than class. And, I would argue, the young men of the "lost generation" so volubly lamented in public and private memorialization rites hover as silent ghosts behind the "dead poets" Woolf would bring to life.

Woolf, of course, does not note such presences directly. Rather, her argument proceeds through what Melba Cuddy-Keane has called, in a different context, a "trope of substitution" (36).[26] Most fully materialized in the insertion

---

"Women, then, have not had a dog's chance of writing poetry" (*AROO* 112). Hence her emphasis on "money and a room of one's own." It may not be insignificant that Sir Arthur Quiller-Couch's *The Art of Writing*, from which Woolf culls this quote, was published in 1916.

[25] Here, as elsewhere, Woolf's language echoes the iconography of doomed youth and the conditions of trench warfare. She deploys similarly charged rhetoric in her discussion of Charlotte Brontë as her representative example of a nineteenth century writer; Woolf insists "she will never get her genius expressed whole and entire . . . . How could she help but die young, cramped and thwarted?" (72-73). For Woolf's public writings on the dilemma of the soldier-poet, see "Two Soldier Poets" (*E*2 269-272), "Mr Sassoon's Poems" (*E*2 119-122), "Rupert Brooke" (*E*2 277-284), "These are the Plans" (*E*3 73-77), and "Maturity and Immaturity" (*E*3 127-131).

[26] Even when Woolf expressly raises a ghost or phantom, as in the possible twilight appearance of Jane Harrison—"could it be the famous scholar, could it be J—— H—— herself?" (17), the figure of the woman scholar appears where other ghosts might have been expected. The materialization of "J—— H——" follows close on the narrator's extended meditation on the War ("Shall we lay the blame on the war," 15); indeed, the narrative takes a sudden swerve to get us to this figure, "For truth . . . those dots mark the spot where, in search of truth, I missed the turning up to Fernham" (15). The J—— H—— sighting breaks off abruptly with the invocation of "youth," a culturally loaded term in the context of recent war losses: "For youth — / Here was my soup." Ironically, Harrison would literally have been a ghost at the time of her presumed appearance, having died in April 1928, five months before the October day that serves as the departure point

of Shakespeare's sister in the dead soldier-poet's place, such substitutions run through the entire work, shadowing even its most foundational claims: "a woman must have money and a room of her own if she is to write fiction" (4). For a room of one's own—"let alone a quiet room or a sound-proof room" (54)—is precisely what soldiers fighting in the trenches did not have.[27] Five hundred pounds a year, moreover, the symbolic figure Woolf selects as a necessary competency to achieve independence—the figure, incidentally, T. S. Eliot set as the minimum annuity that would allow him to quit his job at the bank and devote himself entirely to writing poetry—is a shorthand she first introduces in her diary in 1915 in reference to Leonard's brothers, enlisted in the war effort. Speculating on what they will do after the war is over, Woolf notes "Cecil would like to stay in the Army, which however, one can't do, unless one has money, & neither of them has a penny. Five hundred a year is considerably more valuable than beauty or rank" (*D*1 34). With the cessation of war, Woolf returns to this theme, writing on 15 November 1918: " The first effect of peace on our circle is to set Desmond loose, & to bring Gerald Shove up to London saying that he must find a way of making £500 a year. Before long the crowd of out of work intellectuals looking for places will be considerable" (*D*1 218). When Woolf urges her audience to earn five hundred pounds a year, then, she inserts them in the place of the crowd of out of work intellectuals that preceded them: the returning soldiers, civilian volunteers, and conscientious objectors, displaced by the War.[28]

Woolf herself was not immune to the myth of a lost generation. "Our

---

for Woolf's narrative. In her diary entry for 14 October 1917, Woolf describes a visit to Kingston Barracks for Leonard's medical examination for his exemption from war service: "I waited in a great square, surrounded by barrack buildings, & was reminded of a Cambridge college—soldiers crossing, coming out of staircases, & going into others; but gravel & no grass" (*D*1 59). It might not be entirely fanciful, then, to assume that when Woolf visits Cambridge University in 1928 she is reminded of the barracks. Hence perhaps the corpse-like vision of the world at sleep: "All human beings were laid asleep—prone, horizontal, dumb. Nobody seemed stirring in the streets of Oxbridge (24).

[27] In his study of the relationship between sense perception and lyric voice in Owen and Rosenberg's poetry, Santanu Das reminds us of the centrality of sound to the soldier's experience of the war. "'You couldn't; you can't communicate noise,' noted Robert Graves in an interview; 'Noise never stopped for one moment—ever'; and we have Sassoon's soldier 'going stark, staring mad because of the guns'" (76). When Woolf introduces this idea of a "sound-proof room," she does this immediately after noting the empty bookshelves, a kind of metonymy for the "lost generation": "But for women, I thought, looking at the empty shelves, these difficulties were infinitely more formidable. In the first place, to have a room of her own, let alone a quiet room or a sound-proof room, was out of the question . . ." (*AROO* 54).

[28] Desmond MacCarthy served with the Red Cross, as an ambulance driver, attached to the French army. Gerald Shove was a conscientious objector.

generation is daily scourged by the bloody war," she wrote in her diary in June 1920; "Even I scribble reviews instead of novels because of the thick skulls at Westminster & Berlin" (*D*2 51). And a few months later she returned to the theme, noting that it is "life itself, I think sometimes, for us in our generation so tragic—no newspaper placard without its shriek of agony from some one" (*D*2 72-73). In opening *A Room of One's Own* with a fictive visit to Oxbridge, however, Woolf situates her work where a particular version of the myth was at that moment being solidified: the myth of the loss of an entire generation of brilliant young men who served as junior officers in the war.[29] In this context, Woolf's meditation on the cost of privilege—her critique of Oxbridge for the toll it extracts from those who are locked in as well as those who are locked out—takes on an added significance, given the very different way that "cost" was being construed in contemporary public discourse. For at the heart of this new myth was the idea that it was the elite who bore the major burden of the war and that the loss of so many cultivated intelligences had left the world sadly and irreparably depleted. This myth, Wohl suggests, was not entirely without foundation: "The younger the junior officer and the more privileged his education, the more likely he was to be killed" (114). The more likely, it could be added, he would have been a soldier-poet, given the intellectual emphases of the most privileged public schools and universities. Indeed, "the propensity of Oxford and Cambridge men to join up early," and thus "to receive a commission from an early date," can be explained in part by the fact that they had the leisure as much as the character to do so; they were also, Winter explains, more likely "to serve in the infantry rather than in specialist units, where some scientifically trained undergraduates of other universities were directed," resulting in losses higher even than those of most other universities. As Winter concludes, "The privileges enjoyed by Oxford and Cambridge men in 1914 were paid for by higher than average losses in the First World War" ("Oxford" 19-20).

[29] Woolf was well aware of the class bias that went into dominant versions of this myth. In her diary, for example, she repeats Arnold Toynbee's catty attack on the Oxford war heroes, apparently enjoying the opportunity to cut them down to size: "He knew the aristocratic heroes who are now all killed & celebrated—Grenfells, Lister, Shaw Steuart, Asquith, & loathed them; for one reason they must have thought him a pale blooded little animal. But he described their rows & their insolence & their quick snapping brains, always winning scholarships, & bullying & bringing bath chairs full of rats into Chapel—& admitting no one to their set, so that in the end they were almost abolished by the Colonials, who hated them back. It reads much like a Mrs Ward novel" (*D*1 108-09). And in her review of Lady Glenconner's memoir of her son, Edward Wyndham Tennant, she rags on its subject's all encompassing "aristocratic point of view," concluding that "there is something indecent, though childish and disarming, in the amazing aristocratic irreticence which is displayed—the assumption that everybody must know you, and be interested in hearing all about you" (*E*3 127, 128).

These losses did not go unnoticed by the guardians of these institutions. The imagined rooms in Oxbridge, for example, that Woolf describes in *A Room of One's Own* with such a mixture of envy and ambivalence were, in reality, at this time, well-established memorial sites. In Merton College, Oxford, for example, there was a tradition of putting up wooden plaques in rooms bearing the names of former inhabitants who died in the war (Utechin 59). And by the mid-1920s, virtually every college in Oxford and Cambridge had its own war memorial, where the names of "sons of the college" were inscribed in stone on a wall of the college or engraved in brass plaques. Even without these marks on the wall, however, the rooms were haunted by the young men whose university careers had been aborted or interrupted—often permanently. "'I did not go back to Oxford after the war', Harold Macmillan recalled in old age. 'I just could not face it. To me it was a city of ghosts'" (Harrison, "College Life"). The "famous library" that bars Woolf's narrator from its premises, then, also has other ghosts to answer for, as Woolf herself recognized; in "These Are the Plans," for example, she laments the young poet "ordered from a Cambridge library to the front with the likelihood of death" (*E3* 73). But the rooms were haunted as well by the motley crew of outsiders who became the temporary and unlikely occupants of these seats of privilege, when the colleges in Cambridge and Oxford were nearly emptied out: Belgian and Serbian refugees; soldiers in training; officers, who were sometimes billeted in college rooms and invited to eat at high table; injured and disabled soldiers; and even women, like Vera Brittain and her Oxford women cohorts, displaced into vacated men's rooms in Oriel College when Somerville College became a war hospital. The grounds as well, where Woolf's narrator is not allowed to walk, have their own history of prior usurpation, with the Trinity Backs having been transformed into a temporary hospital, with a permanent hospital installed on the Kings and Clare cricket grounds.[30]

Karen L. Levenback has argued that Woolf "studiously avoided ritualistic and stylized commemoration of the dead" (*Virginia Woolf* 28-29). Not surprisingly, then, Woolf's accounts of her trips to Cambridge make no mention of the university's

[30] For the history of Cambridge during the war, see Brooke. The occupation of Cambridge continued on a smaller scale even after the War: "After the armistice a number of American soldiers were settled in Cambridge awaiting transport home, and about 200 matriculated in the Easter Term 1919. Meanwhile arrangements were made from January 1919 till 1922 for short courses for naval officers, to give them a brief period of recovery from the stress of war and expose them a little to the academic and more to the social life of Cambridge" (334). The following anecdote might have amused Woolf: "'I reached Caius ravenously hungry,' writes one of those who came in 1920, 'and . . . being told that I could sit anywhere I selected a comfortable chair and had a jolly good meal after which I discovered that I had been dining with the Fellows.'" (334)

many memorial sites. Nor does she mention the statue of the returning soldier, "The Homecoming," that stands as one of Cambridgeshire's two major tributes to native sons who fought in the war. Although K. S. Inglis notes, "When you arrive in Cambridge by train, the first monument you pass on the way into town is a war memorial" (583), Woolf never acknowledges taking in this sight. Indeed, she appears to go out of her way *not* to notice it. Thus while she recounts, in February 1923, eight months after the unveiling of this memorial, her walk from the train station to the bottom of Station Road, she does not mention the monument that stands at precisely this location, the intersection of Station Road and Hills Road.[31] And she does not mention it in any of her subsequent journeys to Cambridge, by train or car, including her October 1928 visit. The omission would appear to be pointed, given Woolf's sense of the unhomeliness of Cambridge for those not natural inheritors to the uninterrupted flow of gold and silver that endowed fellowships, chairs, and lectureships and furnished libraries and laboratories. For similar reasons, perhaps, "the glorious dead"—the soldier-poets and aristocratic heroes so obsessively celebrated in postwar commemorations—appear in *A Room of One's Own*, even on their home ground, only through their absence, through the figures Woolf installs in their place.[32]

"From the 1990s onwards," Gail Braybon notes, "there has been an increasing interest in the complexity of the war's impact on different societies and social groups, and a growing recognition that there was no one 'war experience'" (Braybon 5). This has led to a reevaluation of the way our understanding of the war has been shaped by the experience and posthumous reputation of a relatively few privileged men, the members of the junior officer class, and more particularly, the canonized war poets.[33] Stacy Gillis, for example, has argued, "While the reasons for the resonance of these myths surrounding the literary output of the war have been the subject of much work, what has received less attention is the way in which the myths surrounding these literary figures have resulted in the exclusion of other accounts of the war, accounts which spoke to other kinds of experiences

[31] The other major site was the memorial in Ely Cathedral; a third complementary memorial project "has lost all meaning because it is part of an abandoned hospital building" (Inglis 585). Inglis provides a fascinating account of the contradictory features of this monument and the complex deliberations that went into its making. His work here, and in subsequent publications, has been pathbreaking in opening to analysis the culture of memorialization.

[32] Interestingly, when Woolf's narrator, in the fictionalization of Woolf's Cambridge visit, forebears even attempting to enter the chapel, she avoids the opportunity to witness its recently installed war memorial, for as Angela Ingram notes, "At the time when Virginia Woolf spoke at Girton and Newnham the most recent addition had been—what else?—the King's College Chapel War Memorial to the fallen of the First World War" (142n14).

[33] Braybon, for example, notes, "It is a sad fact that more words have been written about the British war poets than about all the non-white troops put together" (28n54).

and traumas" (101). One direction this reevaluation has taken has been to attempt to recover women's experience of the war by recovering the extensive body of women's "war poetry."[34] In putting the woman artist, or would-be artist, in the dead soldier-poet's place, however, Woolf was not particularly interested in reclaiming women war poets, even where their poems might be seen to explore concerns very much like hers.[35] Rather, Woolf's text works through a complex series of displacements whereby the woman artist (in Woolf's formulation, a person who never existed) can, in effect, rescue "poetry"—what comes from the mind of the artist "whole and entire" and uncontaminated (*AROO* 58)—from "war poetry," the poetry that is not poetry, that has taken its place.[36] Woolf, in fact, might have

[34] Claire Buck notes, "of the more than 2,000 poets published during these years a quarter were women. By contrast soldiers on active service wrote less than a fifth of the total output" (426). As Gillis notes, however, most of the women who wrote and published poetry during the war "resist the easy designation of 'war poet'" (105).

[35] Gillis, for example, notes, "The war offered women a creative space in which to engage with . . . new identities"; citing Ouditt, she elaborates, "the war allowed women to 'work, think and practise as artists'" (105). "These new employment opportunities—and, more tacitly, the social freedoms contained therein—are the subject of several poems, largely written by middle-class women, some endorsing and others opposing these freedoms" (107).

[36] As Woolf remarked on numerous occasions, for example, Rupert Brooke could not be deemed a poet. In her reviews of lesser known poets, and in her private comments, she repeatedly notes the failings of their poetry—poetry that most likely would never have been written and certainly would not have been published if it hadn't been for the war. Of Cecil Woolf's poems, for example, she admits, "They're not good" (*D*1 124). Of Geoffrey Dearmer, one of the soldier-poets she reviews alongside Sassoon, she acknowledges, his "imagination is neither strong enough nor trained enough to do the work he asks of it"; "The war, perhaps, has brought these pieces forth before their time," she offers by way of apology (*E*2 271, 272). Of the poet she reviews alongside Charles Sorley, she observes, "Mr. Donald Johnson does not make us feel that he was by nature a poet. No doubt he would have written poetry, and no doubt he would have burned it. But things being as they were, his friends killed, his life changed, himself ordered from a Cambridge library to the front with the likelihood of death, feelings that would have faded unrecorded, some that would never have been felt at all or without such intensity, were necessarily expressed, and poetry was less of an effort, more of a disguise, than prose" (*E*3 73). Even of Sassoon, she notes, "At the same time, it is difficult to judge him dispassionately as a poet, because it is impossible to overlook the fact that he writes as a soldier"; "Mr Sassoon's poems are too much in the key of the gramophone at present, too fiercely suspicious of any comfort or compromise, to be read as poetry" (*E*2 269, 270). Of Blunden, she writes in 1924 that he was "despairing, drooping, crow-like, rather than Keats' like. And did we really all believe in Blunden's 'genius' Had we read his poems? How much sincerity was there in the whole thing?" (*D*2 297). Of Graves she writes, after her first meeting, "No I don't think he'll write great poetry: but what will you? The sensitive are needed too; the halfbaked, stammering stuttering, who perhaps improve their own quarter of Oxfordshire" (*D*3 14).

appreciated Vincent Sherry's wry formulation, "This dearth of 'combat modernist verse' might be taken as one more grim statistic of war dead—how many proto-modernist poets perished in the trenches?" but she would have appreciated as well his re-direction of our gaze to "the other major modernist poets who lived out the war in London, specifically Pound and Eliot and Yeats" (Sherry, "Great War" 191). For ultimately, Woolf invokes her own dead poet to make space for "living" poetry.[37]

Woolf's chain of substitutions, however, is effected through the agency of Shakespeare—Woolf's shorthand for poetry that is timeless, impersonal, and vital. For if Shakespeare's sister stands for great poetry, she does so, quite literally, by standing in for Shakespeare. In 1916, the year of the three hundredth anniversary of Shakespeare's death, a commemorative volume, *A Book of Homage to Shakespeare*, was published by Israel Gollancz, containing entries by 166 contributors from around the world. The volume, as John Lee explains, marked a radically scaled down realization of the pre-War project envisioned by Gollancz, "a memorial that would 'symbolize the intellectual fraternity of mankind in the universal homage' accorded to the genius of Shakespeare" (139)—a project to be implemented through the building of a new theater. The war rudely shattered Gollancz's dreams, and as Lee argues, it also shifted the focus of the commemoration, the collection itself becoming "one of the very earliest anthologies of war poetry, and perhaps the first such international anthology. For, as is suggested by the title given within the book—*1916 / A Book of Homage to / Shakespeare*—many of the contributions, and most of the poetry in English, were more concerned with Shakespeare's relationship to the events of the Great War than with the arrival of the tercentenary itself" (140). Woolf, however, had other ideas about the uses to which Shakespeare should be put, and her own alternative memorial in *A Room of One's Own* could be seen to make good Gollancz's original intention; for Shakespeare's sister, with the promise she holds for intellectual sorority, provides a way to recuperate this "universal homage" by making the name of Shakespeare more truly universal.

Toward the end of *A Room of One's Own*, when the narrative has turned to the present, Woolf's narrator observes "a sudden splitting off of consciousness" if one is a woman, "say in walking down Whitehall," when "from being the natural inheritor of that civilisation, she becomes, on the contrary, outside it, alien and critical" (*AROO* 101). Woolf's choice of Whitehall, of course, is not as arbitrary as she suggests—"say in walking down Whitehall." Indeed,

[37] Recording, on 3 March 1926, her difference with the critic F. L. Lucas, Woolf notes, "He says Tom [T. S. Eliot] &c: have thrown intellect to the winds; given up the ghost; he says Houseman & de la Mare are the real poets. I say poetry is defunct; & Tom &c anyhow try to animate it" (*D*3 65).

Christine Froula has demonstrated that this "sentence cost its author some pains, particularly in respect to the pronouns" (26), and the extended discussion it inaugurates is one of the most worked over in Woolf's manuscripts.[38] The seat of government and power, Whitehall was also, as no contemporary would miss, the site of the Cenotaph and the annual Armistice Day ceremony.[39] In *Mrs. Dalloway*, it is "a pavement of monuments and wreaths" down which Peter Walsh walks, as he follows a group of young boys in uniform bearing a wreath to the empty tomb—a scene David Bradshaw has provocatively illuminated. Over the course of the 1920s Whitehall continued to function as a ready designation for this site of remembrance and its requisite rituals. In May 1925, for example, Woolf records a bus trip—"crossed Westminster Bridge; admired the Houses of Parliament & their fretted lacy look; passed the Cenotaph, which L. compromised by sitting with his hat off all the way up Whitehall"—and a year later she notes, "Silver & crimson guard at Whitehall; the cenotaph, & men bare heading themselves" (*D*3 23, 82). A focal point of collective mourning, the Cenotaph, it was proudly proclaimed at its unveiling, made England "one society"—an assertion reiterated, and even fortified, following the first-ever radio broadcast, on 11 November 1928, of the Cenotaph ceremony and the two minutes silence.[40] But if this society was not one (or not one to which women could naturally belong), Woolf, in appropriating the rhetoric of memorialization that surrounded the Cenotaph, constructs in her "fantastic" conclusion to *A Room of One's Own*, a society of a different sort: a dead poet's society, whose members are linked by the "survival" of Shakespeare's sister in her living counterparts ("She lives in you and in me").

In thus configuring "Shakespeare's sister," Woolf turns her text into a kind of countermonument—one that calls attention to its own creation, to its own essential constructedness.[41] Indeed, from the outset, Woolf makes "Judith

[38] Froula offers a subtle, complex, and compelling reading of the path Woolf tracks to achieve the pronoun "one," and of the performative politics of her pronoun usage (26-28).
[39] As McVicker notes in her discussion of "Abbeys and Cathedrals" and "This is the House of Commons," Whitehall is one of the locations through which Woolf articulates most overtly the theme of monumentalizing the past with its attendant exclusion of women ("Six London Essays," II: 142).
[40] Adrian Gregory, for example, observes, "The crucial feature of the radio Silence was less the actual broadcast than the knowledge that the listener was one of millions doing exactly the same thing" (136).
[41] In making the argument that follows, I am drawing freely on ideas developed by James E. Young in a very different context: holocaust memorials in Eastern Europe. Despite the significant differences in the two contexts—differences that cannot be simply ignored or glossed over—scholars engaged in the study of memorial culture have noted important continuities in memorial (and anti-memorial) practices across these periods and have been attentive to the ways these practices might help illuminate each other. Young's idea

Shakespeare" up—and unmakes her—before our very eyes. In contriving her end, Woolf calls attention to the public dimension of her art, for her monument does not exist apart from its public life. Its meaning *is* its performance, and what its audience makes of it, as Woolf's final flourish makes clear. Woolf's text thus functions as a memory site—a testament to an absent monument, the unmarked grave where the remains of Judith Shakespeare lie; and it remembers this absence by reproducing it, by constituting its phantom shape. Read in this light, the choice of Elephant and Castle for the burial site—a late addition in the evolution of the text—underlines the countermemorial impulse, for it is a location that is markedly not sacrosanct, a locus of urban congestion if not yet urban blight, precisely the kind of location often favored for conceptual art.[42] More specifically, it functions as a kind of negative space, a location defined by the fact that it is decidedly *not*-Whitehall and *not*-Westminster Abbey. Once dubbed the "Piccadilly of South London," by the late 1920s Elephant and Castle would already have seemed something of a distant outpost, "'desperately remote and inconvenient' and 'psychologically. . . miles away' from Whitehall" (Harrison, *Transformation* 303-04).[43] As such it resists the museumification or

---

of a counterindex, for example, is suggestive: "By defining itself in opposition to the traditional memorial's task, the countermonument illustrates concisely the possibilities and limitations of all memorials everywhere. In this way, it functions as a valuable 'counterindex' to the ways time, memory, and current history intersect at any memorial site" (30). In the more immediate context of World War I, Hynes devotes a chapter to anti-monuments, documenting postwar resistance to conventional memorial practices: "These were not buildings or statues or soldiers' graves, of course: those belonged to the state, or were the public gestures of private mourners. They were, rather, all the other forms in which judgements and conclusions about war could be expressed: paintings, poems, novels, histories, plays, music. These were works that rendered the war without the value-bearing abstractions, without the glory, and without the large-scale grandeur. Often they were conscious, aggressive rejections of the monument-making principles; they turned away from celebration, in search of war's reality" (283). While Hynes identifies *A Room of One's Own* as "yet another product of the myth-making years" (468)—the years that saw the displacement of a monument-making ideology by an anti-monumental aesthetic—my interest in the way Woolf occupies the space of memorialization, in ways that simultaneously resist and enact its modes of celebration, might more fully align her practice with Young's theorization of the countermonument. See Hynes, 283-310, for an analysis of anti-monuments.

[42] In the drafts of *Women and Fiction*, Woolf toys with alternative formulations: "buried ~~in~~ under a tomb <in one of the city churchyards> / without a name" (75).

[43] This statement was made by a civil servant in 1969, recalling his "exile" at Elephant and Castle. Since 1939, the civil service had increasingly branched out into other parts of London, with only the highest offices remaining in Whitehall. However anachronistic, the statement captures, I believe, the spirit of Woolf's gesture. See Harrison, *Transformation*.

rigidification of monuments like the Cenotaph, and it stands as a counterpoint to the official structures of ceremonial mourning—the structures that I suggested at the beginning of this essay were turning London into a memorial tract. But if Woolf refuses the consolatory mourning offered by traditional memorial sites—and refuses the patriotic jingoism attached to them—she does so not by simply rejecting their structures but by inhabiting them, and thus opening them to the stories they've left out.[44] In occupying the space the War carved out—the empty shelves where the books of the lost generation were *not*; the tomb of the unknown soldier; the empty tomb of the Cenotaph—Woolf, I am suggesting, establishes the woman author in no-man's land. And in taking up the mantle of authorship by raising a voice and body from the dead, Woolf offers yet another twist to the literary history she rewrites, proclaiming, as it were, "Posthumous was a woman."

A Room of One's Own, as has often been noted, is structured around a "series of turns and counter-turns" (Doyle 136). I want to close this essay with one of my own. Shakespeare's sister, it could be argued, represents in my final formulation a kind of special pleading for women; in another more utopian strain, *A Room of One's Own* gestures toward a time when gender as we know it will cease to be relevant. If Shakespeare's sister, then, functions as a kind of monument, like other countermonuments, it is an ephemeral one—a monument that encodes its own dissolution. For when, at some unknown time in the future, Shakespeare's sister comes to life, "she" will cease to be a site of remembrance. Having been born, she will no longer require a monument to mark her failed existence. At the end of chapter two, Woolf's narrator speculates, in the future perfect voice, on a time, "in a hundred years" when "women will have ceased to be the protected sex" (40). There are no limits, she suggests, to what is imaginable should such a time come to pass: "Anything may happen when womanhood has ceased to be a protected occupation" (41). "Remove that protection," she writes, in a disconcerting illustration, "expose them to the same exertions and activities, make them soldiers and sailors and engine-drivers and dock-labourers, and will not women die off so much younger, so much quicker, than men that one will say, 'I saw a woman today,' as one used to say, 'I saw an aeroplane'" (40-41). Women, Woolf suggests, in a passage laden with Great War references, could be the lost generation. "But what bearing has all this upon the subject of my paper, Women

[44] For an excellent discussion of the feminist ethics of Woolf's commemorative practices in *Jacob's Room* and *To the Lighthouse*, see Clewell. Clewell also links Woolf's practice to countermemorialization strategies: "Anticipating the innovative memorializing acts of Claude Lanzmann's *Shoa*, Maya Lin's Vietnam Veterans Memorial, and the Names Project Aids Memorial Quilt, Woolf's textual practice of endless mourning compels us to refuse consolation, sustain grief, and accept responsibility for the difficult task of remembering the catastrophic losses of the twentieth century" (198-199).

and Fiction?" (41), Woolf asks at the end of this section. If "Shakespeare's sister," as I have been suggesting, offers one way to make the connection by reminding us that "Posthumous was often a woman," Woolf's essay contains the possibility of a potentially even more radical suggestion. For if we recognize gender as socially constructed and historically contingent, we can, Woolf conjectures, envision a more perfect future whose refrain might be, "'Woman' is posthumous."

Works Cited

Barrett, Michèle. "Reason and Truth in *A Room of One's Own*." Berman and Goldman 120-129.

Berman, Jessica and Jane Goldman. *Virginia Woolf Out of Bounds: Selected Papers from the Tenth Annual Conference on Virginia Woolf*. New York: Pace UP, 2001.

Bradshaw, David. "'Vanished, Like Leaves': The Military, Elegy and Italy in *Mrs Dalloway*." *Woolf Studies Annual* 8 (2002), 107-125.

Braybon, Gail, ed. *Evidence, History and the Great War: Historians and the Impact of 1914-18*. New York & Oxford: Berhahn Books, 2003.

Brooke, Christopher N. L., ed. *A History of the University of Cambridge*, Vol. IV (1870-1990). Cambridge: Cambridge UP, 1993.

Buck, Claire. "British Women's Writing of the Great War." *The Cambridge Companion to The Literature of the First World War*. Ed. Vincent Sherry. Cambridge: Cambridge UP, 2005. 85-112.

Cannadine, David. "War and Death, Grief and Mourning in Modern Britain." *Mirrors of Mortality: Studies in the Social History of Death*. Ed. Joachim Whaley. New York: St Martin's, 1982. 187-242.

Clewell, Tammy. "Consolation Refused: Virginia Woolf, The Great War, and Modernist Mourning." *Modern Fiction Studies* 50:1 (2004): 197 -223.

Connelly, Mark. *The Great War, Memory and Ritual: Commemoration in the City and East London, 1916-1939*. Woodbridge, Suffolk: The Royal Historical Society/The Boydell Press, 2002.

Cuddy-Keane, Melba. *Virginia Woolf, the Intellectual, and the Public Sphere*. Cambridge: Cambridge UP, 2003.

Das, Santanu, "War Poetry and the Realm of the Senses: Owen and Rosenberg." Kendall 73-99.

Doyle, Laura. "The Body Unbound: A Phenomenological Reading of the Political in *A Room of One's Own*." Berman and Goldman 129-145.

Dyer, Geoff. *The Missing of the Somme*. London: Hamish Hamilton, 1994.

Froula, Christine. *Virginia Woolf and the Bloomsbury Avant-Garde: War, Civilization, Modernity*. New York: Columbia UP, 2005

Fussell, Paul. *The Great War and Modern Memory.* New York: Oxford UP, 1975.

Gillis, Stacy. "'Many Sisters to Many Brothers': The Women Poets of the First World War." Kendall 100-113.

Gregory, Adrian. *The Silence of Memory: Armistice Day 1919-1946.* Oxford & Providence: Berg, 1994.

Harrison, Brian. "College Life, 1918-1939." In Brian Harrison, ed. *The History of the University of Oxford, Vol. VIII: The Twentieth Century.* Oxford: Clarendon Press, 1994. 81-108.

Harrison, Brian Howard. *The Transformation of British Politics, 1860-1995.* Oxford: Oxford UP, 1996.

Haughton, Hugh. "Anthologizing War." Kendall 421-444.

Hussey, Mark. "Living in a War Zone: An Introduction to Virginia Woolf as a War Novelist." In Hussey, ed. *Virginia Woolf and War: Fiction, Reality, and Myth.* Syracuse: Syracuse UP, 1986. 1-13.

Hynes, Samuel. *A War Imagined: The First World War and English Culture.* New York: Atheneum, 1990.

Inglis, K. S. "The Homecoming: The War Memorial Movement in Cambridge, England." *Journal of Contemporary History* 27 (1992): 583-605.

Ingram, Angela. "'The Sacred Edifices': Virginia Woolf and Some of the Sons of Culture." *Virginia Woolf and Bloomsbury: A Centenary Celebration.* Ed. Jane Marcus. Bloomington: Indiana UP, 1987. 125-145.

Kendall, Tim, ed. *The Oxford Handbook of British and Irish War Poetry.* Oxford: Oxford UP, 2007.

King, Alex. *Memorials of the Great War in Britain: The Symbolism and Politics of Remembrance.* Oxford & New York: Berg, 1998.

Lee, John. "Shakespeare and the Great War." Kendall 134-152.

Levenback, Karen L. *Virginia Woolf and the Great War.* Syracuse: Syracuse UP, 1999.

——. "Teaching *A Room of One's Own* in the New Millennium: The War Continues." Berman and Goldman 170-175.

Lodge, Sir Oliver. *Christopher: A Study in Human Personality.* New York: George H. Doran, 1919.

——. *Raymond; or Life and Death.* New York: George H. Doran, 1916.

Longley, Edna. "The Great War, History, and the English Lyric." *The Cambridge Companion to The Literature of the First World War.* Ed. Vincent Sherry. Cambridge: Cambridge UP 2005. 57-84.

Marcus, Jane. *Virginia Woolf, Cambridge and* A Room of One's Own: *'The Proper Upkeep of Names.'* London: Cecil Woolf, 1996.

Marts, Katie. "Opening Doors to *A Room of One's Own*." Berman and Goldman 176-180.

McVicker, Jeanette. "'Six Essays on London Life': A History of Dispersal," Part I. *Woolf Studies Annual* 9 (2003): 143-165.

——. "'Six Essays on London Life': A History of Dispersal," Part II. *Woolf Studies Annual* 10 (2004): 141-172.

Osborn, E. B. *The New Elizabethans: A First Selection of the Lives of Young Men Who Have Fallen in the Great War*. London: John Lane, 1919.

Owen, Wilfred. *Poems; with an introduction by Siegfried Sassoon.* [1920.] *Project Gutenberg.* 15 May 2009 <http://www.gutenberg.org/etest/1034>.

Rawlinson, Mark. "Wilfred Owen." Kendall 114-133.

Reilly, Catherine W. *English Poetry of the First World War: A Bibliography*. London: George Prior, 1978.

Sherry, Vincent, ed. *The Cambridge Companion to The Literature of the First World War*. Cambridge: Cambridge UP, 2005.

——. "The Great War and Modernist Poetry." Kendall 190-207.

Skelton, Tim and Gerald Gliddon. *Lutyens and the Great War*. London: Frances Lincoln, 2008.

Spater, George, and Ian Parsons. *A Marriage of True Minds: An Intimate Portrait of Leonard and Virginia Woolf*. New York: Harcourt Brace Jovanovich, 1977.

Utechin, Patricia. *Sons of this Place: Commemoration of the War Dead in Oxford's Colleges and Institutions*. Oxford: Robert Dudgdale, 1998.

Winter, J. M. "Oxford and the First World War." *The History of the University of Oxford, Vol. VIII: The Twentieth Century*. Ed. Brian Harrison. Oxford: Clarendon Press, 1994. 3-25.

Winter, Jay. *Sites of Memory, Sites of Mourning: The Great War in European Cultural History*. Cambridge: Cambridge UP, 1995.

Winterhalter, Teresa. "Guns and Big Guns in *A Room of One's Own*." *Re: Reading, Re: Writing, Re: Teaching Virginia Woolf: Selected Papers from the Fourth Annual Conference on Virginia Woolf*. Eds. Eileen Barrett and Patricia Cramer. New York: Pace UP, 1995. 72-79.

Wohl, Robert. *The Generation of 1914*. Cambridge: Harvard UP, 1979.

Woolf, Virginia. *The Diary of Virginia Woolf*. Ed. Ann Olivier Bell and Andrew McNeillie. 5 vols. London: Hogarth, 1977-1984.

——. *The Essays of Virginia Woolf*. Ed. Andrew McNeillie. 4 volumes to date. NY: Harcourt, 1987-2008.

——. *Jacob's Room*. 1922. Annotated and with an introduction by Vara Neverow. Orlando: Harcourt, 2008.

———. Women & Fiction: *The Manuscript Versions of* A Room of One's Own. Ed. S. P. Rosenbaum. Oxford: Blackwell, 1992.

Young, James E. *The Texture of Memory: Holocaust Memorials and Meaning*. New Haven & London: Yale UP, 1993.

"The utmost fluidity exists with the utmost permanence": Virginia Woolf's un-Victorian Sterne

M-C Newbould

Throughout her career as a writer, in both her critical and fictional work, Virginia Woolf repeatedly discloses her fascination with the literary past and seeks new ways in which to make it seem fresh to her early twentieth-century readers, using it both as a site of historical investigation and as a source of fictional inspiration. My concern here is to address how Woolf's keen interest in the eighteenth-century author Laurence Sterne and his work, principally *The Life and Opinions of Tristram Shandy, Gentleman* (1759-67) and *A Sentimental Journey through France and Italy* (1768), shapes her critical and her creative ambitions. Woolf's enjoyment of this period of literature sits alongside that of her contemporaries, Beth Rosenberg noting that "The Bloomsbury group as a whole had a strong affinity to the eighteenth century" (xv); while Woolf captures the vibrancy of its everyday life in *Orlando*, Lytton Strachey describes this "epoch" as one of "the enchanted islands of delight and repose" ("Pope, Addison, Steele and Swift" 11). Yet they also share this interest with the generation of readers and critics that immediately preceded their own; here, I shall examine how the complex relationship of inheritance and rebellion Woolf experienced with the Victorians, and especially with Leslie Stephen, can be fruitfully explored by comparing their writings about Sterne. Woolf's re-evaluation of Sterne's literary legacy, achieved through engaging with and reformulating the opinions put forth by some amongst her father's generation, becomes essential to the modernist enterprise she pursues as an independent author of fiction.

Earlier commentaries addressing Sterne's possible influence on Woolf now seem outdated in the light of more recent critical advances in the study of her relation with the literary past,[1] such as Juliet Dusinberre's focus on sixteenth and seventeenth-century writers in *Virginia Woolf's Renaissance*, and Anne E. Fernald's

[1] Amongst these earlier critiques see, for instance, James Hafley, *The Glass Roof*, or Robert Hunting's article "Laurence Sterne and Virginia Woolf.". Hafley's assertion that *Orlando* is suffused with "Sternesque touches" is unsupported by textual analysis and leads to some dubious conclusions; for instance, had Woolf chosen to present Mr. Ramsay "as a comic figure" he would no doubt be similar to Walter Shandy, Tristram's father, and Hafley makes the opaque claim that Woolf and Sterne had a shared "philosophical perspective" (3, 99). Robert Hunting, by contrast, reinforces Robert Curtis Brown's assertion that it had become "a critical cliché" to claim a link between Woolf's fiction and Sterne's, arguing that Woolf "at no point said anything that might suggest, even remotely, that she had gone to school to Sterne or his methods" (282-3).

Virginia Woolf: Feminism and the Reader. Fernald chooses an eighteenth-century subject for one of her case studies, addressing how Woolf adapts Joseph Addison's spectatorial model of criticism to assert her own position as a woman of letters writing for the periodical press (2, 98, 113). Two other pertinent reference points for this essay are Rosenberg's *Virginia Woolf and Samuel Johnson: Common Readers* and Jane de Gay's *Virginia Woolf's Novels and the Literary Past*. Rosenberg discusses Woolf's relation to "literary tradition" and the importance of Leslie Stephen's role in its mediation, with a particular focus on Samuel Johnson (xv-xx). De Gay, meanwhile, sets out clearly how Woolf connected to a literary past that included her immediate predecessors, amongst them her father, and creatively renegotiated the reading obtained through these complicated access routes in her fiction (3). De Gay presents Woolf's relation with Stephen as one characterized by both inspiration and resistance (12-15, *passim*); the scope of her study, however, does not permit a thorough analysis of the points of contact and of departure between Stephen and Woolf's critical writings on Sterne that she touches upon (136-8). I shall adopt and expand upon De Gay's approach in discussing how Woolf and Stephen's interest in Sterne is necessarily linked; as Gillian Beer points out, "Woolf did not eschew her father's pleasures, reading Sterne particularly with admiration" (95), while by resisting certain key aspects of his critique she moulds her re-evaluation into a model for her own fiction.

Miriam L. Wallace's "Thinking Back Through Our Others: Rereading Sterne and Resisting Joyce in *The Waves*," is clearly important to this discussion. Wallace makes a convincing case for examining Sterne's importance to Woolf as a source of inspiration both for her criticism and her fiction (196). However, Wallace's essay to some extent shares the shortcomings of feminist approaches to studying Woolf's relation to the literary past, such as Dusinberre's and Fernald's, by allowing a heavily gendered reading to inflict a lack of sensitivity toward both the texts Woolf read and how she wrote about them. For instance, Wallace's repeated accusations of Sterne's "misogyny" (198, 204, 216), which she gleans from Woolf's Holograph Reading Notes, her diaries, letters and essays, produce a negatively biased account of Sterne's writings. It is not my purpose to mount an anti-feminist defence of Sterne here–that debate has taken place in greater detail elsewhere[2]– but it does seem that insisting too much on Woolf's resistance to the perceived misogynistic elements of his writings detracts from the really

[2] Ruth Perry, in "Words for Sex: The Verbal-Sexual Continuum in *Tristram Shandy*," argues that Sterne's novel is phallocentric, whilst the opposite case is argued by, for instance Leigh Ehlers, "Mrs Shandy's 'Lint and Basilicon': The Importance of Women in *Tristram Shandy*"; Juliet McMaster, "Walter Shandy, Sterne, and Gender: a Feminist Foray"; Helen Ostovich, "Reader as Hobby-Horse in *Tristram Shandy*"; Paula Loscocco, "'Can't Live without 'em': Walter Shandy and the Woman Within"; Melvyn New, "Job's Wife and Sterne's Other Women."

important points of contact between the two writers' work that Wallace otherwise reveals. As Wallace herself cautions in the conclusion to her essay, "to dismiss Sterne's novel as misogynistic or to focus exclusively on the representation of women in that novel is to miss the possibilities and power of engaged feminist re-reading and critique" (216). It also evades the possibility of a deeper affinity between Sterne and Woolf that surpasses gender, one made possible both through his status as a marginalized figure (rather than as the representative of patriarchal establishment), and through their shared, profound sympathy about the nature of their craft.[3] This is a sympathy generated not only by Woolf's manifest admiration for *Tristram Shandy* but also by his achievements as a writer in general, in the context of which it seems important not to ignore her comments on *A Sentimental Journey*.

While partly wishing to rescue Sterne from the pyre of feminist critique, my main concern here is to address how Woolf herself effects her own recovery of Sterne's writings and reputation from an altogether different inquisition, that of the critical opinions of the other, significant realm of her literary legacy, obtained from the nineteenth-century men of letters who included her father. Despite the potential shortcomings of a discourse resting on the idea of literary inheritance, it can nonetheless provide an informative tool for discussing the relation between two writers who also happen to be father and daughter.[4] The grounds on which

[3] Wallace supposes, for instance, that Sterne appeals to an élite male readership: "*Tristram Shandy* displays all the standard marks of the 'educated' Englishman . . . the 'right reader' of Sterne's novel is the classically educated gentleman," with an Oxbridge background (209). From a different appreciation of Sterne's biography, however, he was the impoverished son of an absent father, sent to Cambridge only thanks to the grudging assistance of a condescending uncle who expected subservient favors in return, and then only as a low class sizar compelled to wait on his fellow students at table in part payment for his keep. His subsequent career was that of an obscure Yorkshire parson cut off from the literary élite of London, who only came to the world's attention with the publication of his book and who, even then, encountered a mixed reception of ridicule and praise by the fashion conscious of high society who leapt on the band wagon of *Tristram Shandy*'s success. See Cash's biography for details. In this light, Sterne was something of an outsider, whose apparent bonhomie with an educated male élite perhaps possesses a more ironical dimension than some analyses allow. He shared more with Woolf than simply a pleasure and pride in the writer's craft: both are excluded, marginalized, and find publishing their writing to be the only means of expressing their voice.

[4] The influence that a writer of one generation can exert over another has been characterized by Harold Bloom as "an irresistible anxiety" (Bloom xviii), in which the younger generation feels inhibited by the achievements of its literary forbears, and so is propelled into an Oedipal struggle to overcome their stifling influence. Jackson Bate, meanwhile, sees it as a "burden" inflicting a "remorseless deepening of self-consciousness, before the rich and intimidating legacy of the past" (4). Fernald rightly warns against the limitations of rigidly

Fernald, for instance, rejects outright any regard for "filiation" are unconvincing: "because family is so powerful so inevitable, so central," she argues, she wants "to try to imagine a version of literary history that would not rely on family metaphors" (5). Woolf's intellectual as much as her biological connection with her father is an undeniable, and above all potentially instructive means of understanding the roots of her emergence as both reader and writer, and how she established her independence in both roles. As De Gay observes, "Woolf's reading of Stephen provided an important mechanism by which she renewed her intellectual heritage, debated with it and found her own way forward" (13). Steve Ellis supports this approach, suggesting that "Woolf remained deeply attentive to the era in which she had been born," which produced "the blend of conservatism and radicalism that informed her outlook" (4, 9). The relation between these two facets of Woolf's identity, as both Stephen's daughter and independent writer, is symbiotic, the "rebellion" providing an exciting stimulus for innovation. As Janis M. Paul explains, "Few writers considered themselves as much in the vanguard of Modernism and theorized as much about the Modernist novel as did Woolf. But, as is true of most other rebels, her revolt was grounded in attraction: she fought as hard as she did against the conventions of the past because they pulled her back. . . ." (6).

Woolf's wide reading is central both to the nature of her relation with her father, through whom she first gained access to books, and to how she writes as both critic and author of fiction. Woolf is profoundly aware that her own love of literature is indebted to her father's generosity in allowing her unfettered access to his books. She conveys a sense of filial gratitude in her essay "Hours in a Library," published posthumously in 1957; the title clearly glances back to her father's work of the same name (De Gay 13), which Leonard Woolf claims to have been "the most popular and probably the best book which he published" in a prefatory note to the essay; yet any indebtedness on Virginia Woolf's part, he suggests, is also conditioned by a natural repulsion:

> Her love of reading and of books and literature owed much to her father, who encouraged her when quite a child to read what she liked in his very extensive library. Like all children of intelligence and originality she rejected and revolted against some things in the mind and philosophy of her father, and she often criticised him rather violently as a literary critic for the narrow Victorian morality which warped his literary judgment of writers, like Sterne, whose books or whose behaviour did not conform

---

following such a line, or of adopting the view T. S. Eliot promotes (to an assumed male readership) in his essay "Tradition and the Individual Talent"; she favors instead Wai Chee Dimock's "idea of resonance" as a more fruitful way of describing one writer's intellectual relation to other writers (3).

> to the standards of Victorian propriety. At the same time she had a great admiration for his love of books and literature and of the way in which he had guided her first steps in the library (Leonard Woolf 7-8).

Here, Leonard Woolf identifies Stephen's treatment of Sterne as a potential source of that dual filial "admiration" and revolt, which solidifies his representative role as an embodiment of the "narrow Victorian morality" influencing his opinion and acts as an important stimulus for Woolf's counter-reaction.

Rosenberg addresses the contradictory nature of this filial connection within a specifically eighteenth-century context by focusing on how Samuel Johnson's writings had, for Woolf, been "mediated by Leslie Stephen" (xv), which proves instrumental to Woolf's own growth as a critic and writer, for it "allows for the transmission of particular notions of reading, writing, and speech, the most important of which is the idea of good writing as good conversation" (xvi). Rosenberg argues that while Woolf encounters Johnson via Stephen, her "need to distinguish her literary identity from her father" forces her "to read Johnson antithetically to Stephen: Woolf reads Johnson as a dialogical writer" (xvi), which she develops in the "dialogical style" characterizing her own fiction. Woolf transforms the potential of writing as conversation found in Johnson from the polished resolution that Stephen identified into a fruitfully combative mode of engagement and so, Rosenberg claims, "changes her literary heritage and Johnson's role within that heritage. The implications of this new heritage for the modern canon are significant" (xx).

It is apt that Rosenberg should select Johnson's "conversational" style as particularly important to the development of Woolf's identity as a "modern" writer, for Sterne is particularly keen to champion how life and writing intertwine, and how verbal modes of human communication are inseparable from their written embodiment: Tristram playfully tells us that "Writing, when properly managed, (as you may be sure I think mine is) is but a different name for conversation" (*Tristram Shandy* 88).[5] The discursive nature of *Tristram Shandy* opens up what Wallace calls an "inter-literary conversation" (195) between Woolf and her predecessors, and offers her an attractive route for establishing a similarly dialectic relationship with her father by arguing with his opinions of Sterne, and which a deeper affinity with Sterne than with Johnson perhaps makes possible.

[5] *Tristram Shandy* has, for instance, appealed to critics who fruitfully draw connections with Mikhail Bakhtin's dialogic model (Rose 131-33).

I

Victorian critical attitudes toward Sterne provided a particularly rich field in which Woolf could forage when seeking to debunk the apparently erroneous opinions of her forbears, and to consider how she might go about creating her own authorial persona as critic and writer of fiction. William Makepeace Thackeray is particularly virulent in his condemnation of Sterne, both man and work, in a series of lectures published as *The English Humorists of the Eighteenth Century* in 1853. Thackeray paints a dark portrait in which the novelist's supposedly reprehensible character traits and conduct are allied to the most objectionable parts of his writing. Various supposed facts about Sterne's life (although actually erroneous)[6] subject him to censure, such as the profligacy that left his widow and daughter destitute after his death, and his supposed ill treatment of his wife. These, in turn, taint appreciation of his writing. Thackeray reproves what he considers to be the grossly indecent nature of some passages, claiming that their notorious bawdiness is the inevitable manifestation of the author's debauched nature: "There is not a page in Sterne's writing but has something that were better away, a latent corruption–a hint, as of an impure presence" (190). Thackeray might find evidence of such "latent corruption" in the entire fabric of the narrative, revolving as it does around the events surrounding and following on from Tristram Shandy's conception, and from which sex is rarely absent; meanwhile, the suggestive wordplay and numerous *double entendres* that feature heavily in *Tristram Shandy* might give offence, such as Dr. Slop's sordid pun on the "curtins and horn-works" that Uncle Toby innocently mistakes as referring to his favorite hobby of military fortification, but which the doctor intends to mean "bed-curtains" and "the horn-works of cuckoldom" (89-90).

Yet Thackeray does not appreciate the sentimental elements of Sterne's writing either, which for some redeem the more scurrilous parts; he claims that Sterne's feeling is both insincere and inescapably tainted by his innate amorality, and that the occasional declarations by his narrators of the heightened feeling they experience are pretended rather than sincere. Parson Yorick, for instance, describes in *A Sentimental Journey* how his aroused sensibility upon meeting a caged starling prompts thoughts about the Bastille and imprisonment in general: "I vow, I never had my affections more tenderly awakened" (60). At such moments, Thackeray claims, Sterne is self-consciously aware of the "effect" that the professed emotion exerts upon his readers, to the extent that one's pleasure is marred by the uncomfortable sense of being watched by the author: "The foul Satyr's eyes leer out of the leaves constantly" (190).

[6] Arthur Cash points out how far Thackeray skews the facts of Sterne's biography for the purposes of his essay; *Early and Middle Years* xii.

As a fellow "Victorian" (in Leonard Woolf's sense) Leslie Stephen, in the essay entitled "Sterne" printed in *Hours in a Library*, confidently condones "The judgment pronounced upon Sterne by Thackeray, which seems to me to be substantially unimpeachable" (133-4). Not only does he approve of and praise this verdict, but he produces further grounds for objecting to Sterne using biographical details that blacken his already sullied portrait, his condemnation couched in even harsher terms than Thackeray's. Announcing that "It is impossible to write [Sterne's] biography . . . without making it a continuous apology," Stephen goes on to accuse Sterne of having "a want of principle," calls him "a consummate sneak," a "patronage hunter" and "servile flatterer," and even insinuates an objectionably "close alliance" with his boon companion, John Hall-Stevenson–the friend whom Woolf more idyllically portrays as Sterne's fellow book lover at Cambridge in her essay "Sterne" (134-7).[7] While forgiving "some of" Sterne's "flirtations" in view of his personal circumstances, Stephen nonetheless objects to "the spirit in which he conducted them," in particular his pursuit of the young singer Catherine Fourmantel, only to drop her when he unexpectedly became famous; Stephen stoutly informs his reader that "a brother of Miss Fourmantelle [sic], had she possessed a brother, would have been justified in administering a horse-whipping" (138-9).[8] He similarly disapproves of Sterne's late-life (unconsummated) passion for the younger, married Eliza Draper.[9]

While thus far concurring with Thackeray's judgment of Sterne's character, and explaining that this partially taints the enjoyment of reading his novels, Stephen nonetheless moderates his condemnation by attempting to balance such incriminating facts with extenuating details about the occasionally trying circumstances of his life: "No doubt Sterne is to be pitied for his uncongenial position," he suggests, in being unable to attain preferment in the clerical profession, "a career for which he was unfitted" but into which he was forced by the impoverishment of an "impecunious father" (and here Stephen's own vexed relationship with "the Church" surely encourages some sympathy with Sterne); Stephen even suggests that "we may pity him for having become tired of his wife whom he seems to have married under a generous impulse–she was no doubt a very tiresome woman" (137). Moreover, Stephen urges that a negative appraisal of Sterne's biography need not necessarily completely tarnish appreciation of his work, which he clearly holds in high regard, claiming that "It is impossible for

[7] Woolf writes of Sterne (albeit with ironic naivety) that "He sat with John Hall-Stevenson under a great walnut tree in the court of Jesus College, reading Rabelais, Rochester, and Aphra Behn, Homer, Virgil, and Theocritus, evil books and good books, so that they called the tree the tree of knowledge" ("Sterne" 88).

[8] Cash gives a more balanced account of Sterne's relationship with Kitty Fourmantel in *Early Years* 291-6.

[9] Not, as Wallace supposes, "Eliza Fowler" (196).

any one with the remotest taste for literary excellence to read 'Tristram Shandy' or the 'Sentimental Journey' without a sense of wondering admiration" (132). Accordingly, Stephen attempts partially to detach biographical from literary criticism:

> I do not, however, wish to preach a sermon upon Sterne's iniquities, or to draw any edifying conclusions upon the present occasion. We have only to deal with the failings of the man so far as they are reflected in the author. Time enables us to abstract and distinguish. (139)

However, while wishing to obtain such a degree of abstraction that his dislike for Sterne the man does not obstruct his admiration for the work, Stephen finds a "considerable difficulty" in the attempt, and knowledge of Sterne's unpleasant characteristics "cannot enter our minds without injuring our enjoyment" (133, 140). As Rosenberg observes, "Sterne is even more severely criticized [by Stephen] than Pope for his immorality. Though we love his writing, we cannot love the man" (132).[10]

The related, suspect ethics of Sterne's writing also remain inescapable. As such, Stephen aligns himself with the "narrow" moralizing tendency of his generation in finding literary merit spoilt by unmentionable features. After all, as Quentin Bell explains, "The coarser passages of Swift and Sterne would have been perfectly familiar to Leslie Stephen, but he could no more have quoted them than he could have alluded to a visit to the lavatory" (xxi). At some moments *Tristram Shandy* might indeed be considered distasteful for those of a delicate constitution, particularly its earliest volumes, but for Stephen even *A Sentimental Journey*, otherwise "a book of simply marvellous cleverness," incurs "disgust and regret":

> The disgust needs no explanation; the regret is caused by our feeling that something has been missed which ought to have been in the writer's power . . . one grows angry when he spoils a graceful scene by some prurient double meaning, and wastes whole pages in telling a story fit only for John Hall-Stevenson. (141-2)

Meanwhile, the potentially redeeming sentimental elements Sterne introduces in his narratives, which might out-balance moments of innuendo, are for Stephen often sickeningly over-indulged, and never divorced from the impression created by Sterne's prurience, as "his sudden excursions into the nauseous are like the

[10] Stephen claims that his historical detachment allows him to enjoy Popean satire whilst knowing it is cruel: "I can admire the keenness of the wasp's sting when it is no longer capable of touching me and my friends" (139).

practical jokes of a dirty boy who would put filth into a scent bottle," and he wastes his "admirable delicacy of genius . . . upon contemptible ribaldry" (142). Stephen reiterates Thackeray's suspicion that the "foul satyr's" sentiment is actually a leering "sham," accusing him of pretending to a "goodness of heart" and elevated feeling:

> Of the literary skill there cannot be a moment's question; but if we for a moment yield to the enchantment, we feel ashamed, at the next moment, of our weakness. We have been moved on false pretences; and we seem to see the sham Yorick with that unpleasant leer upon his too expressive face, chuckling quietly at his successful imposition. (140)

Sterne exemplifies the "bad sense" of "sentiment" as a "word," eluding genuine feeling so as to create a gap between sincere intent and effect that discomfits his readers: "We are never sure that we can distinguish between the true gems and the counterfeit" (153), Stephen echoing here Thackeray's rhetorical "How much was deliberate calculation and imposture–how much false sensibility–and how much true feeling?" (Thackeray 185). For Stephen, the only lasting, redeeming feature of *Tristram Shandy* (and indeed Sterne's oeuvre) is "the presence of that wonderful group of characters who are antagonistic to the spurious wit based upon simple shocks to a sense of decency," most prominent among them Uncle Toby (143). He is "an incarnation of most lovable qualities" shared with some of "the immortal characters in fiction". Although, Stephen qualifies, he is not quite "on the same level" as Don Quixote, Toby nonetheless possesses Cervantic qualities and is "a triumph of art," and even dares to commit the literary heresy of hinting that Toby surpasses those characters of Shakespeare of whom "it is only permitted to speak with bated breath" (133, 156-7). Stephen seems constantly torn between his genuine admiration for Sterne's literary skill, and delight in those passages in which it is most evident, and his profound distaste for the undeniable immorality (by Stephen's standard) that taints them.

Sterne's nineteenth-century reception was, of course, more complex and subtle than such a reductive representation of critical opinions suggests (Howes 27-30). Dickens admired Sterne, and perhaps some of his most lively characters are drawn with a comparable sense of their absurdities, while Bulwer's *The Caxtons* is partly modelled on *Tristram Shandy* (Howes 28, 35). In criticism meanwhile, Uncle Toby was continuously upheld as a heartwarming example of amiable humor. Walter Scott preempts Stephen in describing Toby and his faithful servant, Trim, as "the most delightful characters in the work, or perhaps in any other," while Thomas Carlyle similarly foreshadows Stephen in comparing them to "*Don Quixote*, far as he lies above them" (Howes 374, 380). In the visual arts, meanwhile, *Tristram Shandy* and *A Sentimental Journey* continued to provide inspiration across the century for oil paintings by artists such as C. R. Leslie and W. P. Frith, and for book illustrations from George Cruikshank's of 1832 to Harry Furniss's of 1883.[11] Maria, the distracted "sentimental heroine" who features in both novels, remained popular amongst readers and artists (Gerard 149). Yet even amongst warmer appraisals such as Scott's or Carlyle's, the complaint against Sterne's indecency (both man and work) nonetheless conditions general appreciation.

II

A background of disapproval and of moral rigidity, such as is exhibited in Thackeray's clearly paraded opinions and their more modulated resonance in Stephen, provided Virginia Woolf with a powerful tool in her critical rehabilitation of Sterne. As the Sternean critic Lodwick Hartley notes, hostile Victorian attitudes toward this author motivated "the Bloomsbury writers" to mount "the first significant counter-reaction" against Victorian tastes and moral standards (15). Woolf's reassessment of the "Victorian" Sterne emerges most significantly in her comments upon his literary style and the form of his work, rather than upon biographical details or contestable passages in either of his novels; nonetheless, she focuses on her predecessors' perceived moralizing tendency as a starting point for this undertaking. In her essay "The 'Sentimental Journey,'" Woolf names the author of *The English Humorists*, but replaces her father's admiring approbation of his pronouncement on Sterne with biting sarcasm: "Thackeray lashed him with his righteous indignation" (406).[12] Yet rather than targeting the critic himself, Woolf treats him as a representative of his age: he embodies "the narrow Victorian morality" identified by Leonard Woolf, which characterizes Virginia Woolf's own father; there is even a hint of the "horse-whipping" that Stephen wishes on Sterne in her reproof of Thackeray's "lash." For Woolf, a misguided attitude toward the author as a man, condemned for his supposedly dubious morals as exhibited in certain actions in his life and passages in his writing, deflects from fully appreciating Sterne's work. An altered approach to morality, in which greater

[11] Catherine Gordon's illuminating studies of paintings illustrating Sterne's work reveal the continuing interest in Sterne throughout the nineteenth century as manifested in the visual arts, whilst W. B. Gerard and Brigitte Friant-Kessler's ongoing bibliography of art works relating to Sterne in the journal *The Shandean* provides an important resource for this area of interest.

[12] This essay appears in several different forms; first published in the *New York Herald Tribune*, 23 September 1928, Woolf revised the article for her Introduction to the Oxford World's Classics edition of *A Sentimental Journey*, published in November 1928; the piece was further revised for *The Second Common Reader* (*E5* 408). Citations here are taken from the *Common Reader* version published in *E5*.

permissiveness grants a liberating freedom from the constraints of "righteous indignation," allows Sterne's apparently heinous conduct to be reassessed and his work to be admired anew.

In "Eliza and Sterne" (1922), concerning the youthful object of the middle-aged author's doting affections whom Stephen had cited as amongst Sterne's "flirtations," Woolf scathingly suggests that her Victorian forbears' interpretation of the history, biography or literature of the past was jaundiced by prejudice; they held themselves to be privileged in possessing the "truth" that was "revealed about the year 1850 to the fortunate natives of the British Isles, who need only in future take into account circumstances of date, country, and sex in order to come to a satisfactory conclusion upon all cases of moral eccentricity submitted to their judgment" (100). For Woolf, such judgmentalism can safely be ignored in the freer age to which she belongs; "morality" has acquired an elasticity meaning that what was once scandalous can be viewed with more leniency, even made permissible; consequently, Sterne's misdemeanors seem less pernicious, or can at least be overlooked. Now, Woolf argues, "times are changed"; whereas "in 1850 Eliza would not have been invited to Court . . . in 1922 we should all be delighted to sit next her at dinner" ("Eliza and Sterne" 100). Indeed, she claims elsewhere that blandishments such as Thackeray's become as condemnable as the faults of Sterne's life and writing that he attacks, precisely because they cloud over the admirable qualities of his writing:

> To us at the present time the arrogance of the Victorian novelist [i.e. Thackeray] seems at least as culpable as the infidelities of the eighteenth-century parson. Where the Victorians deplored his lies and his levities, the courage which turned all the rubs of life to laughter and the brilliance of the expression are far more apparent now. ("The 'Sentimental Journey'" 406)

Woolf, however, is certainly not averse to reading biographical fact alongside literary work; indeed, one can fruitfully inform the other, as she presses in her *Times Literary Supplement* essay on Sterne of 1922, but an equilibrium must be maintained. An almost stereotyped, pared down account of the previous generation as moralizing and self -righteous in their opinions about authors such as Sterne allows Woolf to effect her critical rehabilitation, distancing herself from those who miss and even distort the poetic and beautiful qualities she discerns in Sterne's prose by adopting an alternative moral standpoint; as Ellis points out, "Woolf needed the idea of the Victorian, and with it that of the modern, to structure her sense of history," as she formulated her own position in relation to both (6-7).

Woolf's writings on Sterne in fact reveal some notable points of contact with Stephen's essay, yet she articulates her condemnation of certain aspects of his writing and her appreciation for certain shared favorite features (such as Uncle Toby's character) in an entirely different way. In her essay "Sterne," Woolf's reassessment of Stephen's critique partly depends on an altered appreciation of sentiment, pitting her modern dislike against a Victorian fondness for its more tear-jerking manifestations, which Toby seems to embody (particularly in *Tristram Shandy*'s later volumes). She reveals exasperation with Sterne's tendency to over-indulge those features of Toby's character that most successfully capture the loveableness some readers fondly appreciate: "Yet there are moments, especially in the later books of *Tristram Shandy*, where the hobby-horse is ridden to death," and Walter's "invariable eccentricity tries our patience" ("Sterne" 91). Of the sensible feeling expressed in *A Sentimental Journey*, a novel which apparently seems to take as its guiding principle the heightened emotion that Sterne had found to be so popular among the readers of the later volumes of *Tristram Shandy*, Woolf claims that it "sickens us with its sweetness like the drop of pure sugar at the bottom of a cup" ("The 'Sentimental Journey'" 406).

However, Stephen himself is far from admiring sentimental gush ("the nauseous"); indeed, as suggested, one of his principal difficulties with Sterne is that writer's treatment of sentiment, yet his objection is based on different grounds than Woolf's distaste for mushy sentimentalism. While it offers Sterne a disconcerting means of self-posturing, of deception even, more importantly it indicates the essential superficiality of his writing; it represents "sentiment running to waste" in its lack of "any moral, or political, or philosophical application" (145), a view which provides Woolf with the strongest motivation to reject her father's conclusions. Stephen presents Sterne as detached from any real engagement in the pressing concerns of the day; the caged starling incident in *A Sentimental Journey*, for instance, reflects his readiness in "sentimentalizing over jackdaws and prisoners" but has no real practical concern or purpose (Stephen 147).[13] Although the "lovable" Toby provides delight it is of a limited kind, as beyond the "picturesque touches" added to his character he is essentially divorced from reality: "The very essence of the Shandy character implies this absolute disengagement with sub-lunary affairs" (147).[14] Toby offers escapism astride "the magical hobby-horse" upon which he canters into the "enchanted land" of the model fortifications he constructs on his bowling green, with which he plays like "a full-grown child" (148). While Stephen finds pleasure in this

[13] Stephen in fact anticipates the Marxist critique of eighteenth-century sensibility levelled by Robert Markley, for whom Sterne exemplifies the passive philanthropy of a bourgeois elite.

[14] Stephen echoes here Tristram's claim in Volume IV chapter 27, that "When great or unexpected events fall out upon the stage of this sublunary world---the mind of man, which is an inquisitive kind of a substance, naturally takes a flight, behind the scenes, to see what is the cause and first spring of them."

childlike innocence, and suggests that "A man would be priggish indeed who could not enjoy this queer region" (149), Toby's disinterestedness indicates the flimsiness of Sterne's fictional creation in any serious or philosophical sense. This supports Stephen's "thesis" that "all fiction is really a kind of lying, and that art in general is a luxurious indulgence, to which we have no right while crime and disease are rampant in the outer world" (143). While not, of course, condemning "art" outright as a result, the shallowness that Stephen finds beyond the surface pleasure of *Tristram Shandy*, and his admiration of Sterne's style, prevents him from seriously considering this author's achievement as weighty or lasting. Whereas *Don Quixote* reflects "the most profoundly tragic element in human life" in the "contrast" between "lofty idealism" and "the sturdy common-sense of ordinary human beings", Stephen concludes that "It is impossible to find in 'Tristram Shandy' any central conception of this breadth and depth" (157). This shallowness permeates Sterne's fiction, Stephen concluding that "The Shandyism upon which he prided himself was not a very exalted form of mind, nor one which offered a very deep or lasting satisfaction" (163).

Woolf directly challenges these conclusions as she negotiates her own dislike of Sternean sentiment and attempts to assert an alternative reading of his work to her father's. While finding *A Sentimental Journey*'s sentimentality unpalatable, and suspecting (alongside Stephen and Thackeray) that here Sterne is overly concerned with "our good opinion of his heart" and so presents "virtue standing rather too still to be looked at" ("The 'Sentimental Journey'" 406), Woolf does not dismiss the novel; this repulsive quality, or possible pretence to feeling, indicates neither the author's malign character nor a shallowness permeating his work.[15] She claims, instead, that *A Sentimental Journey*, "for all its levity and wit, is based upon something fundamentally philosophic," the most un-Victorian "philosophy of pleasure" (406). Woolf's modern appreciation of both sensual pleasure and the pleasure of the text, which are united in *A Sentimental Journey*, allows her to look beyond her father's suspicions and her own distaste for "sentimentality" to luxuriate in her enjoyment of the prose, and to counter Stephen's lament for his lack of "lasting satisfaction," an appreciation she extends to Sterne's work as a whole.

[15] As regards Stephen's mixed feelings about the fantastical element of *Tristram Shandy*, Woolf to some extent expresses awareness of the dangers of extreme fantasy in her own writing, noting in her diary a conversation with Lytton Strachey about *Mrs. Dalloway*'s composition; he tells her that "You should take something wilder & more fantastic, a frame work that admits of anything, like Tristram Shandy. But then I should lose touch with emotions, I said. Yes, he agreed, there must be reality for you to start from" (*D*3 32), although Wallace presents this conversation as one between an anxious Woolf and Strachey as "the trusted critic" to whom she defers for judgment because he is an educated man, rather that between an author and a trusted friend (209-10).

III

The grounds on which Stephen had based his conditional praise of *Tristram Shandy* and conclusions about Sternean superficiality–the eccentric uncle Toby–furnish those on which Woolf forms her reappraisal of Sterne's writing, using it to reassess her father's stance the better to assert her own in ways which permit fresh possibilities for how she will pursue her own ambitions for fiction. Whereas Stephen is content to categorize Toby merely as a lesser example of a humorist in the Cervantic mould, in "Phases of Fiction" Woolf looks beyond the most easily discernible delineation of character to concentrate on Toby's emblematic role in representing Sterne's wider creative enterprise. A new approach to what "fiction" might encompass prompts Woolf to find in *Tristram Shandy* the substance her father believes to be lacking.

Unlike Stephen, Woolf is more interested in the way in which Toby's character is presented than in his verisimilitude or ability to engage with the world around him. She appreciates that Toby's depiction is part of the creative whole, a necessarily erratic and partially drawn element essential to Sterne's mode of fictional writing. In "Phases of Fiction" she describes how Tristram begins to draw his "portrait" of his uncle ("I was just going . . . to have given you the great outlines of my uncle *Toby*'s most whimsical character"), only to drop it immediately as this easily distracted narrator pursues a digression, then subsequently resumes the picture two chapters later ("If I was not morally sure that the reader must be out of all patience for my uncle *Toby*'s character —" [58, 61]). For Woolf, Tristram's picture of Toby is a sketch rather than a complete portrait; but while Stephen might lean toward such an appraisal when he claims of Sterne that "No one at least shows more inimitable facility in producing a pungent effect by a few touches of exquisite precision" (132-3), Woolf connects this technique to the broader structural nature of *Tristram Shandy*. She recognizes how, paradoxically, fragmentation leads to completeness, how digression drives progression, quoting Tristram's claim that "'the drawing of my Uncle Toby's character went on all the time– not the great contours of it–that was impossible–but some familiar strokes and faint designations of it . . .'" before concurring that

> It is true, for we are always alighting as we skim and circle to deposit some little grain of observation upon the figure of Uncle Toby sitting there with his pipe in his hand. There is thus built up intermittently, irregularly, an extraordinary portrait of a character–a character shown most often in a passive state, sitting still, through the quick glancing eyes of an erratic observer . . . .("Phases" 92-3)

Woolf acknowledges that Sterne's digressions play an important part in enabling his pictures to be "built up intermittently, irregularly"; as Tristram claims, "in all my digressions . . . there is a master-stroke of digressive skill" and "they are the sunshine" (58), each digression fragmenting the picture conveyed so that the reader must mentally reassemble it for him or herself. Woolf's analysis anticipates a vein in Sternean criticism that was not to emerge until the mid-twentieth century. W. B. Gerard effectively describes the technique by which Sterne creates mental pictures of his characters, his "pictorialism," as a process that is "dependent on the reader's imagination subjectively to supply certain elements toward the realisation of a visualized mental picture" (4).

Wallace observes how Woolf's comments on this passage of *Tristram Shandy* feed into the "metonymic narrative strategy" she was to develop in *The Waves* (207); her incorporation of this technique into her own style is, perhaps, motivated by her awareness that Sterne uses it to engross his readers in *Tristram Shandy*'s prose:

> Here our sense of elasticity is increased so much that we scarcely know where we are. We lose our sense of direction. We go backwards instead of forwards. A simple statement starts a digression; we circle; we soar; we turn round; and at last back we come again to Uncle Toby who has been sitting meanwhile in his black plush breeches with his pipe in his hand. ("Phases" 92-3)

Woolf acknowledges here the challenge of reading *Tristram Shandy* that Sterne explicitly poses his readers, to engage in the narrative "conversation," and so in some respects to create it alongside its author; as Wallace describes, "Woolf's reading notes return obsessively to *Tristram Shandy*'s emphasis on the reader's part in making the text work" (203). For Sterne, being a good reader largely rests on recognizing and accepting this interactive role by following his narrator through the twisting, winding maze of *Tristram Shandy*'s digressive, stop-start flow. At an early point in his narrative, Tristram demands that his reader ("Madam") re-read the previous chapter, claiming that she has missed the point it made, meanwhile confiding to the rest of us that

> I have imposed this penance upon the lady, neither our of wantonness or cruelty, but from the best of motives . . . 'Tis to rebuke a vicious taste which has crept into thousands besides herself, — of reading straight forwards, more in quest of adventures, than of the deep erudition and knowledge which a book of this cast, if read over as it should be, would infallibly impart with them. (48)[16]

[16] Sterne's point here is not that all women readers, represented by "Madam," are bad

Woolf's comments on this digressive-progressive narrative style distinguish her from the bad reader Tristram "rebukes"; she finds that the challenge of falling in with the idiosyncratic rhythm of Sterne's prose, as "we circle; we soar; we turn round," stimulates the narrative's progress through activating her imaginative involvement as a reader, just as his partially drawn portraits encourage her to create mental pictures of his characters. As Tristram avers

> . . . from the beginning of this, you see, I have constructed the main work and the adventitious parts of it with such intersections, and have so complicated and involved the digressive and progressive movements, one wheel within another, that the whole machine, in general, has been kept a-going, —(*Tristram Shandy* 59).

Woolf argues that Sterne's partial picture painting enables Sterne to maintain his creative grasp over his fictional creations, just as much as his digressive narrative style engrosses the reader in the wheels within wheels of his unique text, leading her to the rather emphatic conclusion that "Laurence Sterne is the most important character in the book" ("Phases" 93). Yet in this ultimate expression of life-as-art, grounds for opposition such as might rest on the author's character (for Thackeray or Stephen) become irrelevant. Indeed, Woolf elides positive and negative traits of both the author's character and his texts in her appreciation of the all-encompassing representation of life that *Tristram Shandy* offers as its author's creation, the "frame work that admits of anything" which Lytton Strachey identifies (*D*3 32). As such, in "Phases of Fiction," Sterne comes to embody Woolf's aspirations as a writer of fiction both through the dialogic, conversational style he adopts and through the closeness to lived experience his writing attains, an intense realism very different indeed to that of novelists such as Thackeray or Trollope.[17]

In "The 'Sentimental Journey,'" Woolf argues that Sterne's skill lies in conveying the impression of being "more true to life" in his writing through

---

readers, eliciting the knowing male-oriented joke Wallace identifies (203), but that a popular "vicious taste" amongst readers of both sexes has produced a particular *type* of "bad" reader. This is as much a rebuke at the expense of contemporary literary productions than of readers themselves–some authors pander to a fashionable taste for story telling, the "romance" and "novel" writers generally held in low esteem at the time–whereas *Tristram Shandy* is of altogether a different class, quite unique amongst present day publications and so (Tristram hopes) eminently buyable.

[17] And, indeed, to the assumption that such realism can play a role in changing contemporary life, Sterne's apparent failure to do so being part of Stephen's critique. Wallace provides an astute analysis of Woolf's comments on realist fiction in "The Narrow Bridge of Art," and how the idea that "Engaged art must combine the individual-personal with the larger-than-personal" underlies her "perceptive recognition of the limitations of the Victorian novel's allegiance to formal realism for effecting cultural change" (198).

its vivacity, its presence within the moment, its tactility, yet using an overtly contrived medium; as she observes, "Sterne achieved this illusion only by the use of extreme art and extraordinary pains,"

> For though the writer is always haunted by the belief that somehow it must be possible to brush aside the ceremonies and conventions of writing and to speak to the reader as directly as by word of mouth, anyone who has tried the experiment has either been struck dumb by the difficulty, or waylaid into disorder and diffusity unutterable. Sterne somehow brought off the astonishing combination. No writing seems to flow more exactly into the very folds and creases of the individual mind, to express its changing moods, to answer its lightest whim and impulse, and yet the result is perfectly precise and composed. The utmost fluidity exists with the utmost permanence. It is as if the tide raced over the beach hither and thither and left every ripple and eddy cut on the sand in marble (402-3).

Woolf admires Sterne's success in effortlessly uniting art and life to create an intensely "real" reading experience at the very height of its artificiality, an all-absorbing preoccupation that fills "the very folds and creases" of her "mind"; she powerfully impresses the importance of this quality in Sterne's writing to her own ambitions as an author with the aptly Sternean coinage "diffusity" (not recorded in the *OED*).

As a practising author keenly aware of the demands of her craft, Woolf recognizes that it is Sterne's mastery of technical innovation and the art of writing, both of using the malleability of words and the formal features of the text, which enables him to create the impression of lived experience in his prose:

> The jerky, disconnected sentences are as rapid and it would seem as little under control as the phrases that fall from the lips of a brilliant talker. The very punctuation is that of speech, not writing, and brings the sound and associations of the speaking voice in with it. ("The 'Sentimental Journey'" 402)

While offering a direct observation on *A Sentimental Journey* here, Woolf's comments are equally, if not more pertinent to *Tristram Shandy*–indeed she claims that with its opening sentence the second novel places us in the "world" of the first—whose narrator declares the parity between "writing" and "conversation" and which, she claims, "dared to take such liberties with grammar and syntax and sense and propriety and the long-standing tradition of how a novel should be written" ("The 'Sentimental Journey'" 402, 401). For instance, Woolf may have had in mind such moments as that when, during Tristram's passage to

France, Sterne evokes the experience of sea sickness through the disjointed conversation amongst the ship's crew and passengers held together with "jerky, disconnected sentences" and idiosyncratic punctuation:

> — When shall we get to land? captain — they have hearts like stones —— O I am sick! —— reach me that thing, boy —— 'tis the most discomfiting sickness —— I wish I was at the bottom! — Madam! how is it with you? Undone! undone! un —— O! undone! sir — What the first time? —— No,? 'tis the second, third, sixth, tenth time, sir, hey-day —— what a trampling over head! — hollo! cabin boy! what's the matter —
> The wind chopp'd about! s'Death! — then I shall meet him full in the face.
> What luck! 'tis chopp'd about again, master —— O the devil chop it ——
> Captain, quoth she, for heaven's sake, let us get ashore (397).

As Woolf observes, the coalescence of technical skills Sterne brings to bear on his prose captures the vivid, "rapid" sense of real life and talk demonstrating the utmost "control" at the height of its seeming utmost abandonment:

> The order of the ideas, their suddenness and irrelevancy is more true to life than to literature. There is a privacy in this intercourse which allows things to slip out unreproved that would have been in doubtful taste had they been spoken in public. Under the influence of this extraordinary style the book becomes semi-transparent. The usual ceremonies and conventions which keep reader and writer at arm's length disappear. We are as close to life as we can be. ("The 'Sentimental Journey'" 402)

Here, a glance towards those moralizing Victorians creeps in ("privacy," "intercourse," those things which "slip out unreproved"), but these surpass the realm of moral stricture through their abandonment of "the usual ceremonies and conventions," praise Woolf echoes in "Phases of Fiction" by describing *Tristram Shandy* as "a book in which all the usual conventions are consumed and yet no ruin or catastrophe comes to pass" (93).

Indeed, it might not be Sterne's morals as much as his daring approach to novelistic convention that shocks the less open, uncreased mind. While Stephen skates over the technical details of Sterne's written style (despite claiming to admire it) to focus instead on the reprehensible biography and the indictment of vacuity, he nonetheless finds a breath to concur with Goldsmith's virulent (and probably jealous) attack on Sterne as a "charlatan" whose work met with unprecedented popularity and fame, and voices "a passing word of regret that a man of Sterne's genius should have descended so often to mere buffoonery or to the most degrading methods of meeting his reader's interest" (141). Alongside his book's affront to narrative style in its digressions, disconnected syntax and muddled chronology, these "degrading," attention-grabbing "methods" might include the dashes, asterisks, black, blank and marbled pages, and other unusual visual features with which Sterne challenged the expected way in which a book should appear. However, such stylistic quirks, including Sterne's markedly distinctive use of punctuation, help to create the sense of vivacity Woolf admires; his notoriously profuse dashes (he has even been referred to as "the dashite Sterne")[18] and use of symbols (☞) seek to create a vivid impression of the kind of experience normally incommunicable in print: "What could Dr. *Slop* do? - - - He cross'd himself ✝ ——" (*Tristram Shandy* 86). By dismissing such essential features as gimmicks, Stephen closes off an entire realm of fiction's capacity to capture the living moment, which Woolf seizes upon and seeks to emulate. As Anne Henry notes, E. M. Forster compares Woolf and Sterne's ability to portray "'that broken syntax of speech-in-the-mind,'" achieving the "'odd effects'" that characterize both writers' styles through the same "'medium,'" that of typography (Henry 314).

Sterne's success in approximating lived experience brings Woolf to place Sterne on a separate, higher level than the other novelists she describes in "Phases of Fiction," claiming that "Sterne by the beauty of his style has let us pass beyond the range of personality into a world which is not altogether the world of fiction. It is above" (93). Similarly, in "The Narrow Bridge of Art" Woolf sublimates *Tristram Shandy*, describing how Sterne's style goes beyond ordinary prose to assume a poetic quality: "There, one sees, is poetry changing easily and naturally into prose, prose into poetry" (227).[19] As Stella McNichol suggests, Woolf "refers to *Tristram Shandy* . . . as a book in which one sees poetry changing naturally and easily into prose and prose into poetry," which brings her to realize that "The designation 'novel' will no longer be adequate" (McNichol 94).

Woolf finds in Sterne a lyrical quality that not only appeals to her relish of reading his writing but also offers an aspirational model for how she herself would like to write as an author of fiction. The poetic nature of her written style leads Charles Schug to consider Woolf as inheriting and transporting the spirit of Romantic poetry into the modern novel, giving her finest works "the status of the great Romantic odes" (192). Schug identifies Woolf's creative quest as one seeking

> . . . to impose the appropriate form on experience, the form that best helps us deal with it in a meaningful way. That form embodies the underlying principle of the Romantic poetry of experience: that immediate apprehension gained through experience is primary and certain. The effort of all Romantic writers is to make that experience be the experience of their readers . . . (225).

[18] See J. Best Davison, *The Difficulties of English Grammar and Punctuation Removed* (1839), cited in Henry 316.

[19] Wallace provides a thorough analysis of Woolf's description of this quality in "The Narrow Bridge of Art" (198-200).

While this, indeed, rings true as regards the writing and reading of Romantic poetry, the immediacy of experience and urge to communicate that experience to the reader are also poignantly Sternean preoccupations, deftly noted by Woolf's appraisal of how Sterne "brought off the astonishing combination" of making experience seem real through the texture of the written word, the quality that she seeks to attain in her own writing. Wallace suggests that Woolf's "fluid representations of subjectivity" in novels "from *Jacob's Room* through *Between the Acts*" is gleaned from Sterne (206). The narrator of *Jacob's Room* also shares with that of *Tristram Shandy* what Paul calls "a sense of self-awareness and knowledge of the difficulty of writing" (117); yet this "self-awareness" can be exploited for creative ends and the "difficulty" be a painful pleasure in which to engage. Woolf similarly infuses the vivacity she finds in Sterne into her attempt to capture the hubbub of the living moment in the eighteenth-century section of *Orlando*,[20] in which she evokes a densely peopled and object filled world with Sternean "rapidity" and breathlessness, with its "Ladies in flowered silk" and "Citizens in broidered coats," and her listing "of the tobacco, of the stuff, of the silk, of the gold, of the silver ware, of the gloves, of the perfumes, and of a thousand other articles" of a commercialized society, alongside the coffee house culture where conversation and celebrity figures such as Addison, Dryden, and Pope circulate as fluidly as newsprint (159-60).[21]

However, Woolf unequivocally links the poetic transcendence of *Tristram Shandy* to its formal qualities, which she appreciates both as reader and as aspiring writer, what Wallace describes as "the explicit appeal of Sterne's formal structure and stylistic play"; as she observes, "The emphasis on design, formal structure as the tool for combining the material and the poetic, is a strategy she uses herself in *The Waves*" (201). Hunting rightly admires Woolf's appraisal of Sterne's daring approach to "grammar and syntax and sense and propriety and the long-standing tradition of how a novel should be written," and her appreciation of Sterne's "success" in "*speaking directly to the reader*" (288). Woolf's appreciation of writing as a craft, whose substance is words and whose nuts and bolts are syntax, punctuation, print, brings her to admire how far Sterne's apparently loose, unconsidered style is actually the result of "extreme art and extraordinary pains," and how far he challenged "how a novel should be written." The peculiarities that characterize Sterne's style provide Woolf with an inspirational array of technical devices with which to free themselves from the conventional structures of plot, story telling, characterization, to create something fresh and different.

[20] De Gay provides a full account of literary influences on this chapter (133 ff). See also Hafley, who lists numerous instances of supposed "Sternesque touches" in *Orlando*.

[21] Although De Gay observes that this collection of literary dignitaries is probably an ironic homage toward the canon her father establishes of male eighteenth-century authors.

IV

In his *Conjectures on Original Composition*, which appropriately enough appeared in the same year as *Tristram Shandy*'s first volumes (1759), Edward Young describes the process of literary inheritance as one in which "on their father's [sic] decease," the authors of a new generation "enter as lawful heirs, on their estates in fame" (8). The literary legacies that Woolf acquires both from her father and from Laurence Sterne pose something of a challenge to establishing her own independence and originality. Young warns that "Too formidable an idea of their superiority, like a spectre, would fright us out of a proper use of our wits; and dwarf our understanding, by making a giant of theirs. Too great awe for them lays genius under restraint, and denies it that free scope, that full elbow-room, which is requisite for striking its most masterly strokes" (13). Woolf has her "spectres," both Sterne's ghost and her father's;[22] and yet, Young claims, "The mind of a man of genius is a fertile and pleasant field, pleasant as *Elysium*, and fertile as *Tempe*; it enjoys a perpetual spring" (6), and offers hope for both the eighteenth-century modern author and the Modernist writer of the early twentieth century to assert his or her own originality.

As a critic, Woolf can use reappraisal of Sterne's work to differentiate herself from the preceding generation of Victorian commentators that included her father; but as a writer of fiction, the innovativeness of which Sterne was a champion, the liberating freedom from form and convention he promotes, acts as a stimulus for unfettered creativity and the development of her own unique authorial identity. Tindall goes too far, and indeed is misleading, in claiming that Woolf inherits this creative fecundity and flexibility to become "a Bloomsbury equivalent of Laurence Sterne" (209), for this suggests replication where there is innovation. Attempting to imitate Sterne would be an impossible and, moreover, undesirable venture; Woolf imbibes inspiration from Sterne while using the liberating, open-ended experience of reading his text to find the "free scope" and "full elbow-room" that allows her to perform her own "masterly strokes" as an author.

Woolf's reading was absorptive, and her response to previous authors' works in her criticism and her fiction emerged from its complicated origins and from its density. While Leslie Stephen provided a complex access route to that reading, by challenging his published opinions about those earlier Shandean ones Woolf formulates her own authorial persona, in which critical and fictional sources of inspiration merge. Both Woolf and Sterne share a love of words–what Woolf describes as "the medium in which a novelist works" in the same breath as

[22] De Gay describes Stephen as a "Ghost" haunting Woolf (96), whilst Woolf's essay "Sterne's Ghost" provides a fictionalized account of the overhanging presence of an earlier literary figure.

suggesting how deeply *Tristram Shandy* is embedded in "the language in which it is written" ("The Art of Fiction" 54)–and for the technical demands of their craft. In different respects, both Woolf and Sterne weave their chosen words into the rich texture of their witty, provoking, thoughtful prose, both seemingly abandoning formal constraints at the very height of practicing the most careful artistry. As a writer of fiction Woolf finds grains of genius within this eighteenth-century author's writing that stimulate her own creative faculties, liberating her into developing a unique literary style that is as different from the fiction of her Victorian forbears as is her criticism.

Works Cited

Bate, W. Jackson. *The Burden of the Past and the English Poet.* London: Chatto and Windus, 1970.

Beer, Gillian. *Virginia Woolf: The Common Ground.* Edinburgh: Edinburgh UP, 1996.

Bell, Quentin. Introduction. *The Diary of Virginia Woolf.* Ed. Anne Olivier Bell. Vol. 1: 1915-1919. London: Hogarth Press, 1977: xiii-xxviii.

Bloom, Harold. *The Anxiety of Influence: A Theory of Poetry.* 2nd edn. NY: Oxford UP, 1997.

Cash, Arthur H. *Laurence Sterne: The Early & Middle Years.* London: Methuen, 1975.

——. *Laurence Sterne: The Later Years.* London: Methuen, 1986.

De Gay, Jane. *Virginia Woolf's Novels and the Literary Past.* Edinburgh: Edinburgh UP, 2006.

Dusinberre, Juliet. *Virginia Woolf's Renaissance: Woman Reader or Common Reader?* Basingstoke: Macmillan, 1997.

Ehlers, Leigh A. "Mrs Shandy's 'Lint and Basilicon': the Importance of Women in *Tristram Shandy.*" *South Atlantic Review.* 46 (1981): 61-75.

Ellis, Steve. *Virginia Woolf and the Victorians.* Cambridge: Cambridge UP, 2004.

Fernald, Anne E. *Virginia Woolf: Feminism and the Reader.* New York: Palgrave Macmillan, 2006.

Gerard, W. B. *Laurence Sterne and the Visual Imagination.* Aldershot and Burlington: Ashgate, 2006.

Gordon, Catherine. "'More than one handle': The Development of Sterne Illustration 1760-1820." *Words: Wai-te-Ata Studies in Literature.* 4 (1974): 47-58.

——. *British Paintings of Subjects from the English Novel, 1740-1870.* Outstanding Theses in the Fine Arts from British Universities Series. New York and London: Garland, 1988.

Hafley, James. *The Glass Roof: Virginia Woolf as Novelist*. New York: Russell and Russell, 1954.

Hartley, Lodwick. *Laurence Sterne in the Twentieth Century: An Essay and a Bibliography of Sternean Studies 1900-1965*. Chapel Hill: U of N Carolina P, 1960..

Henry, Anne. "'Explorations in Dot-and-Dashland': George Meredith's Aphasia." *Nineteenth-Century Literature*. 61 (Dec. 2006): 311-42.

Holroyd, Michael. *Lytton Strachey: A Critical Biography*. 2 vols. London: Heinemann, 1967-8.

Howes, Alan B. *Sterne: The Critical Heritage*. London and Boston: Routledge and Kegan Paul, 1974.

Hunting, Robert. "Laurence Sterne and Virginia Woolf." *Etudes Anglaises*. 32.3 (1979): 283-93.

Lee, Hermione. *Virginia Woolf*. London: Chatto & Windus, 1996.

Loscocco, Paula. "'Can't Live Without 'em': Walter Shandy and the Woman Within." *The Eighteenth Century*. 32 (1991): 166-79.

Markley, Robert. "Sentimentality as Performance: Shaftesbury, Sterne, and the Theatrics of Virtue." *The New Eighteenth Century: Theory, Politics, English Literature*. Ed. Felicity Nussbaum and Laura Brown. New York and London: Methuen, 1987. 210-30.

McMaster, Juliet. "Walter Shandy, Sterne, and Gender: a Feminist Foray." *English Studies in Canada*. 15 (1989): 441-58.

McNichol, Stella. *Virginia Woolf and the Poetry of Fiction*. London and New York: Routledge, 1990.

New, Melvyn. "Job's Wife and Sterne's other Women." *Out of Bounds: Male Writers and Gender(ed) Criticism*. Ed. Laura Claridge and Elizabeth Langland. Amherst, MA: U of Massachusetts P, 1990. 55-74..

Ostovich, Helen. "Reader as Hobby-Horse in *Tristram Shandy*." *Philological Quarterly*.68 (1989): 325-42.

Paul, Janis M.. *The Victorian Heritage of Virginia Woolf: The External World in her Novels*. Norman, OK: Pilgrim Books, 1987.

Rose, Margaret A. *Parody: Ancient, Modern, and Post-modern*. Cambridge: UP, 1995.

Rosenberg, Beth Carole. *Virginia Woolf and Samuel Johnson: Common Readers*. NY: St Martin's, 1995..

Schug, Charles. *The Romantic Genesis of the Modern Novel*. Pittsburgh: Pittsburgh UP, 1979.

Stephen, Leslie. "Sterne." *Hours in a Library*. New Edition. Vol. 3. London: Smith, Elder and Co., 1909. 130-63.

Sterne, Laurence. *The Life and Opinions of Tristram Shandy, Gentleman*. 1759-1767. Ed. Melvyn New and Joan New. Harmondsworth: Penguin, 1997.

——. *A Sentimental Journey through France and Italy*. 1768. Ed. Ian Jack and Tim Parnell. Oxford: Oxford UP, 2003.

Strachey, Lytton. "Pope, Addison, Steele and Swift." *Characters and Commentaries*. London: Chatto, 1933. 11-22.

——. "Pope." *Characters and Commentaries*. London: Chatto, 1933. 279-96.

Thackeray, W[illiam] M[akepeace]. "Sterne and Goldsmith." *The English Humorists of the Eighteenth Century: A Series of Lectures*. London: Grey Walls Press, 1949. 177-208.

Tindall, William York. *Forces in Modern British Literature, 1885-1946*. New York: Alfred A. Knopf, 1947.

Woolf, Leonard. Note. *Hours in a Library*. New York: Harcourt, Brace and Company, 1957. 7-9.

Woolf, Virginia. "Sterne." *Times Literary Supplement*, August 12 1909. *Collected Essays by Virginia Woolf.* Vol. 3. Ed. Andrew McNeillie. London: Hogarth Press, 1967. 88-93.

——. "Eliza and Sterne," *Times Literary Supplement*, December 14 1922. *Collected Essays by Virginia Woolf.* Vol. 3. Ed. Andrew McNeillie. London: Hogarth Press, 1967. 100-4.

——. "The Art of Fiction." 1927. *Collected Essays by Virginia Woolf.* Vol. 2. Ed. Andrew McNeillie. London: Hogarth Press, 1966. 51-55.

——. *Orlando: A Biography*. 1928. Ed. Rachel Bowlby. Oxford: Oxford UP, 1992.

——. "The 'Sentimental Journey.'" 1928. *Collected Essays by Virginia Woolf.* Vol. 5. Ed. Stuart N. Clarke. London: Hogarth Press, 2009. 401-10..

——. "Phases of Fiction." *Collected Essays by Virginia Woolf.* Vol. 2. Ed. Andrew McNeillie. London: Hogarth Press, 1966. 56-102.

——. *Hours in a Library*. Ed. Leonard Woolf. New York: Harcourt, Brace and Company, 1957.

——. *The Diary of Virginia Woolf.* Ed. Anne Olivier Bell. London: Hogarth Press, 1977-82.

Young, Edward. *Conjectures on Original Composition*. 1759. Ed. Edith J. Morley. 2nd edn. Manchester: Manchester UP, 1918.

"I have had my vision": Empire and the Aesthetic in Woolf's *To The Lighthouse*

James F. Wurtz

The institutionalization of postcolonial studies and the rise of related academic fields, such as Irish studies, marked the beginning of an increasing critical interest in the nexus of relations between literary modernism and the discourses of empire. Indeed, for many critics, "modernism . . . is the true starting point of post-colonial critique" (Booth and Rigby 4). While texts like Forster's *A Passage to India* or Joyce's *Ulysses* explicitly demonstrate art's potential to confront imperial ideologies, the place of empire in Virginia Woolf's writing is not quite as fixable. More specifically, Woolf's engagement with imperialism in her work reveals a profound ambivalence over the role that empire plays in both limiting and making possible her modernist art, a premise which I believe is not sufficiently recognized in the critical discussion of Woolf and empire.

Perhaps nowhere is this ambivalence more apparent than in the letters exchanged in 1940 between Woolf and Benedict Nicolson, the son of Vita Sackville-West. In response to Nicolson's charge that Bloomsbury's focus on aesthetics allowed for the rise of fascism, Woolf discusses the social impact that art should or can have. Her letter of 24 August stands out in particular:

> ...But aren't you taking what you call 'Bloomsbury' much too seriously? I don't think that those people whom I suppose you to mean had the very great gifts to alter society. What puzzles me is that the people who had infinitely greater gifts than any of us had—I mean Keats, Shelley, Wordsworth, Coleridge and so on—were unable to influence society. They didn't have anything like the influence they should have had on 19th century politics. *And so we drifted into imperialism* and all the other horrors that led to 1914. (*L6* 421, my emphasis)

This passage implicitly acknowledges the possibility of art to effect social change, yet Woolf seems resigned that while art "should" have an influence over politics, it doesn't seem to have made much of an impression. In the last year of her life, Woolf would appear to share W. H. Auden's claim that "poetry makes nothing happen: it survives/.../A way of happening, a mouth" (Auden 142). Yet her frustration over art's lack of impact on world politics has not erased her own understanding of the role that art should play, and although it may not directly "alter society," it endures and provides an outlet for the artist to criticize and work for change. The older Woolf sees the younger Nicolson moving towards this realization himself: "Anyhow, I think you've made a good beginning if you hate people who sit on the floor and despise humanity" (*L6* 422). As this letter demonstrates, imperialism was both a major concern for Woolf and a source of disappointment in her realization of the limitations of art.

For Woolf, the artist has a responsibility to "alter society," but by the early twentieth century when she begins her writing career, the scope of what's possible has diminished beyond the point of any real political influence. In answering Nicolson's charges, Woolf reveals that she sees art as a limited site for critiquing structures of power, and "Bloomsbury," despite Nicolson's assertions to the contrary, could never have prevented the emergence of fascist governments. This understanding of the capability of art to confront politics is also crucial in considering the ambivalent place of empire in Woolf's writing. The difficulty with postcolonial analyses of Woolf lies in her work's simultaneous critique of and concession to empire. It appears that, according to Woolf, the artist must denounce imperialism, but cannot expect that denunciation to change the political world. In response to Jeanette McVicker's claim that "to engage in an in-depth postcolonial reading of Woolf today is also to engage in a multi-voiced postcolonial reading of the *criticism*" (214), I approach the question of empire in Woolf's work by focusing on her novel *To The Lighthouse* and examining it through the terms of the critical debate over Woolf's imperialist or anti-imperial tendencies. The discourses of colonialism and empire, I argue, present Woolf's modernist text with its most difficult representational challenge, which critics unravel primarily by situating her work as either critical of or complicit with imperial ideology.

Postcolonial analysis of Woolf's work is significant, for the formal and thematic innovations of literary modernism cannot be separated from its social and historical context; modernism's life-span corresponds with the decline of the British Empire and "old" Europe's death-knell with the Great War, and with the rise of the United States and Soviet Russia in the years following the second World War. In his foundational essay "Modernism and Imperialism," Fredric Jameson claims that modernist art, by its very nature, recognizes the imperial dilemma, and embodies it in its structure. He notes that the colonial society has an integral part of its structure—the colony—outside of and distant from itself, and thus necessarily unknowable: "daily life and existential experience in the metropolis—which is necessarily the very content of the national literature itself, can now no longer be grasped immanently; it no longer has its meaning, its reason for being, within itself" (Jameson 51). Modernist art contemplates this situation: "it is only that new kind of art which reflexively perceives this problem and lives this formal dilemma that can be called modernism" (51). Modernist literature, according to Jameson, must be concerned with the imperial question, and must embody and to some extent seek to address this question within its very form.

While critics have taken up the question of empire's place in Woolf's writing, postcolonial analyses of Woolf since Jane Marcus' landmark article "Britannia Rules *The Waves*" have been problematic insofar as they reduce postcolonial discourse to dialectical oppositions of critical or complicit. This criticism tends to utilize and then attempt to surpass this familiar dialectic, giving the discussion an "either/or" quality. Heidi Stalla's reading of *The Waves*, to cite one example, sees the novel as "an attempt to explore the overlap of opposing forces, such as the intersections between individual and universal, East and West" (29). In a sense, this "overlap of opposing forces" reconfigures the classic New Critical reading of Woolf's modernism as an "attempt to make form and meaning one" (Roberts 842). Stalla's argument substitutes the postcolonial concepts of center and periphery, the Orientalist East/West binary, for the consolidation of form and meaning, in order to answer the question that establishes the dominant dialectic in the scholarly conversation about Woolf and empire: is Woolf critical of empire, or is she complicit with it? In other words, can one say that Woolf is an anti-imperialist writer? For Stalla, as for most critics who participate in this debate, the answer is that Woolf saw her writing "as an opportunity for her to express her own anti-imperialist outlook" (29). In its attempt to subvert the distinctions between self and other that are essential to imperial discourse, this discussion follows the critical/complicit dialectic instead.

Critics do recognize Woolf's deep ambivalence about the imperial, of course, but they frequently approach it as something of a riddle, and attempt to decode it according to the established dialectic. As Christine Froula argues, the disinterested contemplation of art that was a hallmark of Bloomsbury's modernism is the space where "sociopolitical critique is integrated with aesthetics" (12). Froula's reading of Lily's painting, in particular, suggests an anti-imperial project behind Woolf's writing. For Scott Cohen, her "response to imperialism . . . is at once critical and complicit" (87). Yet this recognition only places Woolf in an ambiguous position within the dominant dialectic; the problem with Cohen's reading is that it still relies on this reductive theoretical scheme. Ultimately, Cohen contends, Woolf is critical of empire, and thus is an anti-imperial writer. Marianne DeKoven also sees Woolf's ambivalence as indicative of subversion, with the ability, as Susan Stanford Friedman puts it, to "rupture the ideological coherence of western imperialism" (Friedman 119). Sonita Sarker addresses Woolf's ambivalence about empire by linking it to a gendered reading and ultimately concluding that as a feminist, Woolf opposes "masculinist nationalism" (19). Woolf's entire body of work "projects a multifaceted Englishness" (5) that Sarker reads as the source of Woolf's "ambivalent nationalism" (6). However, "[t]he ambivalence she expresses about loving England but hating a particular kind of Englishness is the point of entry for her feminist anti-nationalism" (18). Sarker clearly acknowledges the central position of Woolf's ambivalence, but continues to utilize the critical/

complicit dialectic to interpret it in gendered terms. On the other side of the debate, John Marx observes that one function of modernist writing was that it "privileged marginality for a cosmopolitan readership," thus revealing itself as complicit even in its ambivalence towards the issue (1).

Instead of binary a priori suppositions, I propose that it would be more productive to return the conversation to the ambivalence identified by Woolf herself, which anticipates Homi Bhabha's warning that ambivalence in and of itself is not constitutively subversive, that it "does not merely 'rupture' the discourse, but becomes transformed into an uncertainty" (127). In *To The Lighthouse*, ambivalence, coupled with a depiction of imperialism as a hegemonic patriarchal project, makes untenable the question of whether Woolf is critical or complicit and deeply problematizes scholars' dependence on the critical/complicit dialectic. Woolf highlights the necessity for and the impossibility of fully subverting (or transcending) colonialism within imperialist discourse through aesthetic critique. Crucially, ambivalence here does not suggest an indecisive wavering between choices but rather the impossibility of choice because of the simultaneity of the critical and the complicit. The question should not be whether she confirms or resists empire, but rather how her modernist writing's intentionally ambivalent relationship to empire indicates the limitations of an aesthetic critique of it from within the imperial structure. In other words, resistance to empire is, as Woolf's engagement with imperialism demonstrates, a constitutive part of the imperial structure. *To The Lighthouse* is a valuable text for examining the ways in which Woolf carries out her imperial critique, as it demonstrates the problems that a consideration of empire brings to her work and gestures towards the inadequacy of the critical/complicit dialectic to address the place of empire in Woolf's modernism.

The question of empire haunts Woolf's writing, and scholars most frequently locate the influence of the imperial primarily in the places of home and family. For feminist critics like Susan Stanford Friedman, Woolf's domesticity presents a fixed space for a critique of empire (125). This focus on the domestic also highlights the impact that empire has on the family in general and, for Friedman, on women in particular (125). To be sure, there are deep and multifaceted connections between gender and imperialism, and one can certainly read Woolf's depictions of domestic life in terms of imperial critique. The performance of gender is intimately tied to the imperialist social structure that Woolf and her characters are embedded in, and the domestic world replicates in many ways the political world that they inhabit.

In thinking through how a critique of empire can proceed through a critique of the domestic, Raymond Williams' discussion of Gramsci's concept of hegemony is helpful. Williams explains hegemony as "relations of domination and subordination" that saturate "the whole substance of lived identities and relationships, to such a depth that the pressures and limits of what can ultimately be seen as a specific economic, political, and cultural system seem to most of us the pressures and limits of simple experience and common sense" (110). In other words, systemic power relations of oppression and submission are unthinkingly incorporated into one's consciousness and accepted as essential characteristics of human life. Hegemony, as Williams interprets it, provides a theoretical base for mapping large-scale power relations (for Williams, capitalism; for our purposes here, imperialism) onto individual examples of power dynamics, such as the Ramsay family in *To The Lighthouse*.

As Urmila Seshagiri points out, the Ramsay family "metonymically suggests the material and ideological goals of imperial enterprise" (67). In his roles as father, philosopher, and professor, Mr. Ramsay is "the primary agent of the imperial" for much of the novel (McVicker 99). While his patriarchal role is fairly clear—he demands sympathy and attention from the females and the children of the family, and the younger men follow him around and strive to emulate his example—his positioning as a philosopher marks his place in Woolf's imperial critique most sharply. When Lily Briscoe asks Andrew what Mr. Ramsay's books are about, he answers "subject and object and the nature of reality," placing his father squarely in the plane of those who "understand" reality and thus by understanding, control it (*TTL* 23). Since the goal of Ramsay's philosophical thinking is to "repeat every letter of the alphabet from A to Z accurately in order," it is worth noting that if this is the "nature of reality," it is a reality with a linear progression from which there can be no comprehensible deviation; a reality that is ordered, defined by, and exists in the English language, the primary and arguably the most devastating colonial weapon of the British Empire. Further, Woolf describes Mr. Ramsay's quest to reach Z using the rhetoric of a leader of an expedition, atop a mountain crag in a far-off land, dying alone and wondering who will mark his grave, as well as the image of the might of empire, "the fine figure of a soldier" (36). The sense of loss, the elegiac quality suggested by this description, is essential to a reading of empire in the novel, for she locates the imperial within a family on an island off of Scotland, surrounded by water and rapidly aging; the younger generation will be wiped out in the war, and the older generation faces an inglorious decline.

Mr. Ramsay's role as professor at Cambridge also indicates his imperial context: he is responsible for training the future civil servants and officers who will keep the British Empire operating smoothly (McVicker 99). His relationship with Charles Tansley demonstrates this. Tansley's imitation of Ramsay, right down to falling in love with Ramsay's wife, provides a source of amusement, but is also profoundly disturbing on a deeper level. Ramsay's world-view is replicated in the younger intellectual, ensuring the continuation of the colonial system supported by that worldview.

However, Mr. Ramsay is not the sole representative of empire. Expanding upon Janet Winston's assessment of how Mrs. Ramsay "functions synecdochically to signify the British Empire," I believe that Mrs. Ramsay is key to reading the novel's critique of the domestic as a critique of empire (49). As mother and wife, she re-inscribes the colonial ethos and serves to keep the processes of empire running smoothly at home. Mrs. Ramsay

> had the whole of the other sex under her protection; for reasons she could not explain, for their chivalry and valour, for the fact that they negotiated treaties, ruled India, controlled finance; finally for an attitude which no woman could fail to feel or to find agreeable, something trustful, childlike, reverential. (*TTL* 6)

From the very beginning of the novel, Mrs. Ramsay shows herself to be deeply embedded within the social structure that supports imperialism. She accepts and attempts to live as society demands a Victorian woman should, and she passes this ideology on to her daughters. Submission to the patriarchal structure and the men it privileges, who rule far-off lands and control the economic systems, is second nature for Mrs. Ramsay, who feels it her duty to give Mr. Ramsay the sympathy and support that he needs: "It was sympathy he wanted, to be assured of his genius, first of all, and then to be taken within the circle of life, warmed and soothed, to have his senses restored to him, his barrenness made fertile, and all the rooms of the house made full of life" (37). Mrs. Ramsay thus creates a domestic space where the men are affirmed in their purpose and are then able to go into the public sphere and exert their control over the subjugated peoples of the British Empire. She lives out the same ideology as her husband, within the means available to her, and demands that her daughters do the same.

In referring to men's "reverential" attitude towards Mrs. Ramsay, Woolf links her female protagonist to the British Empire much more explicitly. On her trip into town with Charles Tansley at the beginning of the novel, Mrs. Ramsay is for a moment silhouetted against a portrait of Queen Victoria: "in she came, stood for a moment silent . . . stood quite motionless against a picture of Queen Victoria wearing the blue ribbon of the Garter; when all at once he realised that it was this:—she was the most beautiful person he had ever seen" (14). As Janet Winston has argued, this superimposition of Mrs. Ramsay upon the familiar portrait of Queen Victoria suggests an allegorical reading of Mrs. Ramsay as Queen and Empress (41). Indeed, various characters identify Mrs. Ramsay as the Queen throughout the novel. Her "royalty of form" makes Mr. Bankes consider it impossible for anyone to have "thought of her simply as a woman" (*TTL* 29). In a moment of hostile reminiscence, Lily Briscoe sees her "presiding with immutable calm over destinies which she completely failed to understand" (50).

Mrs. Ramsay herself is aware of this perception: "Wishing to dominate, wishing to interfere, making people do what she wished—that was the charge against her and she thought it most unjust" (57). The Ramsay children are "called . . . after the Kings and Queens of England" (22) and in the years after Mrs. Ramsay's death, Mr. Ramsay is a "king in exile" (148). As queen, Mrs. Ramsay holds court at the dinner-party that closes the first section of the novel. She takes her place at the head of the table "like some queen who, finding her people gathered in the hall, looks down upon them, and descends among them, and acknowledges their tributes silently, and accepts their prostration before her" (82). Even her crown jewels are from India (81). The consistent representation of Mrs. Ramsay as Queen Victoria speaks to the centrality of the imperial in this seemingly domestic novel. Woolf makes the wife and mother analogous to the maternal figurehead of the British Empire and the fortunes of the Ramsay family parallel in miniature the conditions of the empire.

As the Queen, her role in the novel is pivotal; she affects how every character in the novel sees the world and reacts to it. Lily Briscoe, in creating her final painting, must first come to terms with Mrs. Ramsay's presence, even when Mrs. Ramsay has been dead for years. The legacy of the British Empire, exemplified by the Queen, continues to haunt the artist, and Mrs. Ramsay's effect on Lily's art echoes the effect that empire has on Woolf's novel. Just as Mrs. Ramsay dominates Lily's painting, questions of empire loom over the novel. The central role that empire plays in *To The Lighthouse* speaks to its inescapability, and the decline of the empire at the end of Victoria's life plays out in the dissolution of the Ramsay family at the end of Mrs. Ramsay's life. Accordingly, images of diminishment abound. At what is supposed to be the most triumphant moment of the novel, when Lily finishes her painting and the children and their father arrive at the lighthouse, Lily cries in "anguish" and feels that if she "shouted loud enough, Mrs. Ramsay would return" (180). Simultaneously, Macalister tells the passengers on the boat about the ships underneath them sunk in the storm (164) and Cam imagines their own boat sinking (188). This imagery does not just appear at the climax of the narrative, but motifs of sinking, of submersion, and of deterioration figure heavily throughout the novel.[1]

[1] For instance, Janet Winston's allegorical reading of *To The Lighthouse* incorporates a compelling analysis of sinking imagery in the novel. She claims that images of sinking in the text represent "a pervasive anxiety about the sinking British Empire, whose political and economic hegemony in the world was rapidly declining in the first half of the twentieth century" (47). This notion of decline aligns with the specific decline of the British Empire in a way that neither validates nor repudiates the readings that claim Woolf to be in a sort of mourning for a fading moral or aristocratic order. For further discussion of images of decline and their place in Woolf's imperial critique, see David Bradshaw's treatment of

These images of decline that allegorically indicate the decay of the British Empire are echoed in the creation of the metonymic character Mrs. Ramsay. As representative of Queen Victoria, Mrs. Ramsay demonstrates the extent of the fall of the British Empire. A middle-aged woman, she is aware of her aging, and she accepts the fact that she is no longer young. She refers to herself as an "old woman," and acknowledges her situation: "[w]hen she looked in the glass and saw her hair grey, her cheek sunk, at fifty, she thought, possibly she might have managed things better" (6). If one reads the novel as critical of empire, its critique would seem to proceed effectively by using the Ramsay family as a microcosm of imperial society.

However, there are difficulties with thinking about the place of empire in *To The Lighthouse* in hegemonic terms. As Williams explains, the "specific economic, political, and cultural system" indicated is capitalism (110). Imperialism, in this understanding, is one expression of capitalism. Likewise, patriarchal gender relations also exist as a manifestation of capitalist ideology. While imperialism may be implicated in conflict in the domestic sphere, it only partially constitutes that conflict. Put another way, the part ultimately cannot stand for the whole. Specific instances are, at the last, specific to themselves and not simply representative of wider struggles. By focusing on the connections between domesticity and the imperial in the novel, critics can overlook the siting of gender within a wider continuum of power relations that include race, empire, and economics. In privileging the position of gender in Woolf's engagement with empire, these readings tend to interpret the book in terms of its location within the critical/complicit dialectic.

Woolf complicates the imperial critique by rendering Mrs. Ramsay, as queen, in explicitly aesthetic terms. Charles Tansley elaborates on Mrs. Ramsay, in her appearance as Queen Victoria, as "the most beautiful person he had ever seen." In his further description, she becomes not only a representation of empire, but an aesthetic object as well: "With stars in her eyes and veils in her hair, with cyclamen and wild violets—what nonsense was he thinking? She was fifty at least; she had eight children. Stepping through fields of flowers and taking to her breast buds that had broken and lambs that had fallen; with the stars in her eyes and the wind in her hair—He took her bag" (14). Immediately before this scene, Mrs. Ramsay describes the landscape that the artists now favor, giving a description that calls to mind Impressionist painting:

---

tuberculosis in *To The Lighthouse*, and his alignment of consumption with the wasting away of the British Empire (Bradshaw 201).

> For the great plateful of blue water was before her; the hoary Lighthouse, distant, austere, in the midst; and on the right, as far as the eye could see, fading and falling, in soft low pleats, the green sand dunes with the wild flowing grasses on them, which always seemed to be running away into some moon country, uninhabited of men. (12-13)

Charles Tansley's affection for her is the affection not just of a subject for his ruler, but of a witness to a work of aesthetic beauty. His description of her, following so closely the description of the artists and their paintings, plainly evokes art itself; the "stars in her eyes" and "wild violets" are fit subject matter for the Impressionist painter.

The images of stars and veils repeat throughout the novel, always when Mrs. Ramsay is looking at something beautiful or being looked at herself. For example, on an evening walk, she looks up to see a star above the trees, and she notes "the one star and the draped branches" (73). Charles Tansley's moment of revelation links this imagery with Mrs. Ramsay at the same moment that Woolf identifies her explicitly with Queen Victoria. Indeed, Mrs. Ramsay's identification as the Queen throughout the novel is accompanied by the awareness of Mrs. Ramsay as a beautiful woman, to be gazed at as though she were a work of art. Both Mr. Ramsay and Mr. Bankes see her as an object of veneration for her beauty, and the imperially-named poet Augustus shares a gaze with Mrs. Ramsay/Queen Victoria before "he did her homage" (111). In a remarkable passage that demonstrates the centrality of the ocular to the novel's presentation of empire, Woolf joins the language of consumption with both imperial and aesthetic imagery. At dinner, Mrs. Ramsay "saw that Augustus too feasted his eyes on the same plate of fruit, plunged in, broke off a bloom there, a tassel here, and returned, after feasting, to his hive. That was his way of looking, different from hers. But looking together united them" (97). Mrs. Ramsay, the recipient of the worshipful gaze, does not only "feast" with her eyes, rather, she sees how Augustus is seeing the fruit, and the awareness of this shared sight, this "looking together," connects her and Augustus momentarily before she changes back from viewing subject to aesthetic object.

By tying Mrs. Ramsay's beauty to art, and making all of this conditional upon viewing her as an idealized queen, Woolf demonstrates the connection between her anti-imperialism and the aesthetic. Yet this goes beyond just the figure of Mrs. Ramsay; the novel's entire critique of imperialism is bound up with aesthetics. This connection between social critique and modernist aestheticism presumably leads to Benedict Nicolson's argument with Woolf, and provides one reason why critics initially interpreted modernism as a turning away from the social and the historical, an essentially "apolitical" entity which prioritizes "aestheticism and its ideological commitment to the supreme value of a now autonomous art as such" (Jameson 45). Paradoxically, Woolf's experimental modernist aesthetic both carries and undermines her criticism of empire in *To The Lighthouse*.

If one reads the decline of Mr. and Mrs. Ramsay as part of an assessment of British imperialism, then the natural question to ask concerns what exactly will replace the imperial order that is in its twilight. For Woolf, the character of Lily Briscoe provides the answer. Crucially, Lily is herself an artist; but not an artist working in the Impressionist medium that Tansley translates Mrs. Ramsay into in his worship of her as queen. Rather she is a modernist who creates non-representational art, and who requires her viewer to develop new ways of seeing and conceptualizing art. For instance, Lily's painting, with its geometric shapes and contrasting colors calls to mind the cubist style of Picasso or Braques, the post-impressionism of Cézanne, or even the neo-plasticism of Mondrian. If the key attribute in understanding Mrs. Ramsay as Queen is her status as aesthetic object, then Lily's position as creator supplies the corrective. Vision is central here: Mrs. Ramsay is seen, Lily sees anew and calls for new ways of seeing. Lily's primary physical characteristic is "her little Chinese eyes" (*TTL* 17), and sight becomes the entry point into her work as an artist: "beneath the colour there was the shape. She could see it all so clearly, so commandingly, when she looked" (19). She struggles with her picture, which recasts Mrs. Ramsay as a purple triangle, "reduced," as Mr. Bankes puts it, "to a purple shadow without irreverence" (52). Mrs. Ramsay as the "purple shadow" becomes "the central focus of Lily's picture, the feminine object of a feminine gaze. Even her shadow has a political, as much as formal, significance" (Goldman 183). Indeed, Lily's response to Mr. Bankes reveals the extent to which the imperial weighs on her new art. "There were other senses too in which one might reverence them. By a shadow here and a light there, for instance. Her tribute took that form if, as she vaguely supposed, a picture must be a tribute" (52-53). Lily finds new ways of seeing, but she still venerates Mrs. Ramsay, paying tribute as to a queen, and this is why she cannot complete her painting. She continually labors to fall "under the power of that vision which she had seen clearly once and must now grope for among hedges and houses and mothers and children—her picture" (53). For the bulk of the narrative, Lily cannot finish her painting. The climax of the novel, appropriately enough, comes when Lily makes the abstract concrete by completing the work.

Critics recognize the emphasis on an abstract art as a vehicle for anti-imperial discourse in Woolf's writing. Ironically, however, for these critics the turn to abstraction, the refusal of representation, positions the novel even more firmly on the "critical" side of the critical/complicit binary. For example, Winston remarks that the "privileging of abstract art implicates the representation of Empire in the novel . . . Lily transforms the image of Mrs. Ramsay, standing in for the Imperial Queen and Empire, into an abstraction" (65). Lily, in her role as artist/creator, acts to recast the "monolithic identity and unambivalent authority" (65) of the queen-figure into a color or a shape on a field of many colors and shapes: abstract art becomes the method by which imperialism is finally abrogated. Indeed, Lily's painting is arguably the single most positive moment in the novel, although it is clear that her painting will be stored away, not seen, and not appreciated by many (if any) people. Yet this is not the point. For Winston, the very act of creating this abstract, non-representational art bypasses the rational, imperialist society and relegates it to simply one part of a greater whole (62). Abstraction, it seems, denotes an anti-imperial discourse.

Marianne DeKoven observes that both Lily's painting, and the complexity of high modernist aesthetics act to gloss over the processes of history, yet do not fully achieve this end ("History" 149). She echoes Jameson's critique of the reading of modernist aesthetics as covering up the imperial legacy, yet for DeKoven, this act of covering up history is itself a subversive act, an act of resistance, and an act that allows the art to become at least somewhat socially redemptive ("History..." 150-151). As Herta Newman puts it, "[Lily's] revelation affirms, in the strongest terms that Woolf has yet provided, the power of art to attain to that reality it struggles to convey" (Newman 92). And Christine Froula explicitly links Woolf and Lily's projects in her claim that "[t]hrough an abstract aesthetics that turns away from mimetic representation . . . Lily (and Woolf) picture a hidden 'truth' of the world" (148). In the critical discussion of the text, Lily as creator of non-representational art demonstrates the possibility of such art to transcend the imperial and raise the possibility of a new discursive space from which to operate, the "reality beyond appearances" that Froula argues is the goal of abstraction (147).

Woolf herself seems to support this reading of Lily's painting (and by extension the modernist aesthetic that *To The Lighthouse* promulgates). In "Mr. Bennett and Mrs. Brown," she explains the aesthetic aim of the novel: "it is to express character—not to preach doctrines, sing songs, or celebrate the glories of the British Empire, that the form of the novel . . . has been evolved" (324). However, Woolf recognizes that the novel, despite its stated purpose of "expressing character" has been used to achieve these latter aims—particularly in its form—to reinforce the dominance of empire: "[a]nd so they have developed a technique of novel-writing which suits their purpose; they have made tools and established conventions which do their business. But those tools are not our tools, and that business is not our business. For us, those conventions are ruin, those tools are death" (330). Woolf's political aims in the novel's critique of British imperialism are implicated in her aesthetic sense of how the novel should function. The modernist rejection of a nineteenth-century form that celebrated "the glories of the British Empire" is echoed in Lily's new art (as Woolf's text is part of a movement of "new" art as well). Lily's emphasis on abstraction, the use of geometric shapes and colors, and the predominance of form over all else to preserve "the unity of the whole" in the work of art parallels the traditional understanding of modernist aesthetic experimentation characterized by Woolf and the writers and artists of Bloomsbury (*TTL* 53). Woolf's aesthetics are thus fundamental to her critique of imperialism in *To The Lighthouse*.

However, a key component of abstraction is that it cannot be concretely fixed. Although the conception of abstract art most commonly associated with the Bloomsbury writers demands that art "not seek to imitate form, but to create form" and that the goal of art must "undoubtedly be the attempt to give up all resemblance to natural form, and to create a purely abstract language of form," a truly abstract art cannot be universal, for it requires each viewer to make sense of the work on an individual basis (Fry 190-191). The attempt to derive universal meanings from lines, shapes, and colors can at best devolve into symbolism and thus exist as another form of representation. Indeed, Woolf even suggests that Lily's "tribute" is less genuinely abstract than would appear, for shortly after Lily explains how the "purple shadow" evokes Mrs. Ramsay (52), Mrs. Ramsay, thinking about herself in the third person, reflects that when she is alone, "one shrunk, with a sense of solemnity, to being oneself, *a wedge-shaped core of darkness*" (62, my emphasis). As Jane Goldman notes in her discussion of the feminist aesthetics of *To The Lighthouse*, "darkness itself results from, as well as is illuminated by, the light of successive (patriarchal) empires" (183); thus, Lily's purple triangle may be less a radical recasting of imperial normativity and more of a product of imperial hegemony than critics recognize. Because Woolf's imperial critique privileges an experimental, abstract aesthetic, it, like abstract art itself, can only be ambivalent. Woolf's use of abstraction cannot be read convincingly as a critique of empire.

While the reading of Lily's art as providing a counter-hegemonic discourse to the novel can be persuasive, it does not take into account the influence that the hegemonic order has on her own art. Her use of lines, shapes, and colors remains at least partially representational. The "vision" by which she translates Mrs. Ramsay into a triangle is as likely to be the unconscious expression of the hegemonic order as it is to be an act of resistance. Mrs. Ramsay reveals the influence of empire through her role as wife and mother; Lily may well do the same through her selection and arrangement of colors and shapes on the canvas, starting with the purple wedge. The putting away of the painting at the end of the novel is problematic in this regard, for if Gramsci truly sees only "the capture of the state as the end of counter-hegemonic work," then Lily's painting falls closer to submission than revolution (Lloyd 42). In the end, *To The Lighthouse* reveals Woolf's engagement with empire as ambivalent, a conclusion come to easily enough through even a brief glance at the critical literature. Nonetheless, critics still attempt to decipher this ambivalence in terms of its position on a continuum between confirmation and resistance of the imperial order, and I believe that this limits our ability to understand the role that empire plays across Woolf's career, particularly in texts where she more directly takes on the subject such as *The Waves*, *Mrs. Dalloway*, and *The Voyage Out*.

To The Lighthouse presents a critique of imperialism, but its reliance upon the aesthetic to both censure and provide a possibility for redemption undermines that critique. Mr. and Mrs. Ramsay, the primary representatives of the imperial in the novel, see art as simply decoration (33), and regarding Lily, Mrs. Ramsay observes "one could not take her painting very seriously" (17). Lily's observation of the abrupt change in the conversation at the dinner party "from poetry to politics" points to the distinct separation between those two realms (112) and resonates in Woolf's later question to Benedict Nicolson in their letters of 1940: "will you throw up your job as an art critic and take to politics?" (*L6* 415). In claiming that artists don't have "the influence they should have" on politics, Woolf clearly recognizes that art cannot stem the tide of Nazism, and never could (*L6* 421).

Furthermore, the aesthetic of abstraction at play in the novel rejects terms like "critical" and "complicit" and shows instead that the experience of empire demonstrates the limits of Woolf's modernism as socio-political criticism. The transcendent point of the novel, where Lily's work is done and where she can finally say "I have had my vision" reminds the reader of the intricate links between Mrs. Ramsay, the figurehead of the hegemonic order, and Lily, the creator of counter-hegemonic discourse (209). Not only does the painting reflect Mrs. Ramsay's influence in the colors and shapes, but the entire enterprise is characterized as a "vision," both a way of seeing and something to be seen. Woolf fuses Lily and Mrs. Ramsay together here, and like Mrs. Ramsay, the painting also will be buried by the end of the novel. Just as Mrs. Ramsay makes Lily's painting possible (she is its subject and she provides the material conditions for its creation), she confines it as well: its abstraction ultimately cannot be read as an act of resistance, yet neither does it completely concede to being controlled. Abstraction, at its best, can only be ambivalent, and thus one cannot say that Woolf is critical or complicit, because she is simultaneously both and neither. Her ambivalence does not support empire, true, but neither can it fully reject it.

In her study of gender and history in *To The Lighthouse*, Marianne DeKoven claims that the novel "represents more clearly perhaps than any other the modernist moment . . . of the simultaneity of the impossible dialectic, of dualism that seeks neither unitary resolution in the dominance of one term over the other or in the spurious third term of dialectical synthesis, but rather the two-way passage, difference without hierarchy, never the one without the other" (*Rich* 206). This "unsynthesized dialectic" that DeKoven sees as characteristic of modernist writing is "a function of the modernist writers' irresolvable ambivalence" (*Rich* 4). Although DeKoven primarily examines gender, this is also the way that the novel deals with the question of empire. Woolf's "irresolvable ambivalence" neither complies with nor opposes imperialism, and for this reason, the novel resists postcolonial readings that seek to find in it a fixed anti-colonial perspective or complicity with imperial structures.

In reading the novel from a postcolonial point of view, one must keep in mind Urmila Seshagiri's warning that one cannot "read *To The Lighthouse* merely as an opposition to imperialist or nationalist violence" (78). As Seshagiri demonstrates, race becomes one place in the novel where "social critique and aesthetic innovation" meet, and Woolf's aesthetics are closely connected to the area of social critique. Seshagiri focuses specifically on race, but one might also consider Sonita Sarker's or Susan Stanford Friedman's identification of gender as a meeting point for critique and innovation. As these critics have shown us, close analyses of race or gender are productive and helpful approaches towards understanding Woolf's attitudes towards empire. At the same time, the focus on gender or race as the point of conjunction between aesthetics and politics offers at best only a partial view of Woolf's engagement with empire. Although they are essential components of an imperial system, to concentrate on gender or on race as constituting imperial discourse is to look at only one axis of power as opposed to examining the network of power relations that comprise imperialism. To generalize from Seshagiri's assertion, then, one might observe that in *To The Lighthouse* the connections between "social critique and aesthetic innovation" occur at the moments where Woolf addresses not only race or gender, but the broader category of imperialism. In these moments, Woolf reveals her ambivalence towards empire by linking concrete representations of Mrs. Ramsay as Queen Victoria with the abstract aesthetics of Lily Briscoe's painting. Woolf's deep ambivalence renders the critical/complicit dialectic untenable as an analytical tool, because, as the novel demonstrates, both sides of the divide are essential in the creation of her modernist art.

Bloomsbury has been accused of retreating into the aesthetic and out of the socio-historical realms, a reading that postcolonial criticism has significantly revised. Even so, the difficulties that the question of empire raises in Woolf's writing indicate the problems with reading Woolf's social commentary as anti-imperial. Rather, Woolf demonstrates that empire presents a limit to the effects of her modernism, a boundary past which representation, even representation that is experimental and aspires to abstraction, breaks down and ceases to be possible. Empire makes possible her modernism, but it also circumscribes it. The use of abstract art to bear the weight of the imperial critique in *To The Lighthouse* attests to the ubiquity of the colonial condition. Woolf realizes, even as she criticizes it, that she is part of the imperial structure and cannot (or, more provocatively, cannot want to) operate outside of that structure. All that she can do to resist is to create her art, and she does so with the recognition that while art as a vehicle for critique is preferable to the stasis of compliance, the critique can at best be incomplete. As a British writer emphasizing a non-representational art, Woolf is resistant to and implicated in the discourses of empire, and Woolf's modernism is not so much a turning away from the political and the historical as it is an acknowledgment of the limitations of her art.

Works Cited

Auden, W.H. "In Memory of W.B. Yeats". *Collected Shorter Poems 1927-1957.* New York: Random House, 1964. 141-143.

Bhabha, Homi. "Of Mimicry and Man: The Ambivalence of Colonial Discourse" *October* 28 (Spring, 1984). 125-133.

Booth, Howard J. and Nigel Rigby. Introduction. *Modernism and Empire: Writing and British Coloniality 1890-1940.* Eds. Howard Booth and Nigel Rigby. Manchester, UK: Manchester UP, 2000. 1-12.

Bradshaw, David. "The Socio-Political Vision of the Novels." *The Cambridge Companion to Virginia Woolf.* Sue Roe and Susan Sellers, eds. Cambridge: Cambridge UP, 2000. 191-208.

Cohen, Scott. "The Empire from the Street: Virginia Woolf, Wembley, and Imperial Monuments." *Modern Fiction Studies*. 50.1 (Spring 2004). 85-109.

DeKoven, Marianne. "History as Suppressed Referent in Modernist Fiction." *ELH* 51.1 (Spring 1984): 137-152.

——. *Rich and Strange: Gender, History, Modernism*. Princeton: Princeton UP, 1991.

Friedman, Susan Stanford. *Mappings: Feminism and the Cultural Geographies of Encounter*. Princeton: Princeton UP, 1998.

Froula, Christine. *Virginia Woolf and the Bloomsbury Avant-Garde*. New York: Columbia UP, 2005.

Fry, Roger. "The French Group." Rpt. in *Modernism: An Anthology of Sources and Documents*. Eds. Vassiliki Kolocotroni et. al. Chicago: U of Chicago P, 1998. 189-192.

Goldman, Jane. *The Feminist Aesthetics of Virginia Woolf: Modernism, Post-Impressionism and the Politics of the Visual*. Cambridge: Cambridge UP, 1998.

Jameson, Fredric. "Modernism and Imperialism." In *Nationalism, Colonialism, and Literature*. Ed. Seamus Deane. Minneapolis: U of Minnesota P, 1990. 43-66.

Lloyd, David. *Ireland After History*. Cork: Cork UP, 1999.

Marx, John. *The Modernist Novel and the Decline of Empire*. Cambridge: Cambridge UP, 2005.

McNees, Eleanor. "Colonizing Virginia Woolf: *Scrutiny* and Contemporary Cultural Views." *Virginia Woolf and the Essay*. Ed. Beth Carole Rosenberg and Jeanne Dubino. New York: St. Martin's, 1997. 41-58.

McVicker, Jeanette. "Postcolonial Approaches." *Palgrave Advances in Virginia Woolf Studies*. New York: Palgrave MacMillan 2007. 209-226.

——. "Reading *To The Lighthouse* as a Critique of the Imperial." *Approaches to Teaching Woolf's* To the Lighthouse. Ed. Beth Rigel Daugherty and Mary Beth Pringle. New York: MLA, 2001. 97-104.

Newman, Herta. *Virginia Woolf and Mrs. Brown: Towards a Realism of Uncertainty*. New York: Garland Publishing, 1996.

Sarker, Sonita. "Locating a Native Englishness in Virginia Woolf's *The London Scene*." *NWSA Journal* 13:2 (Summer 2001):1-30. *Project Muse*. Web. 16 November 2009.

Seshagiri, Urmila. "Orienting Virginia Woolf: Race, Aesthetics, and Politics in *To The Lighthouse*." *Modern Fiction Studies* 50:1 (Spring 2004). 58-84.

Stalla, Heidi. "Empire and Elveden: New Light on *The Waves*." *Virginia Woolf Bulletin* 12 (January 2003): 20-29.

Williams, Raymond. *Marxism and Literature*. Oxford: Oxford UP 1977.

Winston, Janet. "'Something Out of Harmony': *To The Lighthouse* and the Subject(s) of Empire." *Woolf Studies Annual* 2 (1996): 39-70.

Woolf, Virginia. *The Letters of Virginia Woolf Volume 6: 1936-1941*. Eds. Nigel Nicolson and Joanne Trautmann. New York: Harcourt Brace Jovanovich, 1980.

——. "Mr. Bennett and Mrs. Brown." *Collected Essays I*. London: Hogarth Press, 1966. 319-337.

——. *To The Lighthouse*. New York: Harcourt, 1927, 1981.

Odds, Ends, and Others: Objects and the Narration of Woolf's Servant Characters

Monica J. Miller

In "Time Passes," only one kind of character can appear without disturbing the reigning "loveliness and stillness" (*TTL* 129). Mrs. McNab does not disrupt Woolf's portrait of an uninhabited house because she herself seems barely animate, a "witless" old woman who "lurch[es]" through the house like a "ship at sea" (*TTL* 130). Her thoughts remain largely inaccessible to her readers and even to her creator, who can only describe her creature's inner life through a hedge of deductions—"Visions of joy there must have been"; "Some cleavage of the dark there must have been" (131). When Mrs. McNab exercises what imagination she does possess, she can only clearly envision members of the Ramsay family. Her memories of her fellow servants, like "Mildred? Marian?" the cook, are hazy, ridden with stereotypes, and repeated almost verbatim in a sing-song manner that strips them of specificity (136). Not even types of meaning-production that breach her mystified interior succeed at elucidating her experiences: when she speaks, her utterances are short and cryptic, and when she sings, it is in a "voice of witlessness" that "rob[s her song] of all meaning" (130).

"Mrs Woolf could never write about her servants," Alison Light tells us in her enlightening study of Woolf's relationship with her own household staff; judging by the ephemerality and formlessness of the servant characters in her novels, it seems at first that we could expand Light's statement to suggest that Woolf could never write about servants at all (Light 83). For the hazy portrait of Mrs. McNab is, to an extent, the only type of portrait Woolf thought it possible to draw of a member of the lower classes.[1] As she contends in "Memories of a Working Women's Guild" (1931), the different experiences of the middle and lower classes opened between them, as between the sexes, an impassable gulf. The kindness and mutual esteem Victorian reformers advocated, while still possible in a modern world wary of Christian charity, would take the form of a detached sense of *noblesse oblige*. The only sympathy Woolf and other bourgeois well-wishers could feel for working women would be an "aesthetic sympathy, the sympathy of the eye and of the imagination, not of the heart and of the nerves, and such sympathy is always uncomfortable" (*CE*4 140).[2] The most productive way to

[1] Though many readers find the caretaker significant, her significance lies more in what she represents—the social unconscious, in Michael Tratner's case, or the artist who violently orders the chaos of nature, in J. Scott Bryson's—than in her individual character. One could even argue that Mrs. McNab is less a character than a force, whether of or against nature.

[2] Virginia Woolf's ideological position in relation to class has long been a fraught subject;

respond to class difference, she argued, was to move beyond it, and thus, as Melba Cuddy-Keane documents, she committed herself to working-class education.

Yet to refuse even to attempt to grant servants inner lives in the meantime, instead restricting depictions of service to the more accessible employer-employee relationship, would be to reduce servants to wheels on their mistresses' coaches, to tweak Henry James's metaphor for minor characters (53). For all Woolf's protestations that middle-class writers should leave working women to write their own stories, she did not avoid confronting the gulf that divides the classes in her own fiction. As Heather Levy notes, Woolf struggled throughout her career to find a means of responsibly depicting working-class characters, repeatedly "revising her strategies of writing the working-class woman's body," though she frequently chose not to publish the results (37). The servants on whom her middle-class protagonists depend, however, are an unavoidable presence in her published work. A "mongrel" with "no roots anywhere," the servant both inhabits and is excluded from the family home, occupying an unusual position between the cracks of feudal and capitalist frameworks (*D3* 220). The tentative techniques Woolf develops in order to characterize working women thus fall even shorter of representing women who are not quite workers, but not quite *not* workers, either.

The unusual position in the household that makes servants so conceptually problematic is also what leads Woolf to the method she develops to represent them. As Hegel was so famously aware, one of servants' primary functions is to mediate between their masters and the world of things; even if they do not entirely belong to the household in the abstract, they are even more familiar than their employers with the material household. An association between servants and objects appears throughout Woolf's work; she sketches even the archetypical Mrs. Chailey of her first novel, *The Voyage Out*, in large part through the "ornaments" with which she adorns her cabin, a collection crowned by the portrait of her dead mistress (24). For Woolf, Light contends, things become "the repository of the immaterial—feelings, obsessions, needs and longings—evidence of a hidden inner life which [can] not be known or explained" (151). I take Light's contention a step further: the objects that clutter Woolf's novels serve not merely as placeholders for unrepresentable inner lives, but rather as oblique representations of seemingly inaccessible interiors. For even if those objects deflect direct metaphorical readings, they rarely remain illegible, whether to the novels' characters or readers. In *To the*

---

most critical assessments of this position have taken the form of condemnations or apologies which weigh her contributions to feminism against her less progressive attitude toward class, as Laurie Quinn recounts in her review of studies of Woolf's class politics. In *Virginia Woolf and the Real World*, Alex Zwerdling provides an account of the "divided motives" that marked Woolf's understanding of her class position (33). She recognized the injustice of the class hierarchy, he argues, but was doubtful of the possibility of change.

Lighthouse, intimate contact with the Ramsays' possessions allows Mrs. McNab to reconstruct the people who use them with remarkable accuracy: as she fills Mrs. Ramsay's old clothes with the image of their late owner, she convincingly resurrects a character readers have come to know well. In fact, if we read Mrs. McNab in light of the more pointed, if still problematic, representations of servants in *Mrs. Dalloway* and *The Years*, the caretaker's "sidelong leer" becomes less a sign of witlessness than an alternative mode of observation (*TTL* 131). In *Mrs. Dalloway*, Woolf refracts servant characters' emotional states through collections of objects and thus allows readers to access characters that they would otherwise reduce to types by viewing them from an angle—or, rather, multiple angles—in a strategy reminiscent of Cubism's attempt to reveal "new relations and a new cause for emotion" by "drawing the greatest number possible of planes of the object to be represented" (Nayral 289).[3] Although the "sidelong leer" never overtakes free indirect discourse as the novel's dominant style, it becomes a valid alternative to the deep depictions of subjectivity for which Woolf is well known. As I argue, through her experiments with Cubism's indirection and attention to surfaces, Woolf attempts to solve a political problem with narrative innovation, seeking a method of characterization better suited to representing the other's interiority.

Yet *The Years*, which at first seems to carry out the promise of this experiment, ultimately reveals a tension between style and politics. Although Woolf develops Crosby into a prominent character by revealing her inner life through the objects that she manipulates, maintains, and treasures, the housemaid's very prominence draws attention to the different way she is narrated. Though at times Woolf also portrays middle-class characters through significant objects, such characterizations supplement rather than replace passages of reported thought. By displacing servants' inner lives almost entirely onto the objects they handle, Woolf sacrifices the intimacy between reader and character that the free indirect style establishes. Her solution to the problem of representing servant characters thus fails to fully reconcile her political and narrative concerns. Nevertheless, her attempt to address the ever-vexing Servant Question has a broader influence on both the political and narrative development of her work: it not only leads her to a means of moving beyond caricatures of servants, but also inspires the experiments with narrative that may be among the roots of her later style's fragmentation.

[3] Woolf's relationship with Cubism has been little discussed, but frequently noted in passing, as by Ann Banfield and Christine Froula. Jack F. Stewart, who sees Cubism as a powerful influence on Woolf's late work, finds it is likely that Cubism was part of the "general ferment of ideas" in which she worked, especially given Roger Fry's interest in the movement (87).

Servant, Self, and Family

The problem of identification that Woolf sets out to overcome is in some sense a knowing fiction; such carefully drawn male characters as Septimus Smith in *Mrs. Dalloway* and Bernard in *The Waves* belie the claim that writing across gulfs is impossible, or at least impossible to do well. Her acceptance of the class gulf as somehow more entrenched than the gender division reflects a common middle-class tendency she herself notes in *Three Guineas*: to defuse potential conflicts between the sexes, men and women "drag in, for example, some old family servant, called Crosby, perhaps, whose dog Rover has died . . . and so evade the issue and lower the temperature" (129). The servant, in other words, becomes a sort of scapegoat for difference.

Ironically, servants' status as others within the family does not eliminate, but rather compounds the interdependence that Woolf objects to in her diaries, and thus makes them necessary inclusions among the "innumerable other characters" Woolf marshals to the support of the "tinselly" Mrs. Dalloway (*D2* 272).[4] In *Mrs. Dalloway,* though the servants remain perpetually at the margins of the household, society, and text, they ultimately become as central to Clarissa's self-fashioning as the friends and family members Woolf more explicitly implicates. Early in the novel, Clarissa acknowledges the role that her servants play in the way she interprets her class status:

> [T]hank you, thank you, she went on saying in gratitude to her servants generally for helping her to be like this, to be what she wanted, gentle, generous-hearted. Her servants liked her. (39)

Gentleness and generosity, both linked to gentility, describe a classed version of kindness: benevolence is possible only in relationships of unequal power. The servants are not entirely powerless, of course, for Clarissa's benevolence depends on their tractability. Nevertheless, their compliance allows her to construe her hierarchical relationship with them as mutually beneficial. They thus function as metaphorical mirrors in which she can adjust her class position to her liking.

In other cases, servants maintain the class position itself. They project a feudal fantasy for Lady Bruton, who employs a retinue of housemaids, "adepts in a mystery or grand deception," to conjure the "profound illusion" that food "is not paid for; and then that the table spreads itself voluntarily" (104). In sparing their mistress all interaction with the marketplace, the servants frame the luncheon in a manner which, as William Handley notes of Mrs. Ramsay's dinner in *To the*

[4] For a more extended account of Woolf's attitude toward the interdependence between mistress and servant, see the third chapter of Light's book ("The Question of Nelly").

Lighthouse, crops out all evidence of an economy external to the household (31). The illusion of the table's voluntary submission to its mistress's will arises from a similar pretense on the part of the servants, who play-act as loyal retainers rather than paid employees. Just as Lady Bruton's pet project, Emigration, shuttles out of sight evidence of the economic system's limitations, so does the fantasy of feudal symbiosis erase reminders of class oppression. Her title artificially reinvested with meaning, Lady Bruton, like Clarissa, can benefit from her class position while maintaining an image of herself as "gentle, generous-hearted" (39).

As scholars of the Victorian novel have convincingly argued, the idealized feudal model that employers like Lady Bruton imagine and writers such as Gaskell advocate transforms servants almost into members of the family, albeit in the role of perpetual children.[5] This quasi-familial status complicates servants' effect on their mistresses' identities, for the structure of the Victorian family encourages a collective rather than individualistic view of selfhood. The familiar ideology of separate spheres does not imply separate souls or interests: John Ruskin, for instance, scoffs at those who speak of "the 'mission' and of the 'rights' of Woman, as if these could ever be separate from the mission and the rights of Man;—as if she and her lord were creatures of independent kind, and of irreconcilable claim" (69-70). Despite their association with opposite genders, the separate spheres denote two layers of a unitary identity gathered under the aegis of the man, such that even the supposedly feminine household reflects the interiority of the man who heads it.

If the nineteenth-century woman blended into her husband's home, her servants were still more submerged. Until the late 1920s, British law perpetuated the ideology of the single-souled house. The service franchise included a stipulation that excluded employees who shared homes with their employers, disenfranchising live-in domestic servants on the same principle that denied adult sons still living at home the vote: the measurement of political rights in terms of households rather than individuals.[6] The same logic that erased servants' presence in the house reinforced their membership in the organic whole, resisting a linguistic trend that gradually narrowed the definition of the family to its nucleus (Robbins 110-112). The servant thus occupied a paradoxical position: she blended so thoroughly into the unified household that she lacked an independent identity, and yet at the same time, as the outsider within, she stood for the differences that threatened the household's unity.

[5] See, for instance, Bruce Robbins (42-43), Dorice Elliott (380-381), and for a historical perspective, Theresa McBride (Chapter 1). This is not to discount Victorian writers' self-consciousness about this tendency; as Julie Nash notes, Gaskell attempts to allay the feudal model's infantilizing effect through her characterization of individual servants.

[6] Male domestic servants finally received the vote along with property-owning women over thirty in 1918; female domestic servants were enfranchised along with young and working-class women in 1928 (Tanner).

In Woolf's novels, the Victorian model of familial identity persists, but not uncontested. Many of Woolf's middle-class protagonists persistently resist subsumption in the collective, attempting to carve out a space for personal identity. Asserting that there is "even between husband and wife a gulf" that "one must respect," Clarissa maintains an attic room cut off from the shared familial space (*MD* 120). However, her withdrawal does not entirely succeed, for the lifestyle she is unwilling to relinquish requires her to "pay back from [a] secret deposit of exquisite moments"—that is, from the substance of deep personal identity—"in daily life to servants, yes, to dogs and canaries, above all to Richard her husband" (29).

Although Clarissa may view her personal identity as opposed to the matter of daily life, the secret moments with which she assembles it nonetheless occur to a surprising extent in the presence of servants. Even the narration reflects servants' involvement in Clarissa's construction of a private self. The novel's famous first line is spoken to her maid, Lucy. Indirect speech then blends with thought to the point of becoming nearly indistinguishable: "For Lucy had her work cut out for her," while likely internal, could conceivably be spoken aloud (3).[7] By the end of the paragraph, however, the narration unambiguously represents Clarissa's interior monologue, which spills into her recollection of a formative experience at Bourton—her most abundant source of "exquisite moments." Although blending of speech and thought is common in the novel, the degree of fluidity between Clarissa's interior monologues and addresses to Lucy suggests a surprising mental confluence between mistress and servant that belies the persistent sense of an impassable gulf between them.

The destabilized boundary between speech and thought becomes less surprising in light of servants' position in the household: almost always present at the margins of the room, even if not acknowledged by the text, servants linger in a liminal position between presence and absence, functioning not only as silent witnesses to their mistresses' seemingly private moments, but also, as in the novel's opening, as half-noticed springboards for introspection. As Clarissa herself implies, her employees frequently serve as mirrors in which she can catch sight of her character, enabling the sort of self-examination that is in large part self-construction.

[7] In *Unspeakable Sentences*, Ann Banfield convincingly argues that the sentence cannot reproduce speech, but since free indirect discourse need only represent direct discourse, the ambiguity remains (66-67).

Furnishing the Soul

How, then, can Woolf allow servants to perform this mirroring function without reducing them to mirrors in the process? Interestingly, she addresses the problem of objectification by embracing rather than counteracting the association between servants and objects. At first, servants' ability to fade into the woodwork—to merge with the houses they maintain—only underscores the role they play in furnishing their employers' identities. As Woolf writes in "Street Haunting" (1927), living spaces, replete with "objects which perpetually express the oddity of our own temperaments and enforce the memories of our own experience," become part of "the shell-like covering which our souls have excreted to house themselves, to make for themselves a shape distinct from others" (*CE*4 155-156). Woolf's objects express their owners' temperaments in a way that reveals the complex network of social, psychological, and economic contexts that give rise to them:

> That bowl on the mantelpiece, for instance, was bought at Mantua on a windy day. We were leaving the shop when the sinister old woman plucked at our skirts and said she would find herself starving one of these days, but, "Take it!" she cried, and thrust the blue and white china bowl into our hands as if she never wanted to be reminded of her quixotic generosity. So, guiltily, but suspecting nevertheless how badly we had been fleeced, we carried it back to the little hotel where, in the middle of the night, the innkeeper quarreled so violently with his wife that we all leant out into the courtyard to look, and saw the vines laced about among the pillars and the stars white in the sky. The moment was stabilized, stamped like a coin indelibly among a million that slipped by imperceptibly. There, too, was the melancholy Englishman, who rose among the coffee cups and the little iron tables and revealed the secrets of his soul—as travelers do. All this—Italy, the windy morning, the vines laced about the pillars, the Englishman and the secrets of his soul—rises up in a cloud from the china bowl on the mantelpiece. (*CE*4 155)

The moment and the past that produces it, the place, the people, market forces, the relationship between nations, and even the weather inhere in the china bowl. Once it enters the narrator's possession, the bowl's meaning must be read back through the filter of personality: it contains its owner's experience of those multiple contexts and the effects they produced on her. Like the famous red carnation in *The Waves*, the bowl as phenomenon presents various faces to various viewers, although its status as property alters these faces to reflect the influence of its owner, while the bowl as an instance of the idea of a bowl possesses certain stable aspects of meaning. As Bill Brown says of the central object of *The Golden Bowl*, it is interesting not in its metaphorical significance, but rather in its ability to "crystallize events, relations, situations" (171).

As Ruth Hoberman persuasively argues, Woolf not only includes kitsch in the array of noteworthy objects, but in fact privileges kitsch objects as hubs of emotional associations. Particularly in *The Years*, objects wallow in their physical materiality, taking on an "emotive power that transcends their aesthetic limitations" in a system that devalues "'social' emotions and 'literary' associations" (Hoberman 81; 85). As kitsch—and, I would add, purely functional—objects produce meaning alongside objects recognized as art, the household, filled with the tools and knickknacks dragged in by each of its inhabitants, comes to reflect a multiplicity of souls rather than that of its owner alone.

Mrs. Dalloway makes room for multiple souls within a single home by exchanging the house for the room as symbol of the individual self: Clarissa locates "the heart of life" in her "attic room" (31). The room not only reflects the particularities of her character, but also provides her with a private space in which to dissociate her identity from her husband's. Yet this private space is not entirely private. Richard may be exiled from the attic room, but Lucy is not: a lady's maid has access to all of the same spaces as her mistress. Although Woolf avoids mentioning Lucy's mobility, perhaps in order to strengthen the metaphor of rooms as private selves, elsewhere in the novel, she recognizes the association between servants and bedrooms: looking through the windows of Buckingham Palace, Emily Coates thinks "of the housemaids, the innumerable housemaids, the bedrooms, the innumerable bedrooms" (19).

Though the subdivision of the household into rooms creates a space for female subjectivity, it initially perpetuates the servant's objectification, for according to the logic of the bedroom metaphor, the presence of servants in Clarissa's room incorporates them into her identity. Although Lucy is not an accretion of her mistress's soul in the same way as is the narrow bed, the fiction of ownership in the employer-employee relationship exacerbates the objectifying tendency the class difference creates by introducing an implication of possession, however temporary and contingent. Servants remain incomprehensible others in both philosophical and political senses: they are separate individuals who belong to a different class. While Clarissa acknowledges their humanity, she encounters them as unified, closed wholes collected under their identities as her servants. The narrator maintains this opacity even while ostensibly giving voice to the servants, for their interior monologues almost entirely reflect on the upper classes. Any glimpses we may catch of deeper selves—Lucy's fantasy of herself as a lady, for instance, or Mrs. Walker's cantankerous indifference to her mistress's famous guests—still ultimately direct our gazes back upstairs.

In her essays, Woolf depicts gazes from either side of the class divide as equally objectifying. "If my father was a blacksmith and yours a peer of the realm," she insists in "Three Pictures" (1929), "we must needs be pictures to each other" (*CE*4 151). In *Mrs. Dalloway*, too, Clarissa's servants at first appear equally unable to see beyond the "picture" of their mistress. When Clarissa expresses her dismay that Richard will be lunching out without her,

> Lucy share[s] as [Clarissa] meant her to her disappointment (but not the pang); felt the concord between them; took the hint; thought how the gentry love; gilded her own future with calm; and, taking Mrs. Dalloway's parasol, handled it like a sacred weapon which a Goddess, having acquitted herself honorably in the field of battle, sheds, and placed it in the umbrella stand. (29-30)

The formulation almost exactly reproduces the "aesthetic" and imagined sympathy the daughters of educated men feel for working women rather than an experiential sympathy. Lucy's sympathy is disembodied, lacking the "pang," and she soon transforms Clarissa's emotion into information, anthropological evidence of "how the gentry love."

Lucy builds her fantasies of the gentry out of images she has collected while observing their appearances, actions, and possessions:

> They would come; they would stand; they would talk in the mincing tones which she could imitate, ladies and gentlemen. Of all, her mistress was loveliest—mistress of silver, of linen, of china, for the sun, the silver, doors off their hinges, Rumpelmayer's men, gave her a sense, as she laid the paper-knife on the inlaid table, of something achieved. (38)

Her conception of her mistress relies almost entirely upon surfaces, and thus initially seems to resemble the inaccurate portraits that Woolf's hypothetical descendants of blacksmiths and aristocrats assemble of each other. However, for all its whimsy, Lucy's fantasy reveals a startling understanding of her employer: in the midst of a playfully superficial depiction of her mistress, she turns to "the sun, the silver, doors off their hinges, Rumpelmayer's men," a list which echoes Clarissa's early monologue in both form and content in a manner too precise to be entirely attributed to Woolf's style.

In fact, given the symbolic weight that objects bear throughout Woolf's work, not to mention their metaphorical status as accretions of the soul, Lucy's method of appreciating the gentry through the surfaces of their bodies and possessions may actually provide an effective means of understanding them. As in Cubist painting, such a method bypasses the impenetrable surface of the totalized whole by breaking it into parts, creating new surfaces that can be juxtaposed in revealing ways. As Gertrude Stein explains, it is a means of accessing "the inside as seen from the outside" (156). The Cubist method spreads out the substance of deep identity into an array of observable objects, which detach from the individual who accretes them, shaking off the stigma of otherness that would otherwise divide observed and observer. The objects, like the Mantuan bowl of "Street Haunting," can thus become reinvested with the affective content that fills the hollow spaces of a sympathy based solely on knowledge.

Woolf uses such a method to briefly characterize the Dalloways' cook, Mrs. Walker:

> It made no difference at this hour of the night to Mrs. Walker among the plates, saucepans, cullenders, frying-pans, chicken in aspic, ice-cream freezers, pared crusts of bread, lemons, soup tureens, and pudding basins which, however hard they washed up in the scullery seemed to be all on top of her, on the kitchen table, on chairs, while the fire blared and roared, the electric lights glared, and still supper had to be laid. All she felt was, one Prime Minister more or less made not a scrap of difference to Mrs. Walker. (165)

The characterization, like Lucy's of Clarissa, is limited, but even so, the cascade of objects provides the reader with an easier point of entry than would an image of the cook herself scurrying from place to place—an image that would not only throw up the usual barrier of mysterious otherness, but would also provoke the divisive emotions that accompany evidence of class difference. What the reader sees are the plates, saucepans, and tureens scattered across tables and chairs and, hence, the sense of agitation those objects convey, rather than the all-too-familiar image of the cook scurrying about a busy kitchen. The passage thus confronts the reader not with another person's frenzy of activity, but with an image of clutter that evokes the reader's own past experiences of frenzied activity, and thus provides the reader with grounds for identification. Though the scene's success is tentative—to communicate a single moment of a working-class character's inner life is hardly to broach the class divide—it offers a point of entry into a mind that would otherwise seem inaccessible to Woolf's middle-class readers.

"There Was a Pause"

The barriers to communication that *Mrs. Dalloway* attempts to surmount continue to recur throughout Woolf's work, perpetually complicating relationships between the classes. A persistent reminder that *Mrs. Dalloway*'s project remains incomplete, the female servant posted at the intersection of gender and class haunts the late novels, particularly *The Years*. Here, *Mrs. Dalloway*'s briefly sketched creatures of sunshine and fresh air put on palpable flesh in the form of Crosby, the Pargiters' long-serving housemaid. In drawing an extended portrait of a single servant, however, Woolf brings to the foreground complexities of service that *Mrs. Dalloway*'s broader but shallower representation of service is able to elide—complexities that compound the need for an indirect method of representation even as they bring it into question.

Some of the pessimism of the later depiction of service may result from the historical moment at which the novel begins; Lucy, after all, is a Georgian servant, Crosby a Victorian one. Though the modern servant's ability to flit in and out of the drawing room implies an ability to flit out of the house altogether should she choose to give notice, it is the loyal retainer who, like the "inscrutable" Victorian cook of "Mr. Bennett and Mrs. Brown" (1924), seems more estranged from the family. It is only fitting that *The Years*, a family history that reveals underlying fissures in the Victorian patriarchal home and eventually oversees its fragmentation into various modern houses and apartments, emphasizes the servant's role as a scapegoat for the breaches in understanding so imperfectly hidden by the trappings of family. Woolf may include signs of Crosby's presence in the pool of sensations the Pargiters deem "familiar": the shuffles, chinks, and clicks of her work provide the ambient music of home (20). But the empty spaces interspersed among these signs of familiarity—the pauses between the chinks and clicks—mar the intimacy between the servant and her employers. Such silences mark the distance that divides people from one another, and thus fall most abruptly when indicating class difference. Among members of a single class, silence is a state of being—"they [eat] in silence" or "they [are] silent" (12; 16)—but a servant's arrival, if noticed, actively silences conversation. Thus Delia breaks off mid-sentence when Crosby comes in with the tray (20), and Eleanor stops and starts, unable to "say what she mean[s] with Crosby in the room fidgeting about" (152). Even when members of the family are able to continue talking, they cannot do so freely, instead "adapting [their speech] to the presence of servants" (207).

Recognizable markers of class often instigate abrupt pauses, as when Crosby arrives bearing the tools of her trade or when Eleanor adopts "the tone of the Colonel's daughter; the upper middle-class tone" with the working-class Duffus, making "him turn sullen before her eyes" (100). However, the novel's persistent refrain, "There was a pause," occurs more frequently, albeit nearly always passively, in conversations between members of the immediate family. Furthermore, the novel's partitioned structure, with its conspicuously empty spaces dividing blocks of text, suggests overwhelming, universal pauses that seem to render questions of greater or lesser degrees of silence trivial.

An incontrovertible estrangement among all people, even members of that bastion of modern society, the nuclear family, is a difficult proposition to accept, given Western political philosophy's frequent claim that all of civil society grows out of such bonds between individuals. As Hegel writes, society emerges on the model of the family, in which "one's frame of mind is to have self-consciousness of one's individuality within this unity [i.e., the family] as the absolute essence of oneself, with the result that one is in it not as an independent person but as a member" (§158). Following this logic, an unsurpassable distance between individuals in a family would make it impossible to identify as a unit within a unity, and thus as a member of a society. Though some of *The Years*'s middle-class characters follow Clarissa in criticizing this model—"It was an abominable system, [Martin thinks]; family life" (222)—they can never quite relinquish it.

The servant, an outsider in terms of interrelated conditions of class and ancestry, and in many cases nationality, gender, and race as well, can be exempted more easily from civil society. Descriptions of Crosby metaphorically exile her to the world before modern civilization: she "pile[s] the coals into a great black promontory" as if building a pagan monument (29), and rings the dinner gong "like a savage wreaking vengeance upon some brazen victim" (34). The frequent parallels both the narrator and characters draw between Crosby and the old family dog, Rover, likewise diminish her to a loyal pet or "a frightened little animal" (223). By using the dog to symbolize Crosby's service—his death, after all, almost immediately succeeds her retirement—Woolf perpetuates the myth that service arises out of a sort of instinctive devotion rather than the modern need to make a living. Thrust back into a time before the rule of English law, Christian religion, and to an extent even full humanity, Crosby no longer factors into a society bounded by those systems. The Pargiters' estrangement from her thus appears to result from her actual strangeness.

The novel's middle-class characters can thus transpose the universal disconnection that risks undermining civil society into the class disconnection that can be regretted, then disregarded, as the inevitable price of capitalism's conveniences. When the Pargiters experience moments of isolation from each other, their thoughts veer sharply toward the old family servant. After a chance meeting at St. Paul's, Martin and Sarah eat "in silence" as he struggles to "make her talk" (230). Their failure to understand one another propels them through a series of rapid substitutions: when the literal-minded Martin asks the imaginative Sarah what she thinks of the service, she shifts the subject of the question:

> 'What do *they* think of it, Martin?' she asked. 'The woman praying and the man with a long white beard?'
>
> 'Much what Crosby thinks when she comes to see me,' he said. He thought of the old woman standing at the door of his room with the pyjama jacket over her arm, and the devout look on her face.

> 'I'm Crosby's God,' he said, helping her to Brussels sprouts.
> 'Crosby's God! Almighty, all-powerful Mr. Martin!' She laughed. (230)

The first substitution establishes the technique of shifting communicative failures to others; Sarah acknowledges Martin's inability to understand her by comparing her incomprehensible emotion to that of a pair of strangers whom no one expects him to understand. Martin attempts to answer her rhetorical question by in turn comparing the strangers to the standard scapegoat for misunderstanding, Crosby. What he sees as an answer to her question is instead only a further deferral of the communicative failure: his glib caricature of Crosby's devotion as religious belief reveals his inability to understand either the servant's feelings or mystical experience, which in turn reveals his inability to understand his cousin.

In keeping with the profound ambivalence toward servants that Light detects in Woolf's work, even as she examines and at times mimics the methods by which the Pargiters transform Crosby into a scapegoat for difference, Woolf makes it difficult for the reader to accept the servant's estrangement. During the decades that *The Years* tracks, the live-in system of domestic service was gradually unraveling as staffs shrank and started to be replaced by part-time service. The new forms of technology symbolized by the "shower-bath" that Eleanor installs toward the end of the novel promise to one day eliminate the need for servants altogether. Yet Woolf does not let the historical sweep of her novel brush Crosby away. Rather than outline the shift from Crosby to Lucy and then to the charwoman who "lives out," Woolf follows Crosby even after the servant's retirement, suggesting a permanent imbrication with the family that extends beyond the period of employment.

"All the Solid Objects"

Woolf also challenges Crosby's isolation by revising the oblique method she develops in *Mrs. Dalloway* in a way that hints at an even more profound intertwining of the Pargiters' and Crosby's identities than the more evident interdependence between Lucy and Clarissa. Crosby first enters the novel alongside the Pargiter children, and in almost the same way: we first see Milly Pargiter attempting to boil water in a kettle, a chore that could as easily fall to Crosby, whose first utterance is, fittingly enough, an offer to boil the water herself (10). The kettle forms a link between the girl and the woman, both of whom are engaged in a kind of domestic service, and both of whom wait impatiently for the recalcitrant kettle to boil.

As in *Mrs. Dalloway*, Woolf depicts her character's mind through that character's gaze at objects, and Crosby's mind, like those of her predecessors, is often fixed on those she serves. What in *Mrs. Dalloway* was a symptom of the author's acknowledged limitations here becomes an aspect of character. So intense is Crosby's identification that after her retirement, she must recreate some semblance of what she knows as life out of the "odds and ends" from Abercorn Terrace she has been hoarding during her years of service, from portraits of the family to a walrus she has rescued from a waste-paper basket (218). If objects are accretions of the soul, then Crosby's collection seems to reveal a soul scavenged from cast-off pieces of her employers' souls. Even her moments of seeming agency work through rather than against her emotional investment in her employers: when Martin holds her at a distance, she repossesses him metonymically by gathering his "injured pyjama tenderly to her breast," expressing her emotion through the sort of figurative code he considers beyond her and, perhaps, repaying his objectification of her by projecting him onto an object (221).

Although the extent to which Crosby's inner life depends on the family she serves risks reducing her to a Victorian type rather than to a unique character, Woolf humanizes her not only through these brief moments of agency, but also through the genuine sympathy that objects allow to flow between her and her employers, particularly during the scene in which she finally leaves Eleanor's service. When not cast as a buffoon, the servant character is frequently an object of pity, as is Mrs. Chailey, whom Light identifies as a "conventional figure of pathos" (67). By contrast, sympathy, which requires an ability to imagine another's emotional state, is less common between mistress and servant. When Eleanor first sees Crosby's tears, she experiences the servant's pain only in the abstract, as an emotion that belongs to another person, and feels only discomfort at her culpability in Crosby's grief. It is only after imagining Crosby's interaction with objects that Eleanor is able to gain access to the servant's emotional state:

> She had known every cupboard, flagstone, chair and table in that large rambling house, not from five or six feet of distance as they had known it; but from her knees, as she scrubbed and polished; she had known every groove, stain, fork, knife, napkin and cupboard. They and their doings had made her entire world. And now she was going off, alone, to a single room at Richmond. (216)

The objects mediate the transmission of emotion between the women: Eleanor does not think of Crosby's attachment to the family, which would remind her of the class difference and thus reinstate a sense of estrangement, but of Crosby's attachment to the material household. Though Eleanor is only familiar with the objects from "five or six feet of distance," an imaginative leap of a few feet is easier to make than one that crosses the gulf between classes. Familiarity and a premature sense of nostalgia can thus emerge from the array of objects unimpeded by the complexities the servant herself produces.

Objects transmit not only powerful emotions, but also the simple, everyday moods and predilections upon which feelings of familiarity rely. Crosby in particular understands the Pargiters by obliquely approaching them through arrays of objects they own or handle. She takes the process we witnessed in *Mrs. Dalloway* a step further, diffracting the objects themselves:

> Crosby held open the door of the dining-room as she waited for them to come down. The silver paid for polishing, she thought. Knives and forks rayed out round the table. The whole room, with its carved chairs, oil paintings, the two daggers on the mantel-piece, and the handsome sideboard—all the solid objects that Crosby dusted and polished every day—looked at its best in the evening. Meat-smelling and serge-curtained by day, it looked lit up, semi-transparent in the evening. And they were a handsome family, she thought as they filed in—the young ladies in their pretty dresses of blue and white sprigged muslin; the gentlemen so spruce in their dinner jackets. She pulled the Colonel's chair out for him. He was always at his best in the evening; he enjoyed his dinner; and for some reason his gloom had vanished. He was in his jovial mood. His children's spirits rose as they noted it. (35)

The first objects she glances at present different faces to her and to her employers: the servant who polishes them designates them "the silver," while the family that eats with them sees them as the "knives and forks." Because as "solid objects" they escape the veil of class division that separates employee and employer, Crosby can see both of their faces, defining the same objects in two ways. The silverware thus represents the differences between its observers while serving as a point of connection between them.

The room provides a space in which objects significant to all of the members of the household can mingle: the oil-paintings and daggers that indicate the family's decorative tastes, but that Crosby "dust[s] and polishe[s] every day," for instance, or the sideboard that helps Crosby serve meals, but that is "handsome" enough for the Pargiters' eyes. The room as a whole presents different aspects to its occupants, "meat-smelling and serge-curtained" for Crosby alone, but "lit up, semi-transparent" for the collected household. Its earthy, heavy daytime appearance efficiently expresses the mood of Crosby's daily drudgery, and its evening glamour represents the atmosphere of mealtimes in both descriptive and symbolic senses.

On the other hand, the room reveals the limitations of oblique characterization by tantalizing readers with the prospect of unconstrained communication. The fashionably late dinner hour, when custom brings the members of the household together and their spirits are highest, functions similarly to Mrs. Dalloway's party and Mrs. Ramsay's dinner: here, the veils between people become the lightest, the most transparent. As the family files in, the unusually open ambiance allows the narrative voice to shift easily between Crosby's thoughts and those of the Pargiter children. However, such moments are so striking because of their ephemerality. The barriers fall ever more starkly when the meal is interrupted by Mrs. Pargiter's turn for the worse. "It was a pity," Crosby thinks; "the dinner was spoilt" (39). Once again, she must read the family through the objects they touch: "dinner" now refers to the food rather than the event, or to be more precise, only refers to the event through the food. Fluid conversation and clear thought have dried up and crusted over like the meat and potatoes she returns to the table, and instead of handing around the food as she did in the previous scene, Crosby shuts the door on the family as they begin to eat.

Accessing others through objects thus seems little consolation for the loss of such moments of direct understanding. Woolf reveals the failure, or at least the incomplete success, of her formal experiment when she attempts to make the transition from indirect characterization of Crosby to a direct transcription of her thoughts. In "1918," as Crosby slowly walks out of the novel on her aching legs, the narration feints at moving into her consciousness. The narrator scans Crosby's body for motions that can be read as signs of interior activity: her face twitches "as if her muscles had got into the habit of protesting, involuntarily, against the spites and obstacles that tormented her," the tentative "as if" tracing the boundary of knowledge (302-303). Crosby mutters her monologue to herself in a manner that resembles narrated thought but does not quite allow the narrator access to her mind. Eventually the narration shifts from direct to indirect speech and then to direct thought, but before we can dip into Crosby's interior monologue, "the long-drawn note of a siren" (304)—already established as a sign of division in "1917" (288)—jolts us back into the external world. As Crosby totters across the road, she disintegrates into a series of images of London at the end of the war that at most represent her sense perceptions but more likely distract us from our continuing ignorance of those perceptions.

Woolf's failure to successfully effect a transition from oblique to direct representation of Crosby's inner life is, like the novel's failure, a deliberate one, for in a scene she excised during the final stages of revision, Woolf allows us to hear the gunshots that end the war through Crosby's ears. Afterward, the narrator continues to follow Crosby's point of view as she spots Edward and Kitty's car, then watches it fade away. However, the omitted scene's deeper attention to Crosby's thoughts and emotions leaves her still more of an accessory to the novel's middle-class characters, for her inner life revolves so tightly around them that she even seems to become more herself in their presence: "her eyes [become] bluer, more prominent"—that is, more characteristic—when they catch sight of Edward and Kitty (Radin 450). When allowed to think on the page at length, Crosby reverts to an earlier iteration of the line of servant characters derived from Sophie Farrell: *The Voyage Out*'s Mrs. Chailey, whose directly reported thoughts almost exclusively concern the family she serves. While the published version of the scene, which contains only snippets of reported thought, keeps Crosby at a distance and even risks encouraging the reader to dismiss her as inscrutable, it leaves her the possibility of an inner life that transcends the limitations of the servant type.

A conception of identity as something that possesses depth, that, for all its dependence on thin threads of connection to friends, social groups, and servants, requires tunnels of memory and a self-aware consciousness, makes unsatisfying a mode of characterization that depends on sidelong glances grazing off surfaces. The contrast between the obliqueness with which Woolf depicts Crosby and the immediacy of other characters' streams of consciousness lends the servant's characterization a sense of incompleteness. Rather than a legitimate alternative to interior monologue, the Cubist method seems to be a means of getting to know the other until her deeper consciousness becomes accessible, but the other's consciousness never becomes fully accessible, for the mode of understanding that objects generate is not the same kind of understanding as that created by interior monologue. The knowledge objects convey remains bonded to their particular arrangement within the novel, much in the way the facets of a Cubist painting become meaningful only in tandem. To extract a single object from the portrait of Crosby is, fittingly enough, to reify the insight it allows us in order to add it to our personal collection of facts—in other words, to harden a delicate and mutable kind of understanding into stereotype. The only meaningful objects in "1918" are Crosby's pained legs and feet. Without other objects to resonate with, alienated even from their owner's body, they express only what we already assume about Crosby.

Yet in *Between the Acts*, Woolf's final novel, the absence of a concerted attempt to move beyond oblique representation of servants into their interior monologues raises its own problems. Though Woolf occasionally reports brief segments of servants' thoughts, she for the most part characterizes their inner lives only through their interactions with objects. We encounter Mrs. Sands the same way we encountered Mrs. Walker: in a bustling kitchen, surrounded by a cascade of objects that seems an adequate alternative to free indirect discourse's cascades of clauses (33). Yet elsewhere, the oblique method confines her to the realm of the material:

> [Mrs. Sands] could see the great open door. But butterflies she never saw; mice were only black pellets in kitchen drawers; moths she bundled in

> her hands and put out of the window. Bitches suggested only servant girls misbehaving. Had there been a cat she would have seen it—any cat, a starved cat with a patch of mange on its rump opened the flood gates of her childless heart. But there was no cat. The Barn was empty. (100-101)

The passage is, rather than a stream of consciousness, a stream of perceptions, a list of objects whose associations are almost entirely practical. Servants in Woolf's final novel are so tied to the material that they lose a sense of the abstract: when the household's bourgeois guests tour a larder that was once a chapel, they see a space haunted by history and religion, whereas the servants who work there believe it haunted by literal ghosts. The kitchen even has a separate language from the drawing room, a diminutive, familiar, and irreligious tongue that transforms Sung-Yen into Sunny, the Master into Bartie (32).

The tensions the complexities of class raise in *The Years* thus resolve in *Between the Acts* into an impression of incontrovertible difference. Narrative technique bleeds into content as the inner lives conveyed by way of objects come to concern almost solely those objects themselves. Even questions of class shift away from the servants; it is Miss La Trobe, as Georgia Johnson notes, who takes up that mantle, reaching for the ideal of the classless intellectual that Cuddy-Keane identifies as central to Woolf's political thinking. It is perhaps surprising that a novel frequently read as disjointed and fragmented—even, in Jack F. Stewart's estimation, Cubist—should depict servants with such thematic consistency, eliding the paradoxes of service that trouble Woolf's previous novel. At the same time, Stewart's reading of the novel's "superimpositions" of "idea and substance, image and thing," which allow "contrasting realities" and conflicting mental states to exist simultaneously, reveals the lasting influence of the oblique method (76). The two narrative modes that Woolf's previous novels divide along class lines combine, one superimposed on the other, to form a fragmented, multidimensional style. But once again, Woolf does not apply the style to servants: without interior monologues on which to superimpose meaningful objects, they must rely on objects alone.

Like mistress and servant, style and politics remain in tension despite and because of their interpenetration. The stylistic innovation Woolf develops in response to the problem of the servant must move away from its political origin if it is to blend with free indirect discourse and form a new narrative mode, while the combination of oblique characterization and failed interior monologue in *The Years*, which on the one hand lends such a sense of unevenness to the portrait of Crosby, on the other hand better reflects Woolf's political objectives by suggesting that it is not the simplicity of the servant psyche but the limitations of representation that prevent the identical treatment of characters of all classes. As Tratner reminds us, foregrounding her own inability to solve the problem of class is a way for Woolf "to keep the struggle alive" (4); her failure, in other words, is a productive one.

Works Cited

Banfield, Ann. "Time Passes: Virginia Woolf, Post-Impressionism, and Cambridge Time." *Poetics Today* 24.3 (2003): 471-516.

——. *Unspeakable Sentences.* Boston: Routledge and Kegan Paul, 1982.

Brown, Bill. *A Sense of Things: The Object Matter of American Literature.* Chicago: U of Chicago Press, 2004.

Bryson, J. Scott. "Modernism and Ecological Criticism." *Modernism.* Vol. 2. Ed. Astradur Eysteinsson and Vivian Liska. Amsterdam: John Benjamins Publishing Company, 2007. 591-604.

Childers, Mary. "Virginia Woolf on the Outside Looking Down: Reflections on the Class of Women." *Modern Fiction Studies* 38.1 (Spring 1992): 61-79.

Cox, Neil. *Cubism.* London: Phaidon, 2000.

Cuddy-Keane, Melba. *Virginia Woolf, the Intellectual, and the Public Sphere.* Cambridge: Cambridge UP, 2003.

Elliott, Dorice. "Servants and Hands: Representing the Working Classes in Victorian Factory Novels." *Victorian Literature and Culture* (2000): 377-390.

Froula, Christine. *Virginia Woolf and the Bloomsbury Avant-Garde: War, Civilization, Modernity.* New York: Columbia UP, 2005.

Handley, William R. "The Housemaid and the Kitchen Table: Incorporating the Frame in *To the Lighthouse*." *Twentieth Century Literature* 40.1 (Spring 1994): 15-41.

Hegel, G.W.F. *Hegel's Philosophy of Right.* Trans. T. M. Knox. Oxford: Clarendon Press, 1965.

Hoberman, Ruth. "Aesthetic Taste, Kitsch, and *The Years*." *Woolf Studies Annual* 11 (2005): 77-98.

James, Henry. "Preface." *Portrait of a Lady.* New York: Penguin, 1963.

Johnson, Georgia. "Class Performance in *Between the Acts*: Audiences for Miss La Trobe and Mrs. Manresa." *Woolf Studies Annual* 3 (1997): 61-75.

Levy, Heather. "'These Ghost Figures of Distorted Passion': Becoming Privy to Working-Class Desire in 'The Watering Place' and 'The Ladies Lavatory.'" *MFS* 50.1 (2004): 31-57.

Light, Alison. *Mrs Woolf and the Servants.* London: Penguin, 2007.

Lukács, György. *Studies in European Realism.* Trans. Edith Bone. New York: Grosset and Dunlap, 1964.

Marcus, Jane. "*The Years* as Greek Drama, Domestic Novel, and Götterdämmerung." *Bulletin of the New York Public Library* 80 (1977): 276-301.

McBride, Theresa M. *The Domestic Revolution: The Modernisation of Household Service in England and France, 1820-1920*. London: Croom Helm, 1976.

Middleton, Victoria S. "*The Years*: 'A Deliberate Failure.'" *Bulletin of the New York Public Library* 80 (1977): 158-71.

Nash, Julie. "'Ruled by a Powerful and Decided Nature': Servants and Labor Relations in Gaskell's 'Condition of England' Novels." *Nineteenth-century Feminisms* 6 (2002): 19-40.

Nayral, Jacques. "Preface." *Exposició d'Art Cubista.* Barcelona: Galeries J. Dalmau, 1912. Rpt. in *A Cubism Reader: Documents and Criticism, 1906-1914.* Ed. Mark Antiff and Patricia Leighten. Chicago: University of Chicago Press, 2008. 75-78.

Quinn, Laurie. "A Woolf with Political Teeth: Classing Virginia Woolf Now and in the Twenty-First Century." *Virginia Woolf: Turning the Centuries: Selected Papers from the Ninth Annual Conference on Virginia Woolf.* Ed. Ann Ardis and Bonnie Kime Scott. New York: Pace UP, 2000. 325-330.

Radin, Grace. "'Two Enormous Chunks': Episodes Excluded during the Final Revisions of *The Years.*" *Bulletin of the New York Public Library* 80 (1977): 221-251.

Robbins, Bruce. *The Servant's Hand: English Fiction from Below.* New York: Columbia UP, 1986.

Ruskin, John. "Of Queens' Gardens." *Sesame and Lilies*. Ed. Deborah Epstein Nord. New Haven: Yale UP, 2002.

Salmon, Lucy Maynard. *Domestic Service*. New York: Macmillan, 1897.

Stein, Gertrude. *The Autobiography of Alice B. Toklas*. New York: Vintage Books, 1933.

Stewart, Jack F. "Cubist Elements in *Between the Acts*." *Mosaic* 18:2 (Spring 1985): 65-89.

Tanner, Duncan. "The Parliamentary Electoral System, the 'Fourth' Reform Act and the Rise of Labour in England and Wales." *Historical Research* 56.134 (1983): 205-219.

Tratner, Michael. "Figures in the Dark: Working Class Women in *To the Lighthouse*." *Virginia Woolf Miscellany* 40 (Spring 1993): 3-4.

Woolf, Virginia. *Between the Acts.* San Diego, New York, and London: Harcourt, 1941.

——. *Collected Essays*. 4 vols. Ed. Leonard Woolf. London: Harcourt, Inc., 1966-1967.

——. *The Diary of Virginia Woolf.* 4 Volumes. Ed. Anne Olivier Bell. London: Hogarth Press, 1980.

——. *Mrs Dalloway*. 1925. San Diego, New York, and London: Harcourt, 1953.

——. *The Pargiters*. Ed. Mitchell A. Leaska. New York: The New York Public Library and Readex Books, 1977.

——. *Three Guineas*. 1938. San Diego, New York, and London: Harcourt, 1966.

——. *To the Lighthouse*. 1927. San Diego, New York, and London: Harcourt, 1955.

——. *The Voyage Out*. 1915. New York: Bantam, 1991.

——. *The Waves*. 1931. San Diego, New York, and London: Harcourt, 1959.

——. *The Years*. 1937. San Diego, New York, and London: Harcourt, 1965.

Zwerdling, Alex. *Virginia Woolf and the Real World*. Berkeley, CA: U of California P, 1986.

A Thoroughly Modern Melancholia: Virginia Woolf, Author, Daughter

Janice Stewart

> But why was I bored? Partly because of the dominance of the letter 'I' and the aridity, which, like the giant beech tree, it casts within its shade. Nothing will grow there.
>
> —Virginia Woolf, *AROO* 96

Elaine Showalter writes in *A Literature of Their Own*, "It is customary to make Leslie Stephen the heavy in Virginia Woolf's personal drama" (266). Woolf's feminism, Jane Marcus notes in her introduction to *New Feminist Essays on Virginia Woolf*, "is too often lightly assumed . . . a traditional form of rebellion against a Victorian father's oppression" (xii-xx, xix). However, if Leslie Stephen's role in Virginia Woolf's identification of herself as an author and a feminist is examined, rather than codified and solidified as a singularly dark patriarchal archetype of paternal possession, aggression, and suppression, the figure and authorship of Virginia Woolf are opened to alternative re-readings. Despite Sara Ruddick's cheerful assertion in "Private Brother, Public World" that "We have always welcomed attention to the powerful effect fathers have on their daughters' lives" (185), the figure of Leslie Stephen has been too easily dismissed as a crippled temperamental tyrant, rather than examined in its possible relationship to the formulation of Virginia Woolf's identity as an author.[1] Allowing that the figure Leslie Stephen was a significant, sometimes tempestuous and possibly damaging force in Woolf's psychological landscape does not preclude the possibility that Woolf did more than merely crumple or simply rebel in the face of that force.

In "As Miss Jan Says" Louise DeSalvo contends that, because of Woolf's propensity for situating people within historical categories, she could not see her father as an individual man; "he became representative, to her, of the archetypal Victorian father, with all the difficulties inherent in that historical type" (106). Perhaps it might be more accurate to suggest that Leslie Stephen has become representative *to critics*[2] of the dark archetypal Victorian father. Admittedly, we, like Woolf, may not always be comfortable with that which was learned "at her father's knee," with the student/pupil dialectic, or the patrilineal model it evokes.

[1] Critical scholarship that also addresses this theme includes Katherine Hill, "Virginia Woolf and Leslie Stephen: History and Literary Revolution," Louise DeSalvo's *Virginia Woolf: The Impact of Childhood Sexual Abuse on her Life and Work*, and Virginia Hyman, "Reflections in the Looking-Glass: Leslie Stephen and Virginia Woolf."

[2] Brenda Silver's *Icon* is an excellent discussion of the role of critics.

Perhaps we must agree with Woolf when she drolly suggests in "Miss Mitford," "That is the worst of writing about ladies; they have fathers as well as teapots" (195).[3] However, facing the "worst" and rereading Leslie Stephen as an influential model of the author in Woolf's texts allows us to glimpse the ways in which the narrating subject of those texts perceives the role of author.

One way of approaching Woolf's relationship with her father is through theories of object relations and one way of approaching theories of object relations is to read those theories through Virginia Woolf's relationship with her father. Rather than simply applying a stock psychoanalytic model to Woolf, and cutting and pasting until she fits, what I hope to do is to explore the ways in which several psychoanalytic texts, for the most part Freud's, can be used to give an understanding of Woolf's texts, as well as the ways in which Woolf's texts offer an interesting perspective on Freud's theories of object relations. Freud and Woolf wrote contemporaneously, and both dealt with interiority in ways that were innovative and had lingering impact upon the ways we read and understand both literature and generational dynamics today. In "Modern Fiction" Woolf contends that,

> For the moderns . . . the point of interest, lies very likely in the dark places of psychology. At once, therefore, the accent falls a little differently; the emphasis is upon something hitherto ignored; at once a different outline of form becomes necessary, difficult for us to grasp, incomprehensible to our predecessors. . . . The emphasis is laid upon such unexpected places that at first it seems as if there were no emphasis at all; and then, as one's eyes accustom themselves to twilight and discern the shapes of things in a room we see how complete the story is, how profound. (162-163)

Woolf's 1919 description of modern fiction could quite easily be mistaken as a summary of psychoanalysis, which was just then barely beginning to become known in England. However, Woolf's disdain of Freudian theory is manifestly

[3] In her review of *Mary Russell Mitford and her Surroundings*, by Constance Hill, Woolf contrasts the carefully constructed image of the cool "lady" who has the fine porcelain teapot (in Miss Mitford's case it was Wedgwood), and the emotional "woman" who has a less than admirable father. One of Woolf's principal criticisms of *Mary Russell Mitford and her Surroundings* is that the biographer takes far too much effort to assure her readers that Miss Mitford was indeed a "lady" of the finest caliber, and, in consequence, tends to downplay the less refined aspects of her life, such as her delinquent father. Hence the problem arises for the biographer, who is determined to create a portrait of a lady; that ladies tend to have fathers as well as teapots. Woolf's ironic comment, then, seems to suggest that writing about less-than-exemplary fathers has a tendency to give a "truer" picture of the woman author's life—and consequently shatter idealized notions of the woman author in question—something which Woolf finds many biographers unwilling to do.

evident five years later when she writes to Molly MacCarthy that after having read some of the proofs for the Hogarth Edition of Freud (or at least a case study in lecture 17 of *Introductory Lectures* which she harshly caricatures in the letter) she claims that psychoanalysis proves very little except perhaps the "gull-like imbecility" of its advocates (*L*3 135). Freud's opinion of Woolf must be inferred from their sole meeting in 1939: all that we know is that Freud gave Woolf a single narcissus.

What are we as readers to do with the blatant and veiled animosity between Woolf and Freud? Woolf's remark in *A Room of One's Own* that "books have a way of influencing each other. Fiction will be much the better for standing cheek by jowl with poetry and philosophy" seems an important comment here (104). In what follows, I will address these and other questions directly and indirectly, through a reading of some of Freud's and Woolf's treatments of melancholia and creativity. Although Woolf and Freud may not have been directly influenced by each other, nor might either of them have welcomed the suggestion of such an influence, today readers of each author are influenced by the other, and reading Woolf and Freud cheek by jowl impels a re-thinking of the various prejudices and assumptions which continue to power a perceived split between Woolf the daughter, Woolf the author, and the ways the narrating subject perceives the roles of daughter and author.

Freud, Object Relations, and Identification

In May of 1915, Freud completed the final draft of "Mourning and Melancholia." As in earlier works, Freud uses the term "object" to denote either a real or imaginary "Other" toward whom the drives are directed. Although the drives and their aims are inherent, the "object" is a phenomenon of experience. The "object" is, at this point for Freud, simply the vehicle or the means whereby gratification of the drives is achieved or thwarted. In other words, Freud imagines a theory of one body rather than a relationship between two bodies. Here the relationship with the object is a result of drives and defenses, with antagonism and violence being enacted between the id and the ego of a singular body. In "Mourning and Melancholia," he discusses the means by which, through a splitting of the ego, an aspect of oneself that has been modeled upon the lost external object internally replaces this object:

> An object choice, an attachment of the libido to a particular person, had at one time existed; then, owing to a *real slight or disappointment* coming from this loved person, the object relationship was shattered. The result was not the normal one or a withdrawal of the libido from this object and a displacement of it on to a new one, but something different, for

> whose coming-about various contradictions seem to be necessary. The object cathexis proved to have little power of resistance and was brought to an end. But the free libido was not displaced on to another object, it was withdrawn into the ego. There, however, it was not employed in any unspecified way, but served to establish an *identification* of the ego with the abandoned object. Thus the shadow of the object fell upon the ego, and the latter could henceforth be judged by a special agency, as though it were an object, the forsaken object. In this way an object loss was transformed into an ego-loss and the conflict between the critical activity of the ego and the ego as altered by identification. (257-258)

The pathological condition evoked by this splitting of the ego and the replacement of an external object with an internal object is, according to Freud, melancholia. It is important to recognize that, in Freud's evaluation, melancholia involves two *active* aspects of the individual who has undergone this bifurcation of ego. The self is thus divided, split by defensive processes, into the subject-self and the object-self which entombs the lost other.

In his 1938 essay "Splitting the Ego in the Process of Defence," Freud discusses the ways in which splitting of the ego allows an individual to know and not know simultaneously, to function defensively with two disparate understandings of reality. In "The Ego and the Id" (1923) Freud noted that although normal processes of identification are not *harmful*, that when identifications become "unduly powerful and incompatible with one another a pathological outcome will not be far off. [However], there remains the question of conflicts between the various identifications into which the ego comes apart, conflict which cannot after all be described as entirely pathological" (370). From these three disparate Freudian discussions of object identification, what I would like to extract specifically is the notion that the ego, upon real or imagined loss of an object, attempts to preserve that object within itself through a fracturing of the ego, an event which may incur a conflict with other identifications. Special attention needs to be paid to Freud's assertion that the conflict arising between identifications is not necessarily pathological. Reading the experience between subject and object is not necessarily reading pathology, it is the reading of the primal interaction between the subject and the object, a savage meeting, a primitive crossing, in which domination and mastery are at stake. In every identification there is a conflict of power, a struggle of contrary instincts, through which the subject comes to define itself.

Against Proper Objects: Narcissus, A Thoroughly Modern "I"

Miglena Nikolchina notes that among Woolf critics "there is a general tendency to privilege Woolf's *Diary* (or her manuscripts for that matter) as the authentic place where the 'real' Woolf can be found. In Woolf's case such privileging disregards her quite conscious strategies for beating the system" (17).[4] In *A Room of One's Own*, Woolf claims that "'I' is only a convenient term for somebody who has no real being" (6). Following Woolf's example, and reading the narrating subject, the "I" of the diary, as a character, a narrator, or a portrait mapped *by* Woolf, rather than as a veritable textual supplement *of* Woolf, challenges the critical assumption that the language of the diary and the essays is a looking glass through which Virginia Woolf is immediately apprehensible both psychologically and physiologically. When I speak of Virginia Woolf, then, I am speaking of a character created by many authors, a compilation of fictions over time, a character which is connected to the author of the texts, but which is less the author herself than she is the theories of the author textually realized. I suggest that it is through the "I" or perhaps the many "I's" of her texts that Woolf the author offers up her own theory of creativity and female authorship.

I propose that, to use Freud's theory, Virginia Woolf is depicted in her autobiographical and pseudo-autobiographical texts as undergoing an object identification and concomitant splitting of the ego resultant upon the loss of her father; thus a conflict is seen to arise between her feminine body-ego and her masculinized object identification with the paternal ideality of the melancholic author (these are Freud's terms and not Woolf's). On the basis of Woolf's depictions of her father and her own textually evident fascination with the connections between her *madness* and her creativity, I believe that melancholia was an important aspect of her internalized identification with her father *and* the corollary intra-psychic condition which that identification evoked.

In other words, Woolf identified a part of her ego with her self-proclaimed melancholic father, and the splitting of the ego, which that identification provoked, resulted in her own melancholic condition. An argument such as this, what might be seen as something of a psychoanalytic ouroboros, blurs not only the distinctions between self and other, subject and object, but also those between cause and effect. Addressing Woolf's melancholia as a doubled problem of identification is obviously not an exhaustive answer to all of the questions evoked by descriptions of Woolf's psychological disquiet. However, it does provide a context within which her work might be better understood, insofar as it allows for a reading of Woolf which does not present her life merely as a flight, a fight, a denial, a defeat, a sacrifice, a substitution, but rather as a tactic, an artful strategy, enabling her to become the prolific and ingenious writer that she was.[5]

[4] Eminent literary critics like Showalter and Silver have likewise emphasized the precariousness of any interpretation of Woolf's texts that presupposes a stable narrator.

[5] I have taken the notion of splitting the ego as an *artful* strategy from Freud, who notes in his discussions of a young boy's disavowal of castration anxiety in "Splitting the Ego in

Much Ado about "Daddy"

Just after Adeline Virginia Stephen was born in January of 1882, James Russell Lowell, United States Minister to the Court of St. James in London, was asked by his old friend Leslie Stephen, who was on holiday in Switzerland at the time of Virginia's birth, to become the child's godfather. Sending a silver posset dish, Lowell included with his gift the rather poetic wish that "the child would be/ A sample of heredity."[6] As James King records in *Virginia Woolf*, when Virginia turned two, Leslie Stephen was again away on holiday in the Alps, and "wondered aloud in a letter to Julia why he and Virginia were so alike" (34). Seven years later, *again* on holiday, Leslie wrote to his wife: "today is Ginny's birthday—she is certainly very like me, I feel, though I cannot say how—but much more life in her than I had at her age."[7] Examining these scraps of epistolary evidence for Woolf's early relationship with her father, what becomes quite evident is that Leslie Stephen *wanted* his youngest daughter to be like him and identified her as such at a very early age.

Melanie Klein first introduced the concept of projective identification, a term which has subsequently been used to denote the ego which projects itself, or aspects of itself, onto an external other and then identifies with the object which it has imaginatively filled with itself.[8] Through a splitting of the ego, the projected aspects of the ego may be either wanted or unwanted elements; they are invested in the other for safety and an alleviation of anxiety. In the instance of unwanted elements being projected, it is the safety of the self, which is protected from the badness of the projected elements. On the contrary, where *valued* elements

the Process of Defence," "This way of dealing with reality [splitting the ego], which almost deserves to be described as artful, was decisive as regards the boy's practical behaviour" (464).

6 James Russell Lowell, quoted in Aileen Pippett, *The Moth and the Star: A Biography of Virginia Woolf*, 3. Posset is a drink made of hot milk curdled with some form of alcohol (wine, sherry, etc.) and often flavoured with spices. It was a beverage regularly prescribed as a remedy for minor maladies. It is interesting that in wishing Virginia "to be/ A sample of heredity" Lowell sent a vessel which, while often used in case of infirmity, is in sterling silver, so that, unlike other lesser posset dishes, it might be an article of display, pleasure, and privilege. The silver posset dish seems to carry with it a silent recognition that Leslie Stephen was a man for whom infirmity was not wholly unpleasant. In giving the newborn Virginia the dish, there also seems to be a suggestion that if she *is* going to be "a sample" of heredity she will be, like her father, plagued by maladies.

7 Leslie Stephen letter to Julia Stephen of 25 January 1891, quoted in James King, *Virginia Woolf*, 48.

8 Klein was also the first to introduce the concepts of the "internal object" and "internal object relations." Internal objects are the internal experiences (phantasies) of external objects.

of the self are projected, the safekeeping and survival of the good elements is assured. Leslie Stephen's attitude toward his daughter indicates some evidence of a projected identification of valued elements of authorship and intellectual prowess. Although a deeper analysis would need to be done in order to glean the full implications of Leslie's identification with his daughter, for the purposes of this paper it is interesting to note that Leslie Stephen began to instill in his family, and in Virginia, the ideality that she was the child in the family who was most like him and thus most likely to be a writer.

If Leslie Stephen was so supportive, perhaps even directive, of Virginia's youthful forays into both the reading and writing of literature, why would Woolf's diary entry for 28 November 1928, the ninety-sixth anniversary of Leslie Stephen's birth, suggest that while alive he was a forceful impediment to her authorship?

> 1928
> Father's Birthday. He would have been 1832 96, yes, today:
> 96
> & could have been 96 like other people one has known; but mercifully was not. His life would have ended mine. What would have happened? No writing, no books;—inconceivable. I used to think of him & mother daily; but writing The Lighthouse, laid them in my mind. And now he comes back sometimes, but differently. (I believe this to be true—that I was obsessed by them both, unhealthily; & writing of them was a necessary act.) He comes back now more as a contemporary. I must read him some day. (*D*3 208)

The first five sentences of this extract have been cited to demonstrate the incessant and stifling demands the dying Leslie Stephen placed upon his daughter during his two-year battle with cancer,[9] illustrating the difficulty of being a daughter and being an author. This diary entry clearly does suggest that if Leslie Stephen had not died, Woolf would never have written a book; however, rather than examining the *physical* impossibility of taking on the role of full time nurse and author, I would like to examine this diary entry by reflecting upon why Woolf believed it a *psychological* impossibility to write before the death of her father, why she felt that his death somehow freed her to become an author. If we follow some of the clues we already have, perhaps it is more accurate to suggest that, as long as Leslie Stephen lived, Virginia Woolf's restrictions and prohibitions were self imposed.

[9] For accounts of the gendered division of labor involved in caring for Leslie Stephen, I refer the reader to the work of Heather Ingman, Phyllis Rose and Elaine Showalter.

Death, Loss, and Melancholia

Sir Leslie Stephen died on 22 February, 1904. After the arduous business of the funeral was completed, the Stephen children and George Duckworth went on holiday for about four weeks at the seashore in Manorbier. During this extended holiday in Wales a certainty that she was capable of writing a book suffused Virginia. In *Virginia Woolf*, James King reports that, in deep mourning for her father, "Virginia sustained herself with the certainty that she somehow knew all that was necessary for writing a book. That vision came to her with brilliant clarity at Manorbier as she walked along the cliffs by the sea" (89). Bringing together these two moments—the revelation at Manorbier and the pensive recollections written almost twenty-four years later at Rodmell—it becomes clear that Woolf believes that if her father had lived there would have been "No writing, no books—inconceivable," but immediately after his death she suddenly feels it is *within* her to write a book. The authorial capacity of Leslie Stephen has seemingly been passed on to, and internalized by, Virginia Stephen. Virginia identified her father as the quintessential man of letters, a man almost entirely engaged in authorship and the appreciation of literature. In "Impressions of Sir Leslie Stephen," all but two introductory sentences are devoted to a lengthy recitation of the many ways in which Sir Leslie appreciated literature. Woolf's suggestion that she "must read him someday" also suggests that Woolf saw her father foremost as a creator of books: an author. But as Wiley points out "The subjugation of the household's females by Stephen and its other authoritarian men (which extended to physical violence and sexual abuse),[10] enflamed by the worry and poor health that his monumental biographical project brought to him, led Woolf to connect with the genre with Victorian patriarchal domination and female oppression" (390).

The identity of author, while embodied in her father was not—could not—be hers; but the loss incurred by his death impels a recuperative gesture whereby she takes into herself the capacity of authorship—takes into herself a part of her father. In the November following her father's death, Virginia submitted her first article for publication, "Howarth, November 1904," to Margaret Lyttelton the editor of the *Guardian*, a weekly newspaper for the clergy. Virginia's first attempt at writing a publishable essay was completed and submitted nine months after her father's death. One way to read Virginia's move to authorship is to consider that given the lengthy illness and death of Sir Leslie, the domestic economy of

[10] Whereas it is a particular form of historical realism to address issues of "abuse" from the perspective of their veridicality, here I am concerned (much like King), rather, with what Ken Plummer has called, "sexual stories"—the narration of gender, sex, and what could be constituted as "abuse" specifically, or as "violence" more generally, across both autobiographical and biographical sources.

the Stephen household had deteriorated somewhat, and it is quite possible that Woolf felt impelled to venture out into a paying career, and hence began to write essays—one of the few jobs she felt appropriate for a woman of the upper-middle-class. What I find of interest, is that after Leslie Stephen's death, Woolf begins conceiving herself as a writer and she delivers her first manuscript to the *Guardian*.

In "Mourning and Melancholia" Freud writes that the inception of melancholia is notable for its orality: "The ego wants to incorporate this object into itself, and, in accordance with the oral or cannibalistic phase of libidinal development in which it is, it wants to do so by devouring it" (258). In devouring the object the subject repudiates the death of the object, disavows the separation and desertion incurred by the loss of the object, and, in taking the object into the self, *revives* the object. To return to Woolf, the concomitant identification of herself as a writer and her first attempt at publishing, suggests that the incorporation of her father, or a part, or parts of her father, was experienced as a creative fomentation insofar as the lost object is revived within Woolf. The death of the father offers to Woolf a primary, and until this critical transition, unavailable, identificatory model; namely, as one who might create—as author.

According to Freudian theory the illusion of control, which is gained over the object through incorporation is an anodyne against future abandonment by the object, but it is also a form of vengeance, as the object was an ambivalent one—the target of both love and hatred. In *Totem and Taboo*, Freud explains that, in the primal horde, the sons of the patriarch feel both love and hatred for the father, ultimately killing him and ritually eating him, and that "in the act of devouring him they accomplished their identification with him" (203). Behind the murderous and cannibalistic impulses of the sons of the patriarch are powerful and ambivalent feelings of love and hate, which, as Kristeva notes in *Black Sun*, are "without doubt the substratum of an unsuspected sexual desire" (11). Thus, the apparent incorporation of the father by the daughter works as the fulfillment of an Oedipal desire, and as an imagined sexually charged taking of her father into herself, creating the liberated daughter as author.

However, it should be obvious that Freud's Oedipal model is forged by means of a relentlessly problematic and rigid set of assumptions concerning sex and gender and concomitant gender politics, politics that were of significant concern to Woolf. As Parveen Adams points out in "Of Female Bondage," "It is one thing to say that the Oedipus complex is the source of all neurosis; it is quite another to recognize that the Oedipus complex pathologizes femininity and feminine sexuality" (249). Rachel Bowlby sheds some light upon the classic Oedipal conundrum of femininity and what a woman wants when she notes in *Still Crazy after all these Years*, that in Freud's model the wish for a baby simply acts as a substitute for, takes the place of, and camouflages the wish for a penis.

Consequently,

> There is no place of femininity at all; femininity itself is still the 'masculine wish for the possession of a penis'. Even the properly feminine woman is still caught up in the masculinity complex, still hankering after a penis, even if this is covered over by the wish for a baby, and still repudiating the femininity she is said to have obtained. (144)

Although laden with problems, most of which I have not even mentioned here, the Oedipal model does, in its most general terms, mark a girl's desire for *something* her father has, and which her experience of reality has indicated she cannot or should not have. Consequently, the desire for what is prohibited may at least partially be recast as a desire for the condoned. If Virginia Woolf's ambivalent love for her father is considered vis-à-vis this less rigid framework of Oedipal prohibition, her essay "Howarth, November 1904" may be seen as the condoned manifestation of a prohibited desire. Interpreting the circumstances of Woolf's first foray into the literary world allows for an understanding of Woolf's notion of the creative process insofar as it demonstrates a woman's adroit coping strategy—a way in which she could simultaneously disavow the loss of her father *and* make money, a way in which she could simultaneously refuse reality and accede to its demands. She might seize, through her father's death, his position as author.

Emphasizing the agentic elements provided by the event of Woolf's melancholy, rather than the supposed pathology of Woolf's melancholy, allows for a reading which does not suggest that Woolf became a great artist *because* she was melancholic, but rather contends that Woolf's ability to construct an artful reality, her ability, as articulated by Vita Sackville West in a letter, to "see things aslant rather than dully straight," (Noble 165) was a capability she brought *to* her melancholy, not an ability emerging *from* her melancholy.

Freud, on the other hand, seems to believe that the creativity of the artist arises *because* he is melancholic. Freud reasserts and reifies the well-established and privileged insight of masculine melancholy in his discussion of Hamlet in "Mourning and Melancholia." There, Freud avows that the melancholic "has a keener eye for the truth than others who are not melancholic. . . [and] it may be, so far as we know, that he has come pretty near to understanding himself; we only wonder why a man has to be ill *before* he can be accessible to a truth of this kind."[11] Jacqueline Rose has suggested that Hamlet, in this passage and many

[11] "Mourning and Melancholia" 255. Italics mine. It is interesting to note that Freud seems to construct his own creative process as one involving a foray into classical creative melancholy: "I am not pleased with anything here, and am in that bodily and mental state to which I am accustomed during intensive inner work—or, rather, the preparation for such. It is a kind of misery; I am rarely productive when I feel well" (Sigmund Freud in a

other psychoanalytic texts, is "given the status of truth" (133). I would suggest alternatively that Hamlet is given access *to* truth through his melancholy, which, in turn, gives him the status *of* truth.

In the same passage of "Mourning and Melancholia" in which Hamlet appears, Freud speaks of a markedly generic and unnamed "good, capable, conscientious woman" (255), who does not seem quite the same as the flamboyantly tragic figure of Hamlet, Prince of Denmark. Suffering from melancholy, the "good, capable, conscientious woman" speaks hyper-critically of herself (just as Hamlet does), but seems to be no more than the competent yet bland, feminine foil to Hamlet's great male melancholia. Freud contends that the "good, capable, conscientious woman will speak no better of herself after she develops melancholia than one who is in fact worthless; indeed, the former is perhaps more likely to fall ill of the disease than the latter, of whom we too should have nothing good to say" (255). It seems that, according to Freud, melancholia provides an internalized privileged point of access to self-knowledge for men and an externalized privileged status to the male melancholic. However, the female melancholic must be satisfied with a suggestion that if she is melancholic, it is unlikely that she is entirely worthless.

Woolf's Refusal of a Binary Division of Gendered Creative Labor

If we ask Freud, or our reading of Freud's texts, to attend to Virginia Woolf, or a reading of her texts, we might find something substantive, rather than a reduction of the complex to the aporia suggested by woman and melancholia. In *A Room of One's Own*, Woolf offers a socio-political, rather than a psychologistic and deterministic explanation as to why a "good, capable, conscientious woman" is not likely to have access to the same exalted status of truth as the male artist.

> Intellectual freedom depends upon material things. Poetry depends upon intellectual freedom. And women have always been poor, not for two hundred years merely, but from the beginning of time. Women have had less intellectual freedom than the sons of Athenian slaves. Women, then, have not had a dog's chance of writing poetry. (103)

Woolf's explanation suggests that for a daughter there is the added burden of discouragement, there "would always have been the assertion—you cannot do this, you are incapable of doing that—to protest against, to overcome" (53). Taking into consideration some of the historical and material disparities between the male artist and the female artist, Woolf's argument grapples with a reality that is elided in Freud's essay: most women did not have the leisure time, the money,

letter of Nov. 5, 1911 to Sandor Ferenczi. Quoted in Ernest Jones, *The Life and Work of Sigmund Freud*, 2: 353).

the education, or the encouragement that was afforded to Shakespeare's layabout prince. By definition, a "good, capable, conscientious woman" was a woman who knew her place was in the home tending to the needs of her family—the woman who missed Woolf's lecture in *A Room of One's Own* because she was "washing up the dishes and putting the children to bed" (108). This is, of course, a classic feminist point. But what is perhaps less well remarked is that Woolf seems to want to talk about, and to, the "one who is in fact worthless" in Freud's estimation, the woman who is not quite so enmeshed in the domestic model of good, capable, conscientious womanhood; a woman who also has desires for something else. In *A Room of One's Own*, Woolf's depictions of artists capable of creativity include women, women who, like men, will create ideas and books.

Judith Butler asks "How useful is a phenomenological point of departure for a feminist description of gender?" (522). I want to argue here the utility of a critical assessment of Woolf's phenomenological commentary concerning the problems attendant to a binary division of gendered creative labor. While her father lived, Virginia, the daughter, was consigned to inhabit and to enact a psychological relationship to her father predicated on each staying affixed to a stable enactment of gendered capacities. In Woolf's case, this included a relation as daughter to a father who inhabits the masculinized role of writer. As Butler points out regarding gender and its "truth effects," "as a strategy of survival, gender is a performance with clearly punitive consequences. Discrete genders are part of what 'humanizes' individuals within contemporary culture; indeed, those who fail to do their gender right are regularly punished" (522).

Locating images that portend attention to the gendered aspects of authorial creativity and its creative labors in Woolf's texts is not a difficult exercise. In the diary entry of 28 November 1928, the same one in which she records her father's birthday and death, Woolf reflects on her writing of what would eventually turn out to be *The Waves*: "As for my next book, I am going to hold myself from writing till I have it impending in me: grown heavy in my mind like a ripe pear; pendant, gravid, asking to be cut or it will fall" (*D*3 208). The reference to a pear tree is most telling here. Woolf underscores an analogy of sexual and textual creativity by insisting on an image of fomentation, therein refusing a more protypically feminine metaphor of creativity as birth.

Androgyny as a Form of Gender Trouble

Woolf's admiration for Coleridge's theories of the androgynous mind are oft-cited and well known, and seem quite closely connected to the model through which Woolf may have understood her own creativity. In *A Room of One's Own* Woolf claims "If one is a man, still the woman part of his brain must have effect;

and a woman also must have intercourse with the man in her" (94). The brain is not uniformly androgynous, but has two fully distinct heterosexual components: "two sexes in the mind corresponding to the two sexes in the body" (93), which must undergo a "marriage," enter into "intercourse" and "collaboration" to "celebrate . . . nuptials in darkness" (99), in order to achieve "complete satisfaction and happiness" (93). "It is when this fusion takes place that the mind is fully fertilized" (94). The sexuality upon which Woolf's diction insists comes back again and again to metaphors of conception. As Elizabeth Abel writes, "Texts are mothered, not authored, in *Room*" (87). For example, in *A Room of One's Own*, in considering the Italian fascists' desire to "'develop the Italian novel'," Woolf contends, "it is doubtful whether poetry can come out of an incubator. Poetry ought to have a mother as well as a father. The fascist poem will be a horrid little abortion" (98). What might be extracted from this pastiche of nativity metaphors is not only their insistence upon the sexuality of the act of creation, but an assertion of female control over that creativity that is not compelled to remain within the bounds culturally ascribed to the feminine, when the author is a woman. Whereas Woolf, one must note, insists that "in the woman's brain the woman predominates over the man" (93-94) it is also the case that she insists "it is fatal for anyone who writes to think of their sex. It is fatal to be a man or woman pure and simple; one must be woman-manly or man-womanly"(169).

In *A Room of One's Own*, Woolf is also speaking with a wry wit, in her choice of self-appellation: "call me Mary Beton, Mary Seton, Mary Carmichael or by any name you please" (6). Knowing quite well that the name Mary Carmichael was the name under which Marie Stopes, England's most vocal advocate of birth control, published *Love's Creation* in 1927, Woolf cryptically emphasizes the political need for female control (self control) of women's bodies and women's minds, sexual and textual production.

Indeed, in writing a mother into the act of textual creation in *A Room of One's Own*, Woolf responds to the depiction of masculine cultural production as childbirth, which was well developed by the late nineteenth century. Early organic metaphors of spiders spinning webs, seeds sprouting, and plants blooming gave way mid-century to metaphors of male gestation and midwifery. As Christine Battersby points out in *Gender and Genius*, "The artist conceived, was pregnant, laboured (in sweat and pain), was delivered, and (in an uncontrolled ecstasy of agonized–male–control) brought forth. These were the images of natural childbirth that the male creators elaborated" (73). The male artist was mother as well as father to his creation. The most that a female artist might hope for was to give birth to a male child, who might, in turn, give birth to a great work of genius.

Creativity and The Feminine

Virginia Woolf's production of texts and her failure to produce children have incurred a great deal of critical comment over the years. I have chosen as examples some of the arguments I think tend to exemplify a rather stale insistence that women must choose to be *either* mother or author. Jacqueline Rose proposed that Woolf herself believed and feared that writing was an act that made her an unnatural woman, and sequestered her from the gratification of domestic and maternal joys that other women experienced (212). Ronald Hayman concludes that for both Katherine Mansfield and Virginia Woolf "stories and characters are a substitute for living and having children" (21). Hayman does not seem to feel, or at least does not mention, that for authors such as Leonard Woolf and E.M. Forster stories and characters were a substitute for living and having children. Michael Holroyd agrees that the pursuits of art and maternity are mutually exclusive, and, in the case of Virginia Woolf, "children with their wetness and noise would surely have killed off the novels in her: and it was about novels that she cared most" (qtd. Showalter 273). Frank Barron tidily sums up the argument that biological production precludes cultural production:

> The creative act is a kind of giving birth, and it is noteworthy that as an historical fact creativity has been conspicuously lacking in women, whose products are their children. At the risk of making too much of a linguistic parallel, it might be said that nature has literally arranged a division of labour. Men bring forth ideas, paintings, literary and musical compositions, organizations of states, inventions, new material structures, and the like, while women bring forth the new generation. (221)

Herbert Marder declares that Mrs. Ramsay, who is notable for her *lack* of artistic production, must be seen as the female ideal of Woolf's model of the androgynous artist because of her stereotypically feminine domestic excellence: "Mrs. Ramsay as wife, mother, hostess, is the androgynous artist in life, creating with the whole of her being" (128). One might respond by saying that Marder seems to have confused androgyny with the angel in the house.

Granted, I have extracted some of the more extreme critical conclusions drawn from Woolf's nulliparity; however, they do come together to suggest that the ideality of the truly feminine does seem to exclude cultural production, which allows us a better understanding of why it was only by means of the internalization of her father as object that Woolf produced a form of gendered complexity that might permit repression of a determinative femininity and in so doing, providing access to the (at that time) seemingly masculine potentialities vested in authorship.

Beyond the Sexual Binary: Creativity and Gender

Woolf offers yet another reflection on the psychological constraints imposed by a rigidly gendered enactment of creativity in *A Room of One's Own.* In considering what is meant by "the unity of the mind," Woolf articulates what states of mind might be most conducive to creative insight, and takes as her example a woman who is walking down the street and suddenly feels herself to be an outsider:

> Clearly the mind is always altering its focus, and bringing the world into different perspectives. But some of these states of mind seem, even if adopted spontaneously, to be less comfortable than others. In order to keep oneself continuing in them one is unconsciously holding something back, and gradually the repression becomes an effort. But there may be some state of mind in which one could continue without effort because nothing is required to be held back. (93)

Woolf's discussion of the ideal state, the "unity of mind," seems to reframe psychoanalytic ideas of repression and the unconscious to formulate an argument that it is not through a selective process of repression that creativity can emerge. Rather it comes from nothing being held back—neither sorrow nor joy, neither sanity nor madness, neither passivity nor violence. And it is here critical to underscore the argument that for Woolf (as for Freud) it has historically been the purview only of men to be able to access, and to make creative use of, the psychically uncomfortable, difficult and disturbing insights yielded up by the unconscious. This, for Woolf, is the severely constraining calculus of a rigid binary division of the forms that gendered labor can take within the imagination.

It is then by now clear that for Woolf, a woman writing in this manner—freely—is a woman writing beyond socially approved boundaries. Woolf asks in "Professions for Women," if the major psychological barriers and material obstacles were no longer in her way, what stands in the way of the female author just being herself in her writing? Woolf does not know, and does not believe that anyone else knows either. She contends that the reason the question is unanswerable is that women have been historically unable to overcome social constraints against a woman speaking freely and honestly about the body and its unwieldy desires. The language Woolf uses to make the point is highly figurative and oblique and becomes an example in itself of the impossibility of speaking directly of the body and desires. Although the account is rather long, it is worth quoting in its entirety.

> I want you to figure to yourselves a girl sitting with a pen in her hand, which for minutes, and indeed for hours, she never dips into the inkpot.

> The image that comes to my mind when I think of this girl is the image of a fisherman lying sunk in dreams on the verge of a deep lake with a rod held out over the water. She was letting her imagination sweep unchecked round every rock and cranny of the world that lies submerged in the depths of our unconscious being. Now came the experience, the experience that I believe to be far commoner with women writers than with men. The line raced through the girl's fingers. Her imagination had rushed away. It had sought the pools, the depths, the places where the largest fish slumber. And then there was a smash. There was an explosion. There was foam and confusion. The imagination had dashed itself against something hard. The girl was roused from her dream. She was indeed in a state of the most acute and difficult distress. To speak without figure, she had thought of something, something about the body, about the passions which it was unfitting for her as a woman to say. Men, her reason told her, would be shocked. The consciousness of what men will say of a woman who speaks the truth about her passions had roused her from her artist's state of unconsciousness. She could write no more. The trance was broken. Her imagination could work no longer. (104)

It is specifically the institutions of social conventions delimiting arbitrarily the apparent stability of the sex/gender system, that have made writing, for women—even the thinking—of the body and of desires, structurally foreclosed from the outset, and as such, impossible. Thinking about shattering these conventions paralyzes the female author's imagination. To give her audience even a vague image of what she is thinking Woolf turns to the body of the fisher*man*, suggesting that the female authorial body must be read, must be interpreted, through the male body, "against something hard"; it cannot be understood on its own.

Writing the female authorial body was a problem that vexed Woolf throughout her career. Insofar as she imagined the ideal state of creativity as one of holding nothing back, the female authorial body was, in effect, a limiting, and as such, horrifically stable container. The imagined violence of mind and body meeting is startling in the midst of the pastoral scene: "then there was a smash. There was an explosion." Smashing and exploding, foam and confusion result when the female imagination exceeds the feminine bodily position. The female author's inner life, her fishing expedition into the unconscious is rich, complex, even daringly adventurous, but the limitations of the female authorial body draw that imagination up short of artistic realization. It was only when the female artist was out of her skin that she could delve into the dark recesses of the pool, but is returned with smashing and exploding into her own skin.

We might then, to return to our initial goal of rendering unto Woolf a certain measure of agency in her efforts to disentangle the enframing contours of sex from those that give shape to authorial opportunities, read this passage as indicative of an effort to be engaged with the incompatibility of holding nothing back and the selectivity of the discipline of writing. To write is to be "conscious of what men will say," and, to be conscious of what women will say. It is also, and perhaps most importantly, to be conscious of the self and capable of sorting the imaginary gendered miscellany into a creative article. The pure visionary cannot translate internal experience to an external world. In *The Waves* Woolf writes of Rhoda, a fragile and intuitive woman who seems to live almost entirely in the realm of the mind and spirit. Rhoda is so disconnected from her own body and the world around her that she must press her toes against the footboard at night to maintain contact with the world. As van Buren Kelley says, Rhoda is Woolf's archetype of an individual who lives entirely within the realm of the visionary and the spiritual, and who consequently experiences outside realities as intrusive violations (152). The only way that Rhoda can see of escaping the buffeting and alienation of the external world is to commit suicide. Woolf knows that pure visionary and imaginative existence is not only lonely, but cannot survive, and most certainly cannot create.

In Woolf's narrative of the fishing author it is suggested that the constrictions imposed upon women radically restricted any possibility of writing the feminine experience and imagination without withholding, without keeping something back, something hidden. The passage also hints that between the internal imagination and the external world, between the imagining and the writing, one must overcome, or at least experience, the violence, the "smash" and "explosion" of the meeting of internal and external. It is evident in the narrative that *all of this occurs in the imagination*. The violence of the confrontation between imagination and object occurs in the deep pool of the unconscious; both quantities exist in the unconscious, not within a realm of conscious recognition. There is only the imagined internal confrontation of the feminine imagination smashing against a hard internalized object that is posited as the voices of men.

In Woolf's narrative the imagination of the young author fails when confronted with the "something hard" buried within the deepest recesses of her imagination. The violence of the confrontation overwhelms the young woman, startles her out of her reverie, and consequently "She could write no more." In Woolf's story, the young girl's imagination is shut down, effectively destroyed, by its violent confrontation with an internalized resisting object. The something hard is left lurking in the depths of the unconscious. What is not said in Woolf's narrative, and perhaps even more important because of that, is that for the female imagination to survive, the resistance of the *something hard* has to be destroyed, its absolute authority must be demolished. The battle between an imagination that is gendered female, and the boundaries that are erected in the wake of culture's imposed forms of repression in this binary division of creative labor, must be won by the imagination if the young female author is to be able to write.

To examine what might comprise the resistance of something hard which needs to be overcome, destroyed, I refer back to the diary entry of 28 November 1928, and Woolf's comment that "writing of them [Julia and Leslie Stephen] was a necessary act. . . . He comes back now more as a contemporary. I must read him some day." As I have remarked above, the last sentence is most intriguing because it suggests, rather surprisingly, that Woolf is, here, effecting a temporal shift in her own relation to the imaginative object constituted by her father's work. Clearly, Virginia had read Leslie Stephen's numerous texts but the fact that she wished to remind herself or to deceive herself, in her own diary, that while he lived she had not *read* Leslie Stephen, but that after his death had *written* Leslie Stephen is a statement of transition: a transition of power from one generation to the next. It is specifically a relationship between father and daughter, as Julia Stephen does not *come back* to Woolf as a contemporary, but seems to be left in the past. The transition of authorial power, the movement from reading (or not reading) to writing, is, for Woolf, movement from muse to writer, the movement from daughter to author.

In *Playing and Reality*, psychoanalyst D. W. Winnicott suggests that for an individual to be able to use an object the object must be able to be destroyed and yet still survive in unconscious fantasy. The destroyed object "develops it own autonomy and life, and (if it survives) contributes in to the subject according to its own properties" (90). The object is always being destroyed or having to survive the ravages of destruction, and it is these repeated efforts at destruction of the object in which its expulsion into the external is managed. This allows the subject to experience the other-than-me substances of the object. Entrance to a shared reality is dependent upon destruction of the object and the placing of the object outside of the subject's omnipotent control, that is, out in the world. Winnicott writes, it is thus, "the destructive drive that creates the quality of externality" (93). The narrative of Woolf's *failed* creativity as the destruction of the imagination by the rigid contours of the unconscious object must be read alongside her narrative of success and satisfaction in finally writing her father. In this way, I suggest that it is only through the repeated imaginary destruction of the internalized object of Leslie Stephen that Woolf comes to be able to identify with herself as a writer. Woolf thus shifts her identification with her father to a relation not as circumscribed by the paternalistic bond, but as a peer—a fellow author. And it is only through such a transformative experience that this authorial identification take place within a shared reality—neither strictly his nor hers. In both narratives Leslie Stephen, the father-to-the-daughter, is destroyed, but he is nevertheless resurrected in the unconscious fantasy: once Woolf succeeds in writing, he emerges *outside* of the pool of the unconscious.

This psychic operation, marked by an internalization of the paternal object, is again noticeable in Woolf's interesting relationship with her father's books—their reading, their writing, and their possession. The Woolfs built their library on the substantial collection of books that Virginia inherited from Leslie Stephen. She covered her father's books in brightly colored paper and did not write in them,[12] although she wrote marginalia in those she or Leonard had purchased or had been given as gifts from others. Decorated and preserved unsullied, Woolf's covering over of her father's books attests to a desire to both hide and draw attention to her father's inclusion in her library—simultaneously making them an integral part of *her* library by covering them with dust jackets of *her* choosing, but also making them stand out apart from her own uncovered books. The reluctance to deface her father's books with her own impressions, opinions, or commentary suggests a return, a memory, of the time before Stephen's death, when Woolf seemed to feel a prohibition against writing, the impossibility of writing, when/where her father had written, the impossibility of writing over, or overwriting, her father. He cannot be broken down, broken into, digested, but is preserved whole, as he was, just covered over.

I have discussed some of the possible interpretations of Woolf's relationship with her father insofar as it relates to Woolf's melancholia and her capacity as a creative artist. Along the way I have counterpoised Freud's texts with Woolf's, examining possible ways in which the texts speak to each other. Posing the possibility that Woolf's disavowal of her father's death and an internalization of a part or parts of him incurred within her a melancholic state of being, I have proposed that the experience of this melancholic union of object and subject was not only the impetus for but also the model through which she understood her own creativity.

I have elaborated how it is that a careful analysis of Woolf's relationship with her father allows us, by means of a critical application of object relations theory, to reassess this complex association with the paternal, and in so doing, avoid either a utopic or a dystopic engagement with Woolf's many gendered- and sex-based anxieties. This close reading allows us to think conscientiously, and with an attention to complexity and a non-reductionism, about the connections between what Hermione Lee has identified as a relation to the father structured by "wanting to do *nothing* that father did" (72) and its inevitable correlative double

[12] Alan Isaac has described Woolf's idiosyncratic bookbinding practices, and Silver has described at length Woolf's reliance on reading notebooks in place of her father's standard practice of intra-textual marginalia (see also King and Miletic-Vejzovic on the Woolfs' library and related bookbinding and annotation practices).

—a relation of idealization and imitation. I have undertaken here to theorize with a measure of historical precision, the significance of Woolf's reflections regarding sex, gender, kinship and creativity. As Kelsey (1932), and Showalter (1977) (and others) have carefully argued, it is by means of a critical reading that one can engage systematically with Woolf's phenomenological reflections on sex, gender and patriarchal systems without the overly hasty imposition of a contemporary ideological label, like "feminism." Woolf's melancholic relations with gender and these various ties (e.g., her relationship with "the father") are, then, properly, here, understood as thoroughly "modern" vis à vis the instability produced by these locations of creative and imaginative engagement, and therein, Woolf's deliberate and bold engagements with the multiplicity of the seemingly stable sexed self. I have emphasized that Woolf's model of creativity was repeatedly refigured by means of her thoroughly modern relation to an unstable account of the gendered self, and its various differences, which allows us insight into what Woolf meant by a "state of mind in which one could continue without effort because nothing is required to be held back" (*AROO* 93).

Works Cited

Abel, Elizabeth. "'Cam the Wicked': Woolf's Portrait of the Artist as her Father's Daughter." *Virginia Woolf and Bloomsbury*. Ed. Jane Marcus. Bloomington: Indiana UP, 1987. 170-194.

Adams, Parveen. "Of Female Bondage." *Between Feminism and Psychoanalysis*. Ed. Teresa Brennan. London: Routledge, 1989. 247-265.

Barron, Frank. *Creativity and Personal Freedom.* London: D. VanNostrand, 1968.

Battersby, Christine. *Gender and Genius: Towards a Feminist Aesthetics*. Bloomington: Indiana UP, 1989.

Bowlby, Rachel. *Still Crazy After All These Years: Women, Writing, and Psychoanalysis*. London: Routledge, 1992.

Butler, Judith. "Performative Acts and Gender Constitution: An Essay in Phenomenology and Feminist Theory." *Theatre Journal*. 40.4 (1988): 519-531.

DeSalvo, Louise A. "As 'Miss Jan Says': Virginia Woolf's Early Journals." *Virginia Woolf and Bloomsbury*. Ed. Jane Marcus. Bloomington: Indiana UP, 1987. 96-124.

——. *Virginia Woolf: The Impact of Childhood Sexual Abuse on her Life and Work.* Boston: Beacon, 1989.

Freud, Sigmund. "Anxiety and Instinctual Life." *New Introductory Lectures on Psychoanalysis*. London: Penguin, 1973.

——. "The Ego and the Id." *On Metapsychology: The Theory of Psychoanalysis.* London: Penguin, 1984. 339-407.

——. "Mourning and Melancholia." *On Metapsychology: The Theory of Psychoanalysis.* London: Penguin, 1984. 246-268.

——. "Splitting of the Ego in the Process of Defence." *On Metapsychology: The Theory of Psychoanalysis.* London: Penguin, 1984. 457-463.

——. "Totem and Taboo: Some Points of Agreement Between the Mental Lives of Savages and Neurotics." *The Origins of Religion.* London: Penguin, 1985. 43-224.

Hayman, Ronald. *Literature and Living: A Consideration of Katherine Mansfield and Virginia Woolf.* London: Covent Garden P, 1972.

Hill, Constance. *Mary Russell Mitford and Her Surroundings.* London: William Brennon and Son, 1920.

Hill, Katherine C. "Virginia Woolf and Leslie Stephen: History and Literary Revolution." *PMLA*, 96:3 (1981): 351-362.

Hyman, Virginia R. "Reflections in the Looking-Glass: Leslie Stephen and Virginia Woolf." *Journal of Modern Literature.* 10.2 (1983):197-216.

Ingman, Heather. *Women's Fiction Between the Wars: Mothers, Daughters, and Writing.* London: St Martin's Press, 1998.

Isaac, Alan. *Virginia Woolf, The Uncommon Bookbinder.* London: Cecil Woolf, 1988.

Jones, Ernest. *The Life and Work of Sigmund Freud.* 3 vols. New York: Basic Books, 1955.

Kelley, A. van Buren. *The Novels of Virginia Woolf: Fact and Vision.* Chicago: U of Chicago P, 1971.

Kelsey, Mary Electa. "Virginia Woolf and the She-Condition." *The Sewanee Review.* 39.4 (1932): 425-444.

King, James. *Virginia Woolf.* London: Penguin, 1995.

King, Julia and Laila Miletic-Vejzovic. *The Library of Leonard and Virginia Woolf.* Pullman, WA: Washington State UP, 2003.

Klein, Melanie. "A Contribution to the Psychogenesis of Manic-Depressive States." *The Selected Melanie Klein.* Ed. Juliet Mitchell. Penguin: Markham, 1986. 115-145.

Kristeva, Julia. *Black Sun: Depression and Melancholia.* Trans. Leon S. Roudiez. NY: Columbia UP, 1989.

Lee, Hermione. *Virginia Woolf.* London: Chatto & Windus, 1996.

Marder, Herbert. *Feminism and Art: A Study of Virginia Woolf.* Chicago: U of Chicago P, 1968.

Nikolchina, Miglena I. "Meaning and Matricide: Reading Virginia Woolf Via Kristeva." Diss. University of Western Ontario, 1993. Print.

Noble, Joan Russell, ed. *Recollections of Virginia Woolf by her Contemporaries*. London: Owen, 1972.

Pippett, Aileen. *The Moth and the Star: A Biography of Virginia Woolf.* Toronto: Little Brown, 1969.

Plummer, Ken. *Telling Sexual Stories: Power, Change and Social Worlds*. NY: Routledge, 1994.

Rose, Jacqueline. *Sexuality in the Field of Vision*. London: Verso, 1991.

Rose, Phyllis. "Mrs. Ramsay and Mrs. Woolf." *Women's Studies* 1 (1973): 199-216.

Ruddick, Sara. "Private Brother, Public World." *New Feminist Essays on Virginia Woolf.* Ed. Jane Marcus. Lincoln: U of Nebraska P, 1981. 185-215.

Showalter, Elaine. *A Literature of Their Own: British Women Novelists From Brontë to Lessing*. Princeton: Princeton UP, 1977.

Silver, Brenda. *Virginia Woolf Icon*. Chicago: U of Chicago P, 1999.

——. *Virginia Woolf's Reading Notebooks*. Princeton: Princeton UP, 1983.

Wiley, Christopher. "'When a Woman Speaks the Truth About her Body': Ethel Smyth, Virginia Woolf, and the Challenges of Lesbian Auto/Biography." *Music and Letters*. 85.3 (2004): 388-413.

Winnicott, D.W. *Playing and Reality*. London: Tavistock, 1971.

Woolf, Virginia. *A Room of One's Own*. Toronto: Triad Grafton, 1987.

——. *The Diary of Virginia Woolf.* 5 vols. Ed. Anne Olivier Bell. NY: Harcourt, 1978-84.

——. "Impressions of Sir Leslie Stephen." *The Essays of Virginia Woolf 1904-1912*. Vol. 1 Ed. Andrew McNeillie. NY: Harcourt, 1986. 127-130.

——. *The Letters of Virginia Woolf.* 6 vols. Ed. Nigel Nicolson and Joanne Trautmann. New York: Harcourt, 1975-1980.

——. "Modern Fiction." *The Essays of Virginia Woolf.* Vol 4. Ed. Andrew McNeillie. London: Hogarth, 1994. 157-165.

——. "Professions for Women." *The Crowded Dance of Modern Life*. Ed. Rachel Bowlby. London: Penguin, 1993. 101-106.

——. *The Waves*. London: Grafton Books, 1977.

When Freud Gets Useful: Retaining the Commonplace in Virginia Woolf's *Pointz Hall*

Nicky Platt

In or around 1939, the nature of Virginia Woolf's relationship with Freudianism changed. This is a story familiar to Woolf scholars, particularly since the publication of Hermione Lee's justly influential psychoanalytically-informed biography in 1996. What is less clear is why 1939, and why during her writing of *Pointz Hall*. This essay traces the pre-history of Woolf's "turn" to Freud, and examines how the gradual evolution of Woolf's understanding of herself as an artist led to the development of a communitarian ideal in which the ideas of Freud, while still disturbing, risible and even maddening, become for the first time *undeniably* useful.[1] This discussion focuses on the first typescript of *Pointz Hall* because, as with so many of Woolf's novels, it is in the unedited immediacy of this early draft that the cultural/political ideas driving the fiction can most clearly be located. Many of the passages quoted below have been heavily edited or cut entirely from the posthumously published *Between the Acts*, just as *The Years*, for example, successfully disguises many of the overt political references of its preceding drafts.[2] But in this case, I would argue, it is the early, "full flood" draft that is in its raw state the more engaging story and in many ways the better read (*D5* 200; and see note 16).

A Family Affair

The problem with being "the daughter of an educated man," in the *Three Guineas* definition, born into the upper middle-class intelligentsia, was that virtually every major intellectual debate could not help but become a family affair. If the Anglo-Indian branch of Woolf's family meant she was as much a "daughter of the Empire" as a vigorous opponent of imperialism, as much an establishment insider as outsider, the eminent "men of letters" branch equally bound her in peculiarly intimate ways to the academic discourses of her time. The current critical debate about exactly when Woolf read Freud's texts is necessary and productive. It is of equal importance, however, as Murray Roston has implied

[1] In taking as the premise of my argument Woolf's evolution of a communitarian ideal in the late 1930s, this essay draws upon and intersects with Jed Esty's thesis in *A Shrinking Island: Modernism and National Culture in England*.

[2] Where passages quoted from *Pointz Hall* have been significantly edited in *Between the Acts*, I have marked with *. Where phrases or passages have been cut altogether, ** appears.

(154), to locate Woolf's response to the discipline of psychoanalysis before 1924, when the Hogarth Press became Freud's publisher in English, and indeed before 1914, when Leonard began to read Freud's work and enthuse about it privately and in print, to those "eminent Victorians" of her father's circle who were debating the existence of a "subconscious." In 1884, two years after Virginia's birth, British psychologist and Stephen family friend James Sully published a book which Freud would later acclaim and which "fascinated [Leslie] Stephen" by its discussion of the co-existence of "conscious" and "unconscious [...] region[s] of the mind" (Roston 154). From a young age it is likely, therefore, that Woolf was exposed to some of the language and ideas of the emergent discourse of psychoanalysis and that it was through her father and her father's friends that she first encountered its key terms.[3] When in the late 1930s Woolf writes of her "ambivalence" towards her father, in an autobiographical sketch that is clearly informed by her concurrent reading of Freud, her father is a Freudian subject in more than one way: he is, in a sense, the originator of the ideas to which Woolf now makes him subject (Woolf, "Sketch" 160).

Two years into her marriage, the family ties increased when in preparation for writing a review of A. A. Brill's just-published translation of *The Psychopathology of Everyday Life*, Leonard undertook a study of *The Interpretation of Dreams*, and thereafter became a considered but staunch advocate of psychoanalytic theory.[4] Lytton Strachey, arguably Virginia's closest male friend at this time, became the next Bloomsbury advocate of Freud, publishing the psychoanalytically-informed *Eminent Victorians* in 1918 and the first "psycho-biography," *Elizabeth and Essex*, a decade later. Freud, in turn, admired Strachey's work, and when Ernest Jones (the chief promulgator of early psychoanalysis in Britain) sought an introduction for Lytton's brother James, Freud was eager to oblige. James travelled to Vienna with his wife of a few months, Alix (née Sargant-Florence), where both underwent a course of analysis that Freud himself conducted. When they returned, it was to devote the rest of their working lives to translating and explicating Freud's work for the British audience, beginning, in 1924, with the publication by the Hogarth Press of the first of the Collected Works.[5] By this time, Woolf's younger

[3] George M. Johnson writes: "Though underemphasized, Leslie Stephen's intellectual legacy to his daughter Virginia included his knowledge of philosophical psychology" (141).

[4] It is also worth noting that, as Merry Pawlowski argues, Woolf was writing about psychoanalysis in her Diary (*D*1 80) as far back as 1917, when she mentions her reading of Wilfred Trotter's *Instincts of the Herd in Peace and War*, through which Woolf "would have been exposed to Trotter's quarrel with Freud's 'psycho-analytic' psychology..." (43).

[5] A fascinating insight into the encounter of James and Alix with psychoanalysis can be gained by reading the letters they wrote to each other at this time. These are collected in Perry Meisel's *Bloomsbury/Freud: The Letters of James and Alix Strachey, 1924–1925*.

brother Adrian and his wife Karin had also succumbed to the charms of Ernest Jones. Both Adrian and Karin, in fact, took Jones' advice even more seriously than James and Alix, and agreed to train first as doctors before becoming professional psychiatrists specialising in psychoanalysis.

James and Alix, Adrian and Karin; but not Leonard *and* Virginia. Did psychoanalysis perhaps seem a peculiarly familial band-wagon, and was that why Woolf was so resistant, and for such a long time, to engage with the real debates? Instead, right up until the later 1930s, Woolf responded to discussions of Freud with a flippancy that is otherwise difficult to account for in a thinker of such brave and formidable intellect. It is only paralleled, in fact, by the apolitical stance she assumed when, if she could not beat Leonard in the political arena, she certainly would not join him.[6] Woolf made a number of disparaging comments in her letters, including the often-quoted remark about the "gull-like imbecility" of the Freudians (*L3* 134–35), but there were more sustained and powerful rebuttals. In a review of J. D. Beresford's *An Imperfect Mother* (entitled "Freudian Fiction," written and published in 1920), Woolf argues that the insights of psychoanalysis "simplif[y]" and "detract" in their attempt at scientific objectivity:

> The triumphs of science are beautifully positive. But for novelists the matter is much more complex … Yes, says the scientific side of the brain, that … explains a great deal. No, says the artistic side of the brain, that is dull and has no human significance. (195–97)

For Woolf, "characters" should not be "cases" in fiction (197), to be examined by the kind of bullying (male) doctors to whom her own ill health had made her subject. It is "society's pychic policemen," as Briggs puts it (*Inner* 133), who are largely held responsible for the suicide of Septimus Smith in *Mrs Dalloway*. Clearly linked to this suspicion of the medical establishment is Woolf's fear of becoming the subject of Freudian "psycho-biography" speculation. This anxiety may have been made all the more acute by the suspicion that her recurrent mental illness would be rich pickings for the analyst-cum-writer.

By the late 1930s, however, Woolf seems deliberately to have been laying herself open to such acts of analytical interpretation. Concurrent with the composition of *Pointz Hall* is a memoir, possibly intended for public consumption at some point, that openly deals with the incestuous sexual abuse to which she was subjected as a child and adolescent (Woolf, "Sketch" 77).[7] For the first time,

[6] As Julia Briggs points out in her biography of Virginia Woolf, Leonard notoriously described his wife as "the least political animal that has lived since Aristotle invented the definition" (*Inner* 335).

[7] It is a matter for debate whether Woolf intended to publish this work. Gabrielle McIntire suggests not, arguing that Woolf "dramatically leaves 'A Sketch of the Past' unfinished

Woolf is reading Freud seriously. She is also taking a little time to get to know the work of Melanie Klein (whom the Press had published since the early 1920s), and find out where her theories differed from those of mainstream psychoanalysis. The answer to what has changed lies not simply in her ennui with the subject of politics and the spread of totalitarianism (which did indeed dominate dinner-table discussions), but with the rather more significant evolution of Woolf's understanding of herself as an artist.

Debate in Bloomsbury circles during the mid-1920s appears to have been especially stimulated by psychoanalytic theories, and in particular the challenge they threw down to artists' sense of their own worth and vision. In Freud's writings, the sole source of art lies in an artist's infantile sexuality, and it is through sublimating this fund of unsatisfied libido into the production of literature, painting, music, and so forth, that the artist prevents her- or himself from becoming the perverted or neurotic individual that would otherwise result.[8] If, in other words, a child's "natural" narcissistic and/or incestuous impulses are not correctly channelled during puberty, these impulses will turn them, as adults, into neurotics, perverts, or artists. Unsurprisingly, those of the Bloomsbury group unaffiliated to Jones and Freud resented being lumped in with the unwanted of society. In 1924, Roger Fry delivered a lecture to the British Psychological Society (later published by the Hogarth Press as *The Artist and Psychoanalysis*) in which he repudiated Freud's position in characteristically measured but determined tones. Just weeks later, Clive Bell entered the argument with equally characteristic bombast, using a column in the *Nation & Athenaeum* to stir up a fight that dominated the correspondence pages, as Abel notes, from June to

(and undestroyed), as though to illustrate performatively her resistance to joining her patriarchal forefathers by writing out her life as a 'whole'" (150–51). Hermione Lee, by contrast, concludes that "A Sketch" was "clearly intended for publication" (18). Lee cites no direct evidence for this, other than drawing attention (as McIntire also does [150]) to Woolf's desire—stated in and of her diaries—to "write my memoirs out of them" (*D*3 125, 3 February 1927). Clearly, it does not necessarily follow that Woolf wanted then to publish these "memoirs," but neither is it made clear that she would not. As a professional writer, it is more likely that if a conscious decision not to publish had been taken, Woolf would have set down some kind of justification for this.

[8] This extract from *Introductory Lectures on Psycho-Analysis Part III* [1916/1917] is illustrative:

> An artist is … in rudiments an introvert, not far removed from neurosis. He is oppressed by excessively powerful instinctual needs. He desires to win honour, power, wealth, fame, and the love of women; but he lacks the means for achieving these satisfactions. Consequently, like any other unsatisfied man, he turns away from reality and transfers all his interest, and his libido too, to the wishful constructions of his life of phantasy, whence the path might lead to neurosis. (376)

October 1925 (15). Exhibiting boundless snobbery, Bell concludes that Freud has about as much understanding of art as a "housemaid" and should, like them, stick to doing the job he knows how to do (qtd. in Roston 190).

Woolf could never tolerate Clive Bell in full, truculent flow, but wrote to Fry to express her agreement with their counter-arguments and to thank him in terms that, ironically enough, have a distinct tinge of eroticism:

> … it fills me with admiration and stirs up in me, as you alone do, all sorts of bats and tadpoles—ideas, I mean, which have clung to my roof and lodged in my mind, and now I'm all alive with pleasure. (*L*3 132)

When in 1928 Lytton Strachey published his second "Freudian" biography, *Elizabeth and Essex*, Woolf was dismayed by what she called "that lively superficial meretricious book … so feeble, so shallow" (*D*3 208–9). Eight years later, however, Woolf's attitude has begun to change. Here in a diary entry for November 1936 is the astonishing (because extremely rare) detail that a dinner with Adrian and Karin and fellow therapist Dr. John Rickman had been enjoyable: "A good deal of p[sycho].-a[nalysis]. talked; & I liked it" (*D*5 32).[9] She adds that it was a "mercy not always to talk politics," but this is clearly only part of the story. Dr. Rickman is commended as "a solid man," and Adrian praised for being "not so aloof as of old" (*D*5 32). Woolf ignores the clear possibility that her "little brother" was less aloof because his big sister was less censorious.

By May 1938 the Freud family felt sufficiently threatened in Nazi-run Austria to seek refuge in Britain. In July of that year Freud's son, Martin, who organized the original publications of his father's work, lunched with the Woolfs; in December, he was asked to dinner (*D*5 155, 191). A month later, Leonard and Virginia (and certainly in that order) were invited to meet the man himself, whose work in translation they had published for the past fifteen years, and who was, in fact, one of the three "consistent money-makers" for the Press (Marcus 130). It was, in Woolf's account, a "[d]ifficult talk," partly because of Freud's increasing infirmity (*D*5 202). Dying of cancer (which she does not mention directly, although she must have known), Freud appears a "screwed up shrunk very old man; with a monkeys [*sic*] light eyes, paralysed spasmodic movements, inarticulate: but alert" (*D*5 202). As so often with friends and acquaintances, Woolf is more repelled by than sympathetic to the suffering inherent in illness and age. Equally, she is ill at ease with the potential for this to turn into an analysis and the unequal power relations that would necessarily result. She and Leonard sit "like patients on chairs," while Freud presides over "a large scrupulously shiny table" (*D*5 202).

[9] Gabrielle McIntire usefully draws attention to the significance of the fact that Woolf "even had a personal shorthand for psychoanalysis, 'p. a.' …" (162).

Perhaps in order to resist this feeling of patient–doctor reliance and subservience (feelings with which she was all too familiar), Woolf chooses to emphasize in her diary account another sensation, the "strain on us too of being benefactors" (*D5* 202). She is careful to record Anna Freud's apparent ingratitude to the patron who has facilitated their new life in London, and that both Anna and Martin are, as "all refugees [...] like gulls with their beaks out for possible crumbs" (*D5* 202). Equally evident, however, is Woolf's fascination and new-found respect for a man of "immense potential," in his advanced years "an old fire now flickering" (*D5* 202). In an untypical move, Woolf begins the diary entry for the following day, without preamble, by recording her further thoughts about the meeting, and returning to what Freud had said about the causes of Hitler's rise to power.

The diary account for 11 March 1939, recording the twenty-fifth anniversary dinner of the British Psycho-Analytical Society, is further evidence of Woolf's growing willingness to engage with Freudian discourse. The dinner itself is unsuccessful. The speeches are "of a vacancy & verbosity incredible," during which most of her table "sit in unmitigable gloom" (*D5* 208). Nevertheless, Woolf is sufficiently enthused by her own developing interest in psychoanalysis to "set upon" Melanie Klein and ask her to dinner (*D5* 208), despite her characteristic reluctance to devote precious "immune" time to new acquaintances. The portrait of Klein later recorded in the diary combines attraction and fear in equal measure, and as such is reminiscent of the entry on Freud:

> A woman of character & force & some submerged—how shall I say—not craft, but subtlety: something working underground. A pull, a twist, like an undertow: menacing. A bluff grey haired lady, with large bright imaginative eyes. (*D5* 209).

Perhaps most significant, however, is the evidence within this portrait that not only is Woolf susceptible to the lure of Klein's status within psychoanalytic circles, but that she is conversant—at least at a general level—with Kleinian theory. As Elizabeth Abel argues, drawing attention to Woolf's incorporation of primitive "underground" forces in this sketch (Klein's Minoan-Mycenean civilization), "Klein's psyche, in this rendition, is isomorphic with her representation of the psyche" (Abel 19).

If Woolf was by this stage familiar with Kleinian theory, the last years of her life saw her develop an undeniable interest in Freud. There is no firm evidence that before 1939 Woolf had read Freud's works in any sustained manner, although it is unlikely in a Press the diminutive size of the Woolfs' that she would have escaped any form of editorial (perhaps last-minute, panic-ridden) duties. During the course of this year, however, Woolf's correspondence and diary testify to a serious attempt to familiarize herself with the major texts, beginning with *Moses and Monotheism* which she records in a letter of July to John Lehmann (Leonard's new publishing partner) "had a very good show [i.e. early sales]—I'm reading it" (*L6* 346).[10] On 2 December she records "reading Freud" (*D5* 248), nearly a week later she is "gulping up Freud" (249), and the next day's entry is focused around the effects of this reading: "Freud is upsetting: reducing one to whirlpool; & I daresay truly" (250). Further entries on 17 December and 9 February 1940 record more reading of Freud's texts (*D5* 252, 266), and it is clear from Woolf's reading notebooks that by the end of 1940 she had read and recorded brief responses to (in addition to *Moses and Monotheism*) *Civilization and Its Discontents*, *Group Psychology and the Analysis of the Ego*, "Thoughts for the Times on War and Death," and "Why War?".[11]

Textual Play

It is appropriate that the great analyst of jokes and their relation to the unconscious should be the subject of such serious comedy in *Pointz Hall*. The first, and perhaps most pointed example is the passage that describes Lucy Swithin, in bed on the dawn of the pageant day, reading "her favourite book, on the antiquity of man" (*Pointz* 42). She spends this time, the third-person narrator condescendingly reports, "thinking of a rhododendron forest in Piccadilly":

> … when the entire continent, not then divided by a channel, but all one, was populated, she understood, by vast elephant-bodied, seal-necked, splay-footed, heaving, surging, slowly writhing, baying and, she supposed, barking monsters; the iguanodon and the mastodon, from whom, presumably, she said, jerking the window open, we descend. (42)

Gillian Beer has argued that "in the twentieth century the unconscious has often been presented in the guise of the primeval," a correlation arising from the "analogy [that Darwin developed] between ontogeny (individual development) and phylogeny (species development)" (*Common* 6). Clearly, the Freudian use of "the primeval" was only one aspect of Modernism's fascination with primitivism,

[10] Elizabeth Abel's discussion of *Between the Acts* includes a fascinating analysis of the echoing of Freud's *Moses and Monotheism* in Woolf's novel, and especially in the storylines of La Trobe's pageant (Chapter 6).

[11] Since the reading of all these works runs concurrently with the composition of *Pointz Hall*, it is not necessary for the purposes of this study to pinpoint precise dates for Woolf's engagement with each text. Given Woolf's tendency to "dip into" a small selection of books at any one time, rather than read from cover to cover in a manner helpful to literary biographers, it is in any case prudent not to be too proscriptive in this regard. (See Brenda R. Silver, *Virginia Woolf's Reading Notebooks* for detailed information.)

which as Marianna Torgovnick details came to the fore among British writers and artists with Roger Fry's organization of "Manet and the Post-Impressionists" in 1910, and his extremely influential essays on "Bushman" and "Negro" art (85–104). However, there is a critical consensus that in her famous remark that "in or about December 1910, human character changed" ("Mr. Bennett" 320), Woolf was probably referring, at least in part, to this exhibition. This is a highly charged statement, which appears to suggest that it is not the prevailing attitude to art or aesthetics that Woolf feels to have been changed by Fry's exhibition, but the current understanding of the mind. It is thus very likely, on this and the evidence below, that for Woolf, as for many artists and intellectuals during this period, Darwinism, the current vogue for so-called primitive art, and the theories of Freud formed a crucial and highly suggestive nexus of ideas.

I would argue, therefore, that the target of textual satire here is not the biology of Darwin, but the psychology of Freud, which was of course dependent on the insights of the former. Nor is it exactly correct to say the character of Lucy is the subject of ridicule. Certainly, she is made to seem naïve and childlike by the way in which, instead of processing the information in the book and delivering it concisely, she repeats all the adjectives she reads in a long mantra of "the primeval." Clearly, she is in thrall to this story, and unable to take any critical distance from it, as the interjection of the rather passive clauses "she understood," "she supposed," "presumably, she said" suggest. (A run of such clauses in Woolf's work nearly always indicates authorial irony.) The real interest of this passage, however, is in its characterization of Freud, not Lucy. Through the depiction of Lucy's wide-eyed fascination with the "antiquity of man" narrative, readers are given their first suggestion of both the danger and the truth inherent in psychoanalytic theory. The danger is that its exotic, colorful "stories" encourage the kind of credulous response Lucy is exhibiting; the truth is in the idea that the primitive lives on in us all. When the "monsters" are described as "baying" and "barking," Woolf is employing the two verbs that are used in her diary of this time to depict the broadcast voice of Hitler.[12] The suggestion that "we descend" biologically from primeval creatures, but psychologically retain them within our psyches is a matter for nervous laughter at best.

The following paragraph capitalizes on the comic potential of the scene, and at the same time sets up a number of key resonances that recur throughout the novel:

> Naturally, it took her at least five seconds in time, actual time, and in mind time considerable ages to separate the actual Grace with the blue teacups

[12] *D5:* "with Hitler baying," 2 October 1938, 178; "Then another bark… & the voice was frightening," 13 September 1938, 169.

> from the leather-covered grunting monster who was about, as the door opened, to demolish a whole branch in the green steamy undergrowth. Naturally, her glance was vague. And how she jumped, when Grace said, putting the tray down, "Good morning!" "Batty," Grace called her, after a moment; for as she felt on her face the divided glance of her mistress, that was half meant for a beast in the swamp for herself, she felt somehow queer in her print dress and apron turned to scaly hide. (*Pointz* 42*)

The repetition of "naturally" as a sentence-opener underscores with irony that Lucy inevitably will find it difficult to tear herself away from stories of the primitive and return to "reality." Lucy is more than engrossed, however. When Grace decides she is "batty" it is, on one level, the verbal equivalent of the forehead-tapping that occurs later in the book and therefore a comic judgement (albeit one not endorsed by the text as a whole, which displays more sympathy for Lucy's whimsicality).[13] All the same, there is real discomfort here for both characters. The primitive has come into Lucy's conscious mind, and when she "jumps" in alarm at the entrance of the maid, the prospect of proximity to "madness" perhaps occurs to them both. Grace is equally thrown: the "glance" of her "mistress" strips her naked, physically and psychologically, in a moment in which the comedy may only be clearly apparent to the reader. In interpreting this moment to be as aggressive as it is comically metamorphic, my reading takes its cue from Abel's persuasive comment that Lucy's "fantasied ancestors are rendered monstrous by their agglomerated parts"; in other words, by the fact that Grace becomes not merely a swamp creature but a "vast elephant-bodied, seal-necked, splay-footed, heaving, surging, slowly writhing, baying and […] barking monster." It is also disquietingly unclear whether this moment is as fleeting as "glance" would suggest, given the suspension of "actual time" that is the prerequisite of this comic sketch.

Unsurprisingly, given the direction of her anti-patriarchal, anti-militarist argument in *Three Guineas*, Woolf chooses to illustrate the retention of the primitive most clearly in relation to her male characters. Bart Oliver is, as Beer memorably puts it, "a nice enough old boy" (*BTA* xxv), but the product of an imperialist, patriarchal age, and it is in this character as well as his son, the proto-fascist Giles, that the reader is encouraged to see "[t]he man of prehistoric times surviv[ing] unchanged in our unconscious" (Freud, "Thoughts" 296). In the one episode in which this grandfather interacts with his grandson, the well-meaning patriarch elicits terror in the young child by "cock[ing] his newspaper" into a snout and surprising him first by the rapid approach of his dog, a panting, coarse-haired "wild beast," then bearing down on the boy as a "terrible peaked eyeless

[13] After Lucy is overheard telling Miss La Trobe "you've made me believe I could have played … Cleopatra," the "villagers winked; and touched their foreheads" (*Pointz* 145).

monster" (45). What makes this moment all the more poignant is that the fright interrupts the child's experiencing of an epiphanic moment of "completeness," during which time all that is right with the world centers in on the flower he is holding.[14]

> Down on his knees on the grass he held that completeness. Then there was a roar and a hot breath; a stream of coarse grey hair rushing past between him and the whole flower; a terror. A great wild beast; rushing, destroying, terrifying. He leapt up; toppling in his fright, and then saw coming towards him a terrible peaked eyeless monster moving on legs; brandishing arms. (45*)

As Beer has suggested, in his ill-fated little game Bart is on one level a personification of Thanatos, those primitive, aggressive, life-destroying impulses that inhabit the unconscious and seek their dark gratification (*BTA* xxv). It could be argued, however, that Woolf is being far more specific than this, and in fact giving her fictional version of Freud's father-figure (which is discussed at greatest length in *Group Psychology*, *Totem and Taboo*, *Moses and Monotheism* and *Civilization and Its Discontents*). In Freud's account of "pre-history," primitive peoples lived in small "hordes," each ruled over by a sole, all-powerful patriarch, who shored up his own position by allowing no other males sexual access to the females in the group and by expelling any younger (male) rivals.[15] Despite her self-confessed dislike of Joycean "indecency" (qtd. in Briggs, *Inner* 73), Woolf was not above crude innuendo, and the use of the verb "cocked" early on in the paragraph alerts the reader to a possible sexual dimension to this story. While the child is static, on his knees, the father-figure advances at his full height, before descending to just above the child's level. The power differential could not be more clear, despite the fact that in his everyday appearance Bart is an old man with declining strength and physical stature. With the apparently irresistible onslaught of the phallicised "peaked eyeless monster," Bart presents during this "joke" a disturbing, mixed threat, his phallus-substitute threatening rape and his "brandishing arms" castration. The grandfather is the daddy, and his "cock" rules.

This is not the only instance in which Woolf uses her novel to "write out" episodes in Freud's writings which particularly interested or troubled

[14] Woolf is drawing on her own moment of epiphany, which she retells in *The Waves* (7-8), and mentions again in "Sketch": "When I said about the flower 'That is the whole,' I felt that I had made a discovery. I felt that I had put away in my mind something that I should go back [to], to turn over and explore" (71).

[15] For a concise and accessible summary (albeit in an early version), see Chapter 10 of *Group Psychology*, entitled "The Group and the Primal Horde."

her. Another key example appears innocuous enough, occurring in the mild-mannered conversation between neighbors that opens the action of the novel:

> "In the Napoleonic wars," old Oliver said, missing some connection, "they had ploughed up the land. Yes, you could see the scar on the hill, where they had ploughed; to grow wheat; in the Napoleonic wars."
>
> "But you don't remember ...?" Mrs. Perry began. No, he did not remember the Napoleonic Wars. Still if you went up in a plane, you could see; he touched his fingers; the lines cut by the Saxons; the Roman road; the Elizabethan Manor House; the mound raised for the beacon; but the scars were almost healed. (37*)[16]

The gentle comedy of the moment, Bart's dry humoring of Mrs. Perry's ignorance, provides light cover for what readers of Freud's *Civilization and Its Discontents* might recognize as an echoing of his Rome conceit.[17] In an extended lesson, over three pages, Freud asks his reader to call to mind all the various transformations the Eternal City has undergone, which he lists just as Mr. Oliver lists the changes

[16] This short extract is a good example of how the text of Woolf's first draft of *Between the Acts* (*Pointz Hall*) differs from the final version, and how the raw draft is significantly more immediate and arresting in the way in which it draws the reader's attention to what is a brief but resonant moment of scene-setting. The final version reads:

> The old man in the arm-chair—Mr. Oliver, of the Indian Civil Service, retired—said that the site they had chosen for the cesspool was, if he had heard aright, on the Roman road. From an aeroplane, he said, you could still see, plainly marked, the scars made by the Britons; by the Romans; by the Elizabethan manor house; and by the plough, when they ploughed the hill to grow wheat in the Napoleonic wars.
>
> "But you don't remember ..." Mrs. Haines began. No, not that. Still he did remember—and he was about to tell them what, when there was a sound outside [...] (5)

The comedy of the moment is all but polished out of the published version, and Bart Oliver is further desaturated by the excision of a few details which in the early draft lend the character color and dimension. In *Between the Acts*, he is distanced as the "old man in the arm-chair," labelled rather than characterized by his professional status in a phrase curiously reminiscent of a newspaper report (perhaps even an obituary): "of the Indian Civil Service, retired." In *Pointz Hall*, he is the more familiar "old Oliver," made fallibly human by having "miss[ed] some connection" in the conversation, and made to appear a three-dimensional, living presence by the way in which the reader sees him counting up, "touch[ing]" his fingers. Similarly, the Freud-derived image itself loses immediacy in the more formal language and syntax of the later version, and by the way in which the scars which are still in the process of healing in *Pointz Hall*, and therefore serve as a living, colorful metaphor, become just "plainly marked" in the revision.

[17] See McIntire for an interesting discussion of this parallel (192).

to the land around Pointz Hall, noting "Aurelian's wall virtually unchanged," "stretches of the Servian wall," and the "scant remains" of "buildings that once occupied this ancient framework" (6–9). He then requests that his reader "make the fantastic assumption that Rome is not a place where people live, but a psychical entity with a similarly long, rich past, in which nothing that ever took shape has passed away, and in which all previous phases of development exist beside the most recent" (8).

In his earlier "Thoughts for the Times on War and Death" (1915), Freud dwells on the negative possibilities of the rule of retention that the Rome metaphor exemplifies, arguing that "the primitive mind" is "imperishable" and "can always be re-established," and that this can present itself in the form of psychopathy:

> What are called mental diseases inevitably produce an impression in the layman that intellectual and mental life have been destroyed. In reality, the destruction only applies to later acquisitions and developments. The essence of mental disease lies in a return to earlier states of affective life and of functioning. (286)

Hermione Lee uses Freud's essay to argue that the theory of psychic retention presented Woolf with a "relentlessly determinist diagnosis" of civilization and of her own mind, and the idea that there is "no escape" from the primitive "affected her profoundly" (724, 723, 722). This biographical reading is entirely sound: Woolf did indeed fear being "reduced to a whirlpool" (*D5* 250), unable to resist Freud's ideas about madness, and by implication unable to resist her own tendency (as Freud would have it) to "regress." The psychoanalytic linking of her "archaic heritage"[18] to the possibility of "going mad again" must have been extremely difficult to contemplate.[19]

Freud's Rome image, and in turn Bart's landscape eulogy, have equally, however, a positive set of implications. Although Freud was notoriously wary about assigning any concrete value to what would normally be classed as the highest achievements of civilization, including (and especially) art, because of their tendency to mask the true, libidinal dynamics of human life, he did concede that "even the group mind is capable of creative genius" (*Group Psychology* 83). Woolf, of course, goes further than this in her realization of the immense productive potential of the mind according to Freud, choosing to celebrate its chaotic flux. Bart is praised for "his percept[iveness]" by the text for realizing that at the end of the play Miss La Trobe does not want thanks, but an opportunity to get back to creating again (170). The terms he uses are key: what she wants,

[18] This concept is discussed in *Moses and Monotheism*, esp. 132–33.

[19] Woolf's suicide note to Leonard begins: "Dearest, I feel certain that I am going mad again" (*L6* 481).

he decides, is "a whisky and soda at the pub; and coarse words descending like maggots through the water" (170), ready to fish up (to continue the metaphor) what lies submerged in her mind, which is also, by not being assigned specifically to "the playwright," the communal mind.

A few pages on, the scene changes to the pub, and again the mind of La Trobe is deliberately elided with the consciousness of those around her, so that what is emerging from the psychic depths is specifically a shared product: "Words copulated; seethed; surged. Phrases began shouldering up from the mist. Here was the breeding ground, among the very dull; the coarse; the kindly; the imperceptive, yet shrewd" (177**). It is difficult to see beyond Woolf's glaring class prejudice here, but nevertheless her emphasis is on the limitless creative potential of the human mind, however primitive it may be, and however liable to give way to the forces of Thanatos over Eros.

Similarly, although Mrs. Manresa's claim to clairvoyance is wholly derided, when she claims that her husband could not have been killed in the Great War "without her knowing it" instantly, it is criticized for its insincerity not its lack of originality or logic, for being "sentimental; vulgar; not common, human-hearted" (68**). It is as a result, in fact, of this valuation of the "common," the "human-hearted," that Mrs. Manresa's claim to believe the ghost story that Bart tells his guests is treated with a surprising level of sympathy:

> And was she right or wrong? A spring of feeling bubbled up in her from mud that was millions of years old. And perhaps, as she insinuated, they were unfortunate to have laid their mud with blocks of marble; to find it unnecessary, indeed impossible, to believe that sheeps' bones were the relics of a drowned Lady Ermyntrude. Perhaps poetry grew from mud. (69*)

"'… [W]hat rot!,'" Bart exclaims, as the voice of dessicating reason, but the authority remains with Mrs Manresa (69**). There is no direct speech at this point, and no speech tags, but the views expressed are evidently attributable to this "wild child" (76), and at this point in the narrative they distinctly echo other narratorial suggestions that art comes from commonality. Just as Miss La Trobe receives her inspiration amongst the farm labourers in the pub, their "coarse words descending like maggots through the water" (170), so Mrs Manresa may be right not to inhibit the age-old "spring of feeling" inside her (69) nor to disown the potentially unoriginal nature of its expression.

In a radio broadcast of 1937, entitled "Craftsmanship," Woolf celebrated the "truth" (247) and "beauty" (249) of words, which far from being "useful" (247) and concrete, instead wield a vast "power of suggestion" (248). It is "their nature not to express one simple statement but a thousand possibilities," Woolf argues, and gives the following scenario as an example:

> When we travel on the Tube, for example, when we wait on the platform for a train, there, hung up in front of us, on an illuminated signboard, are the words 'Passing Russell Square'. We look at those words; we repeat them; we try to impress that useful fact upon our minds; the next train will pass Russell Square. We say over and over again as we pace. 'Passing Russell Square, passing Russell Square'. And then as we say them, the words shuffle and change, and we find ourselves saying 'Passeth away saith the world, passing away … The leaves decay and fall, the vapours weep their burthen to the ground. Man comes …' And then we wake up at King's Cross. (*CE*2 246)

It could, of course, be argued that Woolf's universalist "we" is misplaced. This word-play, and the specific form it takes, may only occur in the minds of those with the time, skills, inclination and opportunity to engage in poeticizing. It is not the veracity of Woolf's claim that is significant, however, rather the very fact that she wishes to make it, that she wants to establish the existence of a shared, choral voice.[20]

In her diary, Woolf records with excitement and pleasure making up "little poems" for use in *Pointz Hall*, even though she clearly does not rate them as high art,[21] which makes it all the more difficult to sanction a claim made in Alex Zwerdling's groundbreaking study *Virginia Woolf and the Real World* that the "orts, scraps and fragments" of made-up or sometimes misremembered poetry are intended to demonstrate the social and cultural vacuity of England at this moment in history.[22] Zwerdling maintains that "the whole literary tradition has ceased to be meaningful to the characters in the novel":

> When they try to recall the words of the "to be or not to be" soliloquy, a passage from the "Ode to a Nightingale" is the only thing that comes to mind, and even that is mangled ("the weariness, the torture, and the

[20] Emily Hinnov develops a useful related argument (borrowing a term from Falasca-Zamponi) around ideas that "choran community [in Woolf's work] enacts a 'democratic radical' aesthetic" (3).

[21] *D*5: 14 October 1938, 180: "Two things I mean to do when the long dark evenings come: to write, on the spur of the moment, as now, lots of little poems to go into P.H.: as they may come in handy …"; 28 August 1940, 313: "I was so light so free so happy I wrote what I call PH poetry. Is it good? I suppose not, very."

[22] See also Chapter 7 of Gill Plain's *Women's Fiction of the Second World War* for a reading of the choric voice in *Between the Acts* that understands Woolf's response to the community and its pageant to be far more negative than positive, in opposition to what I assert.

> fret" – 68). The poetic tags in both this scene and the rest of the novel become mere cultural detritus, bits of flotsam and jetsam floating about in the characters' minds like fragments of a sunken vessel. (317)

Rather than mangling, Woolf is playing around with literary quotation in a way that, as Jane de Gay also argues, is much more "positive and dynamic" than Zwerdling's analysis would suggest (De Gay, *Novels* 204).[23] Far from the novel portraying "a once vital cultural tradition that has lost its authority and connection with the present" (317), *Between the Acts* is an affirmation of belief in the continuing strength of this tradition, which at the same time refuses to be complacent about the challenges posed by modern life and the fascist threat. In the passage that Zwerdling quotes above, the point is not that Isa and William are ignorant of the speech in question (whether they are or not is undetermined), but how the exchange of poetic fragments allows this small community to maintain itself; in this instance, to bridge the gulf caused by Giles' bigoted revulsion for the homosexual William Dodge. When Mrs. Manresa prompts Giles to continue the *Hamlet* soliloquy, Isa senses that he will not comply and "by way of helping her husband," and rescuing the conversation, "supplie[s] the first words that c[o]me into her head" (*BTA* 76). That these first phrases happen to be Keats's testifies not to cultural dislocation but to the multivalent "suggestive power" of words, which can break loose from their originating source, the author, and take on new significances and agendas (Woolf, "Craftsmanship" 248). Later in the narrative, Giles takes his turn to use literary quotation and misquotation to express his own private emotion and at the same time dispel the desire to take more direct, potentially very disruptive, action. "'I fear I am not in my perfect mind,'" Giles mutters, "glaring at his Aunt Lucy," before uttering a string of cathartic poetic tags that enables him to express his frustration without resorting to the violence of which he is capable (100).

The "poetry" in *Pointz Hall* does not all originate from "high" literature but democratically intertwines (mis)quotations from canonical works with the folk sayings of "anon" and with the audience gossip that is patterned in such a way as to create its own musical quality. Just as Isa finishes telling William how as a child she used to stay with an adored uncle who "made up poems; aloud," Bart caps Mrs. Manresa in a game of cherry-stones familiar to Woolf's readership

[23] See Christopher Ames's "Carnivalesque Comedy in *Between the Acts*" for a Bakhtinian reading of Woolf's (word)play in this novel. Ames urges that "We should recognize that Woolf's treatment of the English literary tradition here is of a piece with the typically modernist anxiety about the disabling and paralyzing potential of authoritative tradition," and that what he sees as Woolf's parodic narrative strategy "subverts the authoritative and potentially monologic discourse of venerated tradition without losing sight of what is valuable in it" (397).

(then and probably now) as a childhood rhyme: "'Tinker, tailor, soldier, sailor, apothecary, ploughboy. It appears that I am a thief,' said old Bartholomew" (73). He suggests taking coffee in the garden and rises; the next lines return to a more self-consciously "literary" vein as Isa, while setting out the seating and thus facilitating the continued social interaction of the group, "murmur[s]" her own lyrical phrases alongside the "maiden virtue" quotation from Shakespeare's Sonnet 66 (73).[24] Not the folk-poetry of "anon," via Bart, nor the imaginings of Isa, nor indeed the line from the Shakespearian sonnet, takes precedence over the others: instead, as Jane de Gay argues, the result is a truly "choric effect" (*Novels* 206). It is perhaps only an occupational habit that critics and students of literature (not exempting myself) feel the need to attribute quotations to their sources. In *Pointz Hall* Woolf's deliberate jumbling of literary fragments makes this a difficult, even unsettling task, and the result, in Gillian Beer's phrase, is "the unskeining of literature" (*BTA* xx). It is this "casualness about source" that gives such powerful focus to "the common tongue, the common reader" (xx).[25]

As Beer also recognizes, this "casualness of source" extends to the text's representation of the social interaction at the pageant, whether it is between speakers of the same "type" or different classes. In "A Letter to a Young Poet," published in 1932, Woolf exhorted "him" to be more "interested in what we have in common than in what he has apart" (189), to seek "a whole from all [the] separate fragments" (191) that "get[ting] out, into the world of other people" must necessarily entail (191). Rather than being self-absorbed in his own role as Poet, Woolf prescribes that he "re-think human life into poetry" (191), and it is this inclusionary objective that drives the narrative of her own final novel. Chat, in *Pointz Hall*, is equally as resonant in narrative terms, and equally as important in the task of drawing the reader in to the community of the novel, as the sharing of well-known literary markers. Just as the identity of the authors of these extracts is often withheld, so the identity of the authors of the gossip and commonplace remarks is rarely made clear. Jed Esty makes the important point that whereas in "earlier Woolfian ventures into fugue-style renderings of group voice, each

[24] Julia Briggs establishes a productive link between Isa's "strange and private language that mingles nonsense and poetry" and "Bernard's yearning (as set out in his final soliloquy in *The Waves*) for 'some little language', for stories that don't 'come down beautifully with all their feet on the ground' (*TW* 183)—for an admission that the chaos and flux of nature find their counterparts in the chaos and flux of human thought and conversation" (Briggs, *Reading* 167). Nora Eisenberg also makes this link (254–55), which is variously developed in articles on *Between the Acts* by Tracy Seeley and Jane De Gay ("Bray").

[25] Patricia Laurence, citing her indebtedness to the work of Alex Zwerdling and Mark Hussey, discusses the extent to which Woolf's "communal voice" is also influenced by the relatively new medium of radio, newspaper reports, the gramophone and their collective "fugue" (esp. 227–29).

snippet of conversation could, theoretically, be assigned to an individual speaker," in certain passages here "Woolf gives one voice to a group consciousness" (101). In fact, in a step further, one irreverent story about the King's hair is embarked upon by an anonymous speaker and left incomplete for Woolf's contemporary reader to fill in the rest (112). The Queen is also the subject of a rather pointed allusion to her extravagant furniture-buying habits, and another remark starts to report what the recent newspaper coverage had been saying about the royal couple, without any clue to what it might have been (112). The clue, of course, lies in the mind of the contemporary reader, which therefore sets up a transaction between text and reader that brings another dimension of shared communality into play. There is nothing like sharing gossip, Woolf recognized: the anticipatory excitement; the pleasure of shared knowledge; the kick "we" get as we realize the risk of being compromised, and go ahead anyway.

Freud was not the originator of Woolf's evolving communitarian ideas, nor did his theories in any way delimit her artistry. He did, however, become an unforeseen ally; a specialist, apparently, in the extraordinary, who came to confirm for Woolf the very value of the ordinary, the shared, and the simultaneously fascinating and mundane.

Works Cited

Abel, Elizabeth. *Virginia Woolf and the Fictions of Psychoanalysis*. Chicago and London: Chicago UP, 1989.

Ames, Christopher. "Carnivalesque Comedy in *Between the Acts*." *Twentieth Century Literature* 44. 1998. 394–408.

Beer, Gillian. Introduction. *Between the Acts*. By Virginia Woolf. Ed. Stella McNichol. London: Penguin, 1992.

——. *Virginia Woolf: The Common Ground*. Edinburgh: Edinburgh UP, 1996.

Briggs, Julia. *Reading Virginia Woolf*. Edinburgh: Edinburgh UP, 2006.

——. *Virginia Woolf: An Inner Life*. London: Penguin, 2005.

De Gay, Jane. "'The Bray of the Gramophone and the Voices of the Poets': Art and Political Crises in *Between the Acts*." *Critical Survey* 10.3. 1998. 39–47.

——. *Virginia Woolf's Novels and the Literary Past*. Edinburgh: Edinburgh UP, 2007.

Eisenberg, Nora. "Virginia Woolf's Last Words on Words: *Between the Acts* and 'Anon'." *New Feminist Essays on Virginia Woolf*. Ed. Jane Marcus. Lincoln: Nebraska UP, 1981. 253–66.

Esty, Jed. *A Shrinking Island: Modernism and National Culture in England*. Princeton: Princeton UP, 2004.

Freud, Sigmund. *Beyond the Pleasure Principle, Group Psychology and Other Works. The Standard Edition of the Complete Psychological Works of Sigmund Freud.* Trans. James Strachey, Anna Freud, Alix Strachey and Alan Tyson. Vol. 18. London: Hogarth Press, 1955. 24 vols. 1953–74.

——. *Civilization and Its Discontents.* Trans. David McLintock. London: Penguin, 2002.

——. *Introductory Lectures on Psycho-Analysis Part III. The Standard Edition of the Complete Psychological Works of Sigmund Freud.* Vol. 16. London: Hogarth Press, 1963.

——. *Moses and Monotheism. An Outline of Psycho-Analysis and Other Works. The Standard Edition of the Complete Psychological Works of Sigmund Freud.* Vol. 23. London: Hogarth Press, 1964.

——. "Thoughts for the Times on War and Death." *On the History of the Psycho-Analytic Movement, Papers on Metapsychology and Other Works. The Standard Edition of the Complete Psychological Works of Sigmund Freud.* Vol. 14. London: Hogarth Press, 1957.

——. *Totem and Taboo, and Other Works. The Standard Edition of the Complete Psychological Works of Sigmund Freud.* Vol. 13. London: Hogarth Press, 1955.

——. "Why War?" *New Introductory Lectures on Psycho-Analysis and Other Works. The Standard Edition of the Complete Psychological Works of Sigmund Freud.* Vol. 22. London: Hogarth Press, 1964.

Hinnov, Emily. "'Each is part of the whole: we act different parts but are the same': From Fragment to Choran Community in the Late Work of Virginia Woolf." *Woolf Studies Annual* 13. 2007. 1–24.

Johnson, George M. "'The Spirit of the Age': Virginia Woolf's Response to Second Wave Psychology." *Twentieth Century Literature* 40.1 (1994). 139-64

Jouve, Nicole Ward. "Virginia Woolf and Psychoanalysis." *The Cambridge Companion to Virginia Woolf.* Cambridge: Cambridge UP, 2000. 245–72.

Laurence, Patricia. "The Facts and Fugue of War: From *Three Guineas* to *Between the Acts*." *Virginia Woolf and War: Fiction, Reality, and Myth.* Ed. Mark Hussey. New York: Syracuse UP, 1991. 225–45.

Lee, Hermione. *Virginia Woolf.* London: Vintage, 1996.

Marcus, Laura. "Virginia Woolf and the Hogarth Press." *Modernist Writers and the Marketplace.* Ed. Ian William, Warwick Guild and Warren Chernaik. Basingstoke: Macmillan, 1996. 124–50.

McIntire, Gabrielle. *Modernism, Memory, and Desire: T. S. Eliot and Virginia Woolf.* Cambridge: Cambridge UP, 2008.

Meisel, Perry. *Bloomsbury/Freud: The Letters of James and Alix Strachey, 1924–1925*. Ed. with Walter Kendrick. New York: Basic Books, 1985.

Pawlowski, Merry M. "Towards a Feminist Theory of the State: Virginia Woolf and Wyndham Lewis on Art, Gender, and Politics." *Virginia Woolf and Fascism: Resisting the Dictator's Seduction*. Ed. Merry M. Pawlowski. New York: Palgrave, 2001. 39–55.

Plain, Gill. *Women's Fiction of the Second World War: Gender, Power and Resistance*. Edinburgh: Edinburgh UP, 1996.

Roston, Murray. *Modernist Patterns in Literature and the Visual Arts*. Basingstoke: Macmillan, 2000.

Seeley, Tracy. "(Un)weaving the Shroud of the Fathers: 'A Woman's Sentence' in *Between the Acts*." *Critical Matrix* 7.1. 1993. 81–97.

Silver, Brenda R. *Virginia Woolf's Reading Notebooks*. Princeton: Princeton UP, 1983.

Stonebridge, Lyndsey. *The Destructive Element: British Psychoanalysis and Modernism*. New York: Routledge, 1998.

Torgovnick, Marianna. *Gone Primitive: Savage Intellects, Modern Lives*. Chicago: Chicago UP, 1991.

Woolf, Virginia. *Between the Acts*. Ed. Stella McNichol. London: Penguin, 1992.

——. *A Change of Perspective: The Letters of Virginia Woolf, Volume III: 1923–1928*. Ed. Nigel Nicolson. Vol. 3. London: Hogarth Press, 1977.

——. "Craftsmanship." *Collected Essays*. Vol. 2. London: Hogarth Press, 1972. 245–51.

——. *The Diary of Virginia Woolf, Volume Three: 1925–1930*. Ed. Anne Olivier Bell and Andrew McNeillie. San Diego: Harcourt Brace, 1981.

——. *The Diary of Virginia Woolf, Volume Five: 1936–1941*. Ed. Anne Olivier Bell and Andrew McNeillie. San Diego: Harcourt Brace, 1984.

——. "Freudian Fiction." *The Essays of Virginia Woolf*. Ed. Andrew McNeillie. Vol. 3. London: Hogarth Press, 1986. 195–97.

——. *Leave the Letters Till We're Dead: The Letters of Virginia Woolf, Volume VI: 1936–1941*. Ed. Nigel Nicolson. Vol. 6. London: Hogarth Press, 1980.

——. "A Letter to a Young Poet." *Collected Essays*. Vol. 2. 182–95.

——. "Mr. Bennett and Mrs. Brown." *Collected Essays* vol. 2. New York: Harcourt, 1967. 319-37.

——. *Mrs Dalloway*. Oxford: Oxford UP, 2000.

——. *Pointz Hall: The Earlier and Later Typescripts of* Between the Acts. Ed. Mitchell A. Leaska. New York: University Publications, 1983.

——. *A Room of One's Own and Three Guineas*. Oxford: Oxford UP, 2000.

——. *The Sickle Side of the Moon: The Letters of Virginia Woolf, Volume V: 1932–1935*. Ed. Nigel Nicolson. Vol. 5. London: Hogarth Press, 1979.

——. "A Sketch of the Past." *Moments of Being: Unpublished Autobiographical Writings*. Ed. Jeanne Schulkind. Rev. ed. London: Chatto & Windus, 1985.

——. *The Waves*. London: Penguin, 1992.

Zwerdling, Alex. *Virginia Woolf and the Real World*. Berkeley and Los Angeles: Los Angeles UP, 1986.

Guide to Library Special Collections

This guide updates the information in volume 15.

Name of Collection: The Beinecke Rare Book and Manuscript Library

Contact: Kevin Repp, Curator of Modern Books and Manuscripts
Patricia Willis, Curator of American Literature

Address: Yale University Library
P.O. Box 208240
New Haven, CT 06520-8240

URL: www.library.yale.edu/beinecke/brblhome.html

Hours: Mon.–Thu. 8:30 AM–8 PM
Fri. 8:30 AM–5 PM

Access Requirements: Register at the circulation desk on each visit.

Holdings Relevant To Woolf: General Collection includes autograph manuscript of "Notes on Oliver Goldsmith." Comments on Edward Gibbon, William Beckford Collection. Letters from Virginia Woolf in the Bryher Papers, the Louise Morgan and Otto Theis Papers, and the Rebecca West Papers. Related material: 41 letters from Vita Sackville-West to Violet Trefusis; files relating to Robert Manson Myers's *From Beowulf to Virginia Woolf* in the Edmond Pauker Papers.

Yale Collection of American Literature includes typewritten manuscripts of "The Art of Walter Sickert," "Augustine Birrell," "Aurora Leigh," "How Should One Read a Book?" "Letter to a Young Poet," "The Novels of Turgenev," "Street Haunting." Dial/Scofield Thayer Papers: manuscripts of "The Lives of the Obscure," "Miss Ormerod," and "Mrs. Dalloway in Bond Street." Letters from Virginia Woolf in the William Rose Benet Papers, the Benet Family Correspondence, the Henry Seidel Canby Papers, the Seward Collins Papers, the Dial/Scofield Thayer Papers, and the *Yale Review* archive. Material relating to translations of Woolf in the Thornton Wilder papers. Related material: Clive Bell, "Virginia Woolf" (Dial/Scofield Thayer Papers); 43 letters from Leonard Woolf to Helen McAfee (*Yale Review*); 11 letters from Leonard Woolf to Gertrude Stein.

Name of Collection: The Henry W. and Albert A. Berg Collection of English and American Literature

Contact: Isaac Gewirtz, Curator

Address: New York Public Library, Room 320
Fifth Avenue & 42nd Street
New York, NY 10018

Telephone: 212-930-0802
Fax: 212-930-0079
Email: igewirtz@nypl.org

Hours: Tue.–Wed. 11 AM–7 PM
Thu.–Sat. 10 AM–6 PM
Closed Sun., Mon. and legal holidays

Access Requirements: After acquiring Library card in room 315, check outerwear and *all* containers (briefcases, computer cases, handbags, folders, etc.) in First Floor cloakroom, and proceed to the Berg Collection. Traceable and photo identification required. Undergraduates working on honors theses need letter from faculty advisor.

Restrictions: Virginia Woolf's MSS are now made available on microfilm and CD. URL for Berg finding aid: http://www.nypl.org/research/manuscripts/berg/brgwoolf.xml. N.B. *All the Berg's Woolf MSS are on microfilm and CD published by Research Publications and available at many research libraries.*

Holdings Relevant To Woolf: Manuscripts/typescripts of all of the novels except *Orlando*, including: *Between the Acts, Flush, Jacob's Room, Mrs. Dalloway* (notes and fragments), *Night and Day, To the Lighthouse, The Voyage Out, The Waves, The Years*; 12 notebooks of articles, essays, fiction and reviews, 1924–1940; 36 volumes of diaries; 26 volumes of reading notes; correspondence with Vanessa Bell, Ethel Smyth, Vita Sackville-West and others. Su Hua Ling Chen's Bloomsbury correspondence.

Name of Collection: The British Library Manuscript Collections

Contact: Manuscripts Enquiries

Address: 96 Euston Road
London NW1 2DB
England

Telephone: 0207-412-7513
Fax: 0207-412-7745
Email: mss@bl.uk

Hours: Mon. 10 AM–5 PM
Tue.–Sat.: 9:30 AM–5 PM

Access Requirements: British Library Reader Pass (signed I.D. required and usually proof of post-graduate academic status, or other demonstrable need to use the collections—see www.bl.uk). In addition, access to most literary autograph material only available with letter of recommendation.

Restrictions: Paper Copies, Microfilms, and Photography of selected items available upon receipt of written authorization for photo duplication from the copyright holder.

Holdings Relevant to Woolf: Diaries 1930–1931 (microfilm); Mrs. Dalloway and other writings (1923–1925) three volumes; letter from Leonard Woolf to H. G. Wells (1941); two letters from Virginia Woolf and three letters from Leonard Woolf to John Lehmann (1941); letter written on behalf of Leonard Woolf to S. S. Koteliansky (1946); notebook in Italian kept by Virginia Woolf; notebook of Virginia Stephen (1906–1909); A sketch of the past revised ts (1940); letters from Virginia Woolf in the correspondence files of Lytton and James Strachey; letter from Virginia Woolf to Mildred Massingberd; letter from Virginia Woolf to Harriet Shaw Weaver (1918); letters from Virginia Woolf to S. S. Koteliansky (1923–1927); letter from Virginia Woolf to Frances Cornford (1929); letter from Virginia Woolf to Ernest Rhys (1930); correspondence of Virginia Woolf in the Society of Authors archive (1934–1937); letter and postcard from Virginia Woolf to Bernard Shaw (1940); three letters (suicide notes) from Virginia Woolf (1941); two letters from Virginia Woolf and three from Leonard Woolf to John Lehmann (1941). "Hyde Park Gate News" 1891–1892, 1895 (add. MSS 70725, 70726). Letters of Virginia and Leonard Woolf to Lady Aberconway, 1927–1941. Letter from Virginia Woolf to Frances Cornford. Letters from Virginia Woolf to Macmillan Co. 1903, 1908. Collection of RPs ("reserved photo copies"–copies of manuscripts exported, some subject to restrictions).

Name of Collection: Harry Ransom Humanities Research Center

Contact: Research Librarian

Address: The University of Texas at Austin
P.O. Box 7219
Austin, TX 78713-7219

Telephone: 512-471-9119
Fax: 512-471-2899
Email: reference@hrc.utexas.edu

Hours: Mon.–Fri. 9 AM–5 PM
Sat. 9 AM–NOON
Closed holidays; intersession Saturdays; one week each in late May and late August.

Access Requirements: Completed manuscript reader's application; current photo identification.

Holdings Relevant To Woolf: The manuscript collection includes the typed manuscript with autograph revisions of *Kew Gardens*, and the typed manuscript and autograph revisions of "Thoughts on Peace in an Air Raid." The Center holds 571 of Woolf's letters, including correspondence to Elizabeth Bowen, Lady Ottoline Morrell, Mary Hutchinson, William Plomer, Hugh Walpole and others. Further mss. relating to Virginia Woolf include letters to her from T. S. Eliot and reviews of her work. A substantial collection of the first British and American editions of Woolf's published works, as well as 130 volumes from Leonard and Virginia Woolf's library and a collection of books published by the Hogarth Press, is also housed. An art collection holds a landscape painting of Virginia's garden and a series of Cockney cartoons in a sketch book, signed "V.W." The center also has extensive holdings of materials related to Leonard Woolf, Ottoline Morrell, Mary Hutchinson, Lytton Strachey, Dora Carrington, E. M. Forster, Clive Bell, Roger Fry, Vanessa Bell, Bertrand Russell, Elizabeth Bowen, William Plomer, Stephen Spender and Hugh Walpole.

Name of Collection: King's College Archive Centre

Contact: Patricia McGuire, Archivist
King's College

Address: Cambridge CB2 1ST

Telephone: 01223-331444
Fax: 01223-331891
Email: archivist@kings.cam.ac.uk

Hours: Mon.–Thu. 9:30 AM–12:30 PM and 1:30 PM–5:15 PM. *Closed during public holidays and the College's annual periods of closure.*

Access Requirements: Proof of ID, letter of introduction, appointment in advance.

Holdings Relevant To Woolf: Woolf MSS and letters: Minute book, written up by Clive Bell, of the meetings of a play-reading society, with cast lists and comments on performances by CB. Dec. 1907–Jan. 1909, Oct. 1914–Feb. 1915. Players included variously Clive and Vanessa Bell, Roger and Margery Fry, Duncan Grant, Walter Lamb, Molly MacCarthy, Adrian and Virginia Stephen, Saxon Sydney-Turner. *Freshwater, A Comedy*—photocopy of editorial typescript prepared from the MSS at Sussex University and Monk's House; photocopy of covering letter from the publisher to "Robert Silvers," Jan. 29, 1976. Papers relating to the Virginia Woolf Centenary Conference held at Fitzwilliam College, Cambridge, Sept. 20-22, 1982. TS with corrections of "Nurse Lugton's Curtain." Typed transcript of R. Fry's memoir of his schooldays. Correspondence with Clive Bell, Julian Bell, Vanessa Bell, Richard Braithwaite, Rupert Brooke, Mrs. Brooke, Katharine Cox, Julian Fry, Roger Fry, John Davy Hayward, J. M. Keynes, Lydia Keynes, Rosamond Lehmann, Charles Mauron, Raymond Mortimer, G. H. W. Rylands, J. T. Sheppard, W. J. H. Sprott, Thoby Stephen, Madge Vaughan. Woolf-related archival collections held: Charleston Papers; Rupert Brooke Papers; E. M. Forster Papers; Roger Fry Papers; J. M. Keynes Papers; George Humphrey Wolferstan ('Dadie') Rylands Papers.

J. T. Sheppard Papers; W. J. H. Sprott Papers. Various works of art by Vanessa Bell, Duncan Grant, and Roger Fry, held in various locations around King's College. Access via Second Bursar's secretary.

Name of Collection: The Lilly Library

Contact: Breon Mitchell, Director
Cherry Williams, Curator of Manuscripts

Address: The Lilly Library, Indiana University
1200 East Seventh Street
Bloomington, IN 47405-5500

Telephone: 812-855-2452
Fax: 812-855-3143
Email: liblilly@indiana.edu, mitchell@indiana.edu
chedwill@indiana.edu

Hours: Mon.–Fri. 9 AM–6 PM; Sat. 9 AM–1 PM;
Closed Sundays and Major Holidays

Access Requirements: Valid photo-identification; brief registration procedure.

Restrictions: Closed stacks; material use confined to reading room; wheelchair-accessible reading room and exhibitions (but no wheelchair-accessible restroom).

Holdings Relevant To Woolf: Corrected page proofs for the British edition of *Mrs. Dalloway*; letters to Woolf from Desmond and Mary (Molly) MacCarthy; 77 letters (published in *Letters*) from Woolf to correspondents including Donald Clifford Brace, Robert Gathorne-Hardy, Barbara (Strachey) Halpern, Richard Arthur Warren Hughes, Desmond MacCarthy and Molly MacCarthy; "Preliminary Scheme for the formation of a Partnership between Mr Leonard Sidney Woolf and Mr John Lehmann to take over The Hogarth Press" (includes contract signed by Lehmann, Leonard Woolf, and Virginia Woolf and receipt for Lehmann's payment to Virginia Woolf to purchase Virginia Woolf's share in the Hogarth Press); photographs of Virginia Woolf, Leonard Woolf, Lytton Strachey, Strachey family, Roger Fry, and Vanessa Bell (Hannah Whitall Smith mss.); (Richard) Kennedy mss. (four hand-colored lithographs of Virginia Woolf: artist's proofs for RK's portfolio, VIRGINIA WOOLF: "AS I KNEW HER"; Sackville-West, V. mss. (10,529 items: includes the correspondence of Vita Sackville-West, and Harold Nicolson); MacCarthy mss. (ca. 10,000 items: papers of Desmond and Molly MacCarthy); correspondence between LW and Mary Gaither regarding publication of *A Checklist of the Hogarth Press* (1976, repr. 1986); Todd Avery, *Close and Affectionate Friends: Desmond and Molly MacCarthy and the Bloomsbury Group* (The Lilly Library / Indiana University Libraries, 1999).

Name of Collection: Archives and Manuscripts, University of Maryland, College Park, Libraries

Contact: Beth Alvarez, Curator of Literary Manuscripts

Address: University of Maryland Libraries
College Park, MD 20742

Telephone: 310-405-9298
Fax: 301-314-2709
Email: alvarez@umd.edu

Hours: Dates and hours of operation subject to change. Contact Beth Alvarez before planning a research visit.

Access Requirements: Photo ID.

Holdings Relevant To Woolf: Papers of Hope Mirrlees contain five autograph letters and postcards (1919–1928) from Virginia Woolf to Mirrlees. Also in the collection are 113 letters from T. S. Eliot to Mirrlees, and three letters from Lady Ottoline Morrell to Mirrlees. A finding aid is available at http://hdl.handle.net/1903.1/1536.

Name of Collection: Monks House Papers/Leonard Woolf Papers/Charleston Papers/Nicolson Papers

Contact: Fiona Courage, Special Collections Manager

Address: University of Sussex Library
Brighton
Sussex BN1 9QL
England

Telephone: 01273-678157
Fax: 01273-678441
Email: Library.Specialcoll@sussex.ac.uk
URL: www.sussex.ac.uk/library/speccoll

Access Requirements: By appointment.
Identification to be presented on arrival. Application for access (including contact details of referee) to be completed on arrival.

Restrictions: Photocopying strictly controlled.

Holdings Relevant To Woolf: The University of Sussex holds two large archives relating to Leonard and Virginia Woolf: The Monks House Papers, primarily correspondence and MSS of Virginia Woolf, including the three scrapbooks relating to *Three Guineas*; and The Leonard Woolf Papers, primarily correspondence and other papers of Leonard Woolf. (Monks House Papers are available on microfilm in many research libraries.) The Charleston Papers consist in the main of letters written to or by Clive and Vanessa Bell and Duncan Grant which had accumulated in their home; the library houses Quentin Bell's photocopied set; letters from Roger Fry, Maynard Keynes, Lytton Stachey, Virginia Woolf, Vita Sackville-West, E. M. Forster, T. S. Eliot, Frances Partridge and others. The Maria Jackson letters comprise some 900 letters from Maria Jackson to Julia and Leslie Stephen. The Nicolson Papers complement these three Sussex archives relating to the Bloomsbury Group, and consist of Nigel

Nicolson's correspondence relating to his editorial work as principal editor of the six-volume *Letters of Virginia Woolf*, published between 1975 and 1980.

The Bell Papers. A. O. Bell's correspondence relating to her editorial work on Virginia Woolf's diaries, a parallel collection to the Nicolson Papers.

Collection level description may be accessed at www.archiveshub.ac.uk

Name of Collection: The Morgan Library & Museum

Contact: Reading Room

Address: 225 Madison Ave.
New York, NY 10016

Telephone: 212-590-0315
Email: readingroom@themorgan.org
URL: www.themorgan.org

Access Requirements: Admission to the Reading Room is by application and by appointment.

Holdings Relevant To Woolf: Virginia Woolf. Autograph manuscript notebook, 1931 Sept. 24. 1 item (52 p.) ; 265 x 208 mm. Contains drafts of "A Letter to a Young Poet," a brief letter to the press entitled "The Villa Jones" [ff. 3–5] and a monologue by a working-class woman [ff. 44–46]. MA 3333. Purchased on the Fellows Fund with the special assistance of Anne S. Dayton, Enid A. Haupt, Mrs. James H. Ripley, Mr. and Mrs. August H. Schilling, and John S. Thacher, 1979.

Virginia Woolf. Autograph letters signed (2) and typed letter signed, dated London [etc.], to E. McKnight Kauffer, 1931 Apr. 4–23, and undated.

3 items (4 p.). Concerning a drawing of her and a bibliography of her works. MA 1679. Purchased in 1959.

Vanessa Bell. Autograph letters (83) and postcards (3), signed mainly with initials, and a telegram, dated Gordon Square (London), to John Maynard Keynes, 1907–1936. 87 items (147 p.) Concerning Duncan Grant, Roger Fry, Clive Bell, the Bell children, Virginia Woolf, Lytton Strachey, the Keyneses, & David Garnett. MA 3448. Purchased on the Fellows Fund; a Gramercy Park Foundation (Mrs. Michael Tucker), 1980.

Name of Collection: University Museums and Special Collections Service

Contact: University Archivist

Address: University of Reading
Redlands Road
Berkshire RG1 5EX
England

Telephone: 0118-378-8660
Fax: 0118-378-5632
Email: specialcollections@reading.ac.uk

Access Requirements: Appointment needed to consult material. Permission required to consult or copy material in the Hogarth Press and Chatto & Windus collections from Random House, 20 Vauxhall Bridge Road, London SW1V 2SA, UK. (Jean Rose, Library Mgr. JRose@Randomhouse.co.uk)

Holdings Relevant To Woolf: Hogarth Press (MS2750): editorial and production correspondence relating to publications of the Press including Woolf's own titles. Production ledgers 1920s–1950s. Correspondence between Leonard Woolf and Stanley Unwin about progress with his collected edition of the works of Freud.

Chatto & Windus (MS2444): small number of letters 1915–1925; 1929–1931.

George Bell & Sons (MS1640): 5 letters from Leonard Woolf 1930–1966.

Routledge (MS1489): Reader's report by Leonard Woolf on George Padmore's "Britannia rules the blacks" (1935); "How Britain rules Africa."

Megroz (MS1979/68): 2 letters from Leonard Woolf, 1926.

Allen & Unwin (MS3282): Correspondence with Leonard Woolf 1923–1924; 1939–1940; 1943; 1946; 1950–1951, including letters concerning a reprint of *Empire and Commerce in Africa*, and concerning ill-founded rumors about the Hogarth press.

Name of Collection: Frances Hooper Collection of Virginia Woolf Books and Manuscripts/Elizabeth Power Richardson Bloomsbury Iconography Collection.

Contact: Karen V. Kukil, Associate Curator of Special Collections
Mortimer Rare Book Room

Address: William Allan Neilson Library
Smith College
Northampton, MA 01063

Telephone: 413-585-2906
Fax: 413-585-4486
Email: kkukil@email.smith.edu
URL: www.smith.edu/libraries/libs/rarebook

Hours: Mon.–Fri. 9 AM–5 PM

Access Requirements: Appointment to be made with the Curator.

Holdings Relevant To Woolf: The Hooper Collection emphasizes Woolf as an essayist but also includes many Hogarth Press first editions, limited editions of Woolf's works, and translations. The collection includes page proofs of *Orlando*, *To the Lighthouse,* and T*he Common Reader,* corrected by Woolf for the first American editions, a proof copy of *The Waves* that Woolf inscribed to Hugh Walpole, and the proof copies of *The Years* and of *Flush*. The Collection also has one of the deluxe editions of *Orlando* that was printed on green paper. Other items include twenty-two pages of reading notes from 1926, three pages of notes on D. H. Lawrence's *Sons and Lovers*, thirty-three pages of notes for *Roger Fry*, a six-page ms. "As to criticism," a five-page ms. of "The Searchlight," and a fourteen-page ms. of "The Patron and The Crocus." The Hooper Collection also owns 140 letters between Woolf and Lytton Strachey as well as other correspondence, including a 13 February [1921] letter to Katherine Mansfield and ten letters to Mela and Robert Spira.

The Richardson Collection is a working collection of books and materials used by Richardson in preparing her *Bloomsbury Iconography*. It includes Leslie Stephen's photograph album, ninety-eight original exhibition catalogs dating back to 1929, clippings and photcopies of such items as reviews of early Woolf works, and Bloomsbury material from British *Vogue* of the 1920s. The Collection also has three preliminary pencil drawings by Vanessa Bell for *Flush*.

The Mortimer Rare Book Room also owns Woolf's 1916 Italian ms. notebook and her corrected typescripts of "Reviewing" and "The Searchlight." In addition, there is a 1923 photograph of Woolf at Garsington. Original cover designs for Hogarth Press publications include *The Common Reader, On Being Ill,* and *Duncan Grant*. The Mortimer Rare Book Room also has a Sylvia Plath collection that includes eight of Woolf's books from Plath's library, several of which are underlined and annotated, as well as Plath's notes from her undergraduate English 211 class at Smith (1951–1952) in which she studied *To the Lighthouse.* The collection also includes Woolf's 26 February 1939 letter to Vita Sackville-West, a 1931 bronze bust of Virginia Woolf by Stephen Tomlin, a 1923 Hogarth Press edition of T.S. Eliot's *The Waste Land,* a 1919 Hogarth Press edition of *Paris* by Hope Mirrlees and first editions of Vita Sackville-West publications. Online exhibitions are available on the Mortimer Rare Book Room's web site.

Name of Collection: Woolf/Hogarth Press/Bloomsbury

Contact: Robert C. Brandeis

Address: Victoria University Library
71 Queens Park Crescent E.
Toronto M5S 1K7
Ontario Canada

Email: victoria.library@utoronto.ca

URL: http://library.vicu.utoronto.ca/special/bloomsbury.htm

Hours: Mon.–Fri. 9 AM–5 PM

Access Requirements: Prior notification; identification.

Restrictions: Limited photocopying.

Holdings Relevant To Woolf: This collection, the most comprehensive of its kind with more than 4,200 items, contains all the work of Virginia and Leonard Woolf in various editions, issues, variants and translations; all the books hand-printed by Leonard and Virginia Woolf at the Hogarth Press, including many variant issues and bindings, association copies and page proofs; a nearly comprehensive collection of Hogarth Press machine printed books to 1946 (the year Leonard Woolf and the Press joined Chatto &

Windus) including presentation copies, signed limited editions, page proofs, variants as well as substantial amounts of ephemera, such as the *Catalogue of Publications to 1939* with annotations by Leonard Woolf. The collection is also very strong in Bloomsbury Art and Artists, especially the decorative arts, including important examples of Omega Workshops publications and exhibition catalogues. Materials include the catalogue of the second post-impressionist exhibition, 1912; catalogues relating to Vanessa Bell and Duncan Grant exhibitions; bronze medal of Virginia Woolf by Marta Firlet; oil on canvas portrait of Amaryllis Garnett by Vanessa Bell (c.1958); Portrait sketch of Leonard Woolf by Vanessa Bell; Duncan Grant and Vanessa Bell designed Clarice Cliff dinner plates; original Vanessa Bell and Duncan Grant sketches and designs for dust jackets and novels; bronze busts of Lytton Strachey and Virginia Woolf by Stephen Tomlin (1901–1937); as well as the Marcel Gimond bust of Vanessa Bell and the Tomlin bust of Henrietta Bingham. Original correspondence and mss material includes that by Vanessa Bell; Leonard Woolf; Ritchie family re: Anne Thackeray Ritchie/Stephen family; Duncan Grant; Quentin Bell; S. P. Rosenbaum mss. Large Ephemera Collection including items revealing Virginia Woolf's effect on popular culture.

Name of Collection: Library of Leonard and Virginia Woolf (Washington S U)

Contact: Trevor James Bond
Special Collections Librarian

Address: Washington State University Libraries
Pullman, WA 99164-5610
Email: tjbond@wsu.edu
URL: www.wsulibs.wsu.edu/holland/masc/masc.htm

Hours: Mon.–Fri. 8:30 AM–5 PM

Access Requirements: Letter stating nature of research preferred; student or other identification.

Restrictions: Materials must be used in the MASC area under supervision. Photocopying or photographing is permitted only when it will not harm the materials and is permitted by copyright.

Holdings Relevant To Woolf: WSU has the Woolfs' basic working library including many works which belonged to Woolf's father, Sir Leslie Stephen, and other family members. Over 800 titles came from their Sussex home, Monks House, including some works bought at auction soon after Leonard Woolf died in 1969. Later additions include: 1,875 titles from his house in Victoria Square, London; 400 titles from his nephew Cecil Woolf; and over 60 titles from Quentin and Anne Olivier Bell. WSU has been actively collecting: all works in all editions by Virginia Woolf; all titles by Leonard Woolf; works published by the Woolfs at the Hogarth Press through 1946; books by their friends and associates, especially those by Bloomsbury authors and about Bloomsbury artists; relevant correspondence and original works of art. Original artwork by Vanessa Bell; scattered letters by Vanessa Bell, E. M. Forster, Roger Fry, Leslie Stephen, Lytton Strachey, and Leonard Woolf. Original artwork by Richard Kennedy for illustrations in his book *A Boy at the Hogarth Press*; scattered letters by Roger Fry, Leslie Stephen, Ethel Smyth, and Leonard Woolf. Virginia Woolf's initialed copy of *Cornishiana*; Leonard Woolf's annotated copy of *An Anatomy of Poetry* by A. William-Ellis; Leslie Stephen's copy of *Lapsus Calami and Other Verses*, inscribed by James Kenneth Stephen. Several letters from Virginia Woolf, including two written in 1939 to Ronald Heffer, and a letter to Edward McKnight Kauffer. New in the Hogarth Press Collection are a copy of E. M. Forster's *Anonymity, an Enquiry*, bound in cream paper boards, and what Woolmer calls the third label state of Forster's *The Story of the Siren.*

Name of Collection: Yale Center for British Art

Contact: Elisabeth Fairman, Senior Curator of Rare Books and Manuscripts

Address: 1080 Chapel Street
P.O. Box 208280
New Haven, CT 06520-8280

Telephone: 203-432-2814
Fax: 203-432-9613
E-mail: elisabeth.fairman@yale.edu

Hours: Tue.-Fri. 10 AM-4:30 PM

Access Requirements: Permission needed in order to reproduce.

Holdings Relevant To Woolf: Rare Books & Mss Department: 94 letters from Vanessa Bell and Duncan Grant to Sir Kenneth Clark; Prints & Drawings Department: 4 drawings by Vanessa Bell; 4 drawings by Duncan Grant; 6 drawings by Wyndham Lewis; 1 drawing by Frederick Etchells; Paintings Department: 1 painting by Vanessa Bell, 4 paintings by Duncan Grant (including portrait of Vanessa Bell); 3 paintings by Roger Fry; 6 letters from Lytton Strachey (to Clive Bell, Siegfried Sassoon, et al.).

Reviews

Modernism, Race and Manifestos. Laura Winkiel (Cambridge: Cambridge UP, 2008) vii + 242 pp.

Manipulating Masculinity: War and Gender in Modern British and American Literature. Kathy J. Phillips (New York: Palgrave, 2006) v + 227 pp.

Given the field of modernism's recent interest in recasting its dominant or canonical narratives, pulling them out of their own hegemony, and dissolving the center from which they come, it is no wonder that many studies are beginning to embrace the task of reading major authors alongside lesser-known writers of the "periphery." The field finds itself at an exciting, yet problematic juncture in its attempts to reconfigure the way that we read high modernist writers such as Woolf, Conrad, and Eliot in an effort to displace them from the metropolitan British center, or at least in an effort to balance them with other writers of their period. The trouble, as many critics have noted, is the task of contesting the foundations of a field that is extraordinarily Eurocentric and rooted in the tattered remains of imperialism without appearing to just be playing "catch-up" with postcolonial and cultural studies. Both Laura Winkiel's and Kathy J. Phillips' new books approach this concern with fresh and dynamic readings of peripheral texts not in contrast to, but alongside, canonical themes in modernist scholarship in an effort to "usher in the new while looking backwards and sideways" (Winkiel 237). While the texts are not necessarily in direct conversation with one another, nor are they particularly focused on Woolf, the way in which Woolf's *Three Guineas* (1938) imbues each text suggests a promising direction in the project of recasting larger debates about imperialism, activism, gender, and geography.

By examining the historical and performative elements of the manifesto and its contribution to making and unmaking racial myths, Winkiel's book offers a rich corrective to what she sees as a major blind spot in contemporary understandings of how the genre exposes political and aesthetic tensions along the color line and what they say about the process of modernity (6). She views the manifesto as a liminal genre, capable of looking to the future by critiquing the past. Its genesis comes from moments of crisis that give it its performative power; thus, the manifesto is crucial for a re-imagining of counter-histories. Her argument that manifestos indicate the various temporalities of experiencing modernity paves the way for displacing narrative structure to make room for exposing racial myths and signaling alternate communities (2). Winkiel's book is divided into two sections, "Cosmopolitan London, 1906-1914" and "Transnational Modernisms, 1934-1938," each with a distinctive set of arguments that allow her to explore a wide range of documents born out of myriad social provocations. By digging into the archives, Winkiel upsets progressive narrative in favor of reconstituting a series of socio-political events through the words of the manifestos and the corresponding activism of their readers. In the first section of the book, her model is to show the metropolitan seat of modernism's influence outward onto the periphery (a traditional and familiar way of reading modernism). Her second section reverses that model to show how texts of the periphery infiltrate and alter the dominant colonial narratives of the center, and it is in this section that she considers Woolf's *Three Guineas*. Rather than choosing documents that neatly allow for the rupture of racial myths, many of the texts she explores in the first section are pro-imperialist, nationalistic rewritings of history that "make visible competing versions of community formation" and "open a space for [the] anti-colonial contestations of Anglo-European racial myths" she explores in the second section (2). Because the manifestos operate on radically different agendas and come from many locations, at times it is difficult to maintain a clear vision of Winkiel's argument, and the effect on the reader is a sense of unevenness, uneasiness, and discomfort; yet, it may be the result of Winkiel's attempt to defamiliarize the way we read modernism's trajectories. Through this method, she is able to prepare us for an unexpected repositioning of Woolf's *Three Guineas* alongside the work of C.L.R. James and Aimé and Suzanne Césaire.

The first section, "Cosmopolitan London, 1906-14," establishes a link between the manifesto and performance in the metropolitan center in an effort to destabilize conceptions about the center of modernity's production. Beginning with the women's suffrage movement's use of nationalistic rhetoric, Winkiel shows how in an attempt to recast their role in British society as participants in history, women created a contradiction in how national narratives were perceived and how coloniz*ing* female subjects determined their place in the hierarchy of culture and class (46). She illustrates this by exploring the militaristic language employed by manifesto writers, language that indicated the suffragette's rhetorical adoption of a belief in the unifying condition of war as a period that stabilizes national values (50). Alongside the textual manifestos, women of the suffrage movement employed public entertainment in the form of melodrama and burlesque. Winkiel suggests that these two forms of performance (forms which Rebecca West termed "riotous living" [59]) mobilized women to develop collectivities and adopt theatrical identities by which they could challenge hegemonic narratives by acting out in public spaces such as music halls or urban squares.

From women's suffrage in England, Winkiel moves into territory she argues is more clearly marked by racial myths and anarchic attempts at alternative national discourses as she interrogates the work of the Italian futurists, spearheaded by F.T. Marinetti. Like the suffragette's interruption of narratives in public space through the use of theatricality, the futurists attempted to stall the acceptance of linear time and historical progression by making violent speech acts. Interestingly, Winkiel's reading of futurism links Marinetti quite tightly to British and American avant-garde writers such as Rebecca West, Wyndham Lewis, Djuna Barnes, and Ford Madox Ford, a connection that is often avoided because it exposes various extremes of polemical racism and violence in the works of these writers. In so doing, she is able to continue her own practice of recasting multiple narratives of modernity, even those that cause discomfort. In particular, her reading of Mina Loy's phenomenological imagining of maternal bodies with Marinetti's fascination with machinery creates a powerful link between gender, politics, progress, and art. The third chapter of the section moves back to England and addresses Wyndham Lewis's Vorticist movement through his journal *Blast* and his contributions to the first British avant-garde cabaret, the Cave of the Golden Calf. Winkiel theorizes this space as a Foucauldian heterotopia where racial boundaries were dissolved in the name of art. However, she takes care to show that Lewis's work, especially in *Blast*'s twenty page manifesto, promotes a dangerous alternative nationalism of Anglo-Saxon superiority by both celebrating "a wild and artificial heterotopia" and "contain[ing] and coloniz[ing] the heterotopia's energies" (130, 132). Overall, this first section makes an excellent contribution to the emerging interest in manifestos, because it offers such a comprehensive close reading of the texts within their cultural milieux by aptly demonstrating the complexities and contradictions in the way in which discourse on coloniality permeates calls to action and mass culture just prior to World War I.

Winkiel's second section, "Transnational Modernisms, 1934-1938," will be of use to Woolf scholars interested in the contradictory nature of Woolf's writings on Empire, anticolonization, and women, and the uneven spread of modernism's progression through marginal communities. The first chapter rigorously explores how the rhetoric, tone, and style of earlier manifestos influence and motivate Nancy Cunard and the black transnational texts she collected into her anthology *Negro* to build up pan-African activism and bring it to metropolitan centers. Winkiel's close examination of Cunard's life and work that present evidence of alternative modernisms within diasporic communities is a pleasure to read as it shows her own pleasure in doing her research.

The second chapter in this section takes Woolf to task for the way in which the pageant staged in *Between the Acts* (1941) imagines a postcolonial world that "avoids the question of racial difference" (191). Winkiel asserts that Woolf persists in creating a history that unfolds from a white perspective without irony, a view that counters scholarship that seeks to make Woolf's views more satirical and cosmopolitan than they may have been. In her effort to rescue Woolf from the nationalistic discourse analyzed in the first section of the book, Winkiel asks a difficult question: "how might the call for an avant-garde undoing of representation in Woolf's political rhetoric suggest a space for anticolonial contestation of Anglo-European racial myths, as well as for contesting the gendered boundaries of race and nation?" (193). Her answer lies in *Three Guineas* wherein Woolf acknowledges that while her position is from within the Empire, nationalistic feeling is an "irrational" emotion (*TG* qtd. in Winkiel 193). Winkiel works to reposition Woolf, one of Empire's daughters, by asserting that the limitations placed on women posited in *Three Guineas* can be juxtaposed with the limitations placed on "outsiders" such as C. L. R. James and Aimé and Suzanne Césaire in order to challenge "European universalism and the hierarchies of value that arise from a Eurocentric model of literary historical inquiry" (194). By exposing how Woolf at once employs and critiques the manifesto, Winkiel demonstrates the limitations of the genre. Woolf critiques it for its promotion of masculine ideals, vanguardist tone, militarism, violence, and linear staging of time. However, she also applauds the manifesto for its ability to promote healthy debate within (British) society (200).

Throughout this section, Winkiel alternates between clear analysis of the text that shows Woolf's engagement with creating an alternative modernism and her repudiation of Woolf's racial blind spots that keep her thought process trapped in a Eurocentric space that supports a post-imperial world in which inhabitants on the periphery are catching up to the West. For this reason, the manner in which she sets Woolf alongside C.L.R. James and the Césaires requires her to offer parenthetical apologias for Woolf's dependence on race and class hierarchies within her writing. These small justifications work to keep Woolf and the transnational writers firmly separated despite Winkiel's desire to link them. Nevertheless, by situating *Three Guineas* in dialogue with progressivist manifestos of the mid-1930s, Winkiel succeeds in her objective of exposing the simultaneous imaginings of future possibilities and in showing that multiple modernisms, once visible, rupture linear narratives through literary and performative action.

Similarly, Kathy J. Phillips' newest book works to resituate narratives about masculine bravery, camaraderie, and sexuality during times of war. Wartime is particularly susceptible to the production of nation-building narratives, or myths. The wide scope of Phillips' study contributes to the emerging trend in studies on masculinity from modernism to contemporary literature and explores both British and American texts. This book productively fills a gap by extending her argument about the construction of male identity in collusion with the discourses of Empire during World War I to current debates about gender and the military in the United States' wars with Iraq (and the Middle East) in the past fifteen years. Phillips avoids couching her work in the discourse of trauma studies and does not venture too deeply into psychoanalysis by asking not about what war does to men (and women in the case of the Iraq wars), but why men consent to go to war in the first place. Her argument is clear: "societies which arbitrarily label a number of purely human traits 'feminine' possess a tactic useful to war making, for men are bound to detect some of these human traits in themselves—and then to worry that they have strayed into a feminine, inferior realm" (2). She explores how slang words like "sissy," "wimp," and "wuss" (insults with distinctly feminine etymology) coupled with other kinds of bullying and manipulation appear in literature about soldiering experience in an effort to show the performative nature of enlisting to prove manhood.

Phillips' previous work on Woolf shows as she subtly injects this project with hints of *Three Guineas.* While the book is not in any way about Woolf's position on Britain's great men's inability to prevent war, Phillips urges a Woolfian tone into her own analysis by employing the rhetorical devices of hesitation and reflection within the actual chapter subtitles which all employ a contradictory clause (for example, 2a, "I Fight to Prove I'm Not My Sister (but I Suspect I Am)," is also the subtitle for 3a and 4a). Whereas Winkiel's vast collection of texts feels slippery and difficult to string together into a coherent argument, Phillips' insistence on a strict model within which she applies her argument often traps her close readings. Chapters two through four are about WWI, WWII, and Vietnam, respectively, so by applying the same mode of analysis to each war, and despite historical context and analysis on sexology and gender during each period, these three chapters homogenize the wars. As others have noted of Phillips' work in the past, she is a very strong close reader and each section of the book offers beautiful analysis of a wide variety of war themed memoirs, novels, plays, and poems, many of which are critically overlooked. While Phillips offers a formidable theoretical frame in her introduction, which establishes her feminist reading of masculine manipulation to create national mythologies, she does not apply her lens as rigorously as she could to her close readings of the texts in the war chapters.

Nonetheless, Phillips' statements in her conclusion that "modern Britain and America have pushed men to war (1) by artificially polarizing gender definitions and keeping women secondary and (2) by devaluing pleasure and miseducating people about sex" are both bold and useful claims especially for those interested in the relationship between sex and violence (175). In fact, the concluding chapter is perhaps the most engaging as it responds to these two claims by considering social phenomena like the Kinsey reports, recent discussions in feminist theory on the link between sex, gender, and war, and pop cultural texts that challenge the tight close readings of the previous chapters. The Epilogue opens an important interdisciplinary link between war literature and its sharp gendering of an age gone by and the contemporary examples of war narratives coming from soldiers' experiences in Iraq. Phillips does well to include this preliminary look in her book, because despite the fanfare around the military's attempts toward gender equality, she shows that the language of masculinity is even more sharply reified now. Those who study literature must remain aware of war language's power to manipulate expectations placed on the men and women of the military. Furthermore, this new sort of war will certainly produce a body of work that redefines experiences of humanity in the face of violence and rhetorical tactics.

Winkiel and Phillips engage in asking difficult questions that challenge assumptions and accepted mythologies promoted by dominant rhetoric and are able to open up spaces for peripheral voices. Both texts encourage readers to consider the relationship between speech acts, the written text, and performance as they contribute to or defy nationalism and the place of the individual (and his or her community) within that context. Both authors are committed to exposing writers who remain "outsiders" from the canon, a choice that produces fresh material and perspectives that have the ability to inform Woolf scholarship's commitment to continually resituating Woolf's life and work to reveal new possibilities in understanding it as studies in literature embrace an increasingly global reach.

—Sarah E. Cornish, *Fordham University*

Gifts, Markets and Economies of Desire in Virginia Woolf. Kathryn Simpson (New York and Basingstoke, Hampshire: Palgrave Macmillan, 2008) ix + 200 pp.

Kathryn Simpson's *Gifts, Markets and Economies of Desire in Virginia Woolf* positions itself squarely within the trend of Modernist and Woolf studies which have sought to contextualize the themes and motifs of early twentieth-century British literature in their economic milieu. As she states in her introduction, she places herself in the company of various contemporary critics (among them Michael Tratner, Jennifer Wicke, and Glenn Willmott) who have sought retrospectively the sort of analyses that the Frankfurt School theoreticians were eager to carry out for Continental literature in their own time. In focusing on gendered, or "libidinal," gift economies through a series of close-readings of Woolf's works, though, Simpson departs from this pattern of reading Woolf via Lukács or Keynes, and instead supplements such historical and comparative analyses by posing Woolf as a sort of economic theorist herself.

According to Simpson, Woolf's works champion and exemplify a set of interrelated gift economies which stand as a counterweight to the male-dominated capitalism of her time. At the heart of these is what Simpson refers to as the "alternative feminine libidinal economy," which has the power to destabilize "the heteropatriarchal social order that capitalism seems to keep in place" (2). This basic contrast forms the main significance of Simpson's titular "Desire," a concept which, in turn, dominates her work. "Economies of Desire," for Simpson, are grounded firmly in the French feminist theory of the 1980s à la Hélène Cixous, whom she cites as characterizing a feminine gift economy "premised on generosity, indeterminacy," and acting "as a disruptive force…destabilising hierarchies and rational systems, and undermining property rites" (29). By joining Cixous' model with the main theoretical source on gift-economies in the twentieth century, the anthropologist (and Woolf's contemporary) Marcel Mauss, Simpson derives a concept of the gendered "gift" which allows for its operation in a market-like condition of reciprocity. Via Cixous, she states that it is the gift's basis in a self-perpetuating homoerotic *jouissance* which leads it to exceed and subvert the capitalist sphere's dominating force.

This conception of the gift as concomitant with indeterminacy and excess leads Simpson to two additional identifications of Woolfian gift economies. The first of these is her assertion that Woolf's "textual generosity" by way of "richness, depth and associative connections, [and] syntactic fullness" initiates a reciprocal reader-author *jouissance* of continual, ever-moving interpretation (6). Even a simple metaphor, such as Sally Seton's "diamond" kiss in *Mrs. Dalloway,* serves to introduce a "liminal space" propitious to "an ongoing exchange of meanings, associations and possibilities" (65). This economy, grounded in the mechanics of text, is joined by Simpson's wider description of a gift economy centered on genre and textual form. Simpson includes chapters on Woolf's essays and short fiction in part to argue that the publication practices of these forms, with their experimental possibilities and more direct connection to the market (via the Hogarth Press, for instance), allow for strategies that maintain literature's dual identity as commodity and gift. In doing so, they provide a market-based forum in which to invite the reader toward subversively homoerotic, feminist themes.

In her arrangement of genres and themes, Simpson assembles an elegantly balanced selection of texts: two chapters devoted to the blockbuster novels—one on the various iterations of *Mrs. Dalloway* (short story, draft, and novel), the other on *To the Lighthouse*, *Orlando*, and *Between the Acts*—are bookended by two chapters on the "essays" (including book-length pieces) and short fiction. Simpson's main approach, throughout, is to close-read, and she makes only short forays into historical or biographical context, often distilling the New Historicist work of critics like Anna Snaith in one or two paragraphs before diving into Woolf's writing. In its relative dearth of theoretical heavy-lifting (Cixous and Mauss are by far the most-cited models), Simpson's work departs from theory-laden economic criticism like that of Willmott's recent *Modernist Goods: Primitivism, the Market, and the Gift* (2008). Though Simpson and Willmott might be read productively alongside one another (especially as neither cites the other's work), it is no point of criticism that Simpson does not become overly mired in theoretical underpinnings, as in her single-author volume this provides her with a clearer space in which to take on Woolf's own conceptions.

Simpson begins at the point where these theories are most overt: in Woolf's essays. She mentions various shorter pieces in passing, but focuses primarily on *A Room of One's Own*, *Three Guineas*, "Street Haunting," "Reviewing," and "Thoughts on Peace in an Air Raid." These provide her with a setting in which to outline Woolfian strategies for the evasion of capitalism and the perpetuation of gift-giving, all of which will form the crux of her later chapters. Here Simpson makes clear her prevailing judgment (perhaps a product of our own troubled times) that consumerism is a tainting, controlling force to be combated (20). For her, the key to doing so lies in Woolf's female figures, emblematic of those outsiders whose idiosyncratic involvement with commodity culture undermines its homogenizing values (24). Simpson presents several, rather familiar Woolfian methods for this (e.g. expanding access to scholarly resources, recognizing women's creativity as a "fertilising source," 30), but she is most insightful when addressing Woolf's use of the gift (and concomitantly, anti-consumerism) as a force to resist tyranny and fascism. In applying the gift economy as a frame for Woolf's *Three Guineas* decision to donate funds without conditions—as "free gifts, given freely"—Simpson adds an innovative reasoning to this conclusion; her contrast between a true gift and a tyrannical, demanding rhetoric of gift-giving elucidates the radicality of Woolf's unconditional guinea.

In her following chapter, Simpson turns from politics to perform close (and often symptomatic) readings of the short story "Mrs. Dalloway in Bond Street" alongside *Mrs. Dalloway* and the earlier "Hours." Here, she characterizes Clarissa as the paradigmatic homoerotic gift-giver, whose generous exchanges with shop-women, as well as her conception of party-giving as an "offering," represent the continued outpouring initiated by Sally Seton's original gift at Bourton. For Simpson, Clarissa's gift-giving is also subversive, as it contradicts her husband's capitalist ideology as well as her own intermittent heteronormativity, or, as Simpson terms it, "lesbian panic" (59). In some cases, ambiguities arise regarding the class-bound consumerism by which Clarissa obtains gifts, and Simpson is forced to double-read these scenes as both homoerotic and hegemonic (57). But by and large, Simpson fights to represent Clarissa (and Woolf herself) as manipulating the market economy to more generous ends. Readers may quibble with the short shrift provided to Richard Dalloway's attempts at gift-giving, or the reading of Septimus' suicide as solely "to preserve his homoerotic 'treasure'" (82), yet those looking for a new, charitable explanation of Clarissa's shopping will surely discover it.

Simpson's third chapter combines three novels—*To the Lighthouse*, *Orlando*, and *Between the Acts*—under the thesis that their female artist-protagonists provide gifts both "material and metaphorical" (85). By expanding "artistry" to include not only visual arts but the voices through which Woolf projects her narratives, Simpson argues that the gift can be conveyed or transformed from one "artist" to another. Hence, in *To the Lighthouse* this includes not only Lily's revision of Mrs. Ramsay, but also Mrs. McNab and Mrs. Bast's lower-class perpetuation of the narrative voice in "Time Passes" (98). Simpson makes a similar claim for Woolf's democratization of artistry in her reading of *Between the Acts*' Miss La Trobe as an outsider-artist who generously spreads her creative role to her audience and actors, making her pageant an analog to Woolf's own use of inclusionary literary allusions (117). Yet the strongest of Simpson's treatments in this chapter is of *Orlando*, for which she includes a relatively extensive discussion of the book's historical role (as a gift to Vita Sackville-West and concurrent with the Eliot Fellowship Fund), as well as its dependence on a reification-defying collage of texts and characters (112). She also provides a more nuanced picture of Woolf's economic alignment by remarking that Woolf's most gift-associated novel was also, ironically, her most lucrative. Though Simpson attempts to mitigate this consumerist charge by adding that Woolf's buying-power originated from a subversive homosexual relationship and intense textual experimentation, the acknowledgment of her economic ambiguity remains a crucial point.

In her fourth and final chapter, Simpson's discussion of five stories—"The Mark on the Wall," "In the Orchard," "A Woman's College from Outside," "Moments of Being: 'Slater's Pins Have No Points,'" and "The Legacy"—opens with the premise that their experimental form "derails the possibility of the reader's easy consumption" of their narratives "as a commodity" (132). This anchors Simpson's compelling illustration of Woolf's short stories as the archetype of her gift economy: their formal innovations and allusions encourage the reader's participation in multiple interpretations (138); they maintain "a more transparent and direct relation with the market" through their publication in magazines and collector's editions; and they facilitate the subversive "smuggl[ing]" of extra-monetary, homoerotic female bonds into the heteropatriarchal literary marketplace (130-1). Simpson argues that if feminine gift-giving must persist within a market economy, stories like "Slater's Pins" show how homoerotic, anti-acquisitive *jouissance* and illumination can thrive under the cover of the pointless, commodified pin.

This sort of analysis—close exegesis that portrays Woolf as subverting capitalism and propounding homoerotic subversion—is Simpson's home-element, captured in the hyperbolic wordplay of her conclusion that "one point of Slater's pin/'Slater's Pins,' then, is to prick the bubble of heterosexual romance and open up a different way of relating, bonding, of gaining a sense of identity" (155). Such work will delight some readers and irk others, as it errs on the hermetic side of single-author (and especially Woolfian) criticism, opting for sanctification where other, recent work has pushed increasingly in the opposite direction. Such deference extends, too, to Simpson's treatment of Woolf's female characters; despite recent criticism's reading of Miss La Trobe as a cautionary figure for the artist-as-dictator, for instance, Simpson turns instead to a more traditional praise of her as a creative force in the midst of societal censure. Though Simpson does not offer her readers a criticism that questions Woolf's reign as *miglior fabbra*, her attention to Woolf's innovative role as a portrayer and theorist of gift economies is a significant complement to the surfeit of current works striving to paint the wider picture of Modernism's economic engagements. By bringing Woolf forward as an economically astute and gift-giving novelist, Simpson has done Woolf scholars and Modernists-at-large an important and *generous* service.

—Emily Cersonsky, *Columbia University*

Virginia Woolf: An MFS *Reader*. Ed. Maren Linett (Baltimore: Johns Hopkins UP, 2009) xiii + 443 pp.

I am very glad indeed that Maren Linett persuaded the Johns Hopkins University Press and editor of *Modern Fiction Studies* to collaborate on publishing this thoughtfully designed and very teachable volume. In her prefatory material, Linnet delineates the rationale and organization of the collection, which offers twenty selected articles and an Afterword by Mark Hussey. An appendix provides a helpful guide to which articles address specific works while the bibliography, organized both by date and author's name, lists all articles on Woolf published in *Modern Fiction Studies* from 1955 through 2008. Further, the volume provides a brief index of titles, authors, and topics. In the biographical notes of the contributors, a wistfulness of human evanescence resonates in the relatively recent deaths of James Hafley (2004) and Don Summerhayes (2007). The volume as a whole is both a treasure-trove of pedagogical resources and a refreshing reminder of the continuity of scholarship. Since earlier Woolfian voices should not be forgotten or overlooked or eclipsed by their successors, but all too frequently are, one hopes that, thanks to this collection, researchers will be inspired to consult prior scholarship more rigorously and integrate it into the contemporary discourse.

Offering a compelling overview of Woolf's multi-faceted cultural resonances, the volume begins with Brenda Silver's 1992 landmark article, "What's Woolf Got to Do with It? Or the Perils of Popularity," later integrated into *Virginia Woolf Icon*. The rest of the volume is similarly organized conceptually rather than chronologically. As "Granite, Rainbow and the Lure of Language," the title of the first section, suggests, the selections are multifaceted and resonant. Bonnie Kime Scott's "The Word Split Its Husk: Woolf's Double Vision of Modernist Language" (1988), the first essay, analyzes Woolf's discourse from a richly nuanced feminist perspective. "Virginia Woolf's Pedagogical Scenes of Reading: *The Voyage Out*, *The Common Reader*, and Her 'Common Readers'" (1992) by Susan Stanford Friedman, focuses on the concept of the book as a trope, addressing "the intertextuality of reading life and books" in *The Voyage Out* (66) as well as the evolution of the "common reader" in Woolf's oeuvre. Melinda Feldt Cumings, in her beautifully crafted 1972 article "*Night and Day*: Virginia Woolf's Visionary Synthesis of Reality," examines Woolf's motifs of mystical fusion and transcendence in the novel. Charles C. Hoffman's "From Short Story to Novel: The Manuscript Revisions of Virginia Woolf's *Mrs. Dalloway*" (1968), a detailed and meticulous textual analysis of the manuscript, is very interesting in itself and also offers a strong model for students interested in archival research to emulate. James Hafley begins his very short article "On One of Virginia Woolf's Short Stories" (1956) ,on "Moments of Being: 'Slater's Pins Have No Points,'" by noting "I do not suppose that many people have read Virginia Woolf's short stories with anything like the attention that is given to her novels." Hafley's observation has clearly remained accurate until quite recently—and one must applaud him for his prescient interest in this particular story, which he describes as "a beautifully accomplished artwork" that also "offers a microcosmic illustration of some of Virginia Woolf's techniques in the novels, as well as the other short stories" (116). His extended commentary is almost certainly one of the earliest engagements with the story (thanks to Google Books, I can affirm that prior, much briefer references include Deborah Newton's *Virginia Woolf* [1946] and a reference in *The New Yorker* [1944]). Joseph Allen Boone's "The Meaning of Elvedon in *The Waves*: A Key to Bernard's Experience and Woolf's Vision" (1981-82), which concludes the first section, explores the complex mystical significance of Bernard's visionary story-telling as a medium of healing and a repository of memory.

The second section of the volume, "Subjectivity, Trauma, and Community," includes six articles which speak strongly to each other. The first is Edward L. Bishop's meticulously constructed "The Subject in *Jacob's Room*" (1992), in which he integrates elements of the holograph draft of the novel to argue that "in the figure of Jacob, Woolf is not representing *character*; what she is exploring is the construction, and the representation of, the subject" (137). In "Consolation Refused: Virginia Woolf, the Great War, and Modernist Mourning" (2004), Tammy Clewell, situating her argument in the historical context of the First World War and focusing mainly on *Jacob's Room* and *To the Lighthouse*, addresses what she terms "Woolf's positive reinvention of mourning" (172) as an "anticonsolatory" means of "foster[ing] feminist grievance" (180). Karen DeMeester's "Trauma and Recovery in *Mrs. Dalloway*" (1998), too, is linked to the Great War, exploring the psychological and emotional suffering both Septimus Warren Smith and Clarissa Dalloway endure. DeMeester concludes by observing that only with such works as Pat Barker's *Regeneration* trilogy has the twentieth century been able to come to terms with the harrowing reality of this war—but tragically, she opines that such understanding will somehow "prevent future wars," a flicker of hope almost too painful to contemplate in the aftermath of September 11, 2001. In "'The Central Shadow': Characterization in *The Waves*" (1972), Susan Rubinow Gorsky (who refers, as do other early critics, to "*Mrs.* Woolf") notes in her now-classic article the distinctive recurrent patterns that distinguish each of the individual characters in *The Waves* while also examining the ways these personalities blur and intertwine, thereby "widen[ing] the boundaries of fiction" (235). Don Summerhayes's "Society, Morality, Analogy: Virginia Woolf's World Between the Acts" (1963-64) reflects on Woolf's posthumously published novel as "her last 'will,'" a work in which, for the characters and the readers alike, "the enigma of misapprehension is the only usable reality we have to begin with"

(245). The section concludes with Marilyn Zorn's "The Pageant in *Between the Acts*" (1956), an essay that argues that the pageant itself is an "affirmation of the artist's vision," capturing in "the mirror of Reality . . . the human soul, [and] creating by the radiance of that vision—Harmony" (253).

"The Ethics of Representation," is the most intertextual of the sections. It begins with Jessica Berman's "Ethical Folds: Ethics, Aesthetics, Woolf" (2004), an intricately layered argument that establishes a powerful theoretical standpoint based on the concept of "ethical folds" (266), allowing the interweaving of an overarching feminist ethic with samplings from Woolf's work. "'Robbed of Meaning': The Work at the Center of *To the Lighthouse*" (1992), by Mary Lou Emery, closely scrutinizes both the textualities of the novel and the politics of "Western feminis[t]" discourse by "examining feminist processes of self-representation and exclusion in historically specific ways" (296). Urmila Seshagiri, in "Orienting Virginia Woolf: Race Aesthetics, and Politics in *To the Lighthouse*" (2004), offers a rich and detailed commentary on raciality, drawing on Woolf's cultural and historical context as well as her texts to craft a compelling argument. Karen R. Lawrence's clever and insightful "Orlando's Voyage Out" (1992) traces both Virginia Woolf's and Orlando's own adventures both playfully and seriously, combining the sexual, the textual and the historical in ways similar to those of Woolf's own narrator in the faux biography. In "Sublime Barbarians in the Narrative of Empire; or, Longinus at Sea in *The Waves*" (1996), Laura Doyle offers an intricate inquiry into the politics of the sublime, noting that "It is as the British Empire faces the very limits such narratives of sublimity had promised to transcend that Virginia Woolf writes *The Waves*" (355). The dense intertextuality of the entire section is underscored by Patrick McGee's "The Politics of Modernist Form; Or Who Rules *The Waves*" (1992), an extended and very rigorous rejoinder to Jane Marcus's watershed article "Britannia Rules *The Waves*," published earlier the same year. In the final article, "The Jew in the Bath: Imperiled Imagination in Woolf's *The Years*" (2002) Maren Linett, the editor of the volume, addresses the conundrum posed by Woolf's conflicting anti-Fascist and anti-Semitic perspectives. Mark Hussey's Afterword comments on the future of Woolf studies, identifying five areas of burgeoning scholarship: "the 'new' modernist studies; discoveries of new material; archival research; new editions; and ethics and the role of the humanities" (422). The collection is a valuable and important contribution that traces both the history and the evolution of Woolf criticism over more than five decades.

—Vara Neverow, *Southern Connecticut State University*

Consuming Traditions: *Modernism, Modernity, and the Commodified Authentic.* Elizabeth Outka (Oxford: Oxford UP, 2009) xiii + 214 pp.

In *Consuming Traditions*: *Modernism, Modernity, and the Commodified Authentic*, the inaugural publication of Oxford's Modernist Literature & Culture series, Elizabeth Outka enters into the longstanding debate over the relationship between British literary modernism and popular culture. The "great divide" that Andreas Huyssen described as separating elite modernists from the masses has been challenged on various fronts in recent years. Nonetheless, it remains a source of contention for literary scholars, as definitions of the modernist movement grow increasingly hard to pin down. Outka does not attempt to further this debunking, but rather to reframe the discussion in a more radical way. The overarching argument of her book is that contradictory desires among the turn-of-the-century British public for the "new" promised by modernity *and* for the "authentic" comforts associated with the 19th-century past (or with a non-commercial, upper-class luxury), led to the birth of a commercial culture that did its best to offer its customers both. Affordable, mass-produced goods, which nonetheless had the veneer of authenticity about them, became the order of the day. Everything from cocoa and soap to houses and towns was made to fit the bill and marketed to a middle-class customer base not on the grounds of its intrinsic value, but of its more ineffable qualities.

This large-scale recalibration of consumerism, which Outka terms "commodified authenticity," and which is still with us today in the lifestyle marketing so ubiquitous we hardly notice it in our daily lives (the clothing catalogs that promise glamour, romance, and model-like attractiveness for the price of a sweater; the coffee commercials that suggest your Folgers comes with a leisurely Sunday morning included), permeated not only the act of consumption, Outka maintains, but the literature that emerged at the same time. Consequently, she insists, we are oversimplifying both when we assert that modernists remained aloof from the marketplace, and when we indignantly accuse these writers of complicity in commercial matters. Instead, it is the tension between the two positions (i.e., a commitment to the non-commercial authentic and a rejection of that authentic in favor of new, "modern" reproductions) and modern attempts to occupy both simultaneously that captivates Outka, as she sees this paradox driving not only scholarly debate but much of the modernist work we admire:

> The very idea of the commodified authentic—that one might unite desires for permanence, or commercial purity, or for the absolute original, with the promise that despite appearances such things might be endlessly remade, constructed, reproduced, and exchanged—was an astonishingly powerful paradox; efforts to align modernism or modernity with only one side of

> the equation (with, say, the desire to "make it new") miss how the paradox itself, with its heady promise to sustain the contradiction, functioned as a critical tool within the culture. (5)

Outka focuses her attention mainly on literary works written in the late 19th- and early 20th-centuries. This brief but distinct period, disowned by modernists and Victorianists alike, is a literary moment too often ignored. Many, many valuable Edwardian works have fallen into this abyss. While Outka has chosen only relatively (or very) well-known texts to examine here, it is my hope that her book is indicative of an increased critical interest in this period.

Consuming Traditions covers an impressive amount of ground, as Outka deftly reads E. M. Forster's *Howards End*, along with George Bernard Shaw's *John Bull's Island* and *Major Barbara*, in light of the "model towns and commercial utopias" represented by the Cadbury Brothers' Bourneville and Lever's Port Sunlight, and Virginia Woolf's *Night and Day*, Henry James's "The Great Good Place," and H.G. Wells's *Tono Bungay* in relation to the window displays and innovative sales techniques adopted by Selfridges department store. I admit that I was skeptical when I saw that Outka's longest chapter ("The Past is a Present Country: Model Towns and Commercial Utopias") was a historical account of the company towns built by Lever and Cadbury, a subject that did not immediately pique my interest or announce its own relevance to the matter at hand. Yet while I suspect that Outka could have made her literary claims just as effectively while presenting less of her archival evidence, the materials she shares here (including original advertisements for Cadbury's cocoa and Lever's soap and pictures of the companies' respective planned communities) are so undeniably—and so unexpectedly—fascinating that it is hard to begrudge them the substantial portion of the book that they occupy, except insofar as I would have liked to see in-depth readings of even more writers and more novels. While Outka has constructed a new paradigm for reading modern works in this book, her own interpretations are never formulaic or predictable. One can guess which aspects of a given work would draw her attention, but it is not by any means obvious what her interpretive account of that particular text would look like. The conclusion of the book suggests what a more widespread application of Outka's ideas might produce, as it offers brief readings of three high modernist texts—Woolf's *To the Lighthouse*, Joyce's *Ulysses*, and Lawrence's *Women in Love*—but it really only whets the appetite in so doing. This is, of course, a testament to Outka's argument, as well as to her writing and her literary sensibilities. Her close readings are exquisite and would in and of themselves justify her work.

Outka's thoughtful and original readings of the two novels at the center of her study (*Howards End* and *Night and Day*) offer even the most jaded reader of Forster or Woolf the opportunity to pause over previously unnoticed moments in these works and to reassess fixed views. The chapter on *Howards End* ("Buying Time: E. M. Forster and the Neo-Nostalgic Home") manages to produce suggestive analyses of this much-studied novel (no small feat in writing about a novel with a long and bountiful critical history), particularly in the account of Miss Avery (whose unpacking and arrangement of the Wilcoxes' things at Howards End is a key moment in Outka's reading) and in the apology for Forster's ending, which suggests that the seeming contradiction implicit in the novel's final retreat is actually an attempt on Forster's part to protect not an authentic reality, but "nostalgic desire itself—not a place of actual idyllic beauty, or a space that is actually separate from the commercial, but a place where the desire that these things might be realized can be maintained and protected" (92).

Yet it is her chapter on Woolf's *Night and Day* ("'Lustrous behind Glass': Woolf, Window Shopping, and Authentic Display") that is Outka's real triumph. Her reading of this novel should spark an all-out revaluing—and re-imagining—of this work. Putting aside traditional accounts of *Night and Day*, which see it as caught between 19th and 20th-century modes—and fatally flawed as a result—Outka, reading the novel in light of the development of Selfridges department store that she traces in the previous chapter, again sees the very tension at work in the transition to modernity as the chief point of interest. Not only does this chapter offer new insights into *Night and Day*, but it underscores the vast potential of Outka's argument for reconsidering many books that have been dismissed on the same erroneous grounds of having not entirely aligned themselves with modernity, of still bearing the vestiges of older literary forms and being thereby insufficiently "modern."

The museum-like collection of personal items or "tableau of the dead" that memorializes the Victorian era through Katharine's grandfather is contrasted by Outka (and Woolf) with the department store window displays that offer both figurative and literal light in the modern era, and the idea that authenticity can only be found in what is dead and memorialized (i.e., Katherine's Victorian grandfather) is staunchly rejected. This is a key point, as one of the great dangers of commodified authenticity is an idealization of the past at the expense of the present. As Katharine and Ralph walk the London streets and look in at the store windows, the contrast between the two eras that stand on either side of them is crystallized, and there is much to be said for the present day and the future it promises. Outka's reading of *Night and Day* as a war novel, "capturing through its later scenes of window shopping the overwhelming urge to preserve the prewar era as an oasis of nostalgic authenticity and security"—is a tour-de-force.

Notably, Outka shies away from the most obvious application of her argument—exploring the marketing and sale of books and authors' attitudes toward their own work and its promotion. Perhaps she feels this is an area that has already received adequate attention or that it is not as interesting as her other areas of exploration (fair enough), but it would be helpful to know her views in this regard. At points (perhaps because I saw the reasonableness of her claim early on and did not feel the need for constant reiteration), I felt impatient for her to take the next step and make a larger claim about the implications of this "false" devotion to authenticity for modern literature and modernism generally (perhaps even to expand the claims beyond England, considering them in a more cosmopolitan or at least trans-Atlantic context—what does it mean, for example, that both Henry James and Gordon Selfridge are American by birth?), but overall, this book is worth reading for anyone interested in Woolf or in British modern literature more generally—as well as for those interested in the history of consumer culture.

—Randi Saloman, *Cornell University*

Modernism and the Ordinary. Liesl Olson (Oxford: Oxford UP, 2009) 200pp.

"Make it new," the rallying call of one of the most influential modernist movers and shakers, Ezra Pound, is one that not only helped shape the development of certain kinds of literary modernism, but importantly also became the way in which critical responses to a vast array of literary modernisms have been shaped. One of the central narratives about modernist writing has been a Bloomian one and has had at its core the sense of rupture with what came before, specifically a break with nineteenth-century realism and its narrative conventions which were perceived as inadequate for the task of representing twentieth-century modern experience. As Woolf famously asserts in "Mr. Bennett and Mrs. Brown," the realist "tools" and conventions employed by her realist contemporaries "are death." However, more recently critical attention has shifted toward an exploration of the more complex relationship of modernist writing to its immediate literary forebears. In the sphere of Woolf studies, for instance, this has been explored by Steve Ellis and Jane de Gay. While a reappraisal of modernism's relationship to nineteenth-century realism is not the central focus of Olson's study by any means, realism's attention to the everyday and to the materiality of lived experience is one that Olson sees as reconfigured and re-valued in modernist writing. Her exploration of "modernism's commitment to the ordinary" turns the tables on decades of criticism which has channelled readers' fascination with modernist forms to focus most persistently on the transcendent, epiphanic, crystalline, revelatory and sometimes shocking moments of being which heighten self awareness and signal a new way of perception. Her attention to "a pervasive quotidian" in modernist writing contests this emphasis, arguing that modernists are also preoccupied with "the diffuse and messy particularities of [that] life" (19, 5). She explores the representation of the ordinary in the work of five key writers—James Joyce, Virginia Woolf, Gertrude Stein, Wallace Stevens and Marcel Proust—offering a detailed and nuanced analysis of the difficulties encountered, and of the multiple ways in which the ordinary seems to function—aesthetically, ethically, affectively, socially, politically and philosophically.

Olson considers the influence of philosophers William James and Henri Bergson, and weighs the usefulness of theories of the everyday put forward by Henri Lefebvre, amongst others. What proves most significant for Olson in Lefebvre's theory is the "paradoxical nature" of the everyday and the "impossibility of its representation" (13, 15). She also repeatedly questions whether the ordinary and everyday can remain so, once represented in writing, mediated and to an extent sanctified by language. She makes clear that working to sustain representations of the ordinary *as* ordinary in writing is "a tricky task" (7) as representation of the ordinary inevitably and paradoxically draws attention to a central quality of the everyday which is that it is characterized by being unnoticed, insignificant. Her analysis draws attention to class and gender issues, to the representation of wartime, and returns to a core idea which is that the ordinary and everyday provide a context into which heightened experiences can be subsumed and made useful. The quotidian works to sustain their meaning, creating a space for reconsideration and effecting change beyond the momentary flash of awareness and the shock of revelation. Each chapter explores the different preoccupations with, and "tricky" representations of, the everyday in the work of one of the five main authors.

Joyce's *Ulysses* represents "an environment chock-full of everyday *stuff*" (6) most obviously represented through the lists, which simultaneously "attempt to register and record the variety of ordinary moments that flood experience, while gleefully acknowledging realism's defeat" (35). These detailed lists and Joyce's factual style promise to reconstruct Dublin on 16th June 1904, but inevitably "the ordinary … slips away" (34) as it is either made extraordinary though the process of literary representation, or has its factual details skipped over by the reader in a way that echoes how we overlook details (and so fail to interpret) many of the banal aspects of our everyday experience. Indeed, it is the flood of everyday experiences in *Ulysses* which, Olson asserts, works to counter the possibility and importance of the epiphanic moment of transformation found in Joyce's earlier writing and privileged in critical assessments of his work. Joyce's turn to the aesthetic of the ordinary also has a political dimension in emphasising the importance of engaging with one's context in order to effect change. Ultimately, however, this near documentary representation of the everyday also acknowledges the impossibility of the task as lists both reveal and withhold information, and the variety of styles indicates this novel is a testing ground (but not a definitive model) for ways to represent the ordinary in literature.

Olson's discussion of Woolf's engagement with the ordinary similarly emphasizes Woolf's "commitment to ordinary experience" (58) as well as her recognition of the ways in which the everyday eludes literary representation, and indeed her criticism of representations of the ordinary and political which are too crass. She argues that one of Woolf's aims was to develop a style capable of conveying the experience of non-being and the everyday world of things, alongside that of the inner life as ordinary experience. Rather than seeing "psychological interiority" only as an exceptional, highly subjective experience, Olson suggests that it "is shaped by a myriad of external factors" and repeated actions, making it a shared experience and part of the ordinary (59). Although it is the heightened moments of being that provide the "shock" necessary for insight and artistic inspiration, the important function of ordinary experience is to provide a context in which revelatory moments can be translated into actual processes and can bring about change. The ordinary and everyday also crucially act as a buffer and protection allaying the anxieties and "deformations" wrought by traumatic modern events, notably war, as Olson argues is the case for Septimus and others in *Mrs. Dalloway*. At one point Olson asserts the "power of the everyday to trump trauma" (76), but it is clear in this novel that it is a privileged "ordinary" experience that provides significant protection. Clarissa's class privilege gives her considerable control over her everyday experience, whereas the pleasure of ordinary experience offers only a momentary reprieve for Septimus and Rezia. Olson also makes a strong case that "Clarissa's satisfaction with the ordinariness of events and their transitory quality is her hallmark characteristic," and accepting Clarissa's own (perhaps resigned rather than satisfied) assessment of the routines of her life and everyday events as being "enough" (72). However, I wonder whether this misses another "hallmark characteristic" of Clarissa's, which is a deep-seated sense of something lacking in her privileged life. I think there might be further scope for considering the more problematic aspects of ordinary routine and habit (perhaps as Olson develops in her discussion of Stein drawing on the Jamesian sense of habitual repetition as inhibiting progression), to explore further the ways in which habit and everyday routine can also deter change and gloss over tensions and ambitions which are perceived as out of the ordinary, especially in relation to gender and class. Olson touches on an interesting sense of the ordinary put forward by Auerbach that "the everyday is constituted by moments that are in fact indiscernible to a dominant order" (79) and this could be productively explored to complicate and nuance this argument further here.

In Stein's work radical experiments with form and language articulate the pleasure of the ordinary, domestic life and habit (a preoccupation Olson connects to Jamesian pragmatism). As with Woolf, Olson argues that in Stein the everyday is a crucially important stay and protection against the disruption and trauma of war. However, while a focus on ordinary everyday objects serves to productively disrupt the habitual associations of things in a text like *Tender Buttons*, the preoccupation with daily life in Stein's World War II writing (*Mrs. Reynolds* and *Wars I Have Seen*) is criticized for "an entrenchment in habit" (98) which "marks the limits of her modernism" (99) and which proves "paralysing and troubling" (113). Olson argues that although a focus on ordinary routines and habits may typify the bored and monotonous experience of a vast number of civilians during wartime, and indeed may pose a challenge as the ordinary "accumulates value and takes precedence over war's action" (91), it equally foregrounds "habit's political inadequacy" (101). Unlike novels like *Mrs. Dalloway* and *Between the Acts*, Stein's writing blocks out the violence of war in a way that is "both defiant ... and troubling" (104).

This creates "an extremely problematic escapism" (113) that for Olson is not found in the work of other writers she considers, for example Wallace Stevens, whose preoccupation with the ordinary and the particular has long provoked criticism for its apparent removal from the realities and effects of war. In contrast, Olson argues that his focus on the commonplace "was deeply mindful of the politics of his times," signalling as it does "the necessary negotiations between private life and the public world" (117). Although critical assessments often analyze Stevens' work in relation to what it suggests about the working of the mind, Olson argues that his work values the routines of the everyday over startling revelatory moments of clarity and that his sense of "the commonplace is as much an approach to things as it is the things themselves" and so is "shared" (117, 121). It is both personal and individual *and* part of a collectively experienced environment, as well as what absorbs attention in the face of traumatic extremes (125). Stevens' reflections on his own life, essays, letters and lectures and his long meditative poem "An Ordinary Evening in New Haven" are explored in terms of what Olson reads as Stevens' positive sense of the ordinary as elusive and "always transpiring," and as representative of his understanding and enjoyment of "the paradox of representing the ordinary without transforming it" (118).

Olson concludes her exploration of the ordinary with the earliest writer that she considers, Marcel Proust, and examines how his writing exemplifies the fundamental incompatibility between the diffuseness and atemporality of the everyday and narrative form conceived in an Aristotelian sense. In particular she discusses Proust's use of the imperfect tense coupled with a sense of "habits [that are] engaged with a specific historical world" and that provide a crucial context for epiphanies to register and become meaningful (153-4). As Olson argues in earlier chapters, habits can be "life affirming," offering a protection and safety, but also "life denying" as they guard against change and spiritual experience or transformation (152). Here she also considers habits as "mini narratives" which may give the illusion of controlling time by creating "small narratives within a larger narrative of social and historical time" (154). However, although Proust's *In Search of Lost Time* foregrounds the impossibility of a literary representation that does not transform the ordinary, his modernist representation of the everyday works to counter the limitations of narrative form as it allows for a lack of connection between all aspects of experience and adapts its shape to the unevenness and unexpectedness of ordinary life.

This decision to discuss Proust last invites a sense of chronological disorder that perhaps attests to the way Olson's own text embodies the ordinary through its chronological circling back and suggestion of a two-way continuum—"resisting a moment of summation" (151) or conclusion, just as the everyday resists the teleological logic of narrative. This sense of the ordinary is also generated by repetitions of ideas and interpretations and overlapping elements that each of the chapters have in common. The "animating tension" she identifies in "the fundamental incompatibility of the everyday with narrative form" resonates in the tensions and paradoxes inherent in the form of her own discussion (11). Her argument works through a process of layering and differentiation, highlighting obvious differences as well as more subtle distinctions, and she, like writers she considers here, is engaged in the "tricky task" of putting the ordinary into words while retaining its nebulous qualities and pleasures—a task she does well.

—Kathryn Simpson, *University of Birmingham, UK*

The Formation of 20th-Century Queer Autobiography: Reading Vita Sackville-West, Virginia Woolf, Hilda Doolittle, and Gertrude Stein. Georgia Johnston (New York and Houndmills, England: Palgrave Macmillan, 2007) x + 203 pp.

Georgia Johnston's ambitious new study traces the formation of a distinctive modernist autobiographical practice that simultaneously critiques the so-called "scientific" representations of the perverse lesbian in the sexological and psychological writings of Havelock Ellis and Sigmund Freud. Noting that surprisingly little scholarship focuses specifically on modernist autobiography as a coherent genre in its own right, Johnston finds that the convergence of autobiography and modernism generated a rich and complex "lesbian symbolic," one that necessitated the disruption and refashioning of conventional narrative practices as these four writers explored "lesbian possibilities for self-representation" (2, 5). As Johnston succinctly puts it, "narrative changes in autobiographical content and form are caused by differences in desire" (8): whereas conventional understandings of autobiographical practice foreground gestures of transparency, expressions of lesbian desire necessitated the creation of a set of aesthetic strategies designed both to inscribe lesbian desire and to evade its detection. Given the very real threat of censorship of sexually explicit material during this time, Sackville-West, Woolf, H.D., and Stein deliberately positioned their self-writing in relation to the closet "as a space, as a narrative form, and as a censoring device" (10). Reading through a wide range of genres—memoir, but also fiction, essay, fantasy, and poetry—Johnston sets out to identify these writers' aesthetic strategies as well as demonstrate how, read together, these strategies form discernible patterns that in turn not only link the disparate texts of her study but make the case for a new understanding of modernist autobiography.

Johnston develops her argument over five closely-reasoned chapters, the first focused on the figure of the lesbian in the writing of Havelock Ellis and Sigmund Freud. Ellis and Freud are crucial to Johnston's study: both sought to theorize homosexuality as rooted in biology, rather than in moral vice or mental illness, and hence both became touchstones of narrative possibility for Sackville-West, Woolf, H.D., and Stein. Further, Ellis and Freud both worked with the case study, which Johnston persuasively reads as a narrative form closely related to that of traditional autobiography. But ultimately neither Ellis nor Freud was able to disentangle their representations of the lesbian from their own cultural biases: "the lesbian was, still, for Ellis, perverse, still acted, for Freud, as a remainder of arrested development, a mark of the psychologically ill" (12). Ellis's work oscillated between two poles: "Whereas Ellis aimed to show that homosexuality had a basis in a biological natural realm, at the same time, he kept intact the division between the normalcy of heterosexuality and abnormality of homosexuality. He preached tolerance, while patronizing the homosexual as more prevalent in other races, classes, and nations than his own. Though finding a biological basis in homosexuality, he still presented it as perverse" (32). Freud, particularly in his case studies of Dora and "The Psychogenesis of a Case of Homosexuality in a Woman," imposed his theories of the family romance and the Oedipal complex on the lesbian desires of his patients, thereby equating health with normative heterosexuality: "For Freud, the lesbian woman [sic] was in a state of arrested development, was masculine in type and desire, was morally implicated in her resistance to heterosexuality and men's desires" (46).

Still, both Ellis and Freud became important catalysts for these four writers, Johnston argues, in part because they made a powerful case for the existence of lesbian desire and, in doing so, made lesbian sexuality more visible. And the intersection of theory and representations of the lesbian created the possibility of aesthetic challenges such as parody and caricature, or of alternative self-representations that depicted the lesbian in a more positive, self-defining light (20). Hence Johnston posits the autobiographical texts of Sackville-West, Woolf, H.D., and Stein as constituting an "alternative psychological narrative," one that challenges a "Western cultural system based upon the exchange of women" (22, 23). At the same time, these four writers differed considerably in the success and scope of their challenges. Johnston structures her chapters as a trajectory, beginning with Sackville-West's adaptation of Havelock Ellis, moving through Woolf's and H.D.'s engagement with sexological and Freudian concepts, and ending with Stein's production of a lesbian subjectivity independent of Freud's models. Throughout, Johnston identifies how "[t]he struggle for a lesbian developmental model, when different from those of the scientific theorists, changed their narrative choices, particularly in terms of retrospection, repetition, cause and effect, censorship, gaps, analysis, and subject and object distinction" (25).

Woolf scholars will be most interested in Johnston's readings of Sackville-West and Woolf. Johnston persuasively shows how the autobiographical portions that Sackville-West's son published in *Portrait of a Marriage* draw heavily upon sexological concepts such as inversion; indeed, Sackville-West structured these writings along the lines of Ellis's case studies in the hope that her story would interest future readers because "it will be recognized that many more people of my type do exist than under the present-day system of hypocrisy is commonly admitted" (cited by Johnston, 56). The autobiographical writings in *Portrait* reflect the schisms Johnston identifies in Ellis's theorization of lesbianism: while sexology facilitates the expression of her desire as natural, it simultaneously requires her to cast that desire as abnormal. Johnston terms Sackville-West's autobiographical writing a case of "textual splitting," finding it a "counterfeit autobiography, true in all its facts but misshapen in her chosen rhetoric" (58-59).

By contrast, Sackville-West's novel *Challenge* rewrites the autobiographical facts more positively through a fictional strategy of inversion and cross-dressing: Sackville-West recasts herself as the masculine Julian, her lover Violet Trefusis as Eve, their passion one that can easily pass in a heterosexual world (69). Johnston reads the novel in tandem with the autobiography as a type of palimpsest necessary to inscribe the "truth" of lesbian subjectivity: "It is a genre that . . . must exist palimpsestically, as Julian exists as both cover and shadow to Vita, in experiential life and in the fiction, in both locations counterfeit, first to the dominant rhetoric and second to the lesbian reality" (71).

Johnston's reading of Woolf builds upon this reading of Sackville-West. Woolf's *Orlando* takes up the sexological tropes used by Sackville-West in *Challenge*—Woolf read *Challenge* shortly before beginning her own "biography" of Sackville-West—but, in contrast to Sackville-West, Woolf mocks and parodies sexology. In literalizing gender as sex, for example, Woolf takes the concept of inversion to its logical extreme: "That literal match of sex to gender parallels the sexological idea that normally constituted sexuality corresponds with the sex of the body, and that lesbianism requires a man's soul in the lesbian body. Instead of changing clothes, as does Sackville-West's real-life Julian, however, Orlando changes sex" (75-76). Johnston then moves to a consideration of how Woolf engaged with Freudian thought in the posthumous "A Sketch of the Past," considering in particular Woolf's presentation of memory as an associative structuring device for self-representation. Woolf structures the memoir as if she were herself a patient undergoing a talking cure, Johnston observes, but she undermines "Freud's role as master, by showing that the naïve and uninitiated, the author who 'cannot work this out' can present 'this loose story' [124], retaining control of it" (90). Further, Johnston argues, Woolf's presentation of the family romance, her description of her sexual abuse by her half-brothers, and her narrative use of dreams take up and refashion key Freudian concepts: Woolf's doubled position as insider (her past history as daughter and sister) and outsider (the narrator and spectator looking back) turns Freud's developmental paradigm into a "coercive text" from which Woolf estranges herself and her readers. Similarly, because Gerald's fondling is *not* a fantasy, Woolf implicitly repudiates Freud's seduction theory, whereby fantasies of seduction point to the wish for seduction.

Two final chapters on H.D. and Stein round out Johnston's study. Johnston's reading of H.D. is particularly compelling: demonstrating H.D.'s intense intellectual and personal engagement with both Ellis and Freud, Johnston shows how H.D. refuses to see herself as perverted, "but instead as someone able to develop more fully than others" (99). H.D.'s acceptance of her own sexual experiences, and her expansion of Freud's theory of memory into her own theory of vision, made it possible for her to discern a different relationship between the individual and the group than those models developed by Ellis and Freud: here, "[i]nstead of trying to place the individual in a developmental sexual pattern or classify an individual as a sexual type, she theorizes individual development psychically and through vision, not as a group type" (99). H.D.'s sense of herself as a visionary prophet, someone *inside* myth, resulted in the remarkable memoir *The Gift*, where, employing Freud's methods of free association, H.D. envisions an "I" that "experiences moments that she could not possibly experience through her individual body, inhabiting past sensibilities, and through that transfer gaining knowledge that may help to heal the group in time of war" (115). Key to that visionary persona are H.D.'s relationships with women, with Bryher as co-creator of the visionary experience narrated in *Tribute to Freud* (an experience Freud found symptomatic of H.D.'s megalomania), and with her mother, grandmother, and other female relatives as conduits of prophetic powers in *The Gift*.

Johnston's study ends with a sustained reading of Stein's 1917 prose poem, *Lifting Belly*. Here Johnston takes issue with those critics who read Stein through a psychoanalytic lens. Conceding that such readings are insightful and provocative, Johnston asks, "would it not be possible to read Stein's work without relying upon Freud's theories to explain her, to show how she advocates an alternative culture, even while she is aware that Freud is developing his own understandings of human development within his own patriarchal culture?" (132). In Johnston's view, Stein creates a "version of female eroticism that was not Freud's and which did not rely upon Freud's" (132). Johnston goes on to show how Stein's "conscious nonsense" consists of a set of deliberate aesthetic strategies that textually embody a playful lesbian eroticism of immediacy unmediated by science and cultural paradigms of development. Citing the line "Lifting belly must please me," Johnston comments, "Stein presents the erotics as a matter of awareness and pleasures, as opposed to an erotics displaced from a childhood attachment to the mother, through an Oedipal desire, then, for the father" (136). Stein's use of the "continuous present" opens up multiple possibilities, whereby dialogue and exchange with the lover displace the "commandeering" of the erotic in Freudian theory: "Unlike Dora's desire, observed and recorded by Freud, the erotically charged lesbian subjectivity that Stein constructs . . . is mediated by exchange between the lovers, not based on memory and interpretation from a different point of time or from an observer" (142).

All in all, Johnston succeeds in establishing a new tradition of modernist autobiographical practice, one deeply engaged with sexological and psychological paradigms and deeply inventive in creating strategies for both inscribing and concealing lesbian textuality. Yet Johnston's study does leave some questions unanswered. Johnston's positioning of Stein as the "culmination" of a lesbian "trajectory" points to an issue that periodically surfaces in her analysis, the fact that Stein was the only writer here who unequivocally identified herself as lesbian. Sackville-West and H.D. were bisexual in orientation; Sackville-West and Woolf chose to remain in companionate, sexless marriages. Johnston herself does admit, in writing of the emphatically bisexual H.D., that "curtailing attention strictly to lesbian autobiography does . . . limit an understanding of H.D.'s accomplishments . . . my use of lesbian as a category, particularly with H.D., is, perhaps, still reliant on categorizations used so fully by Havelock Ellis. . . . Doolittle is . . . the writer in this book who most fully reveals such categorizations as obsolete, undermining my critical work while I simultaneously conduct my exploration of her texts in terms of these unsatisfactory categorical terms" (101). Bisexuality as a means of understanding Woolf is relegated to a footnote (162 n.4), in a move oddly reminiscent of Freud's relegation of Dora's lesbian desire for Frau K. to footnotes. I would have liked Johnston to take on more fully the ways in which the categories of bisexual and lesbian do and do not converge for her study, and why she chose to excise bisexuality as a shaping element of the aesthetic strategies she identifies here.

Another area of the study that could use further development is Johnston's reading of Freud, whose early works she considers to the exclusion of his later and arguably more relevant findings. Specifically, the writing on female sexuality that Johnston draws on—the case study of Dora (1905), "The Psychogenesis of a Case of Homosexuality in a Woman" (1920), and "The Dissolution of the Oedipus Complex" (1924)—works well for her argument, but Freud's more radical awareness that heterosexuality—indeed, *all* sexual behavior—is constructed does not come into play. The later essays on female sexuality that Freud wrote between 1925 and 1933 ("Some Psychical Consequences of the Anatomical Distinction Between the Sexes" [1925], "Female Sexuality" [1931], and "Femininity" [1933]) offer more complicated insights that could be used to expand Johnston's analysis. While these essays continue to privilege heterosexuality as a normative endpoint and continue to characterize lesbianism as a regressive retention of an active or "masculine" position, they also demonstrate Freud's growing conviction that heterosexuality is not natural, but a process of acculturation: Freud finds that heterosexuality is tenuously acquired by women, if acquired at all; because of their early erotic attachment to the mother, women retain more of their "polymorphous perversity" than do men; the "difficult development to femininity" is a process "that exhausts the person concerned." Most importantly, these essays show Freud reassessing and complicating his Oedipal model, as he discovers that the girl retains an erotic attachment to the mother that renders movement into the "feminine Oedipus complex"—an erotic attachment to the father and then to other men—deeply uncertain. Hence the Freud of the later essays is uneasily aware that compulsory heterosexuality exacts a heavy toll from women, an insight that Johnston could exploit in her discussions of writers such as Sackville-West and Woolf, whose fractured loyalties attest to their internalized accession to the constraints of a heterosexist culture. Similarly, Freud's account of the daughter's persistent, even lifelong erotic attachment to the mother is congruent with, not opposed to, the biographical mother-daughter portraits of Woolf's "A Sketch of the Past" and H.D.'s memoirs. Nor does Freud ever develop an Electra complex as an analogue to the Oedipal complex (161 n.24); he explicitly rejected this concept, developed by Carl Jung in 1913, precisely because it did suggest that developmental processes between the two sexes were analogous, a simple symmetry he adamantly opposed.

Overall, however, Johnston has usefully shown how significant a role Freud and Ellis played in the lesbian autobiographical tradition she identifies here. Further, her work on these writers' aesthetic strategies builds upon and extends the work on female modernist aesthetics of earlier feminist critics such as Shari Benstock, Sandra Gilbert and Susan Gubar, and Jane Marcus. Most crucially, Johnston locates queer desire as central, indeed constitutive of, female modernism. In that respect, she joins the growing group of critics such as Laura Doan, Jane Garrity, Eileen Barrett, Patricia Cramer, Vara Neverow, and others who have illuminated the "serpentine caves" of women's erotic relationships with each other and have asked readers to join them in that exciting exploration.

—Patricia Moran, *University of Limerick*

The Persistence of Modernism: Loss and Mourning in the Twentieth Century. Madelyn Detloff (Cambridge: Cambridge UP, 2009) xii + 213 pp.

Seventy-one years ago, Virginia Woolf took up Antigone as a figure of resistance within her tripartite treatise on pacifism, *Three Guineas*. Today, Antigone reemerges within the pages of Madelyn Detloff's new book, *The Persistence of Modernism: Loss and Mourning in the Twentieth Century*, which concludes with a compelling appeal for her readers to consider the continued relevance of Sophocles' classical tragedy. Throughout the book, Detloff calls attention to government efforts—both during and after each World War and in the first decade of the twenty-first century—to regulate the meaning of death and mourning and to prescribe "proper" forms of commemoration. She argues convincingly that the modernist works of Woolf, Gertrude Stein, and H.D. provide means for confronting the ethical and political ramifications of extensive trauma and death. Detloff's analysis of their rhetorical and philosophical challenges to dominant discourse constitutes the first half of this book. Readers may begin to glean the originality of Detloff's work from the very description of her methodology. She reads these "queer" women writers as *metics*[1]—outsiders within their culture, in their case due to a "gendered sense of un-belonging" (7), who are uniquely positioned to establish connections across borders during times of bloodshed and imperial disintegration. In the second portion of her book, Detloff demonstrates how the contemporary works of Susan Sontag, Pat Barker, and Hanif Kureishi carry on and extend the projects and ethical imperatives of Woolf, Stein, and H.D. She uses the concept of "patching," taken from the lexicon of computer technology, to argue for the practical value of thinking about the relationship between past and present. Detloff proves that we have much to learn from the ways in which Woolf, Stein, and H.D. confronted "world-shaping and world-shattering events" (4). "Modernism, in its patched form," she argues, "reminds us that there are other, less destructive ways to deal with the ambivalence of ideal loss" (11).

By focusing upon a range of modernist discourses that address loss, this ambitious interdisciplinary work aims to circumvent the definitional debates about modernism that result in binary opposition, including high/low and populist/elitist. This project also works toward forging connections between two divisions of trauma studies that often are theorized separately—the mass trauma caused by historical atrocities, and individual trauma resulting from abuse or familial loss. With a sense of urgency, Detloff demonstrates how connecting communal and

[1] Detloff first defines the term as "subjects who belong, but not quite fully, to a culture" (4). Significantly, she calls attention to its much earlier use within Sophocles. After Creon delivers his death sentence, Antigone claims this identity as an expression of her "statelessness and expulsion from the familial" (7).

private traumas may be a means of countering the efforts to depersonalize the effects of sweeping violence.

Her timely study draws largely from the critical frameworks of queer theory, trauma studies, and post-colonial theory as she reveals how the construction of national subjects is contingent upon the exclusion of others as well as the ongoing performance of national identity. An analysis of rhetoric is central to her argument. Fittingly, she explores "the function of (and the felt need for) apocalyptic rhetoric" (4) during and after times of terrible suffering and loss. Detloff actively criticizes "the ideology of death," a term she borrows from Herbert Marcuse that describes the belief that death gives meaning to life, or that life may somehow be "redeemed" through death. In Woolf, Stein, and H.D., she finds resistance to this dominant ideology, which seeks to generalize loss and use it for political gain. Detloff exposes the efforts of T.S. Eliot, Ezra Pound, and W.B. Yeats to aestheticize and glorify death. The juxtaposition of stanzas from their poems with the more ethically responsible writings of Woolf, Stein, and H.D. brilliantly demonstrates the strength of Detloff's argument. *Trilogy* is a noted exception that Detloff addresses within her chapter on H.D.

The book's guiding questions—How do we represent and commemorate the particularity of loss? How do we formulate "non-lethal (non-suicidal) responses to death-bearing forms of power?" (11). How do we resist apocalyptic narratives?—provide much more than a lens for reading modernist expressions of loss. Through her constant references to present day atrocities such as Sarajevo, Darfur, September 11th, and the war in Afghanistan, Detloff reminds us of the threat to human life when these questions are not addressed.

The first section of Detloff's book, "War, time, trauma," includes individual chapters on Woolf, Stein, and H.D. that examine the treatment of death and mourning primarily through close readings of interwar texts. The chapter on Woolf is arguably her strongest. Detloff addresses *A Room of One's Own*, *Mrs. Dalloway*, and other fiction and autobiographical selections in passing, but she dedicates most of the chapter to *Three Guineas* and *Between the Acts*. Resisting the unsettling assertion that trauma is "unspeakable," Detloff strongly suggests it may be more aptly termed "unhearable," as the listener lacks a social, political, or ethical context for understanding suffering (29). She credits Woolf with creating prose that communicates suffering by tracing its effects. Detloff then shows how Woolf's "radial" style and use of apophasis actively refuse the logic of substitution that permits loss to mean something else.

Reading against scholarship that positions *Between the Acts* as foreshadowing Woolf's suicide, Detloff argues persuasively that the novel is a sign of the author's "political engagement, rather than despair" (34). She contends, "Woolf, by investing the historical moment of June 1939 with many possibilities seen from multiple viewpoints, was able to circumvent the 'irresistible' closed circuitry of tragically emplotting the historical events she was living through" (35). Detloff offers an innovative reading of La Trobe's pageant, which she insists anticipates the theoretical work of Judith Butler and Homi K. Bhabha in its depiction of history and national identity as performative. Detloff's compelling reading of *Between the Acts* calls attention to the profound significance of the pageant and its ability to demonstrate that the constitution of national subjects relies upon citation as well as "the logic of repudiation" (44). Woolf's novel ingeniously reveals that national identity is dependent upon "violent exclusion, rather than the putatively innate bonds of Englishness" (35).

Woolf scholars will appreciate that the writer's influence and resilience remain a thread throughout the entire book. Detloff concedes, "Although it would be foolhardy to suggest that a single author could adequately attend to the concerns outlined in my introduction, Woolf did address many of the issues that still haunt us in a patched but persistent modernism today" (23). She argues that through both form and philosophy, Woolf confronts the particularity of loss, addresses the ethical questions raised by commemorating such loss, and emphasizes the necessity of formulating non-violent responses to destructive sources of power.

Detloff's chapter on Stein begins with a critical evaluation of her iconic status, which many have argued prevents earnest engagement with Stein's texts. Detloff offers a comprehensive overview of scholarly readings of Stein's size, gender, sexuality, Jewish heritage, and flirtation with fascism. By acknowledging the complexity of her circumstances and subjectivity, Detloff refuses to oversimplify the author by placing her in a single category or under a single political rubric. Her discussion then turns to the ethics of Stein's "antimetaphor," wherein the repetition of phrases such as "dead is dead" may be read as a refusal to turn death into a type of rebirth (70). Like Woolf, Stein wanted to reveal the violence inherent in the construction of national subjects, a concern Detloff shows to be especially germane to *The Making of Americans*. Stein's detective stories also operate in service to this analysis by revealing, Detloff argues, "the constructed nature of all historical narratives, even those which leave out the story of their construction" (76).

In her chapter on H.D., Detloff argues that the apocalyptic visions within *Trilogy* bolster the ideology of death prevalent in the poetry of Eliot and Yeats. However, Detloff shows that several of H.D.'s other texts, namely the "Madrigal" trilogy, *The Gift*, and *Pilate's Wife,* more successfully navigate the ethical terrain of commemoration. *The Gift*, for example, demonstrates that the evaluation of the meaning of death is influenced by gender, and subsequently "questions the notion of a 'useful death' altogether" (82).

The second section of *The Persistence of Modernism*, "The modernist patch," begins by refuting Raymond Williams's assertion that modernism lives on only in its aesthetic form and proceeds by examining the persistence of modernism through an analysis of works primarily by Susan Sontag, Pat Barker, and Hanif Kureishi. The Bush Administration's egregious abuse of power and its use of patriotic rhetoric highlight for Detloff the "urgency of articulating the limits of 'sentimental nationalism'" while continuing to resist "cosmopolitan outrage" (122). Detloff examines the role of the witness in relation to Sontag's work and, in doing so, asserts that it is "necessary to examine social conditions that might dull or sharpen our ability to recognize atrocity when we see it, or see it represented" (123). Detloff successfully counters Sontag's frustration with images—"the impossibility of 'our' ever understanding the horror" (127)—by concluding that "this encounter with otherness need not be futile" even though it is partial (128). Drawing on Woolf, John Berger, and Jeanette Winterson, Detloff cogently asserts, "An understanding of one's own location within othering and privileging discourses demands that we be able to recognize a relationship with the other that is dependent upon neither identification nor the premise of absolute alterity" (129).

Detloff suggests that Woolf and Pat Barker's works may offer a way out of Sontag's impasse. Barker emphasizes the importance of self-positioning within *Double Vision*, that is, "find[ing] the proper balance between empathy [...] and appropriation" which depends upon "recognizing our own capacity to do violence, and our own potential vulnerability to violence" (133).

Within this same chapter, Detloff's assessment of Sontag's work duly scrutinizes Sontag's strident evaluations of *Three Guineas*. Although judicious in her criticism, Detloff accuses the theorist of both failing to grasp Woolf's irony and for overlooking the scholarship of Diane Gillespie and Maggie Humm that demonstrates that Woolf "was not naïve about the rhetoricity of photography" (128).

Detloff's subsequent chapter fruitfully explores the ethical consequences that might emerge from "the productive intimacies and transformative counterpublics" of Woolf and Kureishi (137). She suggests that their depictions of queer metic relationships provide "examples of intimacies based on recognition of vulnerability, interdependence, and impermanence, rather than on domination or normativity" (137), and may offer "alternatives to nationalistic bonds that can lead to war, racism, and fanatical violence" (138). Detloff's examination of metic intimacies probes the possibilities and limitations of such relationships in *The Years*, "Old Bloomsbury," Woolf's relationship with Victoria Ocampo, and a handful of Kureishi's novels and screenplays.

Detloff's final chapter examines representations of Woolf's suicide in London newspapers at the time of her death as well as its problematic depiction within Stephen Daldry's film, *The Hours*. She offers a particularly pointed critique of the different interpretations of the suicides of Walter Benjamin and Woolf based on gendered readings of their deaths. Although she recognizes the differing circumstances surrounding their final acts, Detloff notes that Benjamin's suicide has been frequently read as a heroic protest while Woolf's suicide has been cast as selfish and unpatriotic or made to coincide with some imagined failure in her work (156). Detloff labels Woolf's suicide "neither craven nor heroic," but uses Marcuse's analysis of the ideology of death to suggest that Woolf's final act was one of resistance and was "consistent with the pacifist political philosophy that she espoused for most of her life" (159). Although Woolf's premeditated suicide may be read as a refusal to accept death as the *telos* of life and as a challenge to the state's control over an individual's life and death, recognizing her suicide as an act of "freedom" remains unsettling. Detloff is right to challenge the limitations of earlier interpretations of Woolf's death; however, her own analysis seems equally oversimplified. In fact, Detloff's hurried and insufficient treatment of this delicate issue comes as a surprise at the end of this sensitive and rather nuanced study. A thorough examination of Woolf's mental illness and its potential impact upon her work appears within the earlier chapter on the author. While this discussion in many ways anticipates and lays the groundwork for this later assessment, the complex issue of Woolf's suicide demands further attention.

Despite this shortcoming, Detloff's book deserves enormous praise for the immense ground that it covers. *The Persistence of Modernism* performs valuable work within the field of literature while also adding to film and trauma studies. Her incisive analysis of the politics and rhetoric of public mourning seems a timely contribution given our current historical moment. Furthermore, modernist scholars will find that Detloff's work adds fine distinctions and variations to the gendered readings of modernism, taking important work like Bonnie Kime Scott's *The Gender of Modernism* in new directions. Detloff's book, with its emphasis upon the ethical achievements of Woolf, Stein, and H.D. as "queer" metics, makes great strides by addressing important facets of modernism's "unassessed vitality."[2]

—Meghan C. Fox, *State University of New York, Stony Brook*

[2] In her introduction to *The Gender of Modernism*, Scott argues that "in relation to gender, modernism has a great deal of unassessed vitality in form and content, with its own intricate and varied theory." See *The Gender of Modernism: An Anthology*. Ed. Bonnie Kime Scott (Bloomington: Indiana UP, 1990): 3.

Modernism, Media, and Propaganda: British Narrative from 1900 to 1945. Mark Wollaeger (Princeton and Oxford: Princeton UP, 2006) xxv + 335 pp.

Tracing the evolving relationship between modernism and propaganda through the first four decades of the twentieth century, Mark Wollaeger demonstrates not only that modernism came to define itself in opposition to propaganda, but also, and more unexpectedly, that modernism and propaganda had a great deal in common. *Modernism, Media, and Propaganda* offers a corrective to persistent conceptions of modernism and propaganda as antithetical in part by focusing on the role of new media, which, as the sequence of the title suggests, linked the two in shared concerns and even blurred their differences. We are reminded, for instance, that both could be comfortingly totalizing in the face of modernity's overwhelming flows of information and both could be ambiguous. In six chapters, Wollaeger shows how propaganda and modernism were not statically at odds, but rather "sometimes agonistic, sometimes allied, and sometimes indistinguishable" (xiv). Compelling readings of novels by Conrad, Woolf, Joyce, and Ford, and of films by Hitchcock and Orson Welles, place them in the context of the authors' various engagements with propaganda.

In its focus on modernist involvement in contemporary mass culture, the book is, as Wollaeger notes, an instance of what has been called New Modernist Studies. But, whereas much attention of late has been paid to the influence of new technologies on modernist writers, this study contributes a new consideration of modernists' response to, and even participation in, the proliferation of propaganda that the new media made possible.[1] In a fascinating exploration of the complicity of literature with state affairs (and representing a degree of political influence long lost to literature—film would soon be the culturally-dominant medium employed for propaganda), the Introduction describes the British government's creation in the First World War of a propaganda campaign that secretly enlisted well known and influential authors. Conrad and Ford were two among many—including, we might note, Bennett, Galsworthy, and Wells—who published under their own names in commercial and university presses subsidized by the government. In a later incarnation of this campaign, Hitchcock made short films for Britain's new Ministry of Information (MoI) in World War II. Wollaeger's readings of *The Good Soldier*, *The Secret Agent*, *Sabotage* (Hitchcock's 1936 film adaptation of Conrad's *Secret Agent*), and *Citizen Kane* alongside propagandistic work by Ford, Conrad, Hitchcock and Welles, respectively, reveal modernism and propaganda as entangled enterprises.

[1] A Woolf scholar might recall, for instance, Leslie Hankins on film, Michele Pridmore-Brown on gramophones, and many essays in Pamela Caughie's edited collection *Virginia Woolf in the Age of Mechanical Reproduction.*

Wollaeger uses a different approach in the chapters on Woolf and Joyce, who did not write any state-sponsored propaganda. Through analyses of colonial picture postcards as they inform *The Voyage Out* and recruiting posters as they appear in *Ulysses*, Wollaeger is concerned instead with Woolf and Joyce's engagement in "the propaganda of everyday life." These chapters suffer somewhat from the loss of specificity in "propaganda," which in its "diffuse" form begins to seem coterminous with "shared ethos," as he notes, or even "ideology," but the material under examination is compelling and Wollaeger offers an important contribution to our understanding of the novels' intertexts.

Examining *The Voyage Out* in conjunction with colonial picture postcards and Leonard Woolf's first novel, *The Village in the Jungle* (1913), Wollaeger finds the novel "illuminating as a failed version" of what Woolf would later accomplish in *Mrs. Dalloway* and *To the Lighthouse*. He deftly argues that the later novels clearly contest nationalist fictions, *Mrs. Dalloway* by exposing the cultural denial of the trauma of war and the "hidden costs of heteronormativity" (72) and *To the Lighthouse* with its linking of war propaganda with repressive domestic ideology and the bracketed news of Andrew and Prue's deaths. In *The Voyage Out*, in contrast, "propaganda triumphs" (73). Rachel is unable to live either inside or outside propaganda, constituted here as the marriage plot and ethnographic constructions. Though Wollaeger notes that Rachel's death suggests a protest against propaganda, he distinguishes his approach from others (he cites Kathy Phillips) who understand the novel as a "univocal critique of bourgeois domesticity and empire" (76). Rather, he is interested in how the novel "probes [...] into the gap between gendered and racial identities" (77) and locates the key moment for his analysis when Rachel, having gone upriver in South America with her fiancé, encounters a group of indigenous women. This encounter, Wollaeger demonstrates, owes a great deal both to the circulation of colonial images and to Woolf's reading of Leonard's novel, indebted to his experience as a colonial administrator in Ceylon, immediately after their return from their honeymoon. Comparing *The Voyage Out* to its earlier version as *Melymbrosia*, written before the marriage, Wollaeger finds that *The Voyage Out* both undermines and reproduces the imperial hierarchy present in Leonard's novel and in colonial propaganda: "On one hand, insofar as the narrative equates Rachel and the native women, patriarchal and colonial oppression coincide to produce a feminist critique of colonialism. On the other hand, by transforming the native women into a mere backdrop for Rachel's inner drama, Woolf partially reproduces the imperial hierarchy the novel otherwise attacks" (118). *The Voyage Out* "remains suspended between imperial objectification and intimations of an equivalent center of self" (121).

Woolf's writing of her first novel (c. 1904-13) coincided with a craze for picture postcards, a medium that Wollaeger reveals was both an emerging modernist form and used as an early form of propaganda by saturation. His book reproduces eleven colonial postcards dating from the first decade of the century. These postcards are held in the Historical Postcard Collection and the African Postcard Collection at Yale University Library (290, note 27). Though he is not able to say whether or not Woolf saw a colonial postcard (he *is* able to document that she received, posted, and perhaps collected picture postcards), Wollaeger makes a strong case that her depiction of the native women is informed by the widespread diffusion of popular ethnography in the form of postcards and imperial exhibitions. Her essay "Thunder at Wembley" on the 1924 British Empire Exhibition at Wembley provides an opportunity to discuss her relation to exhibitionary culture. However, in claiming that this essay "reads like a halfway house between the later optimism of *The Waves* (1931) and *Between the Acts* (1941) and the early pessimism of *The Voyage Out*, Wollaeger offers a strange chronology: "Reading Woolf's career in reverse, one can see that her later belief that spectacles can catalyze change is steadily displaced by worry over the seductive power of state-sponsored spectacles, and her confidence in the power of individuals to deflect or transform ideological conditioning decays" (84). To put the chronology in its more usual order, the argument seems to be that Woolf was initially worried about the seductive power of state-sponsored spectacles and that this drops away in favor of her later belief that individuals can deflect "ideological conditioning" (84). Perhaps, but I miss a consideration of *The Years* and *Three Guineas*, which I think place Woolf's later view of spectacles far closer to the worried end of the spectrum than to the confident one.

Modernism, Media, and Propaganda offers a new and rich understanding of Woolf's response to "the propaganda of everyday life" in her early career but I would have liked engagement with Woolf's more explicit but no less complex treatment of the more obvious kinds of propaganda in the 1930s. To be sure, the Woolf of *Three Guineas* lurks in the background of this study and makes an appearance early in the book as part of Wollaeger's important historicization of the term propaganda. Here, we learn that propaganda did not always have a sordid reputation; in the late nineteenth century it was a largely neutral term for information and it was only in the early twentieth century, commensurate with two world wars, that the word began to take on the valence of manipulative and partial information, until by mid-century it had become synonymous with sinister deception. It is especially surprising in this context that Wollaeger finds Woolf's use of the term propaganda while at work on "The Pargiters" (later *The Years*) indicative of her sense that to write propaganda is to risk reverting to "Victorian moralizing," quoting her diary entry that "one cant [sic] propagate at the same time as write fiction. And as this fiction is dangerously near propaganda, I must keep my hands clear" (xv). Woolf's diaries and letters make clear what we might already surmise from her published work—that in 1935, when she wrote this entry, she was apprehensive of the more sinister connotations of propaganda. Wollaeger does note that around the same time Woolf saw fascist symbols chalked on London walls, but he discusses the instance only as an indication of her dismay with propaganda's use of repetition, referencing not her diary entry, but how "in a letter to a fellow writer she complains that 'people must have things written in chalk and large and repeated over and over again'" (xv). Though *Three Guineas* is recurrently referenced, there is no consideration of that text's complicated and perhaps conflicted engagement with propaganda—the photographs of pompous judge and general held up for ridicule; the *absence* of the photographs of dead children and ruined houses of which she also writes (photographs taken after the German bombing of Getafe that, as Elena Gualtieri discusses, were used in a propaganda campaign run by the Spanish Communist Party to raise international support); and the book's own status as a masterpiece of polemical writing, for which Woolf wrote that she had "collected enough powder to blow up St. Pauls" (*D4* 77). I would like to have seen how our understanding of Woolf's writing of the 1930s, so explicit in its push and pull with government-sponsored propaganda, as well as the more decentered propaganda of everyday life, might be informed by Wollaeger's analysis of the decade's new media. Wollaeger suggests, for instance, that "Woolf's use of the verb 'propagate' to mean 'propagandize' suggests the degree to which she [associated propaganda] with modernity's new flows of information" (xv) but does not elaborate. Since "propagate" also suggests biological reproduction, as in "to breed" or "to multiply," I'd like to know more about why we should understand it as a reference to technologies of data distribution. These reservations should not, however, detract from the appreciation of Wollaeger's splendid achievement.

Putting canonical modernist texts in dialogue with understudied and largely forgotten propagandistic texts of the same period, and often by the same writers, *Modernism, Media, and Propaganda* is a rich and nuanced study of how modernism and propaganda were formed symbiotically as much as defined by difference.

—Elizabeth F. Evans, *Pennsylvania State University-DuBois*

Works Cited

Caughie, Pamela L., ed. *Virginia Woolf in the Age of Mechanical Reproduction.* NY: Garland, 2000.

Gualtieri, Elena. "Three Guineas and the Photograph: The Art of Propaganda." *Women Writers and the 1930s: Gender, Politics and History*. Ed. Maroula Joannou. Edinburgh: Edinburgh UP, 1999. 165-78.

Hankins, Leslie Kathleen. "A Splice of Reel Life in Virginia Woolf's 'Time Passes': Censorship, Cinema and 'the usual battlefield of emotions." *Criticism* (Winter 1993): 91-114.

——. "'Across the Screen of My Brain': Virginia Woolf's 'The Cinema' and Film Forums of the Twenties." *The Multiple Muses of Virginia Woolf*. Ed. Diane F. Gillespie. Columbia: U of Missouri P, 1993. 148-79.

——. "The Doctor and the Woolf: Reel Challenges—*The Cabinet of Dr. Caligari* and *Mrs. Dalloway*." *Virginia Woolf: Themes and Variations: Selected Papers from the Second Annual Conference on Virginia Woolf*. Eds. Vara Neverow-Turk and Mark Hussey. New York: Pace UP, 1993.

Phillips, Kathy. *Virginia Woolf against Empire*. Knoxville: U of Tennessee P, 1994.

Pridmore-Brown, Michele. "1939-40: Of Virginia Woolf, Gramophones, and Fascism." *PMLA* 113:3 (May 1998): 408-21.

Orts, Scraps, and Fragments: The Elusive Search for Meaning in Virginia Woolf's Fiction. Lisa Coughlin McGarry (Lanham: University Press of America, 2007) v + 177 pp.

The question of human connection, of grasping meaning or the ephemeral "thing beneath the semblance of the thing" (*TW* 118) is not a new line of inquiry in the study of modernism, or in Woolf studies. Throughout her writing, Woolf turned a critical eye to public institutions, problematizing their ability to connect individuals or to provide meaning amidst the devastation of world war and rapid industrialization. What Lisa Coughlin McGarry more pointedly argues in *Orts, Scraps, and Fragments*, however, is that "Woolf's response to the problem of failing (or at least faltering) public institutions is the intensely personal vision and process of art" (15). McGarry's analysis centers on organized religion, marriage, and language as three epistemes that serve to foster division, rather than human connection, in Woolf's novels. Her investigation determines that the *process* of art is the only mechanism that has the possibility to allow for, ever so briefly, moments of understanding for those Woolfian artists—Lily Briscoe, Bernard, Miss LaTrobe—who perpetually undertake that process.

Throughout *Orts, Scraps, and Fragments,* McGarry supplements her argument with rich excerpts from five of Woolf's major novels: *Jacob's Room*, *To the Lighthouse*, *Mrs. Dalloway*, *The Waves*, and *Between the Acts*. The book is helpfully organized into distinct chapters that address Woolf's engagement with organized religion, marriage, language, and art in those novels. That being said, one wonders if focusing on the institutions of religion, marriage, and language alone is too narrow a choice, and if sections on others, such as education or war, would have been worthwhile additions. Of the three institutions McGarry has chosen, she provides a very static picture of Woolf's critical relationship to them, when moments in Woolf's writing betray a more dynamic one. For example, when McGarry argues that, in Woolf, "organized religion is incapable of imparting meaning to a world of chaos" (46) because modern life has become faster than the church, she nevertheless neglects an inclusion of Woolf's later suspicion of religion as a patriarchal institution perpetuating war, as most clearly articulated in *Three Guineas.* Can Woolf's relationship to organized religion, then, be understood not as static, but rather as shifting and changing over time? Vincent Pecora's chapter on "The Modernist Moment" suggests such a reading, noting that Woolf's novels also appear to be embedded in a world shaped by the religious tenets of her ancestors, members of the Evangelical Clapham sect—a sect puritan in doctrine, but whose members were also quite worldly. He persuasively asserts, "it is thus no accident [...] that a Claphamite house party, where seemingly trivial entertainment is grounded in a deeply serious, even religious, belief in the moral significance of social effervescence, plays a central role in two of Woolf's major works—*Mrs. Dalloway* and *To the Lighthouse*" (Pecora 169). In a similar manner, in "An Agnostic Daughter's Apology," Mark Gaipa also reveals Woolf's dialogue with agnosticism in *To the Lighthouse.* Although successfully presenting the religious zealotry of characters like Miss Kilman and Lucy, McGarry nevertheless forecloses opportunities to explore alternate spiritual connections, like those presented by Pecora and Gaipa, that potentially supplant organized religion in Woolf's novels.

McGarry also broadly concludes that Woolf portrays marriage as unfulfilling for all of her characters. In describing the power dynamic that Mr. and Mrs. Ramsay enact throughout *To the Lighthouse,* she notes that although they admire each other, "this unnamed element (love?) is not enough to compensate for the inequity, and in their private moments [Mrs. Ramsay] must hold something back" to the extent that their "marriage is less about natural happiness and more about survival" (82). However, perhaps this reading of marriage as being entirely unfulfilling is too simple. Although the final moment in "The Window" section ends with Mrs. Ramsay "triumphing" over Mr. Ramsay, by not responding verbally that she loves him, the scene can also be read, in another sense, as one of unspoken connection. For, in turning toward Mr. Ramsay, looking at him, and smiling, "though she had not said a word, he knew, of course he knew, that she loved him" (*TTL* 126). In that moment, Mrs. Ramsay thinks, "nothing on earth can equal this happiness" (*TTL* 126). Certainly such a moment is ambiguous, as Mrs. Ramsay's happiness can be read as resulting from her "triumph," from her love for Mr. Ramsay, or from both. Yet, it is just such moments of potential connection that deserve further analysis. Although McGarry focuses her attention on the traditional institution of marriage in this chapter, incorporating elements of Woolf's own marriage to Leonard, the kind of "alternative" marriage that sustained her and her work, would have been a useful inclusion. For, as Natania Rosenfeld shows in *Outsiders Together: Virginia and Leonard Woolf*, while Woolf envisaged the institution of marriage as problematic and confining, she nevertheless viewed marriage, metaphorically speaking, as more of a dialogue, with both partners equally thriving. Additionally, what of other non-institutionalized, "alternate" marriages Woolf presents at times in her novels, such as the relationship between Lily Briscoe and William Bankes? The inclusion of Woolf's own experiences and an evaluation of alternate forms of marriage in Woolf's novels might have led to a more nuanced analysis of her presentation of the institution.

In other moments in the book, McGarry also steers away from deeper criticism of characters like Bernard and Percival. She refers to Bernard's voice as one that "speaks of uncertainty, pain, isolation, and an unsympathetic universe" but one that also "remains a truly inspired voice that imagines the possibility of enduring the battle against the 'central shadow' of life" (61). Yet, in her later endeavor to evaluate Bernard as artist figure, she slightly misreads his attempted mourning. McGarry claims that "he wants to experience his grief fully, to honor Percival by speaking honestly about him with their mutual friends, all of whom loved him as much as Bernard did" (105). However, when Bernard reflects on the numbness that he feels after Percival's death, he spends an ironically, and specifically, short amount of time doing so. He rather over-dramatically ponders, "I am exhausted with the strain and the long, long time—twenty-five minutes, half an hour—that I have held myself alone outside the machine" (*TW* 114). His response is in sharp juxtaposition to Neville's seemingly authentic expression of sympathy, complicating an understanding of the art that Bernard is attempting to pen. Likewise, McGarry does not fully unpack the political implications of Percival's character. Instead, she writes, "the Indian people revere Percival as a God because he can solve the problems that seemed insoluble" (57). Ironically—as Jane Marcus' and Patrick McGee's contending criticism reminds us—it is this same "great man" who died by being thrown from a horse while promoting imperialism. Strangely, there is little reference to Percival's connection to imperialism in McGarry's book, aside from a small footnote in the chapter on language. Although that chapter usefully analyzes the way in which gossip, the overuse of hackneyed phrases, and gender make language an imperfect vehicle, the downplaying of imperialism in her discussion of Percival leads to a missed opportunity for even deeper inquiry. Certainly, one thing Percival is involved in violently spreading while in India is the English language. Not only, then, is language an imperfect vehicle, as McGarry shows, but it is also the problematically false structure upon which the authority of imperialism depends.

The final chapter, in which the process of art emerges as a vehicle to foster human connection, is unfortunately the shortest in McGarry's book. Here, although McGarry argues that the artistic process is the only alternative to institutions as a way of fostering meaning, she also groups different artistic media—writing, painting, theater—together. Yet, how is Bernard, the male, canon-loving, author, necessarily working through a different process than Lily Briscoe, the female, unmarried, woman Woolf describes as having "Chinese eyes"? Tracing the ways in which each of the three institutions McGarry discusses are also linked to patriarchy might have led to a slightly different reading of these artist figures. Of the three, McGarry argues that "Miss LaTrobe is Woolf's final statement about art's immense potential to convey meaning in ways unavailable through social conventions" (158) because of her resilience, and because her vision promotes renewal. While the artistic process is certainly a mechanism for glimpsing meaning, what McGarry argues is that through these three artistic characters Woolf presents "the artistic struggle as the *only* viable response to the need for meaning in an increasingly chaotic world" (145, italics mine). Certainly, the artistic process can be seen as one way of promoting meaning, but are there not other productive responses in Woolf's novels? How do silent, psychic moments, such as those between Septimus and Clarissa, or the dinner party scenes in *Mrs. Dalloway*, *To the Lighthouse*, and *The Waves*, also reveal human connections, or provide glimpses of meaning? Can those dinner parties thrown by Clarissa and Mrs. Ramsay actually be seen as a non-traditional form of "art"? Because McGarry positions the more formal process of art as the only way to glimpse meaning, and situates Miss La Trobe as preeminent example, she dismisses the potential for other characters to connect, or achieve meaning, perhaps too quickly.

Despite these areas for potential expansion, McGarry's book, on the whole, provides an extended analysis of Woolf's critical representations of organized religion, marriage, and language in her major novels. Those newly interested in Woolf or with a broad interest in modernism will find her book helpful as, in addition to the aforementioned chapters, her initial chapter offers an overview of the literary time period, focusing on its relationship to world war and its preoccupation with the chaotic, modern world. Through her own artistic vision, then, McGarry ultimately sets in motion, once more, our unfailing quest for that "thing beneath the semblance of the thing" (*TW* 118).

—Kate M. Nash, *Fordham University*

Works Cited

Gaipa, Mark. "An Agnostic Daughter's Apology: Materialism, Spiritualism, and Ancestry in Woolf's *To the Lighthouse*." *Journal of Modern Literature* 26:2 (Winter 2003): 1-41.

Marcus, Jane. "Britannia Rules *The Waves*." *Decolonizing Tradition: New Views of Twentieth-Century "British" Literary Canons*. Ed. Karen R. Lawrence. Illinois: U of Illinois, 1992. 136-164.

McGee, Patrick. "The Politics of Modernist Form: Or, Who Rules *The Waves*?" *Modern Fiction Studies* 38:3 (Fall 1002): 631-650.

Pecora, Vincent. "The Modernist Moment." *Secularization and Cultural Criticism*. Chicago: U of Chicago Press, 2006. 157-193.

Rosenfeld, Natania. *Outsiders Together: Virginia and Leonard Woolf*. Princeton: Princeton UP, 2000.

Woolf, Virginia. *The Waves*. New York: Harcourt, Inc., 2006.

——. *To the Lighthouse*. New York: Harcourt, Inc., 2005.

The Ethics of Modernism: Moral Ideas in Yeats, Eliot, Joyce, Woolf, and Beckett. Lee Oser (New York: Cambridge U P, 2007) ix + 185 pp.

How do we reconcile modernism's investment in aesthetic experimentation with its attention to renovating culture? Do its various masks comprise a collective ethos? Lee Oser's *The Ethics of Modernism: Moral Ideas in Yeats, Eliot, Joyce, Woolf, and Beckett* admirably undertakes to resolve these substantive issues in an efficient 133 pages (plus notes, a bibliography, and index), which cover both the range of texts represented by the authors in the book's subtitle and key historical antecedents, including, most notably perhaps, Aristotle.

Oser's intricate argument in *The Ethics of Modernism* begins in its opening chapter with a series of dialectical oppositions that proceed by degrees to arrive at his central claim, which is ultimately a corrective on modernist criticism or, more exactly, on how the ethical grounds of modernism have been elided and misunderstood. The book begins by setting up a straw man of sorts, which is then deftly outflanked in order to shift focus to the primary through-line of Oser's position, what he calls "the modernist moral project." That project is constituted by the collective, yet varied effort, "to transform human nature through the use of art" (1). The chapters following the introduction proceed to examine work from the five writers comprising the subtitle before concluding with a chapter that provocatively takes up eugenics as one instance of the modernist faith in the technology of human transformation. More on the conclusion later.

The opening gambit of the introduction posits two possible answers, "both ambitious and imperfect," for the implicit question underlying modernism's attempts to alter human nature (1). On the one hand, Oser presents the case made by the New Darwinist school, represented in his book most expansively by Steven Pinker, which looks askance at the modernist investment in aesthetic efforts to effect social change. Oser argues that Pinker and his cohort assert the preeminence of scientific thought for good actions by humans, vis-à-vis other disciplinary approaches to ethics, giving "high priority to economics, evolutionary biology and probability and statistics" (5).[1] Against the New Darwinism, which serves in this text as a straw man, although worth taking seriously, he offers on the other hand Aristotelian ethics, whose revival in our generation echoes an implicit argument among modernist writers and their immediate antecedents concerning their efficacy. The life of virtue, in Oser's summary of Aristotle's thought, provides a more concrete actuality of morality because it manifests in

[1] Pinker, 235-36. Oser cites Harold Fromm's 2003 two-part article in *Hudson Review* describing this attack on the humanities, as well as several books that constitute this school of thought, including Alan Sokol and Jean Bricmont's *Fashionable Nonsense: Postmodern Intellectuals' Abuse of Science* (1999).

bodily actions the affect and desire of the soul. This Aristotelian body, he argues, "is central to western literature," following a line of critical thought that has attended to mimetic representation and to how a character behaves in response to her human nature in a fictional world (9). Moreover, this tradition of virtue-based ethics counters the alternate filter through which modernism has been read for or against the legacy of Cartesian dualism that privileges psychologism and the disembodied soul, rather than an embodied human nature. Oser finds in William James' writings and notably in Eliot's later texts an understanding that emotion requires a virtuous body acting in the world to achieve its ends.

It is the discussion of the debate between Matthew Arnold and Walter Pater that best demonstrates the subtlety of the argument in the introductory chapter. As the two major "Victorian forerunner(s) of the ethics of modernism," they provide Oser with a set of oppositions—seeing the object v. impressionism, habit v. the aesthetic mind, Aristotle v. Descartes—which he employs to tease out a reading of modernism that runs against a dominant grain of criticism privileging Pater's aesthetics over Arnold's naturalistic and teleological ethics (14). Frank Kermode, Harold Bloom, and David Bromwich are three of the critics who assert the victory of Pater over Arnold, but, as Oser argues, they effectively read modernism from the romanticist perspective that is finally "unmindful of human nature," even though the modernists were not (16). "Pater's chronic flaw," he writes, "the failure of the higher ethics that the modernists would have to rectify, is the gap between the contemplative world of the aesthete and the active world of society" (17). Effectively, then, he establishes with this cross-cut a thoughtful framing for reading Woolf and his other chosen modernists in terms of human nature, but distinct from the classic traditions of character representation.

Oser contrasts the modernist body against the corporeal Aristotelian body because it is, he avers, "an aesthetic body," exemplified by "an image in the mind, an incorporeal voice, a ghost of style [...] epitomized by the persona or mask" (9). His early examples include the myriad faces of Bloom in Nighttown, the voices in *The Waste Land,* and "the bright mask-like look of faces seen by candlelight" in the dinner party in *To the Lighthouse*, out of which Woolf salvages "art from the depredations of time" (10). His argument suggestively locates in these writers various affirmations of and reactions against the modernist ethical project, punctuated by Beckett's suspicion of both aesthetics and morality. But he persuasively proposes for the following readings that modernism inherits from the aesthetic movement a desire for particularized beauty and, from an Aristotelian Arnold, a renewed attention to human nature, habit, and virtue.

The second and third chapters offer nuanced discussions of Yeats' and Eliot's poetics. In the case of the Irishman, Oser argues that Yeats refuses to grant modern science even slight authority about nature, asserting in its stead the private realm of his mind as the basis for his vision of aesthetic and ethical unity. Thus, Yeats shifts the terms of the modernist project: "in some of Yeats's greatest poems [...] the body is an image, an aesthetic body expressing a transcendent vision" (35). That vision, Oser asserts, tends toward metaphysical concerns rather than to the potential for human action. Eliot, on the other hand, is presented by the subtitle of chapter three as "the modernist Aristotle," the Greek philosopher appearing with distinction in *The Sacred Wood.* Moreover, Oser observes that the American-born poet maintains a conflicted intellectual relationship with the thought of his Aristotelian predecessor, Matthew Arnold, even though Eliot's contemporaries abhorred him. Like Arnold, Eliot recognized that literature manifests a "social nature" evinced in part by a "physiological link between art and ethics" (53). In his poetry and drama, he employs irony to portray his exiles in order to disrupt the sympathetic identification of reader or audience with his characters; in so doing, Oser claims, we recognize through our alienation our own spiritual burden to act.

Proceeding in turn through *A Portrait of the Artist as a Young Man, Dubliners,* and *Ulysses,* the approach taken with Joyce's work in chapter four is to view it "as a form of moral education" (67). Indeed, Oser suggests that *Ulysses* positions its readers as disciples who learn from Joyce's characters his moral objectives: "Bloom is an ethical model for the reader, as well as the prophet of Joyce's apocalyptic mission to transform human kind" (76). While this focus on virtuous character might position Joyce as decidedly Aristotelian in a more simplistic analysis, here Oser contrasts the novelist's admiration for the Greek philosopher's metaphysics and aesthetics against Joyce's critique of his ethics. So, rather than embodying virtue, Stephen from *A Portrait* and Bloom become exemplary manifestations of how art transforms human nature in the modernist body.

The chapter on Woolf, subtitled "Antigone triumphant," opens with a historical juxtaposition: he points out that Samuel Butler's *The Way of All Flesh* was published in the same year as G.E. Moore's *Principia Ethica* (1903). The economy of Oser's argument leaves very little ground untilled, and this instance is no exception. Noting that Woolf cites Butler's novel as one of the changes that occurs in December, 1910, he then further elaborates on its pointed satire of Victorian morality and its significance as a historical marker in a changing society: "*The Way of All Flesh* broadcasts the signs of a cultural debacle: England's faltering belief in its institutions, and the waning of its immemorial customs" (85). Moore's text very soon becomes Oser's primary focus, however, and his superlative discussion of its influence on Woolf and her circle, especially insofar as it provided a carefully precise riposte to Aristotelian ethics, is one of the standout moments in this book. Because Moore focused on consciousness as a repository of goodness, rather than on the virtuous body acting in the world, his philosophy provided Woolf with a means "for bringing the authority of ethical discourse into the private realm of aesthetic consciousness, including the lyrical dementia, the apocalyptic derangement of the senses, that recurs throughout her *oeuvre*" (90). Oser offers compelling evidence from both *Jacob's Room* and *Mrs. Dalloway* to demonstrate how Moore's challenge of Aristotelian moralizing is mirrored in Woolf's fiction. Thus, for instance, Septimus Smith's torturers, doctors Bradshaw and Holmes, are repeatedly cast as "human nature" itself, advocating for virtuous action as the cure for his shellshock.

In at least one sense, Oser presents Woolf as the most radical modernist of his group. More overtly political than the three writers who precede her in his study, her writing contains for him two contradictory impulses, an aesthetic vision and a "progressive [...] post-Christian spiritualizing feminism" (91). She is able to reconcile these contraries through Moore's philosophy, which privileges the imaginative conception of essences. Oser also suggests that in her usage in "Modern Fiction" of such concepts as "spirit," "free will," and "utmost sincerity," we see her participation in an "ethics of authenticity" (91) that counters materialist leanings with a redefinition of art and, ultimately, the human being. "Her aesthetic consciousness is a revolutionary will," Oser asserts, "remaking human reality as it purifies the mind" (92). In short, Woolf trusts that artistic power can construct an ideal world, albeit one that exists in unreality, rather than in the real.

Oser's analysis of artistic authenticity and freedom in *To the Lighthouse* is especially acute in this regard. Observing that "unreality [...] emerges as a full blown metaphysical mantra" in the novel (93), he argues that Lily willfully evades the mimetic plot (such as it is), and, by removing the figural depiction of mother and child from her painting, she performatively "dissolves the strongest natural bond in society, and she does so in the name of an aesthetic morality of personal liberation" (95). In other words, Lily and her painting function for Woolf in Moore's terms—her moral "act" is anti-Aristotelian, an act of transforming consciousness rather than of human nature. That "life has changed completely" for Lily is a statement of particular significance for Oser (97)—she has taken on the established order and emerges victorious at the end of the novel. His reading of *The Waves* is less perceptive, however, even though it perhaps would provide a strong supporting case. His reductive account portrays the latter novel as an instance of "Oedipal revolt against parent and authority" (97), and his singular focus on Bernard diminishes both the other voices and the clear distinction between the monologue sections and the interludes. "Bernard has ripped the veil of the temple from top to bottom," he writes in the chapter's closing paragraph, "only to reveal what? Another wave, a repetition, another negation" (101). By linking Bernard's closing utterance to the final line of the novel, Oser judges Woolf's ending as bordering on absurdity, rather than affirming the claim he makes for her aesthetic, that "the good of art transcends the negations of life" (101).

In his penultimate chapter, Oser considers Beckett's work as a crucial rejoinder to modernism's ethics, transcending Eliot's irony with his own apocalyptic satire. He observes that this author's "moments of fulfillment are rare, their outcome ambiguous" (115) but grants in Beckett's seeming despair the possibility that he advances modernism's project, if only by pointing out its hypocrisy and failings. These claims about Beckett suggestively offer a transition into the concluding chapter, which Oser begins by provocatively proposing a modernist defense for its appropriation of eugenical discourse. "Removing eugenics from the jurisdiction of nature," he observes, "the modernists adapt it to art" (120), thus shifting the ground from attempting the management of human bodies through biology to changing human nature through the imagination. Put another way, modernism undertakes to synthesize art and technology, at least metaphorically, in order to transform the human condition. Oser raises the specter of eugenics in order to finally make his persuasive case for modernism's linkage of aesthetics and ethics—that art should be created in order to improve our world.

—Thaine Stearns, *Sonoma State University*

Works Cited

Fromm, Harold. "The New Darwinism in the Humanities, Parts I and II." *Hudson Review* 56 (2003), 89-99 and 315-27.

Pinker, Steven. *The Blank Slate: The Modern Denial of Human Nature*. NY: Penguin, 2002.

Sokol, Alan and Jean Bricmont. *Fashionable Nonsense: Postmodern Intellectuals' Abuse of Science*. NY: Picador, 1999.

British Fiction and Cross-Cultural Encounters: Ethnographic Encounters from Wells to Woolf. Carey J. Snyder (New York: Palgrave Macmillan, 2008) x + 253 pp.

At the heart of cross-cultural encounters, Carey J. Snyder suggests, lies the experience of bewilderment, anxiety, and a destabilized sense of self: think of Marlow's incomprehension at an "inscrutable" Africa in *Heart of Darkness,* Adela Quested's disorientation in the Marabar Caves in *A Passage to India*, and Rachel Vinrace's dissolution of self in *The Voyage Out*. According to Snyder, "the potential with ethnography for unsettling fixed identities" (108) is precisely what connects anthropology and modernist fiction; both require a voyage into foreign cultures and/or altered perspectives and both ask the observer-writer (and the reader) to learn how to see the world and its people through multiple points of view. For Snyder, the foregrounding of the psychological experience of bewilderment is an essential first step in the process of ethnography: by emphasizing obstacles to understanding and undercutting the observer's authority to represent adequately and transparently another culture, the recognition of cultural difference is preserved. By focusing on the role of the self-conscious observer and the idea of the "encounter" across cultures, Snyder crafts a lucid argument for the inter-relationship of ethnography and modernist fiction. As *British Fiction and Cross-Cultural Encounters* convincingly demonstrates, occupying an other's perspective, what Virginia Woolf described as "hanging up looking glasses at odd corners," is the task of both ethnographer and Woolfian "street haunter."

Before turning to this book's value for Woolfians, it is necessary to define Snyder's terms. "Ethnography" can be defined as the practice of describing people, cultures, or communities in writing, often based on direct, observational fieldwork; the modern ethnographer, Snyder tells us, is both observer and writer, fusing the earlier Victorian division of labor between "armchair anthropologists," such as Sir James Frazer, who researched *The Golden Bough* solely through extensive reading, and "data gatherers," missionaries or colonial administrators, who provided the raw material for the armchair crowd. The modern discipline of anthropology is based on the practice of ethnography, of writing based on observations made in the field by a so-called "participant observer," an agent who travels to a foreign culture and who, by "adapting the point of view of the native" (8), functions as an intermediary between cultures. Bronislaw Malinowski's *Argonauts of the Western Pacific* (1922)—a text contemporary with Eliot, Joyce, and Woolf's great works—emerges as the foundational text for this new methodology. As Snyder points out though, one critical difference between ethnographies and modernist fiction of this period is that ethnography tends to marginalize its "subjective impressions," presenting the figure of the participant-observer as one who confidently occupies and communicates the point of view of the "native" (Malinowski's private diaries, expressing his uncertainty or dis-ease among the Trobriand Islanders, weren't published until the 1960s). While adapting the point of view of the native is "new" to ethnographic methodology, and meant to suggest a sympathetic approach to cross-cultural understanding, the imperial connotations implicit in "occupying" this perspective are significant. By contrast, Snyder argues, modernist fiction's rejection of an omniscient perspective allows it to foreground the observer's disorientation in cross-cultural encounters and to emphasize the obstacles to understanding in these relationships, a move that undercuts imperial authority. But is this any less ethnocentric? One might argue that in either case, ethnographers and modernists write for European and American audiences, not for the indigenous people whose point of view they confidently, or anxiously, inhabit.

Although anthropology would come to learn self-reflexivity from modernism, the modernists also learned from the ethnographers. For Snyder, "ethnographic modernism" encompasses modernist texts that emulate ethnographies on the level of content or style, and she makes a compelling argument that the adoption of contemporary ethnographic methodology contributes to modernist representations of de-centered selves and fluid, multiple perspectives. Snyder's focus on modernism is usefully contextualized against a broad range of texts: nineteenth-century "explorer ethnographies," adventure romances, Victorian travel narratives, modernist fiction, and tourist manuals. This wide-angle perspective is useful for Snyder, not only because it demonstrates the range of material that modernists like Conrad, Woolf, Forster, and Lawrence would have had access to, but also because it allows her to show how the trope of bewilderment and anxiety on the part of the ethnographic observer persists in a variety of texts and contexts, even if disavowed. She convincingly demonstrates how the "imperial swagger" of African explorers such as Richard Burton and Henry Stanley emerges from their socially marginal positions in England, arrogance masking insecurity.

By contrast, Victorian traveler Mary Kingsley foregrounds her experience of bewilderment and disorientation in Africa, gendered self-effacement suddenly a valuable tool for cross-cultural understanding. Kingsley, who like Woolf was self-conscious about her lack of formal education, found that "bewilderment is a phase to pass through en route to understanding" (72); it allows the observer to dissolve the prejudices and habits of a fixed, metropolitan identity and therefore to observe and understand the ethnographic "other" from a more flexible, liminal perspective. Kingsley's willingness to "surrender" to feelings of disorientation is in marked opposition to the masculine explorers' machismo, as well as to Marlow's resistance to a similar sense of disorientation in Conrad's *Heart Of Darkness*.

Snyder's chapter on Woolf's "self-nativizing" in *The Voyage Out* was first published in *Woolf Studies Annual* 10 (2004); the term is Clifford Geertz's and refers to how ethnographic research into foreign cultures offers fresh perspectives on "home culture." Placing English culture itself under observation was a career-long practice for Woolf, initiated in her first novel and culminating in her last, when Miss La Trobe's players turn the mirrors on the audience members. Snyder's argument, however, reaches further than a simple focus on the trope of "ourselves exposed" (100): she argues that Woolf's mature style, with its emphasis on multiple perspectives and fluid, unfixed selves, is grounded in and influenced by the ethnographic process of adapting the native's point of view. The obstacles to this process, and the consequent de-centering of personal and national identities can be seen throughout *The Voyage Out*, most intensely in the scene at the Amazonian village where the English find themselves most uncomfortable at being the "objects of the native's gaze" (109), rather than being in control of the encounter (and the gaze). Snyder's larger argument—that thinking ethnographically is a constitutive element of Woolf's emerging literary style—is persuasive, but I found myself wishing for a more extensive close reading of the village scene, specifically the troublesome passage where Rachel appears to faint in an impressionist haze after becoming engaged to Terence at the entrance to the native village. Curiously, Snyder doesn't offer a reading of this paramount example of the disoriented self. If Rachel's dissolving self is partially a product of a self-nativized perspective, then it would make sense to put more pressure on the psycho-sexual undercurrents of their subsequent experience in the village, particularly the encounter with the native woman who stares at the English while breast-feeding her baby. Rachel's latent fears about sexuality and pregnancy are in a sense manifested by the breast-feeding woman, whose gaze at Rachel places English rituals of courtship, engagement, and marriage under observation. In a footnote, Snyder makes the neat observation that Rachel and Terence's courtship proceeds mechanically, "as if on a conveyer belt," evoking the estrangement produced by self-nativization, but such a significant point should not, I think, be buried in the chapter's end-matter.

I have a similar quibble with Snyder's structuring of her discussion of Leonard Woolf's novel *The Village in the Jungle* (1913). This novel and Leonard's experience as a colonial administrator in Ceylon (Sri-Lanka) is, as Snyder notes, an influence on *The Voyage Out* (we might note that ethnographic narratives and courtship/marriage rituals coincide autobiographically here as well). As Snyder observes, Leonard's novel is told from the point of view of the Sinhalese and Tamil natives, an example of the "new method" of ethnography pioneered by Malinowski (209). The problem with Snyder's analysis of *The Village in the Jungle* is that while this observation is placed in a footnote to the

Woolf chapter, her critique of the novel occurs in the Forster chapter, diffusing the analysis. There, Snyder tells us, the problem with Leonard Woolf's novel is that it is told in a transparently realistic style from the native's point of view: Woolf never consciously represents his "outsider" status or discloses any obstacles to his apparently masterful understanding of the Sinhalese world-view. This is an excellent point and a compelling counter-example to Snyder's thesis; as a colonial administrator and "data collector," Woolf is retrograde in his experience and literary style, but progressive (ultimately) in his imperial politics. His ethnographic stance complicates Snyder's argument and deserves a more focused discussion.

Snyder's thesis works best in her analysis of Forster's "fieldwork" in India, as it emerges in his fiction and autobiographical writings. Forster's dramatization of the Anglo-Indian's failure to "connect" with native culture is less about representing India as an exotic enigma, Snyder argues, and more about representing the ethnographic-observer's own position as both insider and outsider to Indian cultures. This stance, as we have seen, is marked by incomprehension and bewilderment, a crucial refusal of omniscient knowledge that undercuts imperial authority by highlighting cultural difference. Snyder usefully suggests the term "sympathetic seeing" as antithesis to the imperial gaze, and proposes that this is the ethnographic practice of Fielding and Mrs. Moore in their relationships with India and Indians. The difference between sympathy and empathy is key here: to understand another's feelings, as when Mrs. Moore removes her shoes before entering the mosque, retains the distance that empathy destroys, as later when Mrs. Moore, identifying with Aziz, says "we shall all be Moslems together now." As Snyder shows quite beautifully, Mrs. Moore's subsequent "spiritual disintegration" and death reveal the dangers of empathy, of a lack of detachment, even as her "post-humous 'nativization'" (140) celebrates "Esmiss Esmoor's" ultimate border-crossing between cultures. Fielding, by contrast, and despite his own desire to sympathize, is overly distanced, his friendship for Aziz inhibited by an "emotional deficiency that bars deep cultural understanding" (143), a deficiency specific to Forster's view of English character, and more broadly to cross-cultural relationships under colonialism. Snyder goes on to analyze brilliantly the gap between these characters' limited point of view and that of the mobile, semi-omniscient narrator, who, despite being able to "occupy" both English and Indian perspectives, nevertheless experiences moments of incomprehension, aporia crucial to undercutting imperial authority.

Snyder's analysis of the influence of ethnographic practices on modernist fiction is a persuasive and fresh exploration of modernist style. Her detailed analysis of the ethnographic observer's disorientation allows her to intervene in long-standing debates about the narrative voice in Conrad and Forster, and provides a new reading of Woolfian impressionism. Her chapter on Lawrence,

Huxley, and "ethnographic tourism" in the American Southwest is fascinating (although it feels like an abrupt shift in focus from ethnographies mainly located within British colonies). One of Snyder's most important moves in this book is to argue that modernist style originates not only in the European urban centers but also "in the bush" of the colonial outposts of European imperialism. By shifting our focus from the metropolis to the peripheries of empire, Snyder contributes to recent scholarship in trans-Atlantic modernism by reminding us that, decades before anthropology's self-reflexive turn in the 1960s and 70s, modernist fiction foregrounds the unsettled nature of identity in cross-cultural encounter.

—Catherine W. Hollis, *U.C. Berkeley Extension*

The BBC Talks of E. M. Forster 1929-1960. A Selected Edition. Eds. Mary Lago, Linda K. Hughes, and Elizabeth McLeod Walls (Columbia: U of Missouri P, 2008) xiv + 477 pp.

Addressing the nation on July 4, 1941, E. M. Forster paid respect to the memory of Virginia Woolf, noting that her death was "in a sense symbolic, and marks the end of an epoch" (145). Referring also to the recent deaths of James Joyce and Hugh Walpole, Forster wondered if a certain Woolfian kind of artist weren't "passing away," taking with her "art for art's sake" as well as something essential to democracy (148). Such claims were common in the radio talks Forster gave from 1928 to 1963, the years in which he did much to shape BBC programming and to popularize a certain idea of culture. How art and democracy sustained each other, mainly through books and their writers, was Forster's main theme across a long broadcasting career—across no fewer than 145 often inspired efforts to connect with the public mind.

Begun by Mary Lago and completed (after her death in 2001) by Linda K. Hughes and Elizabeth MacLeod Walls, *The BBC Talks of E. M. Forster* includes seventy representative radio addresses delivered to England and to India, mainly on the "Third Programme," the high-culture counterpart to the BBC's "Home Service" and "Light Programme." The book's excellent, lengthy introduction gives all the necessary context, including an overview of the development of BBC radio, an evaluation of Forster's war broadcasts, insight into the "ideal relationship" between Forster's sensibility and the Third Programme, recognition of his role not only as public intellectual but as a fireside "beacon for democratic ideals," and an account of "listening for Forster" in the radio-styles he developed over the decades. The introduction prepares nicely for the emergence of the singular figure Forster became in these talks: the "activist litterateur," a kind of new-media Matthew Arnold—one of radio's first and most unlikely stars.

Forster's first talks show this persona beginning to master the style and rhetoric necessary to radio success. Pronouns are key: a lot of "I" and "you" establish candor, modesty, and intimacy, as when Forster confesses, "I don't know who 'you' are," and then proceeds to explain the notion of his audience he has tentatively formed (93). Gentle imperatives—"Do take a firm line with your library"; "Insist on getting what you want"—establish an avuncular authority (94). And plain-spoken judgments give Forster a certain credibility, for example when he professes to like a book because it "gives a clear narrative" and because the writer has "put in his heart" (100-101). When Forster then warms to stronger themes, he has earned public trust. His 1934 claim, "We're certainly not as free as we were thirty years back," is propaganda moderated by a real sense of community, and his 1937 defense of books (they "will wake you up and strengthen you") comes across as the kind of advice you might get from your friendly family doctor. It is fascinating to see Forster develop this style. It is all the more fascinating to study its emergence out of the persona that narrates Forster's novels, since the modest authority that urges radio listeners to read this book or value that freedom is not at all unlike the ironic omniscience that had voiced—only to a far more limited audience—the wisdom of *Howards End.*

Forster's talks almost always come around to democracy, what sustains it, and what does not. Actually, the talks almost always presume a democratic premise: that Forster happily addresses the "man in the street." Everything from this basic rhetorical posture to Forster's reasons for liking the writers he discusses to some of his more passionate arguments proceed from the conviction that we are all the same. It was a conviction radio supported, so even if Forster tended to dislike technology, the medium ironically coincided with his values.

But pursuing democracy for Forster essentially means reading, and his talks are essentially reading lists. Reflecting on his talks, he notes, "the most important moment in each has been the final moment when you have been offered a library list" (118). The reason it all comes down to a library list is an Arnoldian one: books embody culture, and culture civilizes. Arnold is the figure most frequently cited and celebrated in the talks selected in this volume. A talk for January 6, 1944, had Forster reading long stretches of Arnold's poetry, prefaced by the claim that "he is an inspirer of all who long for the light now," "not only a great poet" but "a person who can help us" (263). A talk for June 20, 1945, explicitly champions the Arnoldian definition of "culture," distinguishing it from the pre-war debasements that had produced "cultchaw" and "kultur" alike. "In Matthew Arnold's day, it meant getting to know what is best in human achievements, and trying to pass it on": this folksy take on Arnoldian culture not only reflects Forster's own theory, of course, but his mission as broadcaster. Forster was always "trying to pass it on," and in such a way as to redeem it from history.

But the civilizing mission does not make Forster's recommendations pedantic. Books that are obviously good for you rarely make his lists, which are instead made up mostly of fairly whimsical choices. One great reason to read these talks is for leads on lost titles—for example, *Double Lives* by William Plomer, and *The Road to Bordeaux* by Denis Freeman and Douglas Cooper ("two young Englishmen, cultivated fellows, who knew France before the war, and loved her civilization, her cookery, her people" [151]). Or *Tales of Four Friends* by Pramatha Chaudhuri, "a brief symposium on the subject of womanhood," one of the many works Forster recommends as part of what amounts to an impressive familiarity with Bengali literature (358).

Forster's relationship with India is the most telling test of his skills and his motives. A broadcast for October 15, 1941, seems to indicate a poor start for the program called "We Speak to India," as Forster admits the likely irrelevance of his subject: "Perhaps France to you is something far away and small and dim in the chaos of Europe and perhaps the two books about her tragedy which I am going to recommend will not interest you and may not even be on sale your end" (150). But the recommendation is of a piece with others through which Forster really meant to stress the connections that link different kinds of people. "My home is in England, and I am conditioned by the West," Forster elsewhere confesses, never forgetting that difference, but never allowing that it should disallow cross-cultural understanding. "I shall retain the notion of connection with India"; "You know my thoughts": constant reiteration of such intimacy may well have won him the same regard Forster enjoyed at home. Indeed, a "Message to India" on the eve of the partition begins by noting that "my various Indian friends are now citizens of the new India or of Pakistan" (394), and Forster's notes on Indian fiction tend to trace the personal connections through which the books have reached him. And yet his attitude toward his Indian audience can seem preemptive. When he imagines his "unknown listener" as "an Indian, aged about thirty, educated in India but interested in Western civilization," he raises questions he does not entertain—questions about the likely complexity of the "interest" that may or may not motivate his distant listeners. Then again, he is E. M. Forster, and he did wonder earlier than most if India shared one's feelings. Reporting on the "heavy hand of barbarism" falling upon England in October 1941, he says he is "moved emotionally." And his audience? "Are you? Very likely not" (150).

Two late talks show Forster happy to swing for the fences. Asked in January 1949 to give the opening talk in a series entitled "I Speak for Myself," Forster makes this premise itself a way to stress "our common humanity" (402). He asks "what possible link there can be between us" and answers, "We both of us can speak for ourselves, and if we speak properly can listen. We know we are individuals." Forster somehow manages to make the individualism indicated in the title of the series a function of the power to connect.

On September 29, 1951, Forster defended the Third Programme. He admits it is a "minority program" and that it "cannot be defended quantitatively" but denies that popularity ought to be a decisive factor (414). We should instead respect the space available for "the pioneer, the exceptional, the disinterested scientist, the meditative thinker, the difficult artist" (416). Where else could these figures reach the masses? How else would they survive? The stakes are high: "And if they vanish now, if they dissolve into the modern world's universal grey, what is to happen to the human race in the future? Into what final darkness will it disappear?" (416). Such broad questions finally seem unworthy of the Third Programme as Forster himself characterized it. But as the editors of this volume note, "Forster's high standards for the Third meant that, ironically, he thought he was unfit to broadcast for it" (31). This peculiar situation matches Forster's larger relationship to his radio talks. It reflects the mixture of authority and modesty, of sophistication and "man on the street" plain-speaking that the radio prompted Forster to invent.

That mixture accounts for the tone of questions that might otherwise have been absurd—or, worse, propaganda. "Should there be—do you think there ought to be—a Black List of writers who have collaborated with the enemy during the past war, or indeed have behaved at all suspiciously?" (364). Obviously not, you might think. Should there be public funding ("state subsidies") for the arts? "What do you think?" (408). Yes—probably. And yet these are not just rhetorical questions, because Forster seems humbly to expect that the man on the street may have better answers.

Much more than "our common humanity" and concern for the future of the human race, what makes Forster's talks excellent reading are the smaller surprises. To read Forster praising John Gielgud's wartime Macbeth to an Indian audience, to read why Forster thought *The Death of the Heart* the best novel of 1938, and—best of all—to read the radio-drama dialogue delivered by Forster and his beloved Bob Buckingham in 1932 ("Conversations in the Train") is to return to lost moments of rare charm. It is also charming to imagine Forster's listeners listening. Gillian Beer shrewdly observes (in a passage quoted in this volume's introduction) that since "we cannot know extensively who tuned into whom or how hard they listened," we must only imagine the lost traces of the influence a broadcaster might have had on a fellow writer or artist (14). And it is fun to do so—to think who might have tuned in for Forster on Arnold, on democracy, on art and culture, on Gielgud, Bowen, Lawrence, Wells, Woolf, and others, and what was "passed on" to us as a result.

—Jesse Matz, *Kenyon College*

Modernism's Middle East: Journeys to Barbary. Joanna Grant (New York: Palgrave, 2008) xi + 211 pp.

Virginia Woolf and her fellow modernists came of age when the Middle East (known more typically as the Near East at the beginning of the twentieth century) seemed to be better known by the British public than it is today (Tromans 10). From the end of the eighteenth century to World War I, the reading public was familiar with the "Eastern Question," or what role the West should play in the weakening and eventual dissolution of the Ottoman Empire. As Britain was attaining the height of its own imperial ascendancy near the close of the nineteenth century, its Empire reached into the Middle East (e.g., Egypt, Oman, and Cyprus), and news of its imperial exploits dominated the press. Alongside news coverage, the British could read about the Middle East in the many travelogues written by their fellow citizens journeying eastward as well as about the many archeological finds being unearthed in the Middle East which British citizens could view in the increasing numbers of exhibits made available to the public. Finally, the sensational popularity of artistic productions such as Diaghilev's Ballets Russes, especially *Scheherazade* in 1910 with the legendary Nijinsky, brought the Middle East to British theatrical audiences. In sum, British modernists were provided with a wealth of news, narratives, artifacts, and culture with which "to conceive of a new world and a new art" (Grant 14).

The Eastern Question that most interested British modernist writers, as Joanna Grant writes in her book *Modernism's Middle East*, concerned that of identity. From 1978 on, with the publication of Edward Said's *Orientalism*, it has become difficult to avoid an examination of the West's relationship with the East without resorting to a litany of overly familiarized Orientalisms (Grant 4). Grant's study instead pursues the route suggested by Meya Yeğenoğlu in *Colonial Fantasies*, or "an inquiry into Orientalism" addressing "the constitution of the Western subject" (Yeğenoğlu 2). Grant considers the ways modernists used the *topos* of the desert as a ground on which to build the self anew. While the desert has been a locus for self-renewal from antiquity onward, Grant argues that modernism, with its goal of "make it new," has especially found the desert to be a fertile and vital source for what she terms "reparative identification" (31). In the "desert wastes," regarded as a "zone of authenticity" (6), writers and artists ranging from E. M. Hull to Virginia Woolf located a stage on which to reinvent the self. In the modernist imagination the desert became a proving ground on which high modernists, along with explorers, could toughen up, matching themselves against an extreme environment in order to purge away "all flabbiness and sentiment" (43). Grant connects the harsh conditions of the desert with the "hieratic strain in modernism" (45); in the desert one could mortify the flesh to become not only like the "arid, granitic Arab" (5) but purified into a forceful, visionary, "gifted artist-prince of the desert" (25).

Grant traces a trajectory of modernists' orientalist fantasies starting with a "utopian striving" after the "Arab Other" to an "anguished disappointment," or even horror at being engulfed by desert wastes (3). Across the decades of various modernisms, starting generally with the 1920s and ending in the early 1960s, Grant follows a vector characterized by "increasing dismay and disquiet" (3). Yet, even with the failure to achieve "reparative identification," writes Grant, modernist "yearnings for a kind of separate peace with the Near East never entirely dissipate" (3). What makes Grant's approach an especially valuable one is her selection of modernist works from a wide literary range, including popular fiction to travelogues to autobiographies to fiction, and her synthesis of Orientalism with a variety of approaches informed by thinkers such as Pierre Bourdieu, Jean Baudrillard, and Julia Kristeva. She also employs thick description as she deepens her analyses with biographical, historical, ideological and cultural contexts.

One of the major contemporary discourses driving modernists' quest for "reparative identification" was that of decadence and degeneration. It would have been difficult for a modernist to escape the influence of this narrative, it was so ubiquitous. For modernists, cultural contact with the East allowed for a regeneration of a jaded European civilization. They drew upon Nietzsche, who himself looked to the East for his ideas about the will, which he came to valorize in terms of "the irrational, the unconscious, the cruel, and the forceful" (26), and for his recreation of Zarathustra, the newfound man (34). Grant writes, "[t]he fascination with self-immolation, of the fusion of the self with what is foreign to it, is inextricably intertwined with modernist obsessions with concepts of the will and of force" (16). Grant uses Melanie Klein's theory of object relations, particularly the process of identification, introjection, and disavowal; and her notion of "phantasy," or an "imago," to describe this fusion "between self and other, subject and object, human and divine" (13).

One of the most popular figures to embody this attempted fusion was T. E. Lawrence, or Lawrence of Arabia. Even before his autobiography *Seven Pillars of Wisdom* was published in 1926, Lawrence was well-known as a hero. Grant examines the "Lawrence biography wars" that swirled around this "blond Bedouin," as Lowell Thomas, one of his popularizers, called him. Among those who struggled in this cultural field (here Grant makes uses of Bourdieu) for their version of the "real" Lawrence were Robert Graves, Wyndham Lewis, and Richard Aldington, with Graves at the one end, seeking to preserve the image of Lawrence as a "Nietzschean superman identified with the Arab Other" (95), and Aldington at the other, serving to debunk this image. The cultural field on which these biographers were attempting to advance their position was, at the same time, being invaded by "sun and sand" schlock-mongers, who were threatening to popularize Lawrence of Arabia "out of all good and proper relation to its original" (89), with Valentino's portrayal as *The Sheik* one of the most famous of the sun and sand portrayals. Here Grant employs Baudrillard's work on simulacra to show the real stake in these battles over authenticity versus simulation: preserving the integrity of the canonical hero. Grant tells us that the "regenerative fantasy persisted in the modernist imagination despite the waves of unsavory revelations concerning Lawrence's true nature and achievements" (116).

The reparative fantasy did not survive in the works of the late modernists Lawrence Durrell and Paul Bowles. Grant devotes a chapter to these two underappreciated writers whose works, she argues, are important representations of "the difficulties that arise when West and Middle East meet in the context of imperial decline and incipient nationalism" (134) and allow us to address the question of where modernism ends and postmodernism begins. In the transition between the Lawrence biography wars, and the novels of Durrell and Bowles, we can see the differences between the identification with and fascination for the "Arab Other" typical of the high modernist era, and the abjection and engulfment by this Other representative of late modernism. Grant uses Kristeva's theory of the abject to show how Durrell and Bowles portray the desert as a semiotic space threatening to "respond to the fantasies and drives of Western or Westernized subjects with a vengeance partaking of all the perversity and irony characteristic of the eruption of the abject" (134). The "sublime rapture" that results from this engulfment of all meaning and all humanity is manifested in unsettling laughter; for Grant, "late modernism displays a painful rictus all its own" (139). Focusing on Durrell's *The Black Book* and *The Alexandria Quartet*, and Bowles's *The Sheltering Sky*, Grant explains how these novels delight in the subject's dissolution in the rush of a "much more powerful Other" (136). However, where Durrell ends his quartet with a world only in half ruin, with the hope of finding some redemption and replenishment in heterosexual love (135), Bowles's most famous novel leaves us with a vision of the desert's "complete annihilation of the Western subject," and not "just its salutary gerrymandering" (162).

In contrast to male modernists, female modernists like Woolf and Vita Sackville-West offered "the most enthusiastic and least problematic performance of acts of identification with the Arab Other" (Grant 50) that are treated in *Modernism's Middle East*. Through the discourse of Orientalism, with its "uneasy proximity to supposed deviance" (8), Woolf and Sackville-West could "use their writing as a means of constructing more hospitable folds in patriarchal culture, ones in which they could express their desires and their political and cultural commitments in half-coded, half-explicit ways" (50). From an early age both writers had experimented through masquerade with sex- and race-changing possibilities: Woolf, then Stephen, dressed as Cleopatra at a summer revel in 1909 and participated as an Abyssinian royal in the famous Dreadnought Hoax the following year; and, among other kinds of performances, Sackville-West played a young Caliph in a private theatrical, "The Persian Play," in 1913. Woolf thus had much material to draw from for the sex- and race-crossing characters in *Orlando*, including Sasha and the gypsies, with their voluminous and sexually indeterminate trousers, and above all Orlando him- and herself, whose very essence is androgynous.

Woolf and Sackville-West, interestingly, appropriate the lowbrow genre of the desert romance, a genre designed to put women in their place, for their own subversive ends; writes Grant, both "'play Sheik' at the risk of being outed not just as 'Sapphists,' but also as 'middlebrow lady novelists'" (49). The desert romance revolves around the theme of abduction; Woolf and Sackville-West abduct this staple of the genre as well "to abduct themselves, to steal themselves from the law of the father" (62). Abductions abound in *Orlando*, with one of the most significant that of the gypsy, based on Sackville-West's grandmother Pepita, ravishing Orlando in his role of ambassador. This abduction becomes an inversion of the desert romance formula, with the female character becoming stronger and the male relinquishing his power. Grant concludes that *Orlando* "constitutes the most complete and perfect expression of the sex-changing, race-changing fantasies of Woolf and Sackville-West" (66).

However, just as the romantic relationship between Woolf and Sackville-West drew to an end, so does the West-East erotic fantasy disintegrate, with Orlando seized—abducted—by the conventional marriage plot—by Marmaduke, who, of all characters, writes Grant, "comes to have something sheik-like in his deceptively mild, androgynous appearance" (82). Like Sackville-West's travelogues *Passenger to Teheran* and *Twelve Days in Persia*, *Orlando* demonstrates ambivalence toward and ultimately disenchantment with a true fusion between West and East. Orlando cannot shed his "Western," thinking, writing, conscious self, and the Turks whom he encounters while he is paying homage at the Sublime Porte are as ridiculous in their courtly personae as he is when he plays at being ambassador. Moreover, the gypsies with whom she fraternizes rebuke her and plot to kill her. Nonetheless, spectral images of the East continue to haunt Orlando even after her return to England and, writes Grant, haunted Woolf from the beginning to the end of her writing career. Grant's brief remarks on the desert imagery in her other works of fiction, from *The Voyage Out* to *Between the Acts*, remind us of the work that needs to be done on Woolf and the Middle East. Though critics such as Patricia Laurence, Kathy Phillips, Urmila Seshagiri, and David A. Boxwell, among others, have written on Woolf and Orientalism, there has, to date, been no sustained work on Woolf and the Middle East.

While *Modernism's Middle East* is a fine study of the ways an array of modernists constructed their own versions of the Middle East, one wishes that Grant had spent more time elaborating on varieties of landscape and Middle Eastern Others. For example, Orlando does not disappear into desert wastes while she is in Turkey, but rather into the lush green mountains of Bursa (though Woolf's descriptions sometimes denude them of their greenery). Turks and Farsis (Persians) do not define themselves as Arabs, and Grant might have indicated that. So much does she emphasize the way modernists utilized stereotypes such as the "toughened, arid, granitic Arab" and his mirror image "the effete, luxury-loving, corrupt, decadent Levantine" (5) that she does not explain as much as she might have how these writers attempted to push past these flat, demeaning, and inhuman, representations. It would have been interesting too if Grant had further teased out the significance of gender and the Middle East; why, for example, do modernists seek fusion with the male-gendered "Arab Other"? Otherwise, *Modernism's Middle East* is a concise, sophisticated, informed, well-argued, and rich contribution to the fields of modernism and Orientalism.

—Jeanne Dubino, *Appalachian State University*

Works Cited

Boxwell, David A. "(Dis)orienting Spectacle: The Politics of *Orlando*'s Sapphic Camp." *Twentieth Century Literature* 44.3 (1998): 306-27.

Laurence, Patricia *Lily Briscoe's Chinese Eyes: Bloomsbury, Modernism, and China.* Columbia, SC: U of South Carolina P, 1993.

Phillips, Kathy J. *Virginia Woolf against Empire.* Knoxville, TN: U of Tennessee P, 1994.

Seshagiri, Urmila. "Orienting Virginia Woolf: Race, Aesthetics, and Politics in *To the Lighthouse.*" *Modern Fiction Studies* 50.1 (2004): 58-84.

Tromans, Nicholas. "British Orientalist Painting." Introduction. *The Lure of the East: British Orientalist Painting.* Ed. Tromans. London: Tate, 2008. 10-21.

Yeğenoğlu, Meyda. *Colonial Fantasies: Towards a Feminist Reading of Orientalism.* Cambridge: Cambridge UP, 1998.

Virginia Woolf And The Victorians. Steve Ellis (Cambridge: Cambridge UP, 2007) 224 pp.

No British writer could lay greater claim to the intellectual heritage of the Victorians than Virginia Woolf. Her mother, of course, was the model for photographs by Woolf's great-aunt Julia Margaret Cameron and paintings by Edward Burne-Jones; her father, whose first wife was Thackeray's daughter, was both the compiler of the *Dictionary of National Biography,* the nineteen-volume compendium of the nineteenth century's thought, and the editor of the *Cornhill,* one of the most important literary journals of the day. Together, her parents entertained James, Hardy and Meredith in their home. Thus Woolf, as she herself was aware from an early age, was the product of the Victorian age. As one of the centers of the Bloomsbury Group, however, she has also been positioned as one of the great iconoclasts of her parents' generation together with her friends Lytton Strachey and E. M. Forster, both of whom were also products of what Noel Annan famously termed "the Victorian intellectual aristocracy."

In this new study, Steve Ellis argues for a more nuanced view of Woolf than has been previously espoused by scholars such as Jane Marcus, who have emphasized Woolf's rejection of the past, or by those who have seen her as representing a full contiguity with her forebears. Rather, his book sees Woolf's fiction as representing both a reclamation of her Victorian heritage while simultaneously being committed to a modernist project that would reject it *ipso facto*. This tension, he argues, animates almost the entirety of her oeuvre, starting in the midst of the First World War when her work markedly shifted towards positing itself as self-consciously post-Victorian. On or about 1916, Ellis insists, Woolf's historical understanding changed, and thus all her books following the publication of *The Voyage Out* exhibit her self-consciousness about their modernity by paradoxically returning again and again in their narratives to the Victorian scene. Ellis's book seeks to understand this tension animating her work by a full-length study of all her novels from the 1919 *Night and Day* (the first extended look at the relations between the Victorians and their descendants) all the way through the posthumously published 1941 *Between the Acts* where again the Victorians form an important (if incompletely understood) point of contiguity in the historical pageant enacted at Poyntz Hall.

Arguing against Katherine Mansfield's infamous (and influential) critical understanding of *Night and Day* as reactionary, Ellis reads this poor cousin among Woolf's novels as absolutely critical in its initial articulation of what it means to be "post-Victorian." Such an articulation continues, he argues, among all of Woolf's later major works both fictional and critical. (Despite his broad sweep, Ellis's decision to give only brief attention to two of Woolf's minor works—

the experimental biography *Flush,* and the theatrical *jeu d'esprit Freshwater*—is slightly disappointing, given that they are two of the most extended of her dramatizations of the Victorian age.) He analyzes in *Mrs. Dalloway* how the flux of the present might be firmly anchored in the fixities of the Victorian past. Ellis then argues how *To the Lighthouse* dramatizes an important break not between the periods before and after the First World War, as is often argued (as he cleverly notes, "Times Passes" pointedly downplays the effects the War leaves on domestic life), but rather between the Victorian generation of the elder Ramsays and that of their younger inheritors. In her later years, Ellis argues, Woolf's interest in writing grand narratives of history meant that her attention turned away from her "maternal garden of 1920s nostalgia" towards the more disquieting paternal legacies of the Victorians (145). This turn, he shows, is marked especially in *The Years*, with its *cri de coeur* against the injustices enacted in the world of Abercorn Terrace mixed with its awareness of that world's potencies, and then even more pointedly in *Three Guineas*. Ellis then shows, in his persuasive last chapter, how in her final works (particularly *Between the Acts* but also her essays "The Leaning Tower" and "Anon") Woolf enacts an inability to make the idea of the past cohere closely with the present, so that Mrs. Swithin in *Between the Acts* can say of the Victorians, on the day of the historical pageant at the Hall, "I don't believe there ever were such people."

The arc Ellis traces covers almost the entirety of Woolf's career (omitting only *The Voyage Out* from its study of the major works) in only a matter of barely more than two hundred pages. His command of this corpus is remarkably assured, and he ranges freely—sometimes within even the space of just a few sentences or a paragraph—among Woolf's novels, short stories, essays, letters, and diaries, and offers excellent close readings of materials drawn from all of them. It should be noted that his focus is quite pointed: this work is squarely aimed at Woolf scholars, and gives no quarter to a reader who might not know, say, who Kitty Lushington was, or Jack Hills (to say nothing of Stella Duckworth). The almost absolute focus on Woolf means, unfortunately, that a fuller understanding of Woolf's attitude towards the Victorians receives little contextualization with her modernist contemporaries, many of whom (such as E.M. Forster, Mansfield, and James Joyce) were also deeply involved with considerations of the Victorians and their century. Lytton Strachey's obsession with the nineteenth century could of course hardly be omitted, even though in his case Ellis is unhelpfully vague, arguing both that Woolf's iconoclasm toward the Victorians was much less sharp than that of her Bloomsbury friend (15), and then noting in a footnote that the popular notion of *Eminent Victorians* as "solely an assault on the Victorians" stands as "a curious simplification" (184n)

More troubling, perhaps, is Ellis's reluctance to clarify exactly what Virginia Woolf meant by "the Victorians," even though this catch-all term was one to which she herself repeatedly turned throughout her career. It was Strachey, of course, who claimed in his "Preface" to *Eminent Victorians* that the problem for the moderns with the previous age was that "we know too much about it" (5), and that the overwhelming mass of attitudes, materials, and texts they had left behind were nearly impossible to sort out. Ellis seems to subscribe to this notion, arguing in his introduction that in sorting out and evaluating "the modern" and "the Victorian" Woolf "considers the place of sentiment, romance and individualism in the modern world, together with questions relating to science, politics, social duties, gender, fashion, sexual relations and the practice of reading" (7). This doesn't seem to leave much out, and indeed all of these categories are sometimes lumped together in Ellis's analysis, even though his writing (and his grasp of the materials) is confident enough so that the reader is left almost breathless in his room to maneuver adroitly from one topic to another. It may take, perhaps, other scholars to sort out among all these terms how Woolf defined modern attitudes against those of the Victorians. They will, however, have to use Ellis's helpful, suggestive, and important study as their own starting point in articulating these questions. Certainly at the very least we can hope they will follow Ellis's lead in understanding *Night and Day* not as a one-off or dead end, as has often previously been the case, but rather as a keystone text in Virginia Woolf's lifelong fascination with her Victorian inheritance.

—Jay Dickson, *Reed College*

Works Cited

Annan, Noel. "The Intellectual Aristocracy." *Studies in Social History: A Tribute to G. M. Trevelyan,* ed. J. H. Plumb (London: Longmans, Green, and Co., 1955), 241-87.

Strachey, Lytton. "Preface." *Eminent Victorians,* ed. and introd. John Sutherland Oxford: Oxford UP, 2003.

Woolf Online: An Electronic Edition and Commentary of Woolf's 'Time Passes.' (http://www.woolfonline.com)

I was privileged to meet Julia Briggs only once, at a conference. During her paper I was happy to discover that we shared an interest in digital editions, and I was eager to speak with her about them. We talked briefly, discussing our endeavors to create serious digital resources for scholarly work, and we agreed we should get together to talk about a collaborative project. That talk never happened; Professor Briggs died after a brief illness in 2007. But the digital resource she had conceived and begun to create with colleagues at De Montfort University in Leicester is now available as *Woolf Online: An Electronic Edition and Commentary of Virginia Woolf's 'Time Passes'* (http://www.woolfonline.com), and it offers me a glimpse at what collaborating with Julia Briggs might have been like. For those who study Woolf, it is a wonderful tool for research and teaching; for those who create digital resources for scholarship, it offers some valuable lessons.

In an introductory video, Professor Peter Shillingsburg (who with Professor Marilyn Deegan co-directed the project with Professor Briggs) says *Woolf Online* was designed to be "both a research site and a field for criticism and teaching." "Site"; "field"; "electronic edition"; "commentary": the multiplicity of terms attests to the inchoate nature of scholarly resources that are stored, delivered, and accessed via computers. *Woolf Online* attempts to address all these concepts, and at some it succeeds better than at others.

It is perhaps easiest to conceive *Woolf Online* as an aggregation of resources brought together to aid the study of a particular topic: the textual history of the famous "Time Passes" section of *To the Lighthouse*. *Woolf Online* has created a genetic edition of this text, comprising Woolf's handwritten first draft, a typescript Woolf prepared for French translation in November 1926, page proofs with Woolf's corrections, and the pages of four important printed editions. Each of these texts is represented both as a set of high-resolution digital photographs of actual pages and in transcription.

Supplementing the genetic edition is a variety of materials that help put "Time Passes" and its composition in context. Woolf drafted "Time Passes" in twenty-six days, between April 30th and May 25th of 1926, and *Woolf Online* has gathered passages from Woolf's diary and letters from this period, as well as two essays, "The Cinema" and "Impassioned Prose," which she composed around the same time. As Woolf drafted "Time Passes," Britain was being convulsed by its first-ever General Strike, and *Woolf Online* includes portions of Woolf's diary and several letters showing how closely she was following events as she wrote. The editors of *Woolf Online* have also provided a "diary of events" surrounding the Strike and have included page images from three newspapers as supporting material, along with passages from the diary of fifteen-year-old Margaret Woods to lend another perspective on the turbulent events. The newspaper page images are of poor quality, and they have not been transcribed and so are not searchable. One would like to read the *British Gazette*, the short-lived newspaper published by the Government during the General Strike, but one can hardly decipher it here. It is wonderful to have these contemporary materials near at hand to provide some context, and one hopes the maintainers of *Woolf Online* will continue to refine and expand this portion of the resource. One wishes, too, for greater breadth; fortunately it is one of the great strengths of digital resources that they can, with suitable effort and funding, accumulate materials over time.

To the Lighthouse was profoundly inspired by Woolf's memories of her childhood summers at Talland House, near St. Ives in Cornwall. *Woolf Online* helps illuminate the autobiographical background to the novel with digital reproductions of Stephen family photographs taken during holidays at St. Ives, selections from Woolf's journal from August 1905, when Woolf traveled with her sister and brothers to Cornwall, digital photographs of manuscript and typescript versions of Woolf's unfinished memoir, "A Sketch of the Past," and a miscellaneous collection of digital reproductions (unfortunately without provenance) of postcards featuring St. Ives. An essay by Marion Dell describes Talland house then and now.

John Unsworth has called such aggregations "thematic research collections" and sees them as foundational to the development of digital humanities. An early name for *Woolf Online* seems to have been "The Time Passes Project," and one could wish the endeavor had retained that title, for it derives its depth and strength from its focus on this excerpt and its context: "Woolf Online" is too general a designator for so specific a resource.

Woolf Online is not simply a digital library, however. As a site with a fixed address in the web of Internet-accessible documents and images, *Woolf Online* is an interface whose function is to tie its materials together in suggestive and helpful ways and to make it possible for academic users with different needs to read, view, and compare them.

The heart of *Woolf Online* is its interface to the genetic edition. An overview says the edition has four distinct layers: the holograph draft; the typescript; the proofs; and the printed editions. For each layer several different views are available: transcription text only; image only; text and image displayed simultaneously side by side; and text displayed continuously. For the holograph, there is an additional, chronological view that lets one see what Woolf wrote each day. This view is helpfully linked to diary entries and other context.

The designers have gone out of their way to create an interface that is clean and unobtrusive while providing a variety of tools with which to carry out different readerly tasks. The transcriptions have been encoded and annotated; the interface displays these annotations as notes and color-coded marks that draw attention to points of particular interest. The photographs of the original pages are of high resolution, and the interface provides a variety of ways to zoom in for a closer look at portions of an image.

What one misses is a way to compare the different layers: to compare the corrected proofs with the first American edition, for example, or to see for oneself the differences between the British and American first editions, which the overview says are significant. A view that placed page images side by side, or a kind of "variorum view" that collated the texts and enabled detailed analysis of the variations, would greatly extend the usefulness of these already useful texts; without comparative tools the genetic notion of layers is harder to grasp.

One would also like greater searching powers. The editors have created indexes ("catalogues") that guide a reader to various topics. But one would love to be able to discover, for example, if certain words or phrases occurring in the manuscript also appear at the same time in the diary or the letters, or even in the newspapers. The search-results page is confusing and the presentation of cross-references and linkages even more so.

Indeed, the road to mastery of this resource seems unnecessarily steep. The color-coding of various themes, or sections, or functions seems to gesture at an integration that is not recognizably achieved, and the lack of written help pages in so resolutely literary a resource is disconcerting. The site designers make no apologies for the site's complexity. Professor Shillingsburg's high modernist warning in the introductory video—"it is not expected that anyone will, in two or three minutes, understand its riches"—is rigorous, but as one struggles with the inconsistent display of resources—why can't I read the manuscripts and typescripts of "A Sketch of the Past" with the same interface I can use to read "Time Passes"?—and low-resolution video demonstrations, his warning begins to sound more like an excuse for haphazard design.

Which may be the truth. There are portions of *Woolf Online* that are rudimentary. One can register for a "user account" that allows one to establish a permanent identity, keep a blog, participate in forums, and discover other users with similar interests. This appears to be the "field for criticism and teaching" Professor Shillingsburg describes, but this dimension seems weakly developed: the interface for indicating interests and discovering commonalities with other users is primitive; there seems to be no capacity for creating links among blog entries, annotations, and other content; there is no facility I could find for searching the collective critical apparatus. Without tighter integration with the Woolf materials it is unclear what benefit this field offers over the richer pastures of Facebook, Delicious, and other social networking software.

This is a shame, because real collaboration has already occurred in *Woolf Online*. When Professor Briggs died, a cadre of Woolf scholars from around the world stepped in to help complete the project with commentary and bibliographies. The result is a rich resource that will be invaluable to those interested in studying and teaching the composition of one of Woolf's most famous writings, a resource that will surely grow and mature still further as time passes.

—Clifford E. Wulfman, *Princeton University Library*

Notes on Contributors

Christine Kenyon Jones is a Research Fellow in the Department of English at King's College London and the College's Writer in the Department of External Relations. She has written widely on the history of the College and of the University of London, including *King's College London: In the Service of Society* (2004), and *The People's University 1858-2008* (2008). Her critical publications include *Kindred Brutes: Animals in Romantic-period Writing* (Ashgate, 2001) and *Byron: The Image of the Poet* (editor, AUP, 2008).

Bette London is a professor of English at the University of Rochester. She is the author of *The Appropriated Voice: Narrative Authority in Conrad, Forster, and Woolf* and *Writing Double: Women's Literary Partnerships*. Her articles addressing 19th and 20th century British writers and feminist and postcolonial theory have appeared in such places as *PMLA*, *diacritics*, *ELH*, and *Criticism*. She is currently working on a book project on World War I and the Culture of Memory.

Monica J. Miller is a doctoral candidate in English at the University of California-Berkeley, where she is working on a dissertation on modernist revisions of sympathy.

M-C. Newbould's research activities mainly lie in the field of eighteenth-century literature, with a particular interest in literary adaptation, visual culture, and the work of Laurence Sterne. She has contributed to *The Shandean* and to *Word & Image*. She teaches and conducts research across the long eighteenth century at the University of Cambridge.

Nicky Platt teaches at the University of Reading, UK, and researches the literature and music of the interwar period. She is currently working on a book entitled "Bringing Back Culture with Honor: Munich to the Blitz for T. S. Eliot, Louis MacNeice and Virginia Woolf."

Anna Snaith is a Reader in Twentieth-Century Literature at King's College London. She is the author of *Virginia Woolf: Public and Private Negotiations* (2000) and editor of *Locating Woolf: The Politics of Space and Place* (with Michael Whitworth, 2007) and *Palgrave Advances in Virginia Woolf Studies* (2007). She is currently editing Woolf's *The Years* for the Cambridge University Press Edition of Virginia Woolf and is writing a monograph entitled *Colonial London: Nation, Gender, Modernity 1890-1945* (forthcoming, CUP).

Janice L. Stewart is a Lecturer (Department of English) and Chair, Critical Studies in Sexuality Program, University of British Columbia. Her current program of research engages critically with the stridently positivist promises of Canadian modernism. This research rethinks the contributions of artist and writer Emily Carr as representative of an important voice in the formulation and imagination of an aesthetic nationalism.

James F. Wurtz is Assistant Professor of English at Indiana State University. He has published articles on James Joyce, Elizabeth Bowen, and British First World War narratology, and he has also edited a new scholarly edition of Joseph Sheridan Le Fanu's first novel, *The Cock and Anchor: Being a Chronicle of Old Dublin City*, forthcoming from Valancourt Books. His current research project examines the ways that graphic narrative re-interprets earlier literary texts.

Policy

Woolf
Studies
Annual invites articles on the work and life of Virginia Woolf and her milieu. The Annual intends to represent the breadth and eclecticism of critical approaches to Woolf, and particularly welcomes new perspectives and contexts of inquiry. Articles discussing relations between Woolf and other writers and artists are also welcome.

Articles are sent for review anonymously to a member of the Editorial Board and at least one other reader. Manuscripts should not be under consideration elsewhere or have been previously published. It is strongly advised that those submitting work to WSA be familiar with the journal's content. Among criteria on which evaluation of submissions depends are whether an article demonstrates familiarity with scholarship already published in the field, whether the article is written clearly and effectively, and whether it makes a genuine contribution to Woolf studies.

Preparation of Copy

1. Articles are typically between 25 and 30 pages, and do not exceed 8000 words. Inquiries about significantly shorter or longer submissions should be sent to the Editor at woolfstudiesannual@gmail.com.

2. A separate page should include the article's title, author's name, address, telephone & fax numbers, and e-mail address. The author's name and identifying references should not appear on the manuscript to preserve anonymity for our readers.

3. All submissions must include an abstract of no more than 250 words.

4. Manuscripts should be prepared according to most recent MLA style.

5. Submissions may be sent *either* by email to woolfstudiesannual@gmail.com *or* by mail to Mark Hussey, English Dept., Pace University, One Pace Plaza, New York NY 10038. For mailed submissions, please send **three** copies of the article and abstract.

6. Authors of accepted manuscripts are responsible for any necessary permissions fees and for securing any necessary permissions.

All editorial, review, and advertising inquiries should be addressed to woolfstudiesannual@gmail.com.

Inquiries concerning orders should be addressed to PaceUP@pace.edu.

www.ingramcontent.com/pod-product-compliance
Lightning Source LLC
Chambersburg PA
CBHW070516100726
47907CB00004B/858
* 9 7 8 0 9 4 4 4 7 3 9 9 3 *